MW01259063

The Odds Must Be Crazy

BEATING THE RACES WITH THE MAN WHO REVOLUTIONIZED HANDICAPPING

LEN RAGOZIN
with LEN FRIEDMAN
and RICHARD STEIER

LITTLE, BROWN AND COMPANY
BOSTON NEW YORK TORONTO LONDON

First Edition

Library of Congress Cataloging-in-Publication Data

Ragozin, Len.
The odds must be crazy: beating the races with the man who revolutionized handicapping / by Len Ragozin with Len Friedman and Richard Steier. — 1st ed.
p. cm.
ISBN 0-316-60497-6
1. Horse racing — Betting. I. Friedman, Len. II. Steier, Richard.
SF331.R34 1997
798.401 — dc21 96-37632

10 9 8 7 6 5 4 3 2 1

MV-NY

Published simultaneously in Canada by Little, Brown & Company (Canada) Limited

Printed in the United States of America

Contents

Acknowledgments

Thanks to agent Chris Calhoun — doing a book was his idea.

Thanks from Len Ragozin and Len Friedman to our talented staff. Jake Haddad and Eric Connell today join us in attacking tough variant-making problems from coast to coast. Alex, Paul, Jack, Bryan, and Bob use their computer skills to collate and analyze race charts and reports from our many sharp on-track observers (Lou Rose, Butch, Toby, Mike, Gunar, Pokey, Jack, etc.), while Mike and Danny handle production.

For efforts in former years, thanks to friend and analyst Connie Merjos, Bob Beinish, Brom Kiefetz, and especially Frank Kushi, for many years my lone sidekick, who did not live to see all the fruits of his intense labor.

And a low bow plus a hug to Marion Buhagiar, who always expressed faith that I could do it, always maintained that it was worth doing, and lent her talents to the business and to the book.

The Odds Must Be Crazy

1

J. Edgar Made Me Do It

WHEN I BEGAN WORKING on racing figures in the 1950s, I had no grand vision of transforming the art of thoroughbred handicapping and becoming a millionaire. As a politically blacklisted journalist, I was looking for a way to make a living. The nearest at hand was this hobby that my father, Harry Ragozin, had taken up as a release from his business pressures.

None of us is born to be a handicapper, and becoming one can hardly be traced to a cold, rational decision — considering the fact that the same ability and sweat applied to Wall Street holds the prospect of much larger profits. Racing is, after all, a limited market. The largest and most successful bettors I know can't average a seven-figure income. There just aren't enough losers out there to fund that kind of profit.

My road into this profession was quirky, paved by the political witch-hunting that barred me from a more conventional career. But after the strange detour came an immense amount of hard work. I have the stamina for and love of this work, plus a first-class brain. But with all that, the learning process is slow and difficult enough to make handicapping so financially unrewarding in the early stages that I doubt anyone makes it all the way without another source of income at the start. Mine was poker winnings plus a princely $50 a week from my father for keeping him supplied with betting figures.

So I couldn't starve — and handicapping became my business. And it turned into a remarkably successful business.

Piling up wealth was never my goal, though — and it certainly was never a reason for my interest in handicapping. I would have been happy if horses had given me a modest living — plus, of course, the intellectual delight of beating the unbeatable game.

I'm notorious in thoroughbred racing circles for being arrogant. And I am arrogant — but not about the success of the business or the money. What never ceases to stir my pride is the way I developed figures for thoroughbreds that, for the first time, swept through all the variables of a race — speed, weight, wind, racing surface, and so on — and described with precision how those great running fools performed. I was proud of that achievement and those figures back when I was the only person who could really assess the quality of what I was doing and was barely making a living doing it. I'm not going to pretend to any modesty now.

Growing up, I was a bookworm, with a love for math and science. I dreamed of going to MIT and becoming a physicist. But my parents and teachers talked me out of that. Considering how many youngsters have no idea what they want to do, it now seems criminal to me for them to have interfered with my passion. But science was too narrow a goal for someone with my wide capacity for knowledge, they said. Go to Harvard and get a good liberal arts education. So I did. And that decision, ironically, turned out to be the first step toward becoming a handicapper. Since non-science studies bored me, I eventually used racing as a backdoor way of getting back into mathematics.

But first there were the poker games at Harvard. As a novice cardplayer my freshman year, I lost my entire $100 allowance for the year in a sucker-trap, high-low game. I spent the next few months watching and kibitzing instead of playing. At Christmas I came home and told my parents that I thought I had learned how to play poker and could win back my money if they would advance me my sophomore year's allowance. My father, from good or evil motives, refinanced me. (With hindsight it seems to me a more normal and helpful attitude would have been to tell me to stop wasting my time and their tuition money and stick to studying.)

It turned out I really had learned to play, and from then on my real college major was poker. I won thousands of dollars over the next three and a half years at Harvard, bought a hi-fi and my record collection, a Leica camera and a Speed Graphic — and took friends out to many a dinner. I was eventually expelled for cutting classes — a decision reversed by a high-level dean because I promised to reform and because my grades were good.

In my poker-playing crowd I became a kind of bank to which other players came to borrow money when they thought they had inside information on a horse running at Suffolk Downs or Narragansett. There were days when I loaned so much money to those boys that, if their horse had lost, I would have been scraping by until their rich-parent allowances arrived and they could pay me back.

I never went to the track with them — maybe because the idea of betting into a mutuel takeout didn't appeal to me when I could bet on poker for free. Maybe, though, I resisted those outings because I had some sense that I might become a hooked horseplayer — though I had never even seen a horse race.

Finally, close to graduation, the gang persuaded me to come along. It was early in June 1949. I had finished my thesis on the all-black Dining-Car Workers' Union, which I researched by playing in the weekly poker game these railroad workers ran at their Boston union hall. I was as ready for final exams as I was ever going to be. I figured spending a day at the track couldn't hurt.

Now my father, Harry, entered the picture again. He made his living building textile factories, inventing new textile-making machinery when necessary, and tirelessly finding ways to improve the performance of factories, machinery, and workers. Though he had never been a racegoer, when he reached his forties he wanted a hobby and turned his restless, inventive mind toward finding a way to gauge the performance of thoroughbred horses. He was a problem solver, an improver of systems. He clearly liked the challenge of measuring performance on a racetrack — but that proved to be far more difficult than measuring performance in a factory.

Horse races are run at various distances. How could one compare such efforts? Tracks are constructed differently — another barrier to comparison. Even at the same racetrack, the resilience of the surface varies, depending on the weather and what the ground crew does from day to day. And a horse's time for a race is also affected by the weight it carries, the wind, whether it races near the rail or far outside, and so on. All this makes the process of evaluating and comparing horses' performances a lot more complicated than matching up the records of Olympic swimmers or track athletes.

For instance, rain can make a track surface faster or slower. Wind is considered important enough that records are disallowed in human track meets when runners are aided by a breeze as trivial as 4 miles per hour.

Once Harry recognized how inadequately the two racing papers of that era, *The Morning Telegraph* and *The Daily Racing Form,* coped with these variables, he made corrections to their data in order to develop a race rating that measured the true physical output of a horse each time he ran. This rating was supposed to have absolute meaning. It would allow a handicapper to compare this horse directly with other horses in the race he had just run, to measure his race against his own past efforts in order to judge whether his condition was improving or declining, and to evaluate him against horses he would eventually meet.

Harry wanted figures that would allow precise comparisons even when horses racing against each other had previously competed at different distances, at different racetracks, and over the same racetrack but with differences in the speed of its surface on various days.

This approach was radically different from the traditional ways skilled handicappers rated thoroughbred horses at that time, a half-century ago. Written material on the subject generally boiled down to a debate about the power of "class" as opposed to "speed." Since the speed the theorists talked about was usually uncorrected ratings that included many inaccuracies, it was easy for the class theorists to demonstrate how often the "speed" horse didn't win. You'd do better, they showed, to search out a horse who consistently demonstrated the ability to make a good showing among animals whose presumptive worth (class) was similar to what he faced today.

Still, there remained the tantalizing fact that, by and large, higher-class horses do run faster — that is, show more speed. And since speed is precisely measurable, whereas class is a somewhat vague concept, it remained tempting to try to predict winners through speed.

In this search for rating-figures based on hard data, the obvious approach might have been to anchor ratings by adjusting raw time according to what seem like solid facts, such as the exact composition of the soil, the amount of banking or downhill run in certain portions of the track, the track records, the statistical average time it took to run an extra ⅛ of a mile.

Instead, Harry made a bold leap. He anchored his ratings on a factor that was really an expert opinion rather than a solid fact. His key became the claiming price at which a trainer decides to enter his horse.

When an owner or trainer enters a horse in a claiming race, other owners registered at that track can buy the horse at that price and take it away as soon as the race is run. As a businessman, Harry understood that trainers who weren't able to consistently enter their horses for something very near their real value would soon be forced out of the game.

Try for an easy win by entering your horse for too low a price and it will be claimed away, giving the new owner a chance to win at higher claiming-price levels. The trainer who does this too many times cannot keep his clients. On the other hand, overprotect your horses from claims by always running them for a little more than they are worth and you will rarely win a purse. You won't keep many clients that way, either.

So Harry reasoned that the prices at which mature horses entered claiming races could be used as a reliable indicator of true value, buried within a chaotic host of numbers — the running times of all different kinds of races. He boldly postulated that, on average, equal claiming prices meant equal performance, even if the running times looked different.

Now his task was to get comparable ratings for races run at various distances and/or at various tracks. My father hired a statistics student to average up the times run by horses performing under these varying circumstances at similar claiming prices. Winning an average $25,000 sprint at Monmouth Park would now earn the horse the same rating as that of a horse winning a $25,000 long-distance race at Aqueduct. (Later, we made some small adjustments for page size.)

These claiming-race averages allowed Harry to set what racing analysts now call "par times" for all commonly run distances at all tracks. (Rarely run distances are filled in by analytical extension.) But at the time Harry began these calculations, there was nothing in handicapping books to suggest this was a useful approach.

My father's work in this area he had picked out as a hobby also became another device by which he exerted control over my life. First he had persuaded me to go to Harvard and give up a healthy desire to attend MIT and become a physicist. Next he supported me in the advancement of my poker-playing skills. Now he introduced me to an innovative, intriguing way to handicap thoroughbred horses. When I called him from Harvard to say I was about to go to Suffolk Downs and see my first horse race, he sent me a long telegram listing all the corrections he would make to the *Morning Telegraph* speed ratings for that day's race card on the basis of his new research.

I took just $50 with me so I couldn't get hurt. Using my father's corrections, I hit one of the first seven races, and the winner paid enough so that I had $45 going into the eighth and final race. It was a long-distance race with a $2,000 claiming price and purse — as cheap as races come. As I applied Harry's corrections, a horse named Kardoso was clearly best. The *Telegraph* noted that Kardoso, who was five years old, was a maiden running against winners. But that didn't scare me because I was so green I didn't know that "maiden" meant the horse had never won. All I knew were the ratings I came up with. The tote board had Kardoso at odds of 30–1. I bet $15 across the board.

Kardoso was running eleventh early in the race, then began to rally. By the time the horses reached the three-quarter mark, he was in the thick of the race. They turned for home and he was between horses for a long and furious stretch drive — and got his head in front at the wire. Kardoso paid $69 to win. Counting my place and show bets, I collected more than $700.

The leader of those racetrack expeditions was my close friend Jim Biederman, an enormous intellect who later got a brief (and honest) moment on the scandal TV quiz show *Twenty-One*. Biederman had spent the entire afternoon lecturing me on the fine points of traditional handicapping — but he had no money on Kardoso. At the finish of the race he looked at me with a glum expression and growled, "Good handicapping."

The bitter tone of Biederman's compliment brought home to me in very personal terms what the potential might be in these early results of my father's spare-time hobby. What I viewed as entirely logical, following in a mechanical way the corrections he wired to me for the racing paper's data, was unsettling for experienced handicappers, who relied on "class" or on less accurate speed ratings.

The power of this method didn't end with cheap claiming races, either. At the 1953 Kentucky Derby, I showed it could be applied successfully — at generous odds — to the most famous race in the sport. It wasn't my first trip to Churchill Downs on Derby Day — three years earlier I had taken the train from Memphis, where I was working in a factory, to Louisville, and bet five winners using Harry's methods, including Middleground in the Derby.

But to watch the 1950 Derby, I had climbed onto a railing

way past the finish line to get a view above the mob of racegoers. This time I was going to be in the best box in the house, sitting with a group of wealthy businessmen. The box belonged to Herbert Bayard Swope Jr., a wealthy newspaper publisher who served with my father on the board of directors of my uncle's textile firm, Beaunit Mills. Swope was a society racegoer, with his own box at the New York tracks. My father and he used to talk racing before and after company board meetings but were not exactly friends. With his chauffeur-driven limousine and luxurious home, Swope was out of our league.

So it was something of a surprise when Swope's secretary called a few weeks before the Derby and offered my father the use of his box. Why us? Well, millionaire Swope was something of a pinchpenny. My father had seen him walk around the table after board meetings picking up the pencils other board members left behind. Harry concluded that Swope was offering him the box because Swope's real friends were too Social Register to think of offering him cash if he gave them the box. Harry told Swope's secretary he'd love to use the box but that he insisted on paying the printed price for the six seats — $96. The money was duly accepted — and every year through the end of the 1950s Swope made us the same offer.

The box was adjacent to the one that Churchill Downs kept perpetually vacant in memory of Colonel Matt Winn, the man who built up the Derby. It had a clear, overhanging view of the track, 1/16 of a mile before the finish line. A few boxes away was Alfred Gwynne Vanderbilt, whose unbeaten Native Dancer was the pre-race star for this Derby.

Native Dancer was so impressive as a two-year-old that he shared Horse of the Year honors. Only Secretariat has won that prize as a two-year-old in the years since. And on true speed, at least as the Ragozin figures measure it, Native Dancer at the age of two showed more than Secretariat, who improved more at three.

In contrast with the carefully spaced winter campaigns of today, a common road to the Derby in those days was a long winter layoff and a crowded March–April schedule. Native Dancer won the Gotham Stakes two weeks before the Derby at the old Jamaica track in New York, then came back a week later and won the Wood Memorial, also at Jamaica. Trainer Bill Winfrey was really cracking down. And he would, in fact, get the horse to deliver a top effort in the Derby.

I would have liked to see Native Dancer win that Derby. I admire real champions. But sentiment wasn't going to rule my betting. Native Dancer paid $2.30 in the Gotham and $2.20 in the Wood. He was going to be odds-on in the Derby. He might be worth it, but surely there was not much of a betting edge.

There was, however, another horse in the race, Dark Star, who, using the Ragozin figures plus a little imagination, could seriously be considered as an upsetter.

Native Dancer was fast and consistent. Dark Star rarely ran to his best figure. He was six lengths behind Native Dancer as a two-year-old in the Futurity and thirteenth in the Champagne Stakes a month later, beaten by nearly twenty-five lengths.

But after he was badly beaten in the Florida Derby in March as a three-year-old, Dark Star performed moderately well at Keeneland a month later and then, just four days before the Derby, surged to a four-length win in the Derby Trial. He was improving race to race, but could he continue to do so?

The Ragozin figures said yes. The previous September, just before the Futurity, Dark Star had won an allowance race at six furlongs in 1:09 ⅕. That race, according to the Ragozin rating, was better than his Derby Trial, so he still had room to improve. That effort had been only a shade worse than Native Dancer's steady top-class efforts. But now, in the Derby, Native Dancer was running in a big field with the uninspiring Eric Guerin riding. He was a cinch to lose ground racing on the outside. That could be the equalizer.

If Dark Star could come back to his sprint figure while running 1¼ miles, and if he saved ground while on the lead, and if Native Dancer lost ground and didn't jump to a new lifetime top — lots of ifs — the upset might be accomplished. The odds figured to be long enough to offset the ifs.

All week I had held forth about this, repeatedly and brashly, to my low-paid associates at *Newsweek,* where I was then a would-be writer-researcher, clipping stories from publications all over the world for the magazine's writers to plagiarize. I told my fellow clippers that I was going to the Derby and was playing Dark Star if he was 8–1 or better. Several of them gave me a few bucks to add to my investment.

My father and I drove down to Louisville the day before the Derby from our home at West 103rd Street in New York City. I was lugging a stack of *Racing Forms* and chart books containing races run by several Derby entrants from outside the New York / New Jersey / Florida axis, which our figures covered. In the hours leading up to the Derby, I was going to have to calculate whether any of these "foreigners" showed enough ability to disturb my plans.

So there we were at the world's biggest party and booze-fest, and I had my nose buried in old charts all day. I had no time to look at any of the other races on the card, or even to gaze at any Churchill Downs Derby Day hoopla. This did not necessarily work to my disadvantage as a Derby spectator, since the steady consumption of mint juleps throughout the day creates a state in which, immediately after the Derby horses cross the finish line, the most common expression around the track is, "Wha' happen?"

My research in the chart books concluded that the horses for which we didn't have accurate figures couldn't run very fast anyhow. Meanwhile, my father's business acquaintances who shared the box found my intensive study pretty amusing — sitting off in a corner, no drinking, never getting up to make a bet.

Finally it was time for the Derby. Dark Star was going to be about 25–1. With all the work I'd put in, and the confidence with which I touted the horse at *Newsweek,* I bet a grand total of $50 — $25 to win and $25 to place — on Dark Star. (My salary was less than $50 a week.)

Then I noticed a strange imbalance in the place pool. Native

Dancer was going to pay $3 to place — about the same as he would pay for a win bet. Considering his consistency, this seemed a fine way to "save" my gamble on Dark Star. I threw $100 on Native Dancer to run second. Finally, there was a 40–1 shot named Invigorator to whom the Ragozin figures gave a slim chance, so I bet $5 across the board on him. My father followed my lead but as befit a capitalist among capitalists he bet about ten times as much.

They broke from the gate and headed past the stands with the crowd roaring. Henry Moreno, Dark Star's jockey, did everything right. He used Dark Star's speed to get to the lead, moved him to the rail and saved ground all the way. He also saved the horse's strength by not pushing him to open a big lead. Guerin settled Native Dancer in eighth place early, and after a ½ mile he was ten lengths behind Dark Star. So far I was looking pretty good.

Guerin launched his move, and Native Dancer began picking up horses steadily but not spectacularly. It was the patented Guerin ride — losing plenty of ground by sweeping outside on the turn. When they straightened away for home, Native Dancer was just one and a half lengths behind, but Dark Star was not quitting. They came past where we were sitting, and the lead was less than a length. But it seemed clear that Native Dancer's big move was over. Unless Dark Star suddenly faltered, he was not going to be caught.

Some said later that if the race had been 10 yards longer, Native Dancer would have won. But that's mythology. After the horses passed us they were matching stride for stride and it stayed that way. Dark Star won by a head — the only race Native Dancer would ever lose in a twenty-two race career. Invigorator, incidentally, ran third. If there had been trifecta betting in those days, the score would have been immense.

Elated as I was over the success of the figures, I was still able to think as a journalist-to-be. I had brought along my Speed Graphic press camera, and I was only a few yards away from Alfred Vanderbilt. Here was a way to prove my worth at *Newsweek:* a picture of Vanderbilt immediately after his heavy favorite was beaten might

SEVENTH RACE
8 5 5 2 4
May 2-53—C.D

1 1-4 MILES. (Whirlaway, May 3, 1941—2:01⅖—3—126.) Seventy-ninth running THE KENTUCKY DERBY. $100,000 added. 3-year-olds. Scale weights. Trainer of winner, second and third horses to receive $3,000, $2,000 and $1,000, respectively, of the added money, and breeders of winner, second and third horses to receive $2,000, $1,000 and $500, respectively, of the added money, whether or not they are the owners of the horses when the race is run. Owner of winner to receive a gold trophy.
Gross value, $118,100. Net value to winner $90,050; second, $10,000; third, $5,000; fourth, $2,500. Mutuel Pool, $1,532,731.

Index	Horses	Eq't A Wt	PP	St	½	¾	1	Str	Fin	Jockeys	Owners	Odds to $1
(85175)	DARK STAR	w 126	10	3	$1^{1\frac{1}{2}}$	$1^{\frac{1}{2}}$	$1^{1\frac{1}{2}}$	$1^{1\frac{1}{2}}$	1^{h}	H Moreno	Cain Hoy Stable	24.90
(85023)	NATIVE DANCER	w 126	6	6	8^{3}	$4^{\frac{1}{2}}$	4^{2}	2^{1}	2^{5}	E Guerin	A G Vanderbilt	a-.70
85023^{3}	INVIGORATOR	w 126	4	5	$7^{\frac{1}{2}}$	$6^{\frac{1}{2}}$	6^{1}	4^{1}	3^{2}	W Sho'aker	Saxon Stable	40.90
85175^{4}	ROYAL BAY GEM	w 126	11	11	11	8^{2}	$7^{1\frac{1}{2}}$	$7^{1\frac{1}{2}}$	$4^{1\frac{1}{2}}$	J Combest	E Constantin Jr	6.80
(84881)	CORRESPONDENT	w 126	2	2	2^{2}	2^{1}	$2^{\frac{1}{2}}$	3^{1}	$5^{1\frac{3}{4}}$	E Arcaro	Mrs G Guiberson	3.00
84881^{2}	STRAIGHT FACE	wb 126	9	7	4^{3}	3^{1}	$3^{\frac{1}{2}}$	5^{h}	6^{nk}	T Atkinson	Greentree Stable	10.40
85023^{4}	SOCIAL OUTCAST	w 126	8	10	$10^{\frac{1}{2}}$	$10^{1\frac{1}{2}}$	8^{2}	8^{2}	7^{2}	J Adams	A G Vanderbilt	a-.70
85175^{2}	MONEY BROKER	wb 126	7	9	$5^{\frac{1}{2}}$	$5^{\frac{1}{2}}$	5^{h}	6^{3}	$8^{2\frac{3}{4}}$	A Popara	G & G Stable	45.80
85175	RAM O' WAR	wb 126	3	8	$9^{\frac{1}{2}}$	11	10^{1}	9^{1}	9^{nk}	D Dodson	B S Campbell	85.10
85175	CURRAGH KING	wb 126	5	4	6^{2}	9^{1}	11	11	10^{h}	D Erb	E M Goemans	99.10
84881^{4}	ACE DESTROYER	wb 126	1	1	$3^{\frac{1}{2}}$	7^{2}	9^{3}	10^{1}	11	J D Jessop	Mr & Mrs T M Daniel	91.80

a-Coupled, Native Dancer and Social Outcast.

Time, :23⅘, :47⅘, 1:12⅕, 1:36⅗, 2:02. Track fast.

Mutuel Prices	$2 Mutuels Paid			Odds to $1		
DARK STAR	51.80	13.60	7.00	24.90	5.80	2.50
NATIVE DANCER (a-Entry)		3.20	2.80		.60	.40
INVIGORATOR			9.40			3.70

Winner—Br. c, by Royal Gem II.—Isolde, by Bull Dog, trained by E. Hayward; bred by W. L. Jones, Jr.
REACHED POST—4:32. OFF AT 4:32½ CENTRAL DAYLIGHT TIME.
Start good from stall gate. Won driving; second and third the same. DARK STAR, alertly ridden, took command soon after the start, set the pace to the stretch under steady rating, then responded readily when set down in the drive and lasted to withstand NATIVE DANCER, but won with little left. NATIVE DANCER, roughed at the first turn by MONEY BROKER, was eased back to secure racing room, raced wide during the run to the upper turn, then saved ground entering the stretch and finished strongly, but could not overtake the winner, although probably best. INVIGORATOR, in close quarters entering the backstretch, raced well when clear and closed willingly under urging, but could not threaten the top pair. ROYAL BAY GEM, away sluggishly, was forced to lose ground while working way forward and could not reach the leaders when set down through the stretch. CORRESPONDENT, bumped after the break by ACE DESTROYER, recovered under good handling and raced nearest DARK STAR to the stretch, but had nothing left for the drive. STRAIGHT FACE raced prominently to the mile, then weakened. SOCIAL OUTCAST lacked early speed and was never dangerous. MONEY BROKER swerved into NATIVE DANCER at the first turn, raced well to the stretch, then gave way.

be a shot that a weekly would use: an exclusive, with human interest.

I climbed up on the box railing and balanced shakily. "Hey, Alf!" I yelled. He turned, resignation all over his face. I snapped the shot but my shaky footing betrayed me and the image turned out to be not quite sharp enough to print.

Meanwhile, the businessmen in the box seemed astonished at what Harry and I had just done. With Dark Star paying $51.80, our family profit was about $10,000 — but I don't remember getting any share of my father's winnings.

The score on Dark Star also made me a sort of minor celebrity at *Newsweek*. A month later, however, the FBI came around to see me and I suddenly had a new, very different sort of distinction on the job.

I should have expected it, but I didn't. It was now the height of the McCarthy era — open season on anyone who even wore his hat on the left. But plenty of people I knew who really did consider themselves communists had been harassed by the government long before McCarthy came along. What was about to happen to me at *Newsweek* wasn't the first time my politics had affected my employability.

A few years earlier, when I was trying to get into union organizing by working as a factory hand in Memphis, I bumped into a former classmate from Harvard who was now a cub reporter for the local newspaper. Putting his own career ahead of any consideration for what the consequences for me might be, he handed in a story to his paper about the leftist Harvard grad doing factory work. That made it very easy for local employers to blacklist me. Whatever job I got in Memphis lasted a very short time. Foremen often fired me rather sheepishly, having been given no clear idea, I guess, as to why they were told to do so.

My Memphis experience was terminated when I was drafted — but I turned out to be unemployable even in the U.S. Army. Nothing special would have happened to me in the army if I had kept my mouth shut. But that's not my style. Like a jockey who has yet to take his first spill, I still had all my youthful optimism. I liked risks. I was still acting on my political beliefs — trying to swing people around to a more critical way of thinking about the conditions of their life and work. And here I was with an audience of scared kids, swept off the streets of Brooklyn, the Bronx, and Manhattan, who knew that in nine weeks they would likely be facing bullets from the Chinese Army half the world away from home. I became my camp's anti–Korean War radical blabbermouth.

I still have a collection of threatening letters I kept getting from higher and higher army brass implying dire consequences if I didn't change my behavior. I didn't change. Finally, after more than a year, they blinked — and discharged me.

Now, at *Newsweek,* I was next in line for promotion from researcher to junior editor. Then a couple of FBI agents paid me a visit on the job.

The agents worked in the classic cops' good-guy / bad-guy act. The short, ferretlike character displayed a hot temper, and the tall, friendly performer kept saying, "Go easy. Lenny seems like a good Joe." They wanted me to tell them who had been my pals in communist political activities at Harvard. Despite my nervousness, I could figure out that this question was one to which they must already know the answer, so it was simply a way to test the waters, to get me to start cooperating with them. As calmly as I could — and I was actually plenty panicked — I kept saying that I didn't want to talk with them. After a time, they got right down to business: "You better play ball or we'll get you in bad on your job." I sounded a lot cooler than I actually felt when I replied, "You have your life to live and I have mine."

Not much later, my big *Newsweek* career moment came around. The next editor in the business news department was supposed to be me — on the basis of seniority among the researcher candidates. The business editor, a Southern gentleman with old-fashioned manners, liked my work and, I think, liked me for my somewhat Victorian behavior — I never swapped dirty jokes or tales of sex escapades with the other young guys in the office. He had promised me this job when it opened up. But when I reported to work on the fateful morning, bright-eyed and ready to hear the good news, I was told that there was no promotion. When I asked the editor what was going on, he seemed genuinely distressed.

"I've been ordered not to give you this job, Lenny," he said, as his eyes avoided contact with mine.

To be denied such a minor and routine promotion was unheard of. But it was clear the FBI had stepped in to give me some strong career advice: we can make you an unemployable. I couldn't see staying with this hanging over my head — so I quit.

I had to assume that any other place I went to work, the FBI would come calling again. I needed a way to make a living where I couldn't be fired. The nearest thing at hand was to use the Ragozin data to try to make my way by betting horses seriously. I was already doing it as a sideline, and enjoying it.

I took over all the work of maintaining my father's speed figures. But maintaining soon turned to refining and innovating — to the point where the figures became mine more than his. Eventually, I began using 8″ × 5½″ sheets of custom-designed graph paper to chart each horse's development, which is how my data became known as *The Sheets.*

After the McCarthy era ended, the FBI stayed in touch periodically over the next twenty years. But my most serious brush with the bureau — in 1977 — actually involved horse racing, not politics. By then I had a friend and partner, Len Friedman, who bet for us while I spent all my time in the office generating the figures. That September, Friedman capped a spectacular betting run by having two tickets on a winning triple at Belmont that paid $29,855. A few days later, it was discovered that the winner of that race — a 50–1 shot listed in the *Racing Form* as a cheap South American import named Lebon — was actually a champion runner from Uruguay named Cinzano. The horse had been entered under a false name for a betting coup.

As part of the criminal investigation that followed, the FBI wanted words with me because my partner, Friedman — the only person with two tickets on the winning triple — had (as usual) cashed them in my name. The FBI agent who came to our office didn't look too happy when I said I had to give him a handicapping lesson to explain our wager. Friedman and I tried to educate him on just what we were doing in our little betting factory in Greenwich Village. With an advanced horseplayer or a mathematician it might have been easy to demonstrate that, based on the figures we had calculated for "Lebon" and his opponents, a very normal improvement his second time out in this country would have made him as good as anything in the race. And "Lebon" also had the benefit of five months' rest before his first U.S. outing. Furthermore, we explained to the agent, it was the fall season, and the favorites in the race were going stale after hard, year-long campaigns. Their poor condition meant they wouldn't run to their best ratings. It was all very clear, we showed him on *The Sheets,* that Lebon was a reasonable bet.

I don't think the agent really followed all this. He was probably ordered to interview us because of our bet rather than from any suspicion that we were in on the coup. Anyhow, the FBI didn't impound our winnings.

My next contact with the FBI came after the Freedom of Information Law took effect and made it possible for citizens to get a look at files the government collected on them. In 1984 I asked for my FBI file because I thought it might help me to reminisce. (I've never been the type to keep diaries — my interest is in today or tomorrow.)

But as a nostalgia trip, my 187-page FBI file was a total bust. It only hit the high spots — the things I remembered anyway. Eighty percent of the typing was blacked out by a heavy marker. So much for Freedom of Information.

I can't regret the way my politics steered my life. Along with my successful betting and horse ownership while building *The Ragozin Sheets* into a respected, profitable, and intellectually satisfying enterprise, I also got a long-desired chance to edit a left-wing newspaper during the Vietnam War era. (When my leftist friends there learned that I supported myself betting on horses, some were horrified. Others proposed that I publish tips in the newspaper in order to increase its circulation. Communist morality prevailed, however, and this proposal was rejected.)

Without the FBI's pressures, I might have remained at *Newsweek,* a pleasant but essentially very dull place, and contented myself with remaining an armchair Marxist. As it turned out, life has been far more interesting.

I was never driven by a need to be a big success by the world's standards. I did my work because I enjoyed it. I continue to work at it with pleasure years after I could have comfortably retired. Now, as I look back, I realize that what I did with *The Sheets* was about as high an achievement as I was ever likely to gain. What's to complain?

2

Searching for a Better Method

WHEN MY FATHER AND I began creating our own speed figures, we decided to ignore all printed material on the merits of "class" versus "speed" (after reading all that was in print in those areas). In retrospect, I see that *The Sheets* basically bridge the gap between class and speed. First we comb out variables and arrive at an accurate series of speed figures — the sheet. Then the soundness of the horse, the percentage of times it can run near its best speed figure or improve on it, becomes the missing factor in measuring its class.

By this analysis, it is not surprising when the horse with the best previous speed figure does not win the race. More important: How likely is the horse to run to that figure on a given day? A steady horse with limited speed is, of course, low class. But a horse who runs ten bad races and one extremely good one is also of dubious class. My father and I didn't express our work in these terms; what we did was take the thesis — speed — and the antithesis — class — and come up with our overall synthesis.

Combing out variables was at the heart of our approach. Weight, for example, is a variable that unless taken into account makes final time for a race an unreliable measure of performance. If weight carried didn't affect speed, designers of racing cars and yachts wouldn't spend so much money to reduce it. The question is not whether weight matters, but how much. The more accurately your figures get rid of other variables, the more accurately you can test for the effect of weight.

Early on, my father recognized how key this weight correction was and he made an innovative leap in solving the problem. He must have been a little lucky because he came up with a perfect correction. Every other formula derived in our early days of calculating figures has been revised as we developed ever more accurate figures. But in forty years of working on these figures, I've never had to revise his weight correction.

Originally my father's figures ignored the effect of wind. But once I took an interest in these figures, it seemed obvious to me that wind was often causing horses to run faster (or slower) than they otherwise would. A really strong wind not only created a physical barrier or provided an assist that affected the horses' running times, but it could be so disconcerting that it actually confused some horses or made them extra cautious: in effect, scaring them out of giving anywhere near a normal effort.

The track surface was another unsolved puzzle for most handicappers. Some racing surfaces are built to be faster than others and, regardless of weather, will produce faster running times. This might be caused by the nature of the soil and the subsurface. Chutes — the extra straightaways (some downhill) that allow races to be run using one fewer turn — also speed up a race. Races of 1⅛ miles at Belmont Park, for instance, are run around a single turn by starting from a long chute, so horses will go faster there than at most tracks, where 1⅛ mile races start in front of the grandstand and go around two turns.

Downhill chutes, which exist at racetracks from Monmouth Park to Santa Anita, pose another performance measurement problem, which I spotted as soon as I began to look more closely at my father's figures. It seemed to me that accuracy demanded that we know the degree of slope of chutes at each track where they existed, something my father's initial corrections never considered.

Figuring out the daily change in track speed or resiliency was also a weak link in the approach my father initially developed. The *Morning Telegraph* (New York's old version of *The Racing Form*), which was then a handicapper's chief tool for analysis, printed a "variant" figure for each day that — like today's *Racing Form* figure — very roughly measured differing track conditions. Harry made some modifications to improve this variant in his initial work, but it was left to me to solve this most central problem with much more precision years later.

With his innovations, Harry had a framework for speed ratings that didn't follow *The Racing Form* by depending on an extraordinary — and therefore aberrant — performance like a track record to set the scale. To make his "100" rating something that only the best horses could occasionally reach, he set the cheapest claiming horses at the major tracks (at that time, roughly a $3,000 claimer) equal to a rating of 80. Each 25-percent rise in claiming price was equal to an additional point. One point was how much faster a 25-percent pricier horse ran at that particular distance. Conveniently, it turned out that a 25-percent increase in claiming price was worth about ⅕ of a second in the most common race distance — six furlongs.

After we averaged up performances for all distances and rated them by this claiming-price system, we found that the longer the race, the greater the time spread achieved by a better horse. So a "90" horse would be 10 fifths of a second faster than an "80" horse at six furlongs, but many more fifths faster at 1½ miles. This, of course, is what you would expect — the longer the race lasts, the farther the better horse runs away from its inferiors.

Once the rating scale was set up with claimers, all nonclaiming horses were measured on that same scale.

Obviously, when the track got slow or muddy, the figures needed adjustment. For convenience (remember, this was a hobby, not a business for him), Harry made an admittedly rough adjustment on the very imprecise track variant published in *The Telegraph.* Nevertheless, even the first, somewhat ragged speed figures Harry calibrated were good enough to produce betting profits.

As I worked with my father's figures and looked at a lot of

sheets, I developed strong suspicions that the horses' lines would make more sense, be more predictive, if certain variables that we weren't using were added to our practice. And I was willing to do the work to test those intuitions.

I have an inquiring mind, though more of a refiner's mind than that of a brilliant innovator. But I'm willing to work hard to test my hunches. Back then, there were no computers — it was all hard labor. In terms of effort, I compare it to the drudgery endured by Marie Curie, who spent years in a cold shack stirring pots of ore in order to confirm her idea that radium was in there somewhere.

The two main changes I imposed on the par-time structure I inherited from my father were: wind corrections, and an independently calculated daily track variant to replace his modified *Morning Telegraph* figure. In retrospect, I see that these two fundamental improvements, which broke new ground in speed ratings, were linked. Without wind corrections, you cannot have a single variant that works accurately for both one-turn and two-turn races — because wind often affects those races in an opposite manner. But wind corrections mean extra work — gathering the data track by track for every hour of every racing day and figuring out how the track's various distances are affected by this wind. Most of today's handicappers don't want all this trouble, so they cop out by merely making separate variants for long and short races. If they're lucky, this procedure overcomes the wind differential. But they're pushed into depending on very small samples to make these separate variants, and errors often result.

I tackled the wind correction problem first because wind is physical and real. I also had an excellent way to get a handle on it. They were still running races then out of Belmont's old Widener chute — a six and a half-furlong straightaway. On that track, wind influence was gross, which made it easier to equate wind-speed and horse-speed.

I looked at the figure sequences — the patterns — of all the horses that ran on a windy day and noted that correcting their windy-day times by a certain amount would bring aberrant figures into the horses' normal range and make their sequences much smoother. Soon I knew how much wind per furlong equaled how much time-change.

Next came calculating a daily variant for track condition or resiliency. But the value of making this change was just a theory — actually hardly more than a hunch. In fact, it seemed scary to consider abandoning our finely honed, speed-chart averages on a day when, to the eye, the track surface looked normal. Could we be deluding ourselves by adding or subtracting a claiming-race-based "variant" when the listed track condition was the usual "fast"?

True, a physical reality lay behind the track-variant idea, just as it did for wind corrections. A racetrack is not a synthetic surface, subject to little variation. Its resiliency changes in response to work done by groundskeepers and to moisture. Nevertheless, at first I pussyfooted. I shifted a day's figures only halfway between our basic speed-chart figure and what the variant — based on the day's performance of claiming-race horses — indicated the day's true speed should be.

In other words, if, by and large, all the claiming horses on a certain fast-track day were getting ratings somewhat better than you would expect for animals of their claiming price, I wouldn't give them full credit. I would assume that extra track-resiliency had something to do with it, and shade the figure to include this concept. But since the track carried its standard "fast" label, I was afraid to overcorrect the figure. I sat on the fence and compromised.

The more I worked with these compromise figures, though, the clearer it became that if I hadn't been so conservative, the horses' lines would have become more meaningful and more predictive. Finally, I acted on the courage of my convictions. All figures for the day — not only on wet tracks but on aberrant-looking "fast" tracks, too — became anchored by the claiming-race variant. If all the claimers ran slowly, the assumption for that day became that the track was dull. Horses were given ratings better than their actual speed. The exceptions to this rule were based not upon compromise but rather on analysis of each day. I tried not to correct the occasional day in which I judged that the claiming races looked off-base merely by aberration rather than because of a real difference in track speed.

This judgment meant advanced handicapping, of course, and was possible only as the figures — and my understanding of horses' development — got better.

When all this ground-shaking theoretical work was well under way, I took my few hundred dollars in vacation pay due after my forced exit from *Newsweek* and began betting for real.

How long has this been going on? was my first joyful reaction. My $300 became $6,000 in two months. But the harsh laws of probability soon humbled me. The process of refining the performance figures, which I have never ceased to do, does not automatically produce successful betting results.

The favorite is usually the fastest horse — but if you bet all favorites, you lose. My long-run success began only after I was struck by the patterns of condition revealed in the figures. I asked, Is this horse moving along in a pattern of better, still better, best; or taking a step back after an improvement and then charging forward again; or falling way back after a stupendous effort? Finally I began comparing these various patterns for all the horses in a race and assessing which were the best for betting. That meant finding a horse headed toward a good performance but also with a *Racing Form* line that contained some element of concealment of his good form so as to steer the public off the bet and build the odds. . . .

There were two lean years while I was subconsciously absorbing this "condition" data and losing money on pure speed. I worked hard to refine both the figures and my own analysis of what made a line that was worth betting.

Fortunately, I could fall back on the poker table for subsistence money in emergencies. There were plenty of games in Greenwich Village, where I lived at the time, and a plentiful supply of high-salaried poker addicts who showed up to rub elbows with bohemia. My other antidote to poverty was that I was living happily in a $10-a-week furnished room. This never bothered me and certainly was no stigma in my crowd.

By the end of the 1950s I had come up with the idea that I now realize set me apart from the vast majority of handicappers. I would use these increasingly accurate figures to compare a horse with ITSELF rather than with other horses.

My new approach was to recognize and predict radical changes in what a horse might do today, rather than rely on averaging up old performances. This meant interpreting the inevitable peaks and valleys in the horse's physical condition. Once I recognized how powerful this approach could be, we began entering a horse's numbers on *The Sheets* in such a way that the flow from peaks (which on *The Sheets* today are entered as lower numbers) and valleys (higher numbers) of performance could be easily seen. We "graphed" it. The basic design of today's *Ragozin Sheets* emerged.

I began winning steadily literally from the first day that I gave horses in a race "condition letters" based on their trends instead of just projecting the next number for a horse from an arithmetical reading of previous numbers.

I assigned two condition letters: one for the horse's long-term condition and another for the attractiveness of the immediate pattern. Among other things, this second letter stopped me from betting a horse whose last race was a "big top" — an especially good effort. Others call this the "bounce theory." To me, there is no such elaborate theory. If your figures are really good, mere observation reveals that horses usually bounce to a poorer race after big efforts, with certain exceptions for horses who have not yet fully matured.

I began to bet my best condition letters even if those horses had less average speed than the favorites. The money return on horses with a big condition edge proved startling. Horses in good condition run a better figure than any handicapper is likely to project based on past performance. Even if they don't, their competitors — horses in mediocre condition — often enough throw in a single bad effort, so that the slower-but-fitter horse wins by default. Once I recognized this, I was getting long odds by betting slower but healthier horses. My precise rating of speed was producing overlay bets — against that speed!

3

Getting the Right Number

CONVENTIONAL WISDOM about handicapping never seems to be required to pass any scientific tests. Of course, that's part of the charm of racing — everyone's entitled to his own nutty ideas. And you aren't supposed to ask them the rude question, "Yes, but are you winning?" When you do, the practitioner always implies that he is, or that he would be if his theory wasn't undermined by lack of control at the betting windows. Sometimes I get a little mean and offer to bet such guys that if they mail me just one selection per day, they won't show a profit at the end of a year. So far, none of the barroom theorizers I've met has taken this challenge.

I always smiled at my father's concern that we had better keep very quiet about our valuable theories. But their success has indeed had at least one effect he lived long enough to see. Today the range of serious discussion about approaches to racing is much narrower than it was twenty years ago. Our success — and later, the success of our customers — both as bettors and as horse owners had a great deal to do with this. Serious handicappers today accept that the bedrock of their work must be a speed figure that overcomes the limitations of *The Racing Form* speed rating.

Handicapping based on the idea that horses cycle in and out of form is today considered normal. I never saw a word written about it, however, in the days before Preston King became New York's leading trainer by making claims under *Sheets* guidance, and before he and his millionaire clients talked up *The Sheets.*

One thing hasn't changed much: "The Bible." *The Daily Racing Form* really does contain all the facts you need to start attacking the problem. Seal me in a room and send in *The Racing Form* plus Weather Bureau wind readings, and I'll send out to you passable figures, even without all the special data we now generate to arrive at *Sheets* figures, including private clockings and track observers' notes on who raced wide and who hugged the rail.

But *The Racing Form* shorthand approach of a simple speed rating and variant, which when taken together are supposed to tell you how fast a horse really ran, is just good enough to get you hooked. Eventually, though, you fall short because of its limitations. Despite recent adjustments, these figures are much too imprecise for making decisions about races where the margin of victory will often be less than a fifth of a second. Put it another way: The signal that a horse has turned the corner and is pointing back toward good form may be based on a comparison of efforts that are so close to each other that there is not only absolutely no chance that *The Racing Form*'s speed rating will reveal it but, in my opinion, very little chance that other people's more advanced rating systems will get the figures accurate enough to spot the shift more than half the time. The main purpose of *The Form*'s ratings (they do have a rational basis) is to provide a semicasual player with a foundation for building a "system." This helps keep the betting game going, so as a businessman I guess I should be grateful.

The Racing Form gives you two numbers:

- a speed rating that sets 100 as its usual top, meaning the fastest time run at that distance in the past three years;
- a variant, or speed adjustment, that merely averages up how many fifths of a second all that day's winners fall short of a

> 100 rating. This is a very crude measure of track condition — especially because it is too much affected by the quality of the horses that happen to be running on a particular day. On a lightning-fast racetrack *The Form*'s variant could be as low as zero. More typically, the variant will be around 15 on a fast track, much higher in bad mud.

The Racing Form's idea of how you build your handicapping system is to add the speed rating and the variant together. The horse who has a speed rating of 92 on a day when the variant is 15 is considered faster than a horse who got a speed rating of 95 when the track was more resilient and the variant was 7.

Early on, my father used his own modified version of these imprecise variants to adjust his own speed ratings, which were based on the performances of claiming-race horses rather than record-holders. He knew that he needed a correction that was meant to reflect the condition of the track on a particular day — especially when the track condition was slop or mud. However, Harry's claimer-based ratings were so accurate compared to what other people then had that he began making money on his bets despite the crude variant (not to mention the lack of wind corrections, private clocking, and adjustments for saving ground or racing wide that we now use). With profits coming in, he lacked incentive to improve. I was more of a perfectionist, interested in the work itself, unsatisfied with loose ends or partial solutions.

Harry had made a big step forward in developing his ratings by completely eliminating track records or best times. Some track records are set by top-class horses, but races for rarely run distances might be set by mediocre runners. I claimed a $15,000 horse for my father named Sunny and Mild, who soon moved into stakes company and set a track record at Aqueduct on November 18, 1972. But this was in a low-grade stakes at 1³⁄₁₆ miles. Top-class horses skipped that race, and there were no big stakes run at that distance. Sunny and Mild got a speed rating of over 100 from *The Racing Form* for that race. But the horse really ran a figure not much better than that of a top-class claiming horse.

In recent years, *The Racing Form* has tried to improve matters by pegging its 100 rating to the fastest time run at a distance in the previous three years, rather than the track record. It's hard to understand why this is better. At least when they use the track record you know where you are. You can easily see when and by how much it changes. Since you have to make corrections anyhow, I think it is less confusing to deal with track records, which don't change as often as three-year best times and always change in the same direction — faster.

A second problem with these ratings — a mistake that is made by quite a few sophisticated ratings-makers — is that they allow exactly 1 point for each length behind that a horse runs, regardless of a race's distance. A one-point-per-fifth scale says that there's no difference between a horse being beaten by two lengths at six furlongs and a horse losing by that same margin at 1½ miles. Once you make this error, ratings can't properly reflect the abilities of horses running at different distances. (Even equating one length to one-fifth of a second, as *The Racing Form* and many others do, is a mistake. One-sixth of a second per length is more accurate.)

The fact is, the further horses race, the more distance will separate the good ones from the mediocre ones. This fact is fairly obvious not only in horses but in racing cars and among human runners. A contestant who is one grade better than his competitor will beat him by a wider margin in a longer race. For a rating to be usable as a comparison of true ability, it must allow for this. This is why the owners of quarter horses, who race for large purses at very short distances, long ago insisted on a rating system based upon hundredths of a second rather than fifths.

When my father and I set out to measure what effect distance had on performance, we didn't start with any assumption that a more expensive horse would beat a cheaper horse by an extra amount for each extra furlong in the race. We started with facts. We averaged up what thousands of claiming horses actually did.

If anything, we were expecting a dropping-off curve. We had guessed that cheap horses would probably get very fatigued at around 1¼ miles or so and — compared with a sprint — fall further behind than simple geometry would predict. But our study showed a linear fall-off, with this fatigue factor very minor until the races get longer than 1½ miles.

Since *The Racing Form* does not adjust its rating for extra distance, it is no surprise that a lot more horses get speed ratings in the 90s running in short races than when they go over a mile.

The Racing Form arrives at its variant by taking the winning times of all the horses at the track that day, comparing them to their 100-rating times, noting how many fifths they fell short, and then averaging up these differences. Nowadays *The Racing Form*'s sprint variant is calculated separately from the one for races of a mile or longer, and it uses a separate average for turf races, again divided into sprints and routes.

The Form's use of separate sprint / route variants is a dubious improvement on its old overall average. This approach means a "variant" is often based on a very small sample — sometimes just one race run that day at a particular distance. Such a variant will always give the horses in that race their usual sort of figure, obscuring the cases in which they all ran better or worse than expected.

Another problem with *The Form*'s variant arises when the day includes a race for which the 100 rating is way out of line. For instance, in Belmont Park's 1⅜-mile races on dirt — which are run only when a race is rained off the turf — the winner tends to come too near the 100 rating. Using that race will distort the track variant.

The Form tells you, in its explanation, the main problem with its variant: "The lower the track variant, the faster the track, OR the better the overall quality of the competition." A low variant means a lot of winners got near the 100 rating. This might truly indicate a very resilient racing surface. But it could mean that a lot of genuinely good horses were entered on that day. If you rate your horses by adding speed rating to variant, horses who ran on such a day are going to get cheated by an artificially low variant.

The more you think about this flaw, the more you are drawn to make some kind of allowance for the true class of the horses who contributed to the variant. In other words, you are pulled toward what I do: start with horses of known ability — claimers — and make a variant from what they do. You could extend this idea by grading various kinds of allowance races and stakes and working them into a scale that will compare logically with your claimers. But unless you have some way of combing out the effect of good cards versus bad cards on your track variant, you can't achieve an accurate result.

Toward the end of the early period, when my father was still using *The Racing Form*'s variant, he made a crude effort to overcome at least the most flagrant cases of artificially fast variants. He made a special correction for Saturdays, since those cards were likely to feature better horses. Then he started correcting for Mondays, which in those days often had a lot of maiden races. Well, you can see why I got increasingly restless with the idea of using *The Racing Form*'s variant at all.

In tacit acknowledgment of its own ratings' shortcomings, several years ago *The Form* started printing Andy Beyer's speed figures. This is both better and worse. Better, because Beyer has a good idea of what a par time should be and thus combs out the most obvious of *The Racing Form*'s errors. Worse, if you are using his ratings as gospel.

Since *The Form* doesn't explain how Beyer arrives at his ratings — except to say that he employs a team of experts — they are hard to analyze. His actual figures show he sometimes uses separate variants for long and short races. If he does, he falls into the trap of basing variants on very small samples, especially during times of the season when half the races are run on the turf. But if he sticks to his single variant for short and long, he invites inaccuracy by the fact that he makes no allowance for wind, not to mention weight or ground lost racing wide on the turns. In an effort to compensate for all these problems, if the figures for an individual race "look wrong" to Beyer, he assigns a figure for that individual race based purely on a projection of what these horses showed earlier on his figures — what they "should have" run. You have no way of knowing when Beyer's all-knowing attitude has led him to override both the actual hard data on an individual race and his own variant to assign a "judgment" figure.

In a Las Vegas seminar in 1990, I heard Beyer state that if an individual race comes out "too fast" or "too slow" — meaning that the whole field runs better or worse than the horses' previous Beyer ratings — you should assign a rating on this race purely on projections from those previous numbers rather than using his average variant. His book *Beyer on Speed* says this also.

To me, this is ducking the problem. If I change the variant for one race only, there had better be a thunderstorm. If I change the effective time, there had better be a big wind shift — or even a misplaced starting pole, as sometimes happens on the turf. My figure cannot detach itself from the physical realities of the day just to make the horse's line come out neater.

My father used the facts contained in *The Form*'s speed ratings. He did not arbitrarily override them; he systematically corrected them. He started out with no prejudices. He had never bet and had no misconceptions or fixed ideas. A production man in industry, he just dealt with hard facts. He wanted a figure that told you who was running better regardless of the distance and the track.

Unfortunately, there will be a few erratic mistakes in the printed racing data — especially when temporary rails are put up on the turf course in order to conserve the condition of the grass. In the old days, when I didn't have my own observers, and inaccurate data resulted in unbelievable figures for a race, I was forced to take the Beyer option and just wing it — just rate one race by itself. This might have happened once or twice in an entire race meeting. But with our own observer data, never.

For Beyer, however, breaking a single race out of his general mold is a more frequent occurrence. His approach may be better than submitting to an error, but it also may lead you to assume a nonexistent error on a day when the horses really did run an exceptional race. And it cuts that race out of contributing to your overall variant, leaving you with less data to make your average. To me, it's better to actually track down the error and keep all my figures integrated.

I am trying to give you an idea of how we approach the problem of creating good ratings, so that those who don't want the expense of buying *The Sheets* or who would rather have the satisfaction of making their own figures can get an idea of how to arrive at passable ratings. My mind rebels at the idea of using "passable" data in a game that is so hard to beat. However, you are free to feed on the ideas I introduce to you here and develop your own details.

The value of our painstaking approach to setting the variants has been demonstrated not only by the success of our longtime customers but in a recent analysis by the SPORT-STAT organization. Using *The Ragozin Sheets* and a mechanical betting method, SPORT-STAT showed a profit and did about 15 percent better per dollar bet than using Beyer, on whose figures it showed a loss. Tests it did with another rating service, Thoro-Graph, founded by a former employee of mine who knows my formulas, showed results even worse than using Beyer. (To get SPORT-STAT's study, call them in Las Vegas.) To me, these results demonstrate that even when you have most of your concepts right, as Beyer and Thoro-Graph do, there is a lot of experience and judgment involved in making accurate par times, and — especially — in reaching precise daily variants.

I now make a daily racing variant based on the foundation of our original speed ratings — the average results of all the claiming races that include four-year-olds. Each racing day, at every track, we average up, after first correcting for wind, the first 40 percent of the finishers in these claiming races to see if they are running near their norm or unusually fast or slow. This indicates track speed.

By using these more ordinary horses, you have the advantage of dealing with the typical rather than the exceptional, which is what a track record or a three-year fastest time represents. A mature horse who is running in a claiming race has generally demonstrated his limitations to his trainer. He should be a known quality. Of course, if he was recently claimed by a trainer who has found the latest undetectable miracle method for boosting speed . . . you'll have to adjust! Yes, occasionally, an older claimer overcomes some physical problem — perhaps with some quiet help from medical science — and runs an outstanding race. This could knock the claiming-race average times for the day out of whack, leaving you with the riddle of whether this horse was really that good or whether everything else running that day actually was running poorly. I average in some of the horses who finish behind the winner to try to avoid being thrown by such unusual efforts.

Even then, the claiming-race averages are only my first approximation. Based on this approximation, I use my par times for the given track — plus the beaten lengths — to give a speed rating to every single horse who ran that day. This is where judgment becomes crucial. For the greatest accuracy of every number, these preliminary figures — which use the claiming-race variant — must be modified by looking at every horse. But, modified by how much?

The Sheets at this stage show a single figure for every race run by every horse. Wind, weight, path, and the approximate variant are already allowed for in the figure. When I modify the variant, I look at how closely all the horses ran to what might have been expected, based on trends considering their recent form and their lifetime ability, and recognizing that young horses in good condition may surpass their lifetime tops.

If a lot of horses are in line with what they should logically have run, setting the variant can be simple. But there are plenty of days when the numbers are tough to judge. Getting the variant right on such days is what separates *The Sheets* from the goats. The problem presents itself as a decision between sticking very near to the claiming-race average as an exact judge of that day's track speed (variant); or, deviating a little — or sometimes a lot — because your handicapping judgment tells you that a lot of horses were legitimately ready to run nontypical performances on this day, so the raw averages need to be taken with a grain of salt.

You also have to remember that these aren't just airy numbers; you are governed by the racetrack's physical realities, which create these changes in speed. Seriously underconsidered by Beyer and most other modern analysts is the *likely* speed of the track today, based on weather — especially precipitation — and on the track superintendent's habitual day-to-day changes in grooming the track. Today's variant should relate in an explainable way to yesterday's and tomorrow's. But these physical influences on the variant can't become clear unless you modify running times by wind corrections; otherwise, part of your variant reflects a changed wind and has nothing to do with ground resiliency.

Regardless of your claiming-race averages and your handicapping judgment on all the horses' lines, you don't want to end up with the track extra slow on Friday, extra fast on Saturday, and extra slow on Sunday, unless this can all be justified by rainfall or by a known pattern of this track superintendent of speeding up the surface for the big stakes days. Though you are practicing mathematics, you are also measuring something physical — the resilience of the track — and your answer must make real-world sense. These aren't just arbitrary numbers on a card, and you can't get lost in your own mathematical world.

For instance, during Handicapping Expo '90, a Vegas weekend featuring top handicappers, Andy Beyer went out of his way to query me publicly about my figures giving Easy Goer a "zero" in the Wood Memorial. He himself cut that race loose from all his other analysis of that day, saying that it came up so fast that they must have speeded the track up for that one race (with invisible earth-moving equipment?).

Now I know that this has *never* happened except as the result of a rain shower or a sudden freeze. And, in fact, Easy Goer later ran back to that figure (but Beyer still says it's wrong).

Beyer appears to be satisfied with allowing his magical numbers to override physical realities, as long as he likes the horses' resulting figures. I set tougher standards: the horses' lines must

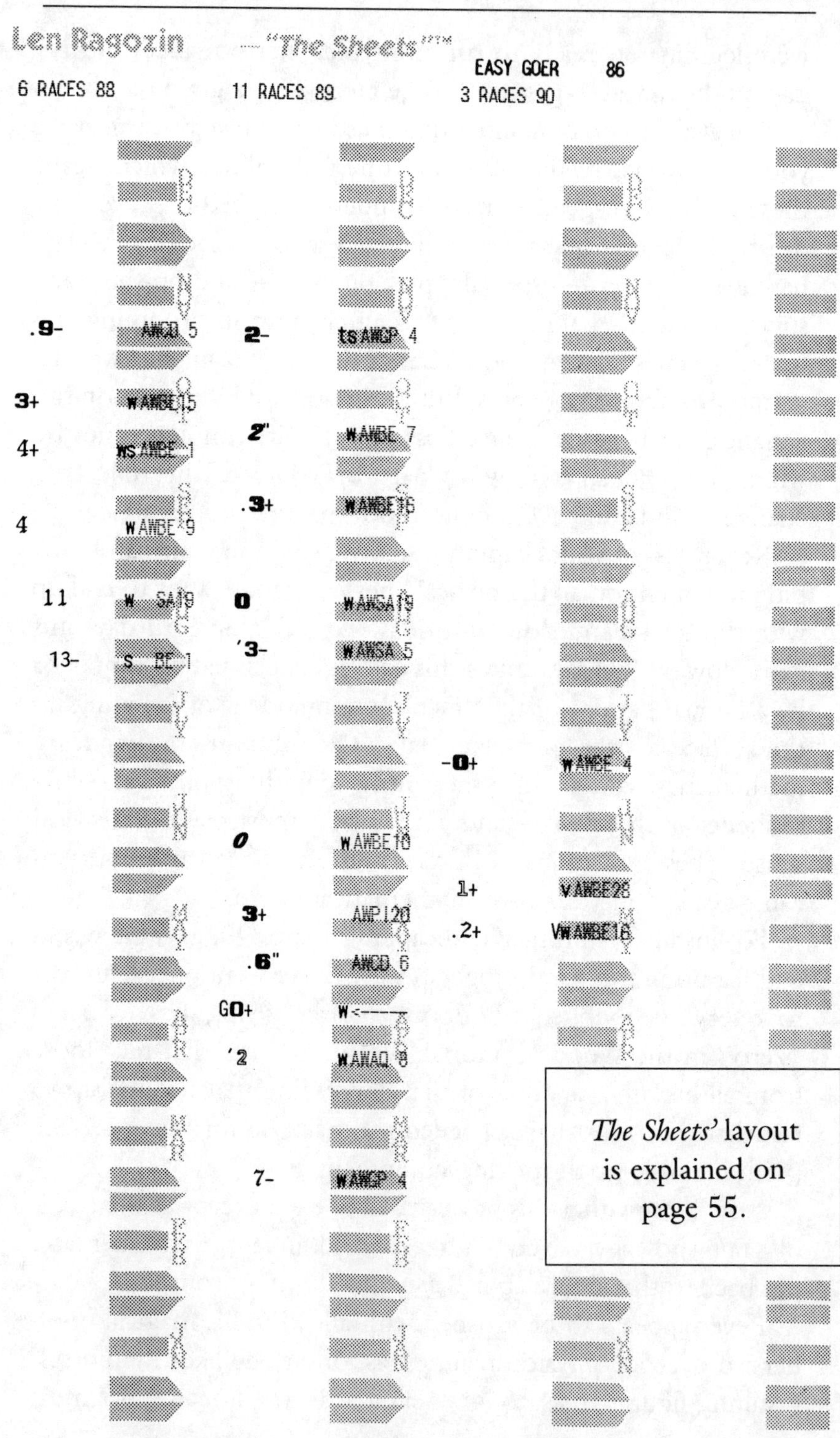

The Sheets' layout is explained on page 55.

look as reasonable as possible — *but all the figures must use the same variant unless rain or a freeze or a thaw changes things.*

Actually, I don't remember doing any particular agonizing when I gave Easy Goer a figure near zero. The rest of the races run that day showed clearly enough what the variant had to be. But, among our competitors, it wasn't only Beyer who didn't want to give the horse that figure. One outfit went so far as to take out a large ad in *The Daily Racing Form* just before the Belmont Stakes was run, telling the world *The Sheets* had blundered on Easy Goer's figure, and including sarcastic remarks about how we were presuming to put this horse in the same league with former champions. Unfortunately for this particular public relations venture, Easy Goer won the Belmont by a city block, running another near-zero rating. The derisive ad became a free ad for *The Sheets.*

Long experience demonstrates that the track speed of the day cannot wildly diverge from what the long history of this particular track suggests it should be on such a day.

It's harder to meet these requirements than it is to merely give the horses the most logical-looking numbers. But it is that occasional funny-looking figure you are stuck with because you respected the physical realities that often brings you a great bet — or a great bet-against — in the future, because others misrated that race. Good longshots pop up later from the hard decisions made on these days.

It becomes increasingly difficult to make a good variant if your original pre-variant figure drifts away from accuracy because of failure to correct for weight, ground loss, and wind. *The Form* tells you what weight the horse carried in the past as well as what it is scheduled to carry today, but both *The Form* and Beyer leave it to their readers to judge what effect weight shifts will have on their performances. Worse, Beyer's instructions for making variants prescribe no role for weight, leading to fuzziness.

Despite the many mystical pronouncements on the effect of weight that are made by trainers and by authors, any decent statistical analysis leads to a tight, formula-driven relationship of weight to the acceleration of a horse. Forty years of experience with hundreds of thousands of horses has proved the accuracy of the formula we use on *The Sheets.*

Ground loss as a horse races further from the rail is another direct physical effect that should be in a ratings figure. At the end of the past-performance line, *The Racing Form* offers a word or two about the horse's trials and tribulations during the race. Usually, the comment gives you nothing you didn't already know by looking at the running positions: "Tired"; "No late bid"; "Early speed." But once in a while *The Form* says something more useful like "Rallied wide." Unfortunately, such comments are tantalizingly vague. "Rallied wide" could mean the horse made a big sweeping move on the turn. Thus, by the laws of geometry, it actually ran much further than the listed distance. Or, it could mean the horse was on the rail on the turn, then swung out in the straightaway, losing virtually no distance. Similarly, a comment like "Four wide" doesn't tell you how soon the jockey steered him out.

To make your own ground-loss correction, go back to the full printed race chart and look analytically at every call from the start to the final turn. Remember that when the race began, the horses were stacked up from Post 1 on the rail to the highest-numbered post on the outside. Visualize as best you can how each horse must have run — closer or away from the rail — and you can eventually come up with a pretty good idea of just where everybody was on the turns. You'll get better at it after poring over ten- or twenty thousand race charts, just as I did.

Today I correct for ground loss at most tracks by using information sent in by observers. But my father and I were successful bettors and horse owners long before I made my first deal with an observer. That deal was with the savvy veteran Connie Merjos, who had been making his own fine ratings for many years and published a selection sheet that was much the best of any available in New York. When Connie saw my marked-up charts estimating who was how far wide, he was amazed that I could be so right so often though I rarely went to the track. It can be done — but it's work.

Wind effects are very crudely reflected in the track variants prepared by Beyer and *The Racing Form* — to the extent that they use different variants for one-turn and two-turn races. Most winds that speed up a one-turn race are likely to slow down a two-turn race. But wind also has a differing effect on one-turn races run at different distances. When the wind is helping the horses down the backstretch, it can knock two or three fifths off the time of a horse whose race starts all the way down the chute. On the other hand, horses running the shortest sprints aren't helped at all, because they run roughly as far against this wind in the homestretch as they run with it in the backstretch. Two-turn races will come up comparatively slow on such a day because horses have to run into the wind through the homestretch twice.

If you use as your variant *The Racing Form* average or a Beyer-type average, it would surely be improved by adjusting all times for wind effects before calculating the variant. And of course this is vital for days on which there is a big wind shift during the racing day. Without wind-shift input, your "averages" are based on data that are not comparable.

Without wind data, the sprint times can't be meaningfully averaged with the route times when making a variant. *The Racing Form* and most modern "figuremen" have found they get better results by making separate variants for shorter races and longer ones, not realizing that the prime reason is the differing effect wind has on a one-turn sprint and a two-turn route. I know they don't realize wind's role because they include mile races at Aqueduct in their averages for a long-race variant — despite the fact that those races go around one turn only, starting from a chute that's over ½ mile away from where the track starts its 1⅛-mile races. At Aqueduct, mile races really should be averaged in with the sprints.

The effect of wind on running time was something I noticed almost from the first day I started working seriously on the figures originated by my father. In fact, the wind correction was my first original contribution. Frankly, it was hard to miss if you were at Belmont Park on October 15, 1954. A hurricane was brewing and a two-year-old filly named Vestment was blown along to what was then a world record for six furlongs — 1:07 4/5 — racing entirely on a straightaway down the old Belmont Widener Chute. In those days, all two-year-olds ran out of the Widener Chute, and as I started working on the figures, their times looked so erratic I figured out that the wind was the culprit. Once I began to make wind corrections, betting two-year-olds in New York became very profitable.

Vestment's future racing career was plagued by that world record, which clearly belonged to the wind. She was not some new Native Dancer. I don't believe she ever won again, because that single performance made her owner shrink from dropping her into claiming races, where she undoubtedly belonged.

Today I pay observers at all major tracks to give me reports on wind, to time each race from when the gates open instead of from the official start (more on this later), and to observe how wide each horse runs on the turns. They can tell me exactly when there is a sudden change of wind during the course of the racing card. When I started my wind calculations more than forty years ago, however, my wind information came by teletype from airports, which, by happy circumstance, are often located near racetracks. I was forced to assume that a 15-knot northwest wind recorded at Fort Lauderdale's airport would also prevail at Gulfstream Park. Once I started using local observers, I found that these assumptions held up well — giving me about 90 percent accuracy. Using the observers, though, makes the wind calculations 99 percent accurate.

The old system of using airport wind data had one ludicrous result. Back in the 1950s I didn't have a computer hookup to bring me wind readings from airports all over the United States, so I would leave my workroom and subway down to the southern tip of Manhattan, where the U.S. Weather Bureau then had its office.

Each airport for which it had readings was listed on the teletype by an abbreviation. As I expanded the number of tracks on which I kept figures, I would ask the resident weather expert for the nearby airport abbreviation. When I added Atlantic City, one of them told me the teletype abbreviation was ATL, so I began taking ATL data.

I didn't do very much betting at Atlantic City. The figures from there were needed mostly to complete the lines of horses shipping to New York or to Monmouth Park. At least, that's my excuse for not catching this error sooner. A year later I was scanning a technical publication and was unnerved at finding that ATL was actually the symbol for Atlanta. The Atlantic City symbol was ACY. This cast more than a little doubt on the accuracy of my wind corrections for races run at Atlantic City.

Do I have a suit against the Weather Bureau for entrapment into losing wagers?

4

Ironing Out the Wrinkles

ADJUSTMENTS FOR WEIGHT, ground lost, and wind can put you on the path to more precise figures, but there are some other tricky bends in the road that come up occasionally. When they do, they make a race look so crazy that it's no wonder a rating "expert" can decide to give up analyzing today's racing data and rate those races solely by projecting from the horses' previous ratings.

The horror stories fall into two main categories: a race run at an inexact distance, and a flaw in the way a race is timed.

Most tracks, either because of the way they are configured or because track management doesn't want to invest money in extra teletimers, are unable to run certain races at their exact distances, particularly on the turf. Gulfstream and Calder are two examples. These tracks run what they call "about" turf distances. To ensure that the grass course is worn down evenly, they often use an additional rail placed some distance from the hedge. The trouble is, the placement of this rail varies — at Calder it might be anywhere from 10 to 30 feet out. The further out the rail, the further the horse must travel to reach the finish line. Naturally the running time is increased — but by how much?

The Racing Form lists "about" races with an asterisk, but

often offers no information on how far the rail was from the hedge. I rely on my local track observers for pretty solid estimates. Without such information, the final times of such races are nearly useless.

On top of this, Gulfstream has now come up with a system that in practice makes such timing unusable even if you do know the placement of the rail. The time published beneath the chart on Gulfstream turf races is not what the teletimer registered. It is adjusted by a computer, which presumably allows for the placement of the rail. Unfortunately, for certain distances, whoever programmed the computer had serious disagreements with Euclid. His geometry is wrong. Meanwhile, the adjusted time is printed as if it were raw data. And some other tracks are now adopting this system.

A ludicrous side effect of the computer correcting popped up after the first few weeks of the track's 1996 meeting. Suddenly, the times of the sprint races on the dirt track became wacky. This led to a column in the January 26, 1996, *Racing Form* by Mark Hopkins, who computes a lot of the Beyer figures. He discussed the error-prone history of Gulfstream's new computer-controlled timers, installed in 1994, explained why he found it hard to believe the times posted for one particular day, then stated, "Given the history of the timer, as a last resort, I decided to hand-time the results."

"A last resort?" Are he and Beyer serious about their numbers or aren't they? If they're at the track anyway, why shouldn't it be a matter of routine for them to click a stopwatch during every race for which they supply *Racing Form* readers with speed figures?

My own assumption was that the Gulfstream computer was "correcting" these races on its own, though I suppose it might have been a teletimer failure of some kind. Since we use our own timing, our figures weren't affected — except that our customers found some unexpected longshots because of the published mistimes.

Another type of error involves mismeasurement of the

course — actually starting the race from an erroneous point. This happens mostly on turf courses that use temporary rails but that do not run "about" distances. To keep the distance exact, the starting point is moved to compensate for each setting of the rail. The problem is that they have so many possible starting points that either the ground crew makes a mistake or the person who activates the teletimers switches on the wrong one. This happens a few times per meeting at Saratoga, less frequently at Santa Anita and Monmouth, and occasionally at Belmont.

Even main-course starting points can be misplaced, although that's rare. Decades ago an evildoer moved the mile-and-70-yard pole at a New England track to louse up the timing, giving him an edge until it was noticed. Right now I have suspicions about the three-furlong start at Hialeah and am checking it. A few years ago, two-year-olds who ran in three-furlong "baby races" at Hialeah were running much worse when they moved on to longer distances. Since they were so young, they figured to improve after the Hialeah meeting. I asked my observer to pace off the course to see if it still actually measured ⅜ of a mile. Track officials wouldn't let him into the area where he could do this. His best judgment, as of late 1995, was that it looked short, and I am now treating the times accordingly. I plan to send him a nautical range-finder so he can measure the course from where he sits.

Until 1994, 1⅛-mile turf races at Calder didn't quite fit into the maximum length of the course. They were actually 110 feet short, and *The Racing Form* designated them as "about." But this creates a problem for the race-chart reader because *The Form* uses the same "about" asterisk to note that Calder has put up a temporary railing for turf races. How is a serious handicapper to know if a 1⅛-mile race is merely "about" — that is, 110 feet short — or "about about" — that is, 110 feet short but lengthened by the temporary rail?

Calder has now lengthened the turf course so 1⅛ miles can be run almost exactly. But similar situations remain at other tracks. In fact, whether a race is run on turf or dirt, you would do well to be suspicious of a distance that is squeezed in by going all the way to the end of the chute. It may be a little short. Even if the distance is perfect, the times may come up too slow by a few fifths because the horses are given practically no room for their usual running start to the timer.

To help you along, *The Racing Form* occasionally includes at the top of a day's charts a small-type line listing a track's dimensions. At Hialeah, after giving the track measurements for the turf course, *The Form* says "all 'about' distances are ten feet longer than the designated distance." This line has been appearing for decades. Ignore it. The real situation at Hialeah is complicated, but the 10-feet fairy tale reflects nothing but inertia. (Perhaps it once was true. And perhaps when this book appears, *The Form* will erase that line.)

The Woodbine track up near Toronto has its own traps for the speed analyst. Turf races are run in various "lanes" — on the hedge, around a rail, around a wider rail, and so on. Yet the track made no "about" designation until my partner, Len Friedman — who should have kept his mouth shut — discussed the matter with the track superintendent. Now they call it "about" when a "lane" makes the distance inexact. More recently, Woodbine officials rebuilt the course to accommodate harness racing in the winter — so, if you finally worked out your "lane" corrections for the track, they are now different, and you had better do it over.

There are different ways of running the same distances at Arlington Park, and the explanations supplied are inadequate. Rockingham's 1⅛-mile turf races have their own very special error. And Santa Anita turf races start on a hillside, which speeds them all up, with some distances getting more downhill run than others. Here we solved the problem by deducing, from tracks with downhill chutes, exactly how elevation affects final time.

Given all this, it can take years of experience to cope with the question of correct par times on the turf. No wonder that when it comes to turf races, some experts would rather make an estimate of the value of each race separately, relying on the prior known class of the horses. At least that way they aren't trapped by misinformation. But just think what an edge you have if you can get a true speed rating. A horse may show an unusual improvement in a maiden race or a minor allowance race — and you will know it. And the more common advantage of achieving precision — the ability to spot small changes in horses' condition — is all yours. Most customers, as well as my staff members who bet, report their best results come from betting turf races. Beyer, relying on the printed data, says turf is tough.

In addition to turf oddities, a fundamental imprecision in all chart timing — including timing of all races run on dirt tracks — is that the distance specified is not the distance actually run. Though this is rarely mentioned, all races are really longer than their designated distance. The reason for this is that horses are given a running start — a "run-up" — from the starting gate to the point where timing begins. If it's a mile race, the time measurement is not, as in a human race, from the standstill starting point to the finish. The mile begins at the timer, which is down the track from where the horses start.

Nothing in the rules of racing sets the run-up distance. It could be any distance and varies, sometimes arbitrarily, sometimes because of track configuration. Most run-ups are in the neighborhood of 50 feet, but there are plenty of odd ones. At Belmont there are run-ups of as little as 15 feet going 1 1/16 miles on the inner turf course with no rail up, and as much as 190 feet going 1 1/4 miles on that same course with a rail up.

With a short run-up, the chart time for that race figures to be slower than normal because the horses are not yet fully in stride when they reach the timer. For instance, if you average up the opening quarter-miles in all races at Belmont in which they use the 15-foot run-up at 1 1/16 miles on the inner turf, you will find that horses run about 3/5 of a second slower than in all other 1 1/16-mile turf races at the track. But of course *Racing Form* data doesn't reveal that the real variable is the run-up.

To keep *The Sheets* ratings precise, we add the run-up distance to the official distance and then time the race from the gate, not from the timer.

Getting the right sort of information is not merely a question of having observers or looking over things yourself. Your rating approach has to be solid enough and your figures already accurate enough that you can sniff out a piece of dubious data. I know what questions to ask my observers to ensure that I'm using accurate run-ups. If necessary, I will personally check a TV tape.

Years ago, both my father and I were successful bettors and horse owners at a time when the only on-track observer was — occasionally — me. Unfortunately, the bettors you are trying to beat today are more sophisticated than the ones we faced. Only precision can give you the edge you need.

When I first started, there was no turf racing, and thus few timing errors, in the northeastern United States. But even with no turf, every now and then I could cope with an ugly-looking main-track race only by assuming the time was a misprint. On the sheet I would add or subtract one full second and write "sec. err." Well, as I got wiser, there were fewer and fewer "sec. errs." When I began buying private clockings, it turned out that on a dirt course, major timing errors were pretty rare. The "err." was in my immature insistence that all horses have smooth race sequences. They don't!

Your biggest edge as a bettor or a buyer of horses is the ability to spot when the unusual is coming — be it a horse's turn for the better or for the worse.

I am so convinced that you must analyze trends that I am almost sorry that the SPORT-STAT study showed a profit from betting on the horses that merely had the best individual figure on *The Sheets* in their last three races and were 4–1 or higher in the betting. The study used a one thousand–race sample. We're testing this with a much larger sample, but we're half-hoping that this mechanical approach won't beat the mutuel take — proving that real success comes only when you are forced to do some creative thinking in applying good numbers.

To improve the figures for an expanding circle of customers, I keep adding observers. By now I get reports from New York, New Jersey, Pennsylvania, Maryland, Florida, Ontario, Kentucky,

Louisiana, Arkansas, Chicago, and California (south and north, including the major fair meetings). I don't have anybody at a few medium-sized tracks that I would like to cover, but we do make very good figures from these tracks by applying careful judgment to *The Racing Form* data plus airport wind, as we did with success in my early days at the New York tracks.

Nor do I have observers at the two West Virginia tracks. It isn't worth it. But I'm certainly curious about what a Charles Town private clocker might be able to tell me. Most of the races there are timed by hand — no electric-eye beam — and it turns out that the capacity for human error is never so large as when the clocker is a human being at a small racetrack, where everyone is living from hand to mouth and desperate for even the smallest betting edge.

A computer analysis done by a longtime Ragozin employee, Jake Haddad, indicates the probability of timing errors at Charles Town that would cause ten-length errors in the figures. If every horse in a race is coming up much faster than usual, it could be an honest mistake — the clocker started his watch too late. If an occasional race comes up impossibly slow, however, either the jockeys held all the horses in a fix, which is very hard to do, or the clocker hoped that listing an abysmal time would build up the odds when these horses ran against other competition. It's a cruel world, gentlemen.

There's another track where the electric timer is activated not by a beam broken by the horses soon after the start but by someone sitting in the press box, ¼ mile or more away. Another one arrives at times for mile-and-70-yard races — believe it or not — by adding exactly 4 seconds to the time it took the horses to race one mile.

Well, enough about timing errors. Let's say you're satisfied that you can satisfactorily rate the winners of enough races to have useful figures. How about the horses who didn't come in first? What times did these horses actually run? Of course, you answer this by using the beaten lengths — the published distances that the other horses finished behind the winner.

During a race, most frequently at each ¼ mile, *The Racing Form*'s chartcaller will estimate how far each horse is ahead of the next. At the finish, however, the photo-finish camera is finally consulted to determine beaten lengths more precisely. This is a unique camera. The shutter is a vertical slit. The camera is actually constantly photographing the tiny vertical segment of the world that is found right at the finish line. But because the film keeps moving, all these tiny vertical areas run together and end up looking like a complete picture of a horse. If you look closely at horses' legs in a photo-finish picture, you'll realize no running horse ever had his legs in such a position. The distortion arises because the camera actually photographed — separately — each millimeter of leg as it occupied the tiny area of the finish line. It never photographed the whole horse at once as a photographer with a conventional camera would do.

Think about it and you will realize that if the film — which is moving steadily behind the slit — were speeded up, the horse's body would look longer in the final photograph. A longer piece of film would be running through the camera during the time between the horse's nose reaching the finish line and the point when his rump passed the slit. This picture — which is formed by a continuous build-up — would be stretched. Also stretched would be the distance by which he beat the next horse.

When the chartmaker reviews the entire photo finish to give *The Racing Form* the beaten lengths, he has a scale that tells him that such-and-such a distance on the picture equals one length, two and a half lengths, et cetera. But if the camera is set to run a little fast or a little slow, the real-life gaps will be stretched or condensed on the picture, and using the scale will give longer or shorter answers. And, unfortunately, the cameras vary in speed.

My observers don't just clock the winner — they clock some beaten horses. So we don't rely completely on the published beaten lengths to tell us how fast a beaten horse ran. Thus, a few years ago I was able to startle the Gulfstream Park photo-finish operator by phoning from New York and asking him why he was running his camera at odd speeds. I could see this because the beaten lengths printed in *The Racing Form* charts didn't at all match our clockings of beaten horses.

He not only admitted he was doing it, but said his backup cameras — used in case of breakdown — were set at yet another speed; and of course you wouldn't know when they were used. Then he generously offered to sell me all this relevant information on his operation of the cameras! I declined his proposition.

The fact remains that even with normal operation, the speed at which these cameras rotate is not precise, and although the day-to-day variation at one track is usually small, from track to track it is larger. At Calder (at least through 1994), one length on a *Racing Form* chart represented about 20 percent more actual time than it did at Belmont. Even Aqueduct as recently as late 1995 was 10 percent different from Belmont. And at almost all tracks the dirt-course lengths come up different from those on turf. My guess is that whoever runs the cameras is trying to make the built-up picture of a horse look normal — not like a giant dachshund or a squashed pony. This means running the camera faster if horses are running faster, and on turf courses they generally do run faster.

If your figures are fairly rough anyhow, you can get by without knowing all this. Use the estimate that six lengths equals 1 second; it's good enough. But once you become convinced, as I am, that successful handicapping nowadays is possible only when you constantly strive to achieve the utmost accuracy, every little improvement counts.

With all such small corrections, you must keep in mind that the main goal is to help get the overall variant right. It might not seem to matter if an occasional rating is off by ½ point. But suppose your most dependable performers on a given day — the horses that are going to influence you heavily in modifying your variant — are sending slightly conflicting signals. Precision in combing out the small errors we have been discussing can help solve this problem. Your most reliable performers will all give you the same signal — showing you that a certain precise variant modification is the best. You are much better off. And your figures have a much better chance of improving from year to year. . . .

Let's explore further why it's better to time a race from the moment the gate opens, rather than waiting for a horse to reach the time-beam at the official starting point.

Simply put, since the horses start even at the gate but are no longer even at the time-beam, the most useful rating would be one that measures their full effort, gate to finish. After all, that's what determines who wins!

But I can make the case even stronger for timing races from the moment the gate opens. Suppose there is an extreme front-runner in the race. He always busts out of the gate at full speed and gets a length or two ahead of the field before the others reach the timer. So he breaks the time-beam, goes off to a big lead, then quits, and the race is clocked in 1:12⅕.

Now suppose this same horse acts up at the gate and is a late scratch. The gate opens. Everybody else does exactly what they did in the case just described. But this time nobody breaks the time-beam so early, and the race is clocked in 1:11⅘.

Do you really want to give all the horses in the first case a much slower rating than they would get in the second scenario? After all, the horses actually did the same thing physically. Will it help you pick a winner next week if today's ratings depend on how fast some rabbit broke the time-beam? On the other hand, if you time from the moment the gate opens, the two cases come out the same. And if you time from the gate, you are rating what really counts: who can run fastest from start to finish.

I don't want to give the impression that esoteric concepts about variants and measurements are being constantly discussed in my office every day. They aren't — except on the odd occasion when some rating smells very wrong. All these concepts are nowadays accepted as "given" in a day's work in my office. The conclusions of all this past analysis are programmed into our computer, track by track. The remaining judgment point, on which the computer output will have to be overridden and modified, is the elusive variable of today's exact track speed — the modified daily variant.

The initial work in processing all the data is done by keypunchers and figure-men in my New York office. These jobs can overlap — the people who start as keypunchers are generally overqualified for that job and are capable of moving up into decision making. This of course helps us because they might spot a problem or an error at a preliminary stage instead of just blindly punching it into the computer.

The work starts with data from *The Racing Form* charts, which provide the most convenient framework for dealing with a race, even though we later correct parts of it. Going into the computer along with the chart excerpts is our own raw data:

- Observer clocking from the gate in 1/100ths of a second
- How much distance the run-up adds to the true length of the race
- Clocking of beaten horses in the same race
- Turf rail, if any: How far from the hedge is it?
- Race-by-race wind speed and direction, taken from observer and / or airport data
- Weight carried by each horse
- Path of each horse: How much ground did he lose on the turn?
- Lengths behind the winner for each horse. This data is, of course, input as part of *The Racing Form* chart, but its lengths will be overridden by our observers' timing of beaten horses.
- How many hundredths of a second should be added for each beaten length at this particular track (This is a function of the motor-speed of the photo-finish camera.)

The computer can take all this data, refer each piece to the par times and wind charts and other relevant solution-formulas for that track, and spit out a rating for each horse, modified by a claiming-race variant and ready for further judgment modification.

Now we "modify" the whole day as a unit, by judging the race-by-race lines of all the horses and factoring in the expected day-by-day development of track resilience at this track, taking into account our data on weather conditions and the past performance of the ground crew superintendent. Turf is naturally a separate unit.

Since we now cover too many tracks for me to do all the rating modifications, for many tracks two of my most experienced associates make an initial judgment — each of them working on the same data independently. If they disagree as to what the modifier should be, they pass the work along to me to help reach a definitive decision.

I can hardly believe that once I did all this by hand!

When I started out, I was young and enjoyed a struggle. I was constantly wrestling with the imperfect concepts. Now that I am older, I prefer the more even keel provided by the help of competent associates, efficient data input, massive computer power, and better racing information. For each racing day, the main struggle I still face as a handicapper is to achieve the final daily variant — making it as accurate as I know how. And by now I am a wise enough old hound that it rarely escapes me.

The first step is the computer-generated provisional rating for each horse, calculated by using a claiming-race average. Time, wind, weight, track peculiarities, paths — all the data we feed into the computer — produce a set of figures whose relationship to each other is locked in.

Now I am ready to change the variant to fine-tune the numbers based on an analytical look at each horse's development — but if I change one figure, I must equally change them all. If I want to change Holy Bull's provisional rating for a 1¼-mile race from 5¼ to the more likely 4, I must subtract 1¼ from every other horse — including sprinters — running on the dirt that day. I can't tidy up the horses' lines by subtracting a point here and adding a point there.

There's no "let's just put something in, it's getting late." Problems must be solved and integrity maintained. The only equivocation allowable is to mark a tough day for review. That means that every time a horse that ran that day runs again, his figure on *The Sheets* for that day is flagged. At some point we reevaluate such numbers in light of the extra evidence now provided by races that day's horses have run since the day it was so difficult to set the variant. Well over nine times in ten, this subsequent review confirms the original figure.

Long ago I felt *The Sheets* were an amazing achievement. I felt this the way any scientist concludes he has a great result: from the consistency, simplicity, and elegance of figures emerging from a mass of chaotic data. Of course, a scientist's ultimate test of his hypothesis is in its value to predict results: if I am right, such-and-such will occur in a predictable percentage of cases. In betting and in claiming horses, *The Sheets* have passed that test.

5

The New Science of Betting

BEFORE GETTING into the next section of the book, let me say that all opinions on betting — even when I use only the pronoun "I" — are based largely on the experience of my partner, Len Friedman. When he has the time to buckle down and really tackle a racing card, he is virtually unbeatable, as people who have attended his trackside seminars can attest. He has bet about $2 million a year for three decades, so naturally this book relies on his opinions about how to bet to win.

The Sheets are the basis of our approach. As our betting strategies are explained in the following chapters, the sheets of horses being discussed illustrate specifically the patterns of condition and the past ratings we talk about.

It will undoubtedly help you to see just what a sheet looks like. This one for Gold Fever is typical. Just to the right of the horse's name is the year in which he was foaled. The extreme left-hand column lists his races as a two-year-old, with the months of the year moving from the bottom up. The next column contains his three-year-old races up to today's race; the adjoining columns would contain races for his four- and five-year-old seasons if he were still running.

In the white space of each column, numbers rating the effort

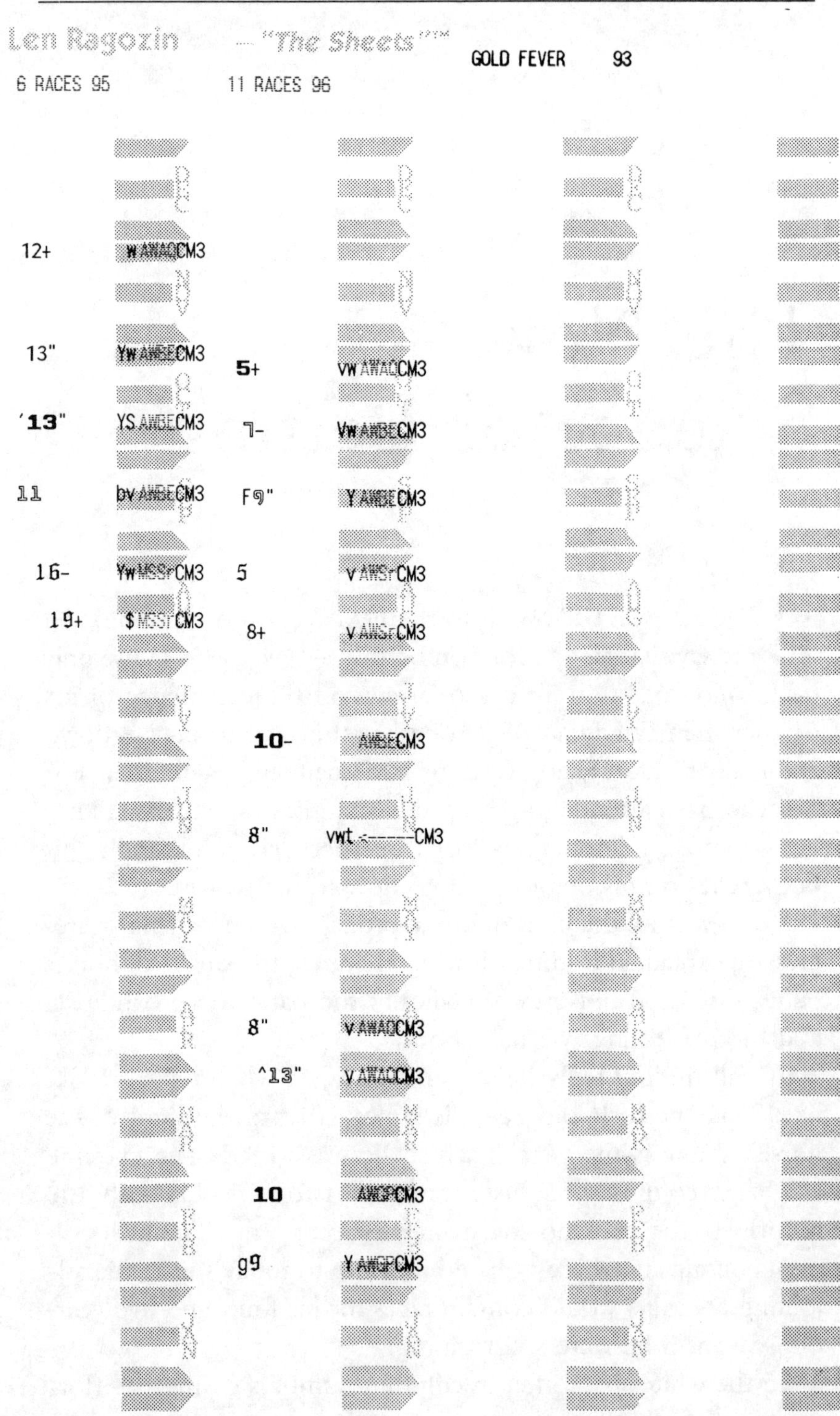
Len Ragozin — "The Sheets"™
GOLD FEVER 93
6 RACES 95
11 RACES 96
12+ wAWAQCM3
13" YwAWBECM3
5+ vwAWAQCM3
'13" YSAWBECM3
7- VwAWBECM3
11 bvAWBECM3
F9" YAWBECM3
16- YwMSSrCM3
5 vAWSrCM3
19+ $MSSrCM3
8+ vAWSrCM3
10- AWBECM3
8" vwt------CM3
8" vAWAQCM3
^13" vAWAQCM3
10 AWGPCM3
g9 YAWGPCM3

RAGOZIN SYMBOL SHEET June 1994

The LOWER the number, the better the race. One year of races per column. The most recent race is at the top of the rightmost column.
SYMBOLS: Generally, the symbols before the figure are more important than symbols after the figure.

BEFORE	AFTER
= turf	& claimed by... w/initials
^= good turf	S off poorly 2 - 4 lengths
.= yielding turf	s off poorly < 2 lengths
:= soft turf	D dwelt - > 4 lengths
' wet fast	P pace too slow
^ good track	Z bled
. wet track	* trainer switch
: very bad wet track	J lost jockey
.. very slow track	m mud caulks
../ ploughed after freezing	u turn-down shoes
.: heavy track	b buried race (better than looked)
F first lasix	Q switched off turf
r rain	w won race
s snow	< bar shoe on
/ frozen track	> bar shoe off
g heavy gusting wind	R ran off before race
G very heavy gusting wind	$ bet for no obvious reason
~ approximate	G unruly at the gate
X ~ fig. stretch call	B bore in/bore out
P~ Adjusted for slow pace	K lame/broke down
P Pace too slow (unadjusted)	k sore
XX = Did Not Finish	t small trouble
circle = missing number	T big trouble
	n no lasix used
+ is a quarter-point	L back on Lasix
- minus quarter-point	] blinkers off
" is a half-point	[blinkers on
	V 4 or more horse-widths wide
A mile race is one turn	v 3 to 3.5 horse-widths wide
at these tracks:	Y rail trip
AP, AQU, BEL, CD	E Fell during race

HERE ARE EXAMPLES OF THE TYPE-STYLES USED AND THE DISTANCES THEY REPRESENT:

less than 5 furlongs	*11 22 33 44*
5 - 5.5	11223344
6	11 22 33 44
6.5 - 7	11 22 33 44
7.5 - 1mile 40yards	11 22 33 44
1mile 70yards - 1 1/8	**11 22 33 44**
1 3/16 - 1 1/4	**11 22 33 44**
over 1 1/4	***22 44 66 88***

Trainer initials (NY & NJ):
3 capital letters = 3 initials.
2 caps and 1 small = 2 initials + last letter of last name.
To avoid duplications, some trainers don't use these rules. List is available.

To the FAR RIGHT is information about the class of race and where and when it was run. The first two characters indicate the class. MS - Maiden race. AW - Allowance, Handicap, or Stakes.

If there's a number, that was the approximate claiming price of the race. For example 10AP29 means a $10,000 claiming race at Arlington on the 29th of the month. For missing races, a summary is provided. "Rui 5X 2/0/1" means five races at Ruidoso Downs. The horse won twice & finished third once. If there's a dollar amount, that's the purse money earned for those races.

he put in during a particular race are graphed, with the better numbers further to the left of the column. The letters at the left of the shaded area are brief comments: for example, the dollar sign listed for his debut race at 2 indicates Gold Fever was heavily bet for no obvious reason; the capital "Y" and the small "w" for his second race tell you that he was along the rail throughout the final turn and won the race. Just to the right of those symbols, you'll notice these notations for both races: "MS," "Sr," and "CM3." "MS" means they were maiden nonclaiming races, "Sr" indicates they were run at Saratoga, and "CM3" is my shorthand for his trainer, Claude "Shug" McGaughey III.

Notations to the left of horses' sheet numbers tell you whether a race was run on turf (any race without an "=" sign in front of the number was run on dirt) and the condition of the track and any adverse weather conditions. For example, the small "g" in front of the number for Gold Fever's first race as a three-year-old indicates the wind was gusting heavily that day; the ^ symbol before his number for his third race as a three-year-old tells you that the track was rated "good" that day, rather than the usual "fast." The accompanying symbol sheet on page 57 explains every notation you will find on *The Sheets.*

When comparing horses for an upcoming race, you must penalize those who are carrying the higher weights. 5 pounds = 1 point. A simple method is to take 115 pounds as a norm and add ⅕ point for every pound over 115 a horse will carry today, or subtract ⅕ point for every pound under 115 today. Don't look at weight carried in previous races — that data is already in the figures. You may also want to add a point or so if you project that a horse will race wide today; or subtract ½ point or so if you project a rail trip.

6

Forsaking Handicapping Myths

FOR MUCH OF MY FIRST DECADE as a professional horseplayer, I gambled in solitude. Going to the track was often a family affair, with my parents or occasionally an aunt with nothing more interesting to do that day accompanying me, but the serious handicapping and the bookie betting were done alone.

Then I met Len Friedman at a party of antiwar activists in 1967. He was a brilliant young man who had grown up between New York and California and gone to law school in Chicago. But he was so confident in his own intelligence that he never bothered to do the rote preparation that proved necessary to pass the bar exam. By now he was assisting lawyers who represented rent strikers and political dissidents, but the law had begun to lose its appeal as he discovered that in practice it was grubby and corrupt. He was mathematically apt, a successful poker player, and though he had no experience betting horses, he showed immediate interest in what I was doing. Since we were politically simpatico, I started calling him every day with my betting picks. My success reinforced his idea that *The Sheets* offered a bettor a substantial edge. Without a lot of coaching, he began reasoning backward from the lettered condition ratings I was then noting on *The Sheets*. Soon he began to play on his own.

It became obvious to me that temperamentally he could make better use of *The Sheets* than I could. Also, since he had time to go to the track, he could make use of the odds. Eventually we formed a partnership in which we were informally financially linked.

I think Len has contributed more to the business than he has gotten out. He feels the same about me, so the only arguments we have ever had about shares consist of trying to make the other fellow take more. Certainly he has made my life not only more successful but infinitely more pleasant. Meeting him was a blessing.

The approach Friedman and I bring to betting horses goes beyond simply producing numbers that are more precise than those given by *The Racing Form* or other publications. It involves looking at races free of the misconceptions that pass for truth among most handicappers and trainers. Of course you can begin to do this successfully only when your figures are accurate.

The Ragozin Sheets paved the way for the speed-figure revolution that punctured one of racing's most enduring myths: that class is all-important. This theory holds that once class is established by a horse, it is a measure that will generally outweigh mere speed and even current physical condition as revealed by the speed a horse has recently shown.

By this reasoning, a once-good horse dropped to lower-level races because of bad form — which probably means physical problems — should still defeat sound but mediocre animals.

Conversely, a horse of supposedly modest class who is suddenly bursting with good health that is reflected in sharply improved performance will nonetheless be humbled once he steps out of his league. The presumption is that if the horse has reached the stretch run still in contention, as soon as one of his high-class superiors "looks him in the eye," he will remember his station in life and retreat to it.

Other old misconceptions about racing still endure, as well as new errors. One that cropped up recently is the notion that a horse coming out of a turf race is a good bet running on the dirt. This idea gets talked up anytime a horse shows improvement in winning a dirt race right after the trainer has run him on turf, particularly if the grass race was nothing special. A more logical explanation is that the horse didn't expend much energy in the turf race and was ready to put in a strong effort his next time out. The same effect is often seen when a horse who is in good shape runs one mediocre effort in the slop or even on his normal racing surface. If there were truly something about racing on the grass that improved a horse's chances in his next dirt start, why wouldn't all trainers work out their horses on turf between their dirt races?

Other common prejudices of thoroughbred bettors include these:

- Never bet a filly racing against colts.
- Never bet a three-year-old against older horses.
- Never bet a horse carrying more than a certain weight.
- Never bet a horse who has just broken his maiden.

Like most stereotypes, each of these beliefs has its roots in some reality — one that has not been deeply analyzed. More often than not, fillies do lose to colts, three-year-olds are defeated by their elders, high-weighted favorites are underlays, and maiden winners lose their next start. But understanding the real reasons behind those losses lets you cash bets at good odds by going against such "rules" in the right situation.

The key to using *The Sheets* properly is to trust the numbers, while analyzing what they mean in terms of horses' condition and development. The numbers on a horse must look reasonably good compared with the competition. But — more important — the development of those numbers must also suggest he is capable of matching or exceeding his best recent effort today. At the right odds, that horse is a bet. And if that horse is bucking one of the prevalent stereotypes, you are pretty sure of getting the right odds.

• Fillies, by and large, have trouble beating colts racing at a comparable level. If you average up the ability of the fifty thousand or so fillies running in the United States, they would come

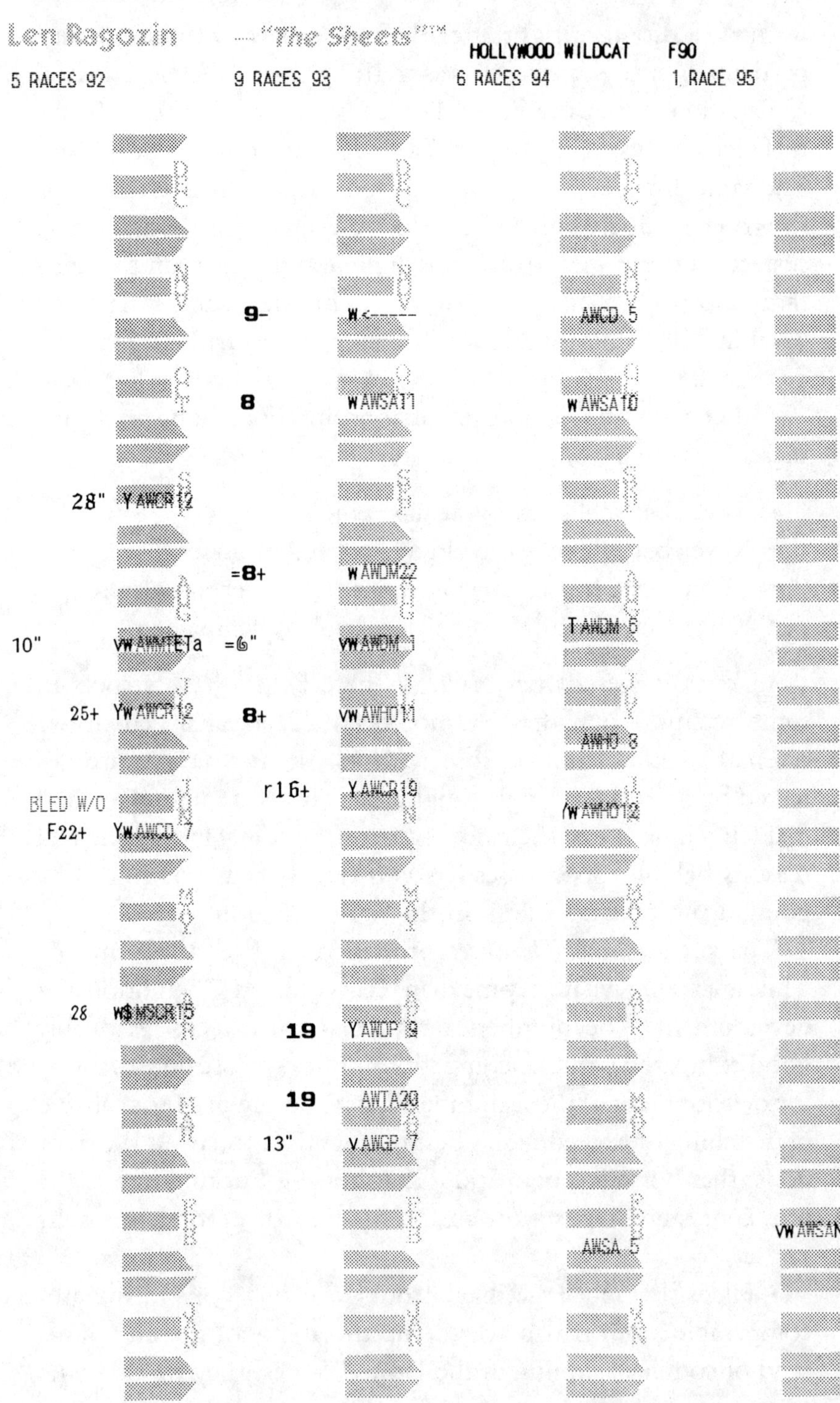
Len Ragozin
"The Sheets"™
HOLLYWOOD WILDCAT F90
5 RACES 92
9 RACES 93
6 RACES 94
1 RACE 95
28" YAWCR12
10" vwAWMTETa
25+ YwAWCR12
BLED W/O
F22+ YwAWCD 7
28 W$MSCR15
9- W<-----
8 WAWSA11
=8+ wAWDM22
=6" vwAWDM 1
8+ vwAWHO11
r16+ YAWCR19
19 YAWOP 9
19 AWTA20
13" vAWGP 7
AWCD 5
wAWSA10
TAWDM 6
AWHO 8
YwAWHO12
AWSA 5
vwAWSAN

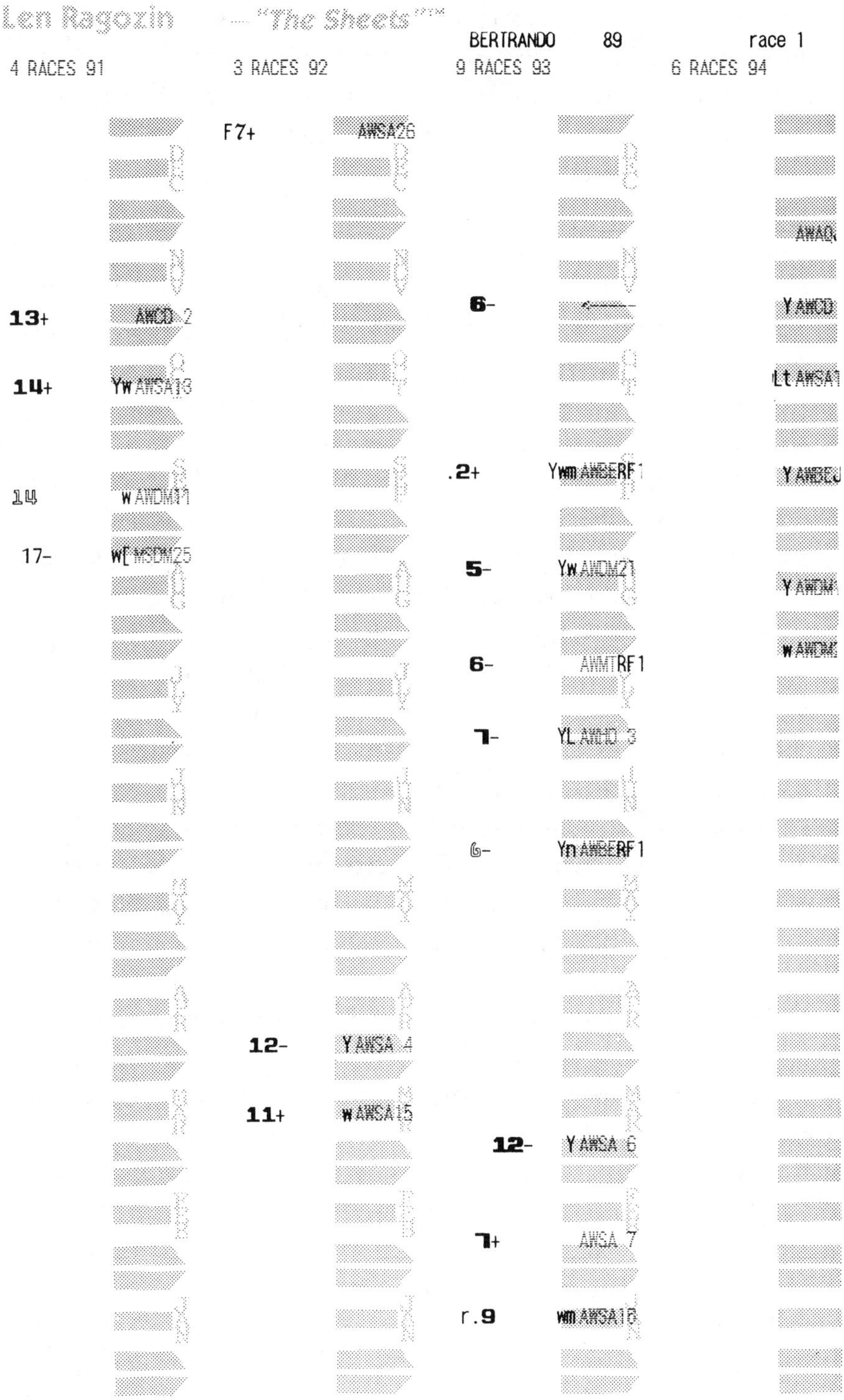

Len Ragozin — "The Sheets"™

BERTRANDO 89 race 1

4 RACES 91		3 RACES 92		9 RACES 93		6 RACES 94
		F7+	AWSA26			
						AWAQ
13+	AWCD 2			6-	←——	Y AWCD
14+	Yw AWSA13					Lt AWSA1
				.2+	Ywm AWSERF1	Y AWSE
14	w AWDM11					
17-	w[MSDM25			5-	Yw AWDM21	Y AWDM
						w AWDM
				6-	AWMTRF1	
				7-	YL AWMD 3	
				6-	Yn AWSERF1	
		12-	Y AWSA 4			
		11+	w AWSA15			
				12-	Y AWSA 6	
				7+	AWSA 7	
				r.9	wm AWSA18	

out about 1 second slower per mile than the males. This is a difference of about 1 percent! However, it translates to a difference of about 3½ points on *The Sheets* — which means that, on the average, a filly's owner is better advised to seek out a filly race. But when an owner or trainer decides to go against these averages, your success will depend not on this overall picture but on how his particular filly stacks up against her field on that day.

Let's look at the sheets for the 1993 seasons of Hollywood Wildcat, who won that year's Breeders' Cup Distaff, and Bertrando, who finished second in the Breeders' Cup Classic. The number at the top of each column is the figure each horse got in the Breeders' Cup. Bertrando's 6– as runner-up to Arcangues was an effort 3 points better than Hollywood Wildcat's 9– in winning the Distaff. Looking further down the columns for that season, Hollywood Wildcat had consistently run about an 8 in winning her four races preceding the Breeders' Cup, while Bertrando was typically running a 6 or 7 — and not always winning.

The obvious conclusion is that Grade 1 races for males are more difficult to win than Grade 1s restricted to fillies and mares, and so even a top filly will have a hard time going against males.

But that was no obstacle to Genuine Risk, who won the 1980 Kentucky Derby against a mediocre group of colts, or to Winning Colors, who won the 1988 Derby against an excellent crop of males. Both fillies happened to be ready to run peak efforts on Derby Day, although the extent of Genuine Risk's improvement was harder to forecast.

Other fillies and mares, particularly in distance races on the turf, have proven that gender is no barrier to beating top males. If a filly's numbers give her a good chance against a field of colts, that's all you need to know.

• A three-year-old colt is the equivalent of a teenager, while a four- or five-year-old is like a man at his physical peak. For this reason, during the first half of the racing year, it's rare to see three-year-olds running in stakes races against older horses.

Later in the year, however, three-year-olds often become excellent bets as their trainers become more willing to try them against their elders. They get weight allowances in those races, but that is not the primary reason to look closely for betting opportunities. Rather, it is because most three-year-olds have gained maturity as the year progresses but still have not been raced too heavily. They are relatively fresh and you can still look for improvement in their form. If anything, they are likely to improve more than you might have anticipated from a mere mathematical reading of their previous numbers. Their odds are likely to be based on a past-performance history that they may be ready to surpass.

In contrast, older horses — except for a few who are rested up for the Breeders' Cup — have been more heavily campaigned. They are likely to begin showing signs of weariness in the fall. If they surprise you, it is more often going to be by racing worse than their recent numbers would suggest. So their odds are likely to be based on a past-performance history they may fail to live up to.

Take those opposite physical trends together, factor in that the developing three-year-old may have never run as well as some of those older horses, and you're likely to get terrific odds on a fairly reasonable proposition. Again, it comes down to analyzing the numbers, not following an arbitrary rule based on age.

• Decades-long analysis convinces me that the effect of extra weight on all horses is steady and quantifiable. Many horsemen believe there is a threshold weight their pet horse can carry, and that one pound more will be the breaking point. Jimmy Croll made reference to this conviction at the start of Holy Bull's four-year-old season when he said his horse was not one of those horses for whom that breaking point applied. I find no evidence to support the breaking-point theory for any horse. I think it's ridiculous to suggest that carrying an extra sixteen ounces will drastically alter the performance of a twelve-hundred-pound animal.

The reality that led to the breaking-point theory is simple. A horse usually carries high weight in a race because he has been winning. In the course of running those good efforts, which earned him the high weight assignment, he probably reached his peak. Now the horse is ready for a decline. So, the day he carries the highest weight, he may well be decisively beaten — not because of a weight-induced breaking point but because of declining physical condition.

Do not conclude from this that low-weighted horses win most of the races. By and large the high-weights have better recent figures, and today's weight will often not be enough to overcome that edge. We make weight corrections in order to come up with accurate figures that can help with predictions — not to bar you from betting a high-weight.

• The biggest climb most horses must make is from maiden races into events in which all their competitors have won at least once. Instead of a field that includes only one or two real runners, the ex-maiden now faces a full group of competitors. Most maiden winners are unlikely to win their next start, regardless of whether they are moving from maiden races into early allowance company or into claiming races for winners.

But there will be exceptions, and not just the royally bred horses who win their first race by ten lengths and therefore are prohibitively short prices the first time they face winners. What you want is to find a maiden winner who, without showing an obviously big race, has run good enough numbers to suggest he has a chance in his next start. There won't be many. But finding the ones that have competitive numbers that are not obvious to the rest of the bettors can be very rewarding in the long run.

Virtually no one claims maidens. The reality is they are generally overpriced in relation to the ability already shown. But when I ran my very small stable, I claimed a half-dozen maidens — more than any owner would dream of. When my trainer would protest, "But he's a maiden," I would reply, "By tonight he won't be!" Only once — with a horse named Admiral Auteuil — was I wrong. He lost the race out of which I claimed him but then won for us against winners.

The common thread for defying all these racing maxims is that you have to be getting good value. The odds are important. And accurate figures are essential to your analysis of the horse's ability and how well he is developing, and in weighing that analysis against his odds.

7

When Price Dictates the Bet

IN DECIDING which horses to bet, we focus on three criteria:

- The "shape" of the horse's prior form leads us to believe that he is ready to run one of his better races. That is, he recently ran better than he had in the near past but still didn't reach his real peak.
- The horse has numbers that make him a contender (sometimes, for younger horses, by projecting an improvement).
- The price must be good enough relative to the horse's chances so that you are offered decent value.

Using *The Sheets* properly does not mean you're going to hit every race on a card. The examples we're giving in this book are usually cases where our methods produced a winner — but at least three times as many could be found where we did everything right but lost.

Our approach to handicapping is virtually guaranteed to cost us some winners in the course of a day because, if we believe the fastest horse in the race legitimately deserves to be 8–5, we do not bet it at 6–5 or even 9–5. In such cases we either pass the race or look to key on another horse who may not be as fast but who is offering good enough value for us to take a chance that the horse who legitimately figures best will find a way to lose. There are no certainties in racing; no "bet to end all bets." That is why getting value is essential.

That was the reason Friedman was able to make a nice score on the eighth race at Aqueduct January 15, 1995, an event that might seem indecipherable. It involved seven three-year-old horses with uneven form. None of the horses in the race had yet shown much ability at the 1⅟16-mile route.

The rail horse, Conduit Street, had done nothing wrong in his four-race career, although he looked slower than most of the other horses. (Basically, the lower the number I assign a horse, the stronger the effort. My scale of rating horses begins at zero and works upward, with each point worth about a half-length in a route race, or almost a length in a sprint.) The sheet for Conduit Street shows his best race as a two-year-old was a 22¼ run more than eight weeks earlier. That was enough time to make it likely that further improvement would come if he could handle his first race around two turns. Healthy young horses often improve in surges spaced two to three months apart.

Roman Rating's numbers were similar to Conduit Street's, but his trend had been in the wrong direction since breaking his maiden in his debut in late October at Suffolk Downs.

Lemming had run two strong races at Aqueduct the previous November, pairing a 14 that was as good as anyone in the field had run. In his most recent race January 2, though, he had run only a 21¼, finishing third over a muddy track in his first try at two turns. Had the two consecutive strong efforts taken something out of him, or was the off-race simply a reaction to the mud (shown by the dot in front of the number) or the wind (the "g" to the left of the dot means gusty)?

Is Sveikatas's line suggested he was a somewhat slower version of Lemming: his two best races had come back-to-back, a 17– and a 19½, and been followed by a decline to a 26– when fifth in that January 2 race behind Lemming.

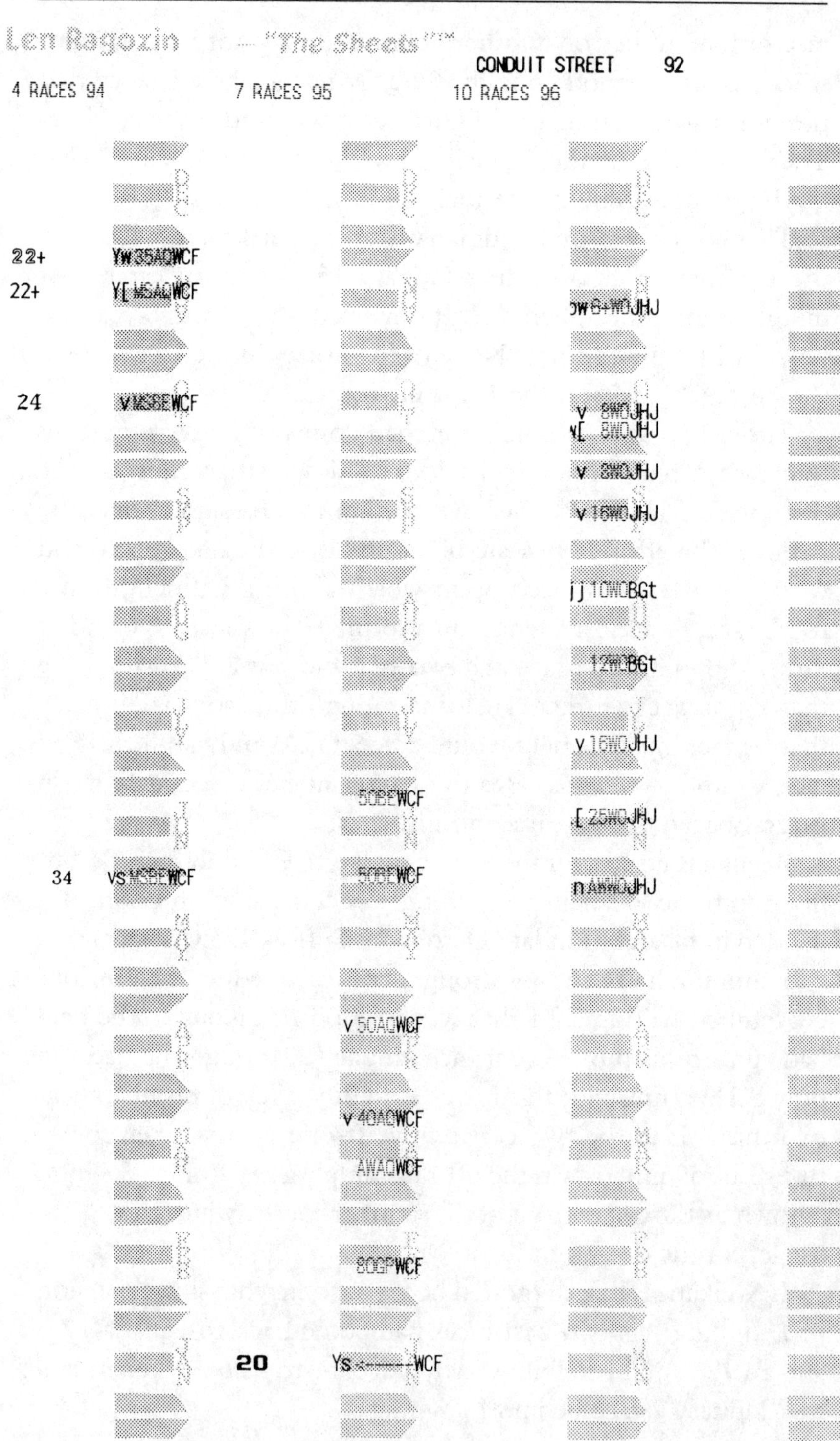
Len Ragozin —"The Sheets"™
CONDUIT STREET 92
4 RACES 94
7 RACES 95
10 RACES 96
22+ Yw35AQWCF
22+ Y[MSAQWCF
24 vMSBEWCF
34 vsMSBEWCF
5OBEWCF
5OBEWCF
v 5OAQWCF
v 4OAQWCF
AWAQWCF
8OGPWCF
20 Ys←——WCF
ow6+WOJHJ
v 8WOJHJ
w[8WOJHJ
v 8WOJHJ
v 16WOJHJ
jj 10WOBGt
12WOBGt
v 16WOJHJ
[25WOJHJ
n AWWOJHJ

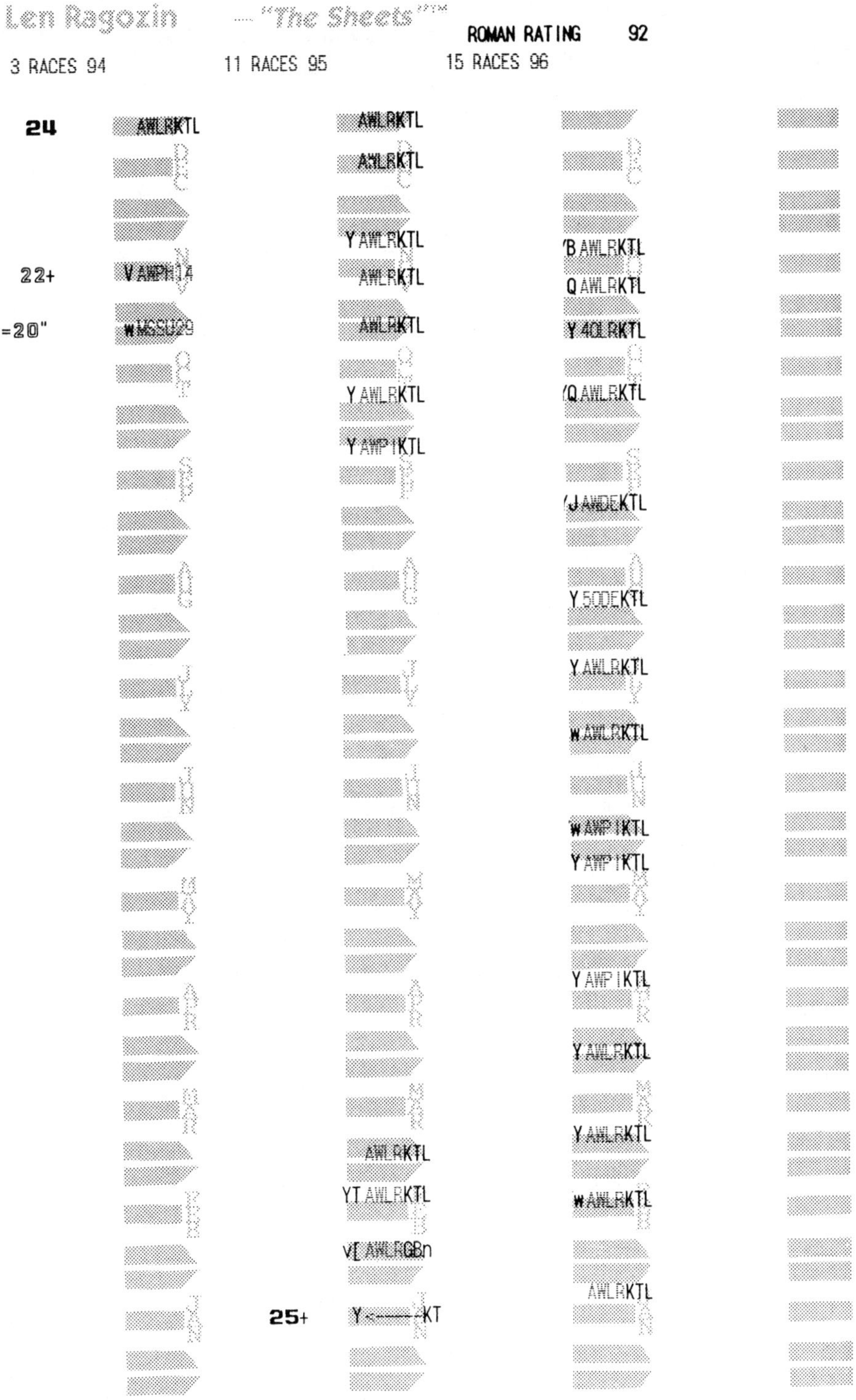

Len Ragozin ... "The Sheets"™

ROMAN RATING 92

3 RACES 94 | 11 RACES 95 | 15 RACES 96

	94		95	96
24	AWLRKTL		AWLRKTL	
			AWLRKTL	
			Y AWLRKTL	'B AWLRKTL
22+	V AWPH14		AWLRKTL	Q AWLRKTL
=20"	w MSSU29		AWLRKTL	Y 40LRKTL
			Y AWLRKTL	'Q AWLRKTL
			Y AWP1KTL	
				'J AWDEKTL
				Y 500EKTL
				Y AWLRKTL
				w AWLRKTL
				w AWP1KTL
				Y AWP1KTL
				Y AWP1KTL
				Y AWLRKTL
				Y AWLRKTL
			AWLRKTL	
			YT AWLRKTL	w AWLRKTL
			v[AWLRGBn	
				AWLRKTL
		25+	Y ------KT	

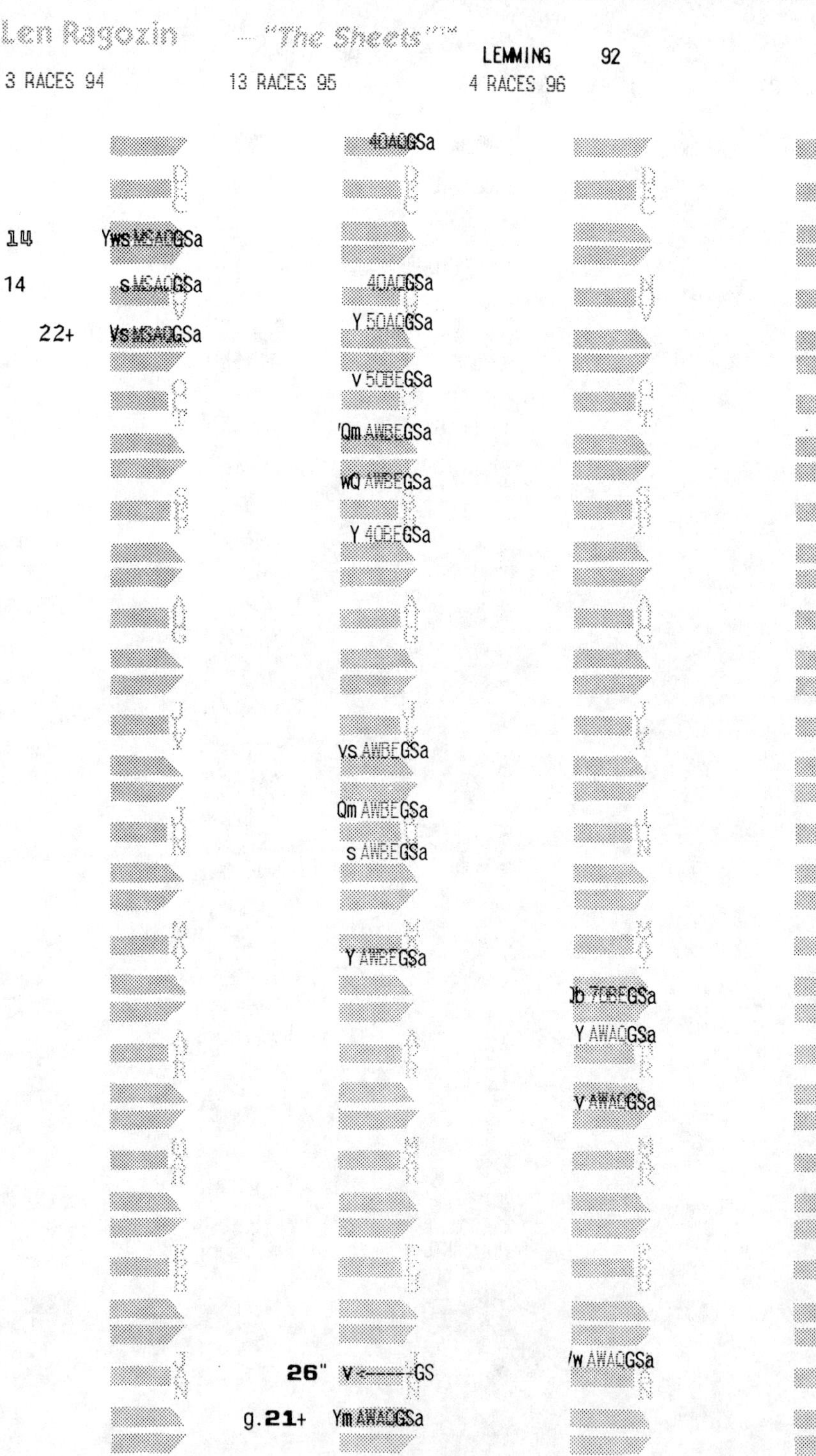
Len Ragozin — "The Sheets"™
LEMMING 92
3 RACES 94
13 RACES 95
4 RACES 96
40AQGSa
14 Yws MSAQGSa
14 s MSAQGSa
40AQGSa
Y 50AQGSa
22+ Vs MSAQGSa
v 50BEGSa
'Qm AWBEGSa
wQ AWBEGSa
Y 40BEGSa
vs AWBEGSa
Qm AWBEGSa
s AWBEGSa
Y AWBEGSa
Jb 70BEGSa
Y AWAQGSa
v AWAQGSa
/w AWAQGSa
26" v ←——GS
g.21+ Ym AWAQGSa

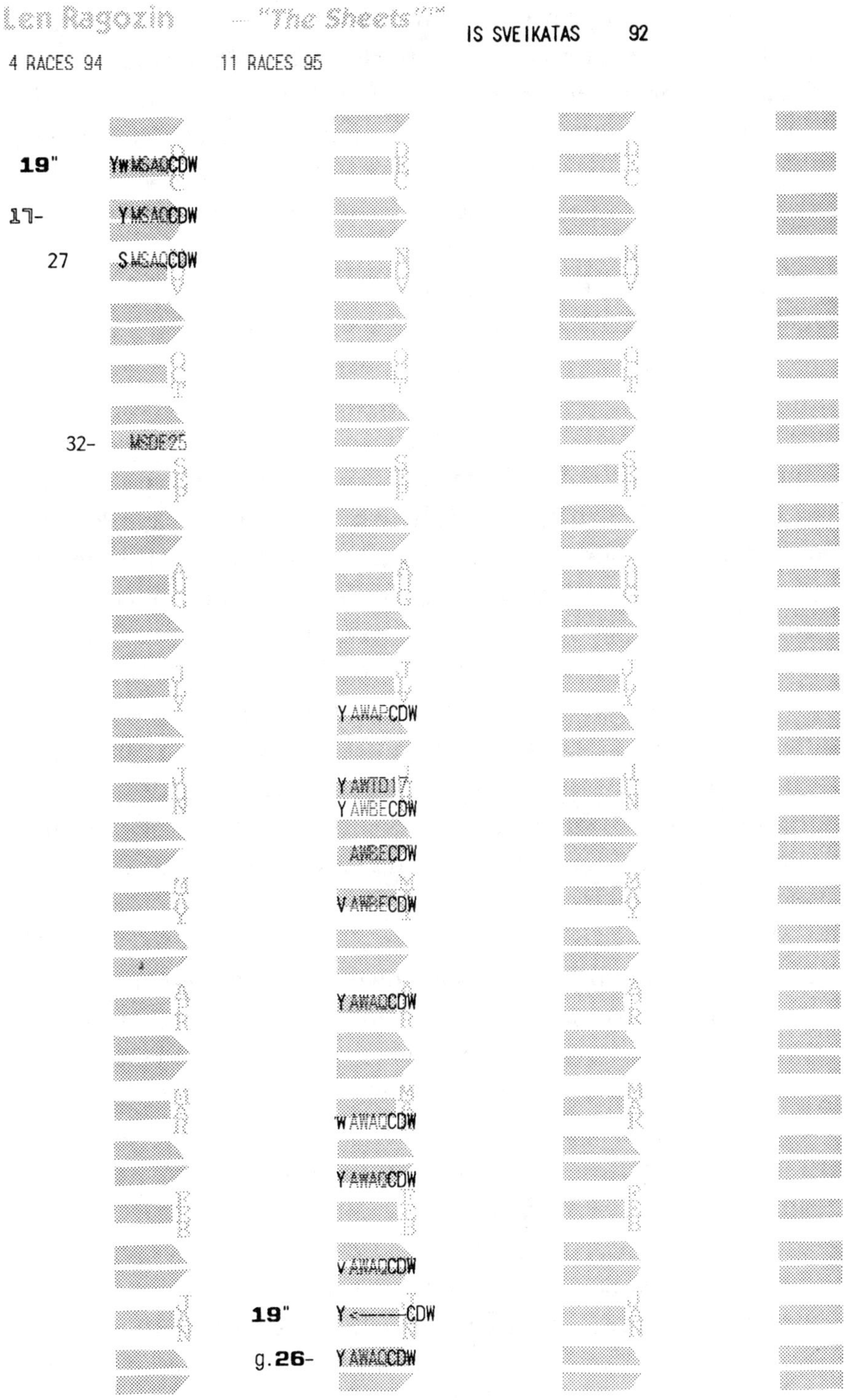

Len Ragozin — "The Sheets"™ IS SVEIKATAS 92

4 RACES 94 11 RACES 95

19" YwMSAQCDW

17- YMSAQCDW

27 SMSAQCDW

32- MSDE25

Y AWAPCDW

Y AWTD17

Y AWBECDW

AWBECDW

V AWBECDW

Y AWAQCDW

wAWAQCDW

Y AWAQCDW

v AWAQCDW

19" Y ←——CDW

g.26- Y AWAQCDW

Paragallo's Hope had finished sixth in that race, but otherwise fell somewhere between the two horses directly inside of him. He had a similar pattern: a 15½ November 20, followed by a 17 December 2, and then a 25 in the January 2 race. Paragallo's Hope and Lemming seemed similar: with two months gone by since each had run his best race, this could be a good day for them to make a comeback to top form.

Guadalcanal had run well in both his starts at 2: an 18− in his debut December 8, then a 13¼ that slightly topped Lemming's best effort. But two factors made it questionable that he would be able to move forward again: the big improvement occurred just two weeks before today's race, and he was racing around two turns for the first time. It seemed more likely that he would react temporarily. The question was, how far would he back up?

The outside horse, Gin On Land, had run his best effort in his debut at Monmouth in late August, breaking his maiden while running a 16−, a good number for a two-year-old at that point in the year. He had backed up to a 17½ six weeks later at the Meadowlands, run poorly over a soft turf course after that, and then run a 19¼ December 9. At Aqueduct December 29 he made his first move forward since his debut, running an 18½ in a sprint. That small progression was encouraging, but the horse was unproven going a distance and figured to lose ground from Post 7 in the short run to the first turn.

Friedman's decisions on how — and whether — to play the race were made for him by the crowd. Lemming was made the even-money favorite, while Paragallo's Hope went off at 10–1. Lemming's two best races were slightly stronger than Paragallo's Hope's best but not nearly enough to account for the wide difference in price, particularly since they were too lightly raced to be exactly governed by their past figures. Is Sveikatas, with a similar pattern to those two, was 21–1.

The most plausible explanation for the way the public regarded these three horses was that it was attaching great weight to who beat whom in the January 2 race in which they had all competed. But our figures showed that none of the three had come close to his

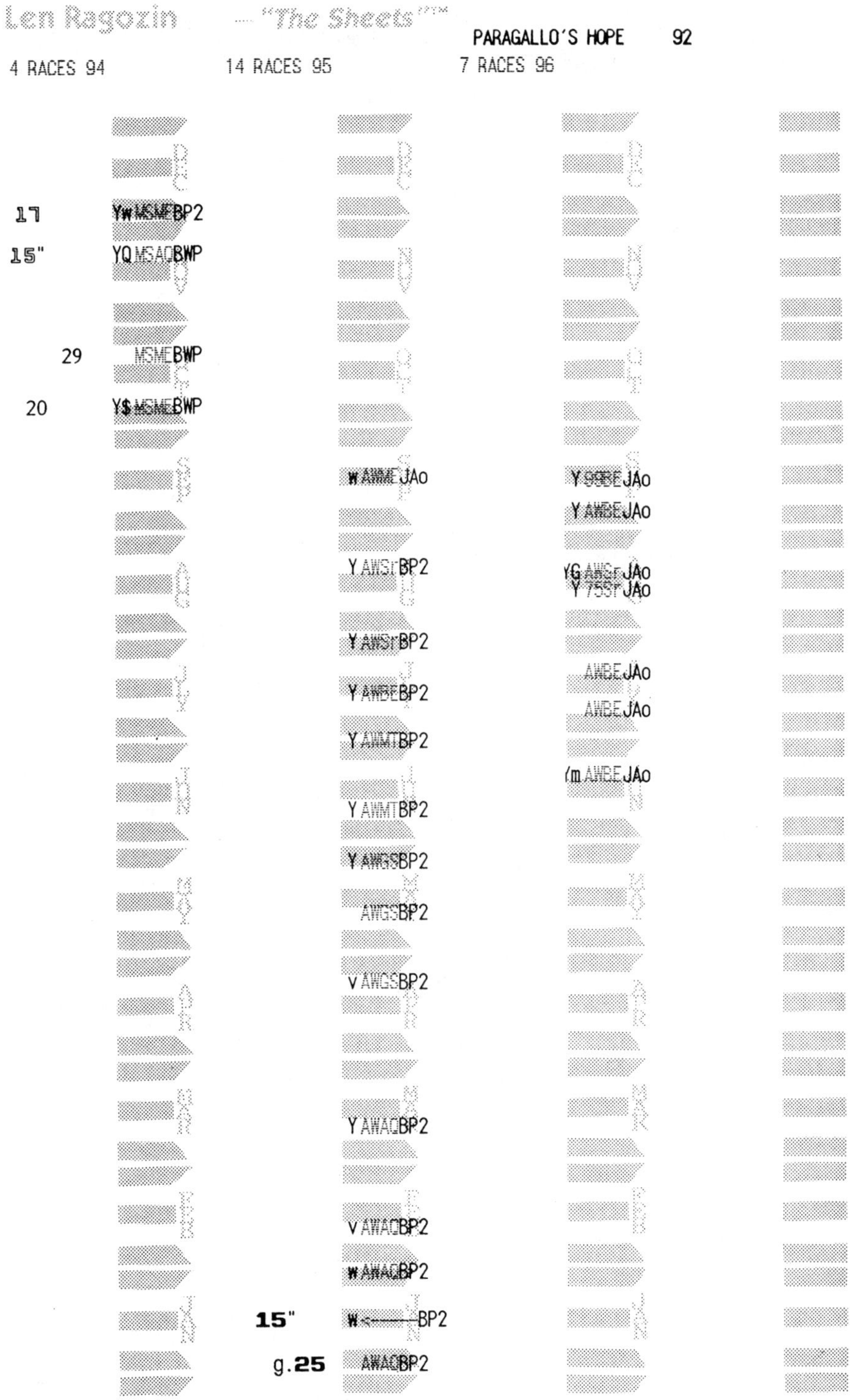

Len Ragozin — "The Sheets"™

PARAGALLO'S HOPE 92

4 RACES 94

17 YwMSMEBP2

15" YQ MSAQBWP

29 MSMEBWP

20 Y$MSMEBWP

14 RACES 95

wAWMEJAo

Y AWSrBP2

Y AWSrBP2

Y AWBEBP2

Y AWMTBP2

Y AWMTBP2

Y AWGSBP2

AWGSBP2

v AWGSBP2

Y AWAQBP2

v AWAQBP2

w AWAQBP2

15" W←——BP2

g.25 AWAQBP2

7 RACES 96

Y 99BEJAo

Y AWBEJAo

YG AWSr JAo

Y 75Sr JAo

AWBEJAo

AWBEJAo

(m AWBE JAo

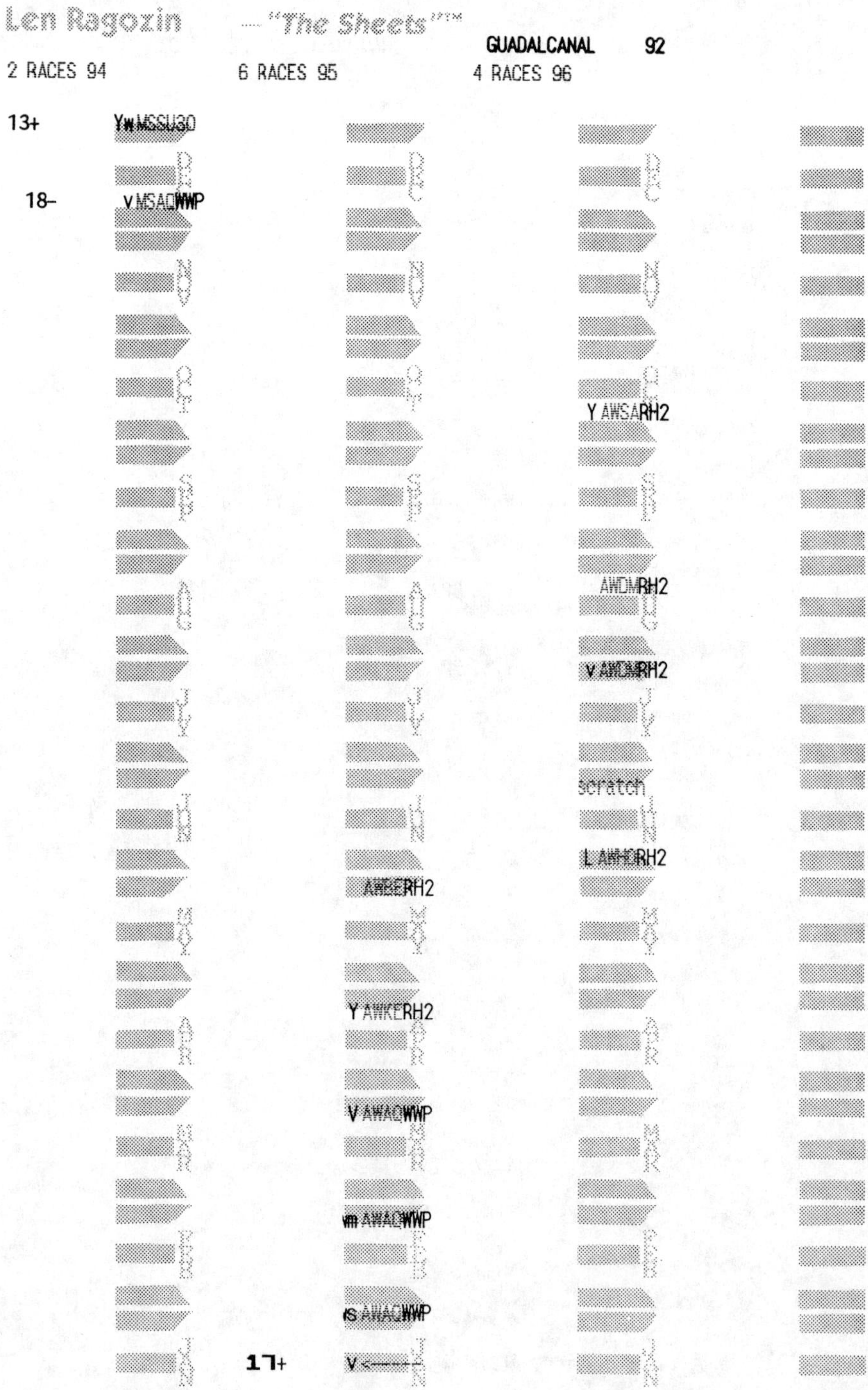
Len Ragozin
"The Sheets"™
GUADALCANAL 92
2 RACES 94
6 RACES 95
4 RACES 96
13+ YwMSSU30
18– vMSAQWWP
DEC
NOV
OCT
SEP
AUG
JLY
JUN
MAY
APR
MAR
FEB
JAN
Y AWSARH2
AWDMRH2
v AWDMRH2
scratch
L AWHORH2
AWBERH2
Y AWKERH2
V AWAQWWP
vm AWAQWWP
vs AWAQWWP
17+
V <-----

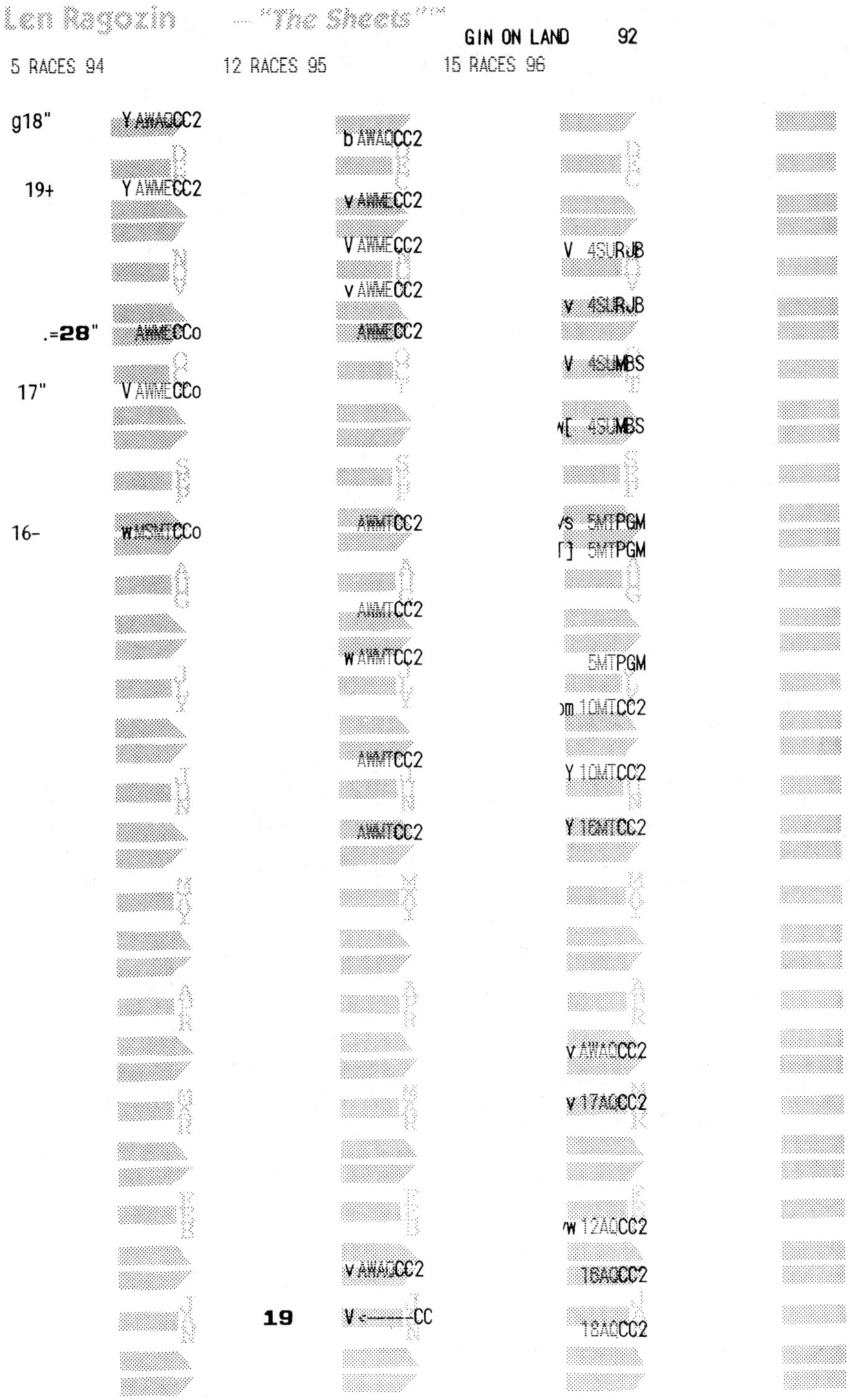

Len Ragozin — "The Sheets"™

GIN ON LAND 92

5 RACES 94 12 RACES 95 15 RACES 96

g18" Y AWAQCC2
b AWAQCC2
19+ Y AWMECC2
v AWMECC2
V AWMECC2
V 4SURJB
v AWMECC2
v 4SURJB
.=**28**" AWMECCo
AWMECC2
V 4SUMBS
17" V AWMECCo
w[4SUMBS
16- w MSMTCCo
AWMTCC2
vs 5MTPGM
[] 5MTPGM
AWMTCC2
w AWMTCC2
5MTPGM
m 10MTCC2
AWMTCC2
Y 10MTCC2
AWMTCC2
Y 16MTCC2
v AWAQCC2
v 17AQCC2
w 12AQCC2
v AWAQCC2
18AQCC2
19 V ←——CC
18AQCC2

previous good numbers, so comparing them in this race was a mistake. Most likely the bad racing conditions led all these inexperienced colts to toss in random poor efforts that day. Friedman treated that race as irrelevant to today's race, which was being run over a fast track without high winds. Once he reached that conclusion, Paragallo's Hope loomed as an incredible overlay, and Is Sveikatas's price was also far higher than it should have been based on his previous fast-track form.

So Friedman bet Paragallo's Hope to win, then keyed him in exactas giving equal weight to Is Sveikatas, the overbet Lemming, and Guadalcanal, the second choice at 5–2.

Paragallo's Hope quickly grabbed the lead on the rail and increased his margin through the stretch to win by six and a half

EIGHTH RACE
Aqueduct
JANUARY 15, 1995

1 1/16 MILES. (Inner Dirt)(1.41) ALLOWANCE. Purse $32,000. 3-year-olds which have not won a race other than maiden or claiming. Weight, 122 lbs. Non-winners of a race other than maiden at a mile or over since January 1, allowed 3 lbs. Of such a race since December 15, 5 lbs.

Value of Race: $32,000 Winner $19,200; second $6,400; third $3,520; fourth $1,920; fifth $960. Mutuel Pool $135,890.00 Exacta Pool $200,434.00 Triple Pool $151,003.00

Last Raced	Horse	M/Eqt.	A.	Wt	PP	St	¼	½	¾	Str	Fin	Jockey	Odds $1	
2Jan95 ^{8}Aqu^{6}	Paragallo's Hope		3	117	5	3	$1^{1\frac{1}{2}}$	1^{2}	1^{2}	1^{5}	$1^{6\frac{1}{2}}$	Rydowski S R	10.10	Ridden out
30Dec94 ^{5}Suf^{1}	Guadalcanal		3	117	6	4	$2^{2\frac{1}{2}}$	$2^{\frac{1}{2}}$	2^{1}	$2^{\frac{1}{2}}$	2^{nk}	Migliore R	2.55	Held place
27Nov94 ^{1}Aqu^{1}	Conduit Street	b	3	112	1	7	4^{2}	3^{1}	3^{1}	$3^{2\frac{1}{2}}$	3^{hd}	Perez R B^{5}	30.00	Broke slowly
2Jan95 ^{8}Aqu^{5}	Is Sveikatas		3	117	4	2	7	7	7	5^{4}	$4^{3\frac{3}{4}}$	Santagata N	21.00	Late gain
29Dec94 ^{7}Aqu^{3}	Gin On Land	b	3	117	7	5	3^{hd}	4^{1}	$4^{2\frac{1}{2}}$	4^{1}	$5^{6\frac{3}{4}}$	Madrid A Jr	7.50	Wide, tired
27Dec94 ^{9}Lrl^{4}	Roman Rating		3	117	2	1	$5^{\frac{1}{2}}$	5^{1}	$5^{1\frac{1}{2}}$	6^{2}	6^{5}	Luzzi M J	4.70	Tired
2Jan95 ^{8}Aqu^{3}	Lemming	b	3	117	3	6	6^{12}	6^{14}	6^{4}	7	7	Chavez J F	1.10	*Checked early, du

OFF AT 3:28 Start Good. Won ridden out. Time, :24, :47^{4}, 1:13, 1:39^{1}, 1:46 Track fast

$2 Mutuel Prices:			
5-PARAGALLO'S HOPE	22.20	9.90	5.10
6-GUADALCANAL		4.80	4.00
1-CONDUIT STREET			5.40

$2 EXACTA 5–6 PAID $109.50 $2 TRIPLE 5–6–1 PAID $1,530.00

Ro. c, (Mar), by Wolf Power–White Hope, by Whitesburg. Trainer Perkins Ben W Jr. Bred by Echo Valley Horse Farm Inc (Ky).

PARAGALLO'S HOPE outsprinted rivals for the early advantage, opened a clear advantage along the backstretch, extended his margin in upper stretch and was never threatened while being ridden out. GUADALCANAL chased the winner slightly off the rail to the top of the stretch but was no match for that one while holding for the place. CONDUIT STREET away slowly, went evenly while saving ground. IS SVEIKATAS far back for six furlongs, failed to threaten while improving his position in the stretch. GIN ON LAND raced within striking distance while three wide into upper stretch and lacked a strong closing bid. ROMAN RATING faded after going six furlongs. LEMMING checked slightly in the early stages and was never close thereafter.

Owners— 1, Paraneck Stable; 2, Be Stables; 3, Leahy Richard & Meriwether John W; 4, Whitaker Clarke D; 5, Parent Arthur F; 6, Brittingham Baird C & Lufkin Daniel; 7, Klaravich Stables

Trainers—1, Perkins Ben W Jr; 2, Perry William W; 3, Freeman Willard C; 4, Whitaker Clarke D; 5, Carlesimo Charles Jr; 6, Leatherbury King T; 7, Sciacca Gary

$2 Pick–3 (2–4–5) Paid $188.50; Pick–3 Pool $112,496. $2 Pick–6 (6–1–4–2–4–5) 6 Correct 10 Tickets Paid $10,117.00 (including $37,946 Carryover); 5 Correct 204 Tickets Paid $111.50; Pick–6 Pool $121,390.

lengths. Guadalcanal ran second throughout and won a three-horse photo for place over Conduit Street and Is Sveikatas. Lemming finished last, beaten 22½ lengths.

Had Is Sveikatas gotten second, Friedman would have taken home half the racetrack. As it was, he cashed a sizable bet on the $109.50 exacta in addition to the $22.20 win price.

How did the actual results compare to Friedman's analysis of *The Sheets*? Paragallo's Hope ran a 15¼, similar to his previous top effort two months earlier. Lemming threw in his second straight poor effort, declining to a 26.

There was no way to project from *The Sheets* that two horses with such a similar pattern in their running lines would veer off in opposite directions on this day. It was simply one of those instances in which the odds board rather than a hair-splitting reading of the horses' form dictated the way in which Friedman played the race, and a good illustration of why such a method is the best way to bet.

A more straightforward example, in which the most consistent horse in the field went off at 12–1, occurred a day earlier in the eighth race at Turfway Park.

A quick glance at *The Sheets* for the allowance race for fillies and mares indicated that six of the eleven entrants were too slow to have a realistic shot of winning. That left Parrish Queen, Blondeintheshower, Cheswell, Viz, and Dawn Deal to be considered.

Parrish Queen showed two strong races the previous fall followed by two slower ones, the most recent one at Turfway. If she could duplicate the 18¼ she had run November 1 at Churchill Downs, she might win this race.

Parrish Queen had two numbers better than 20; Blondeintheshower had run a 19¼ in three of her previous six starts.

Cheswell looked slower than the other contenders, but her recent form had slowly inched forward, giving her a chance to improve and thus an outside shot.

Viz had by far the best number in the field, a 12½ run a year earlier at Hollywood Park. But that race appeared to have knocked her out: she was sidelined for the next seven months, and

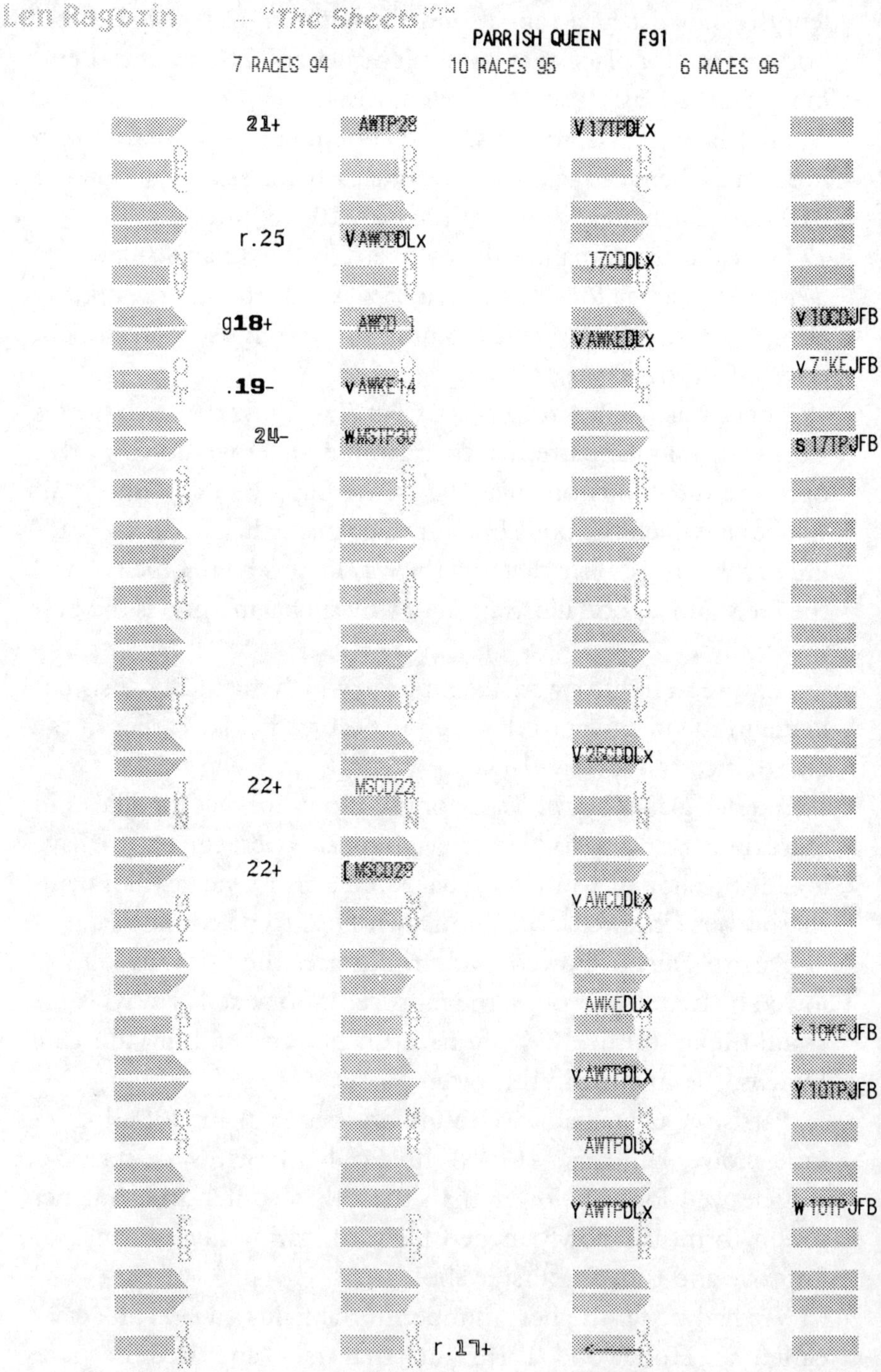

Len Ragozin — "The Sheets"™

PARRISH QUEEN F91

	7 RACES 94		10 RACES 95		6 RACES 96
DEC	21+	AWTP28		V 17TPDLx	
NOV	r.25	V AWCDDLx			
NOV				17CDDLx	
OCT	g18+	AWCD 1			V 10CDJFB
OCT				V AWKEDLx	
OCT					v 7"KEJFB
OCT	.19-	v AWKE14			
SEP	24-	WASTP30			s 17TPJFB
AUG					
JLY					
JUN				V 25CDDLx	
JUN	22+	MSCD22			
MAY	22+	[MSCD29			
MAY				v AWCDDLx	
APR				AWKEDLx	
APR					t 10KEJFB
MAR				v AWTPDLx	Y 10TPJFB
MAR				AWTPDLx	
FEB				Y AWTPDLx	W 10TPJFB
JAN			r.17+	←	

Len Ragozin — "The Sheets"™

BLONDEINTHESHOWER F91

12 RACES 94 | 8 RACES 95 | 20 RACES 96

12 RACES 94

23 vAWTPDJH
19+ V&dh 17CD19
g19+ Vs AWCD 1
21- Vw 35KE15
22+ v[MSTP23
19+ VMSEL31
=22" VMSEL 6
=15 MSEL 4
22" MSCD25
19+ MSCD29
F27" YMSKE17
20+ vS$MSGP 8

8 RACES 95

Yw 17TPDJ
v 20KEDJH
vs 15TPDJH
AWTPDJH
Y 25ELDJH
AWTPDJH
v AWTPPRM
r.16 vw

20 RACES 96

v 8CDMHe
Y 8CDMHe
10HP29
v 10HP18
AWHP12
10HP 6
Y 10TPMHe
10TPMHe
v 8ELMHe
Y 8ELMHe
10ELMHe
Y 10CDMHe
mh 6+CDJG1
st 10CDJG1
v 15CDJG1
V 13TPJG1
v AWTPJG1
Y 17TPJG1
V 13TPDJH
Ys 17TPDJH

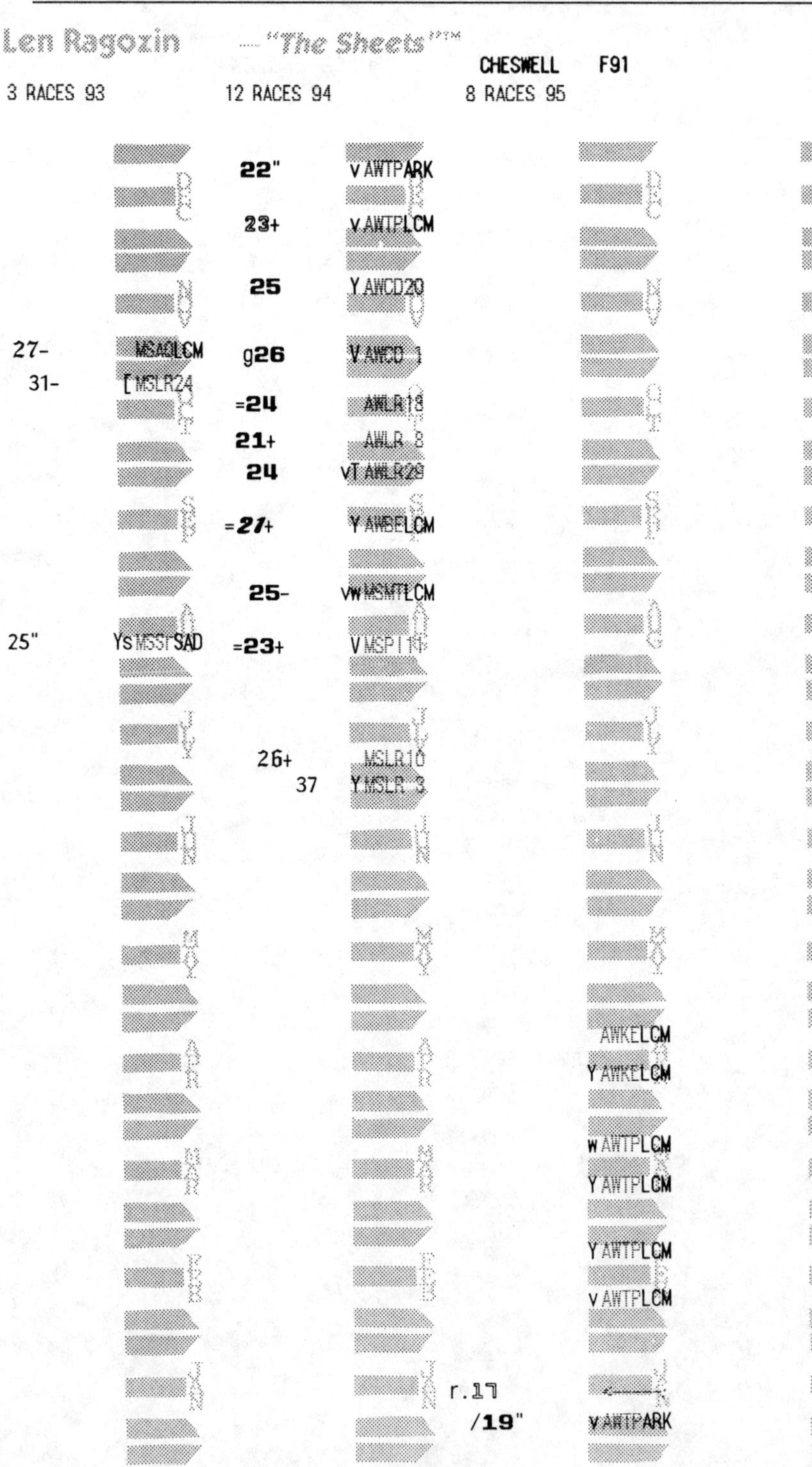
Len Ragozin "The Sheets"™
CHESWELL F91
3 RACES 93
12 RACES 94
8 RACES 95
22" vAWTPARK
23+ vAWTPLCM
25 YAWCD20
27- MSAQLCM
g26 VAWCD 1
31- [MSLR24
=24 AWLR18
21+ AWLR 8
24 vTAWLR29
=27+ YAWBELCM
25- vwMSMTLCM
25" YsMSSrSAD
=23+ VMSP 11
26+ MSLR10
37 YMSLR 3
AWKELCM
YAWKELCM
wAWTPLCM
YAWTPLCM
YAWTPLCM
vAWTPLCM
r.17
/19" vAWTPARK

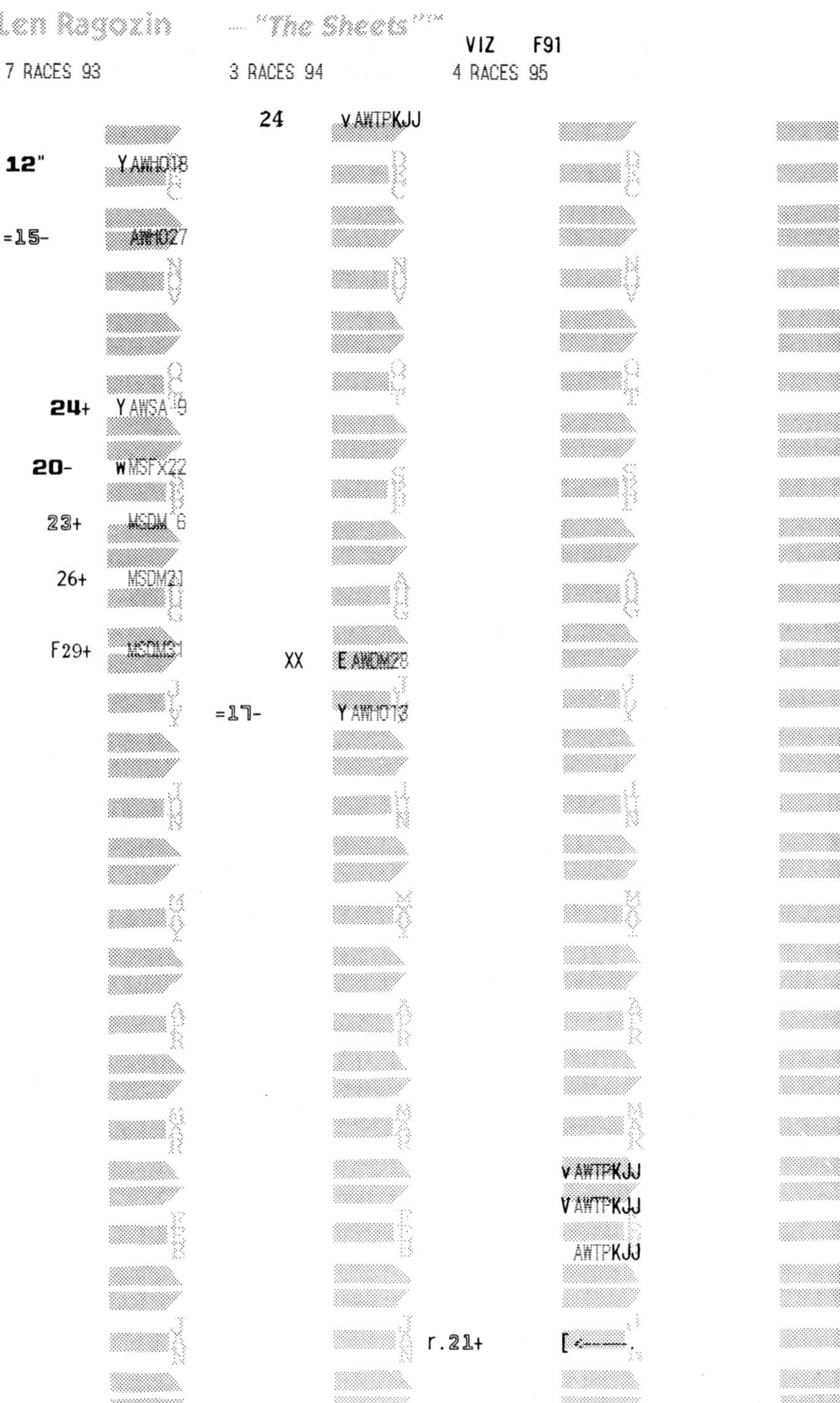

Len Ragozin
"The Sheets"™
VIZ F91
7 RACES 93
3 RACES 94
4 RACES 95
24 V AWTPKJJ
12" Y AWHO18
=15- AWHO27
24+ Y AWSA 9
20- W MSFX22
23+ MSDM 6
26+ MSDM21
F29+ MSDM31
XX E AWDM28
=17- Y AWHO13
V AWTPKJJ
V AWTPKJJ
AWTPKJJ
r.21+

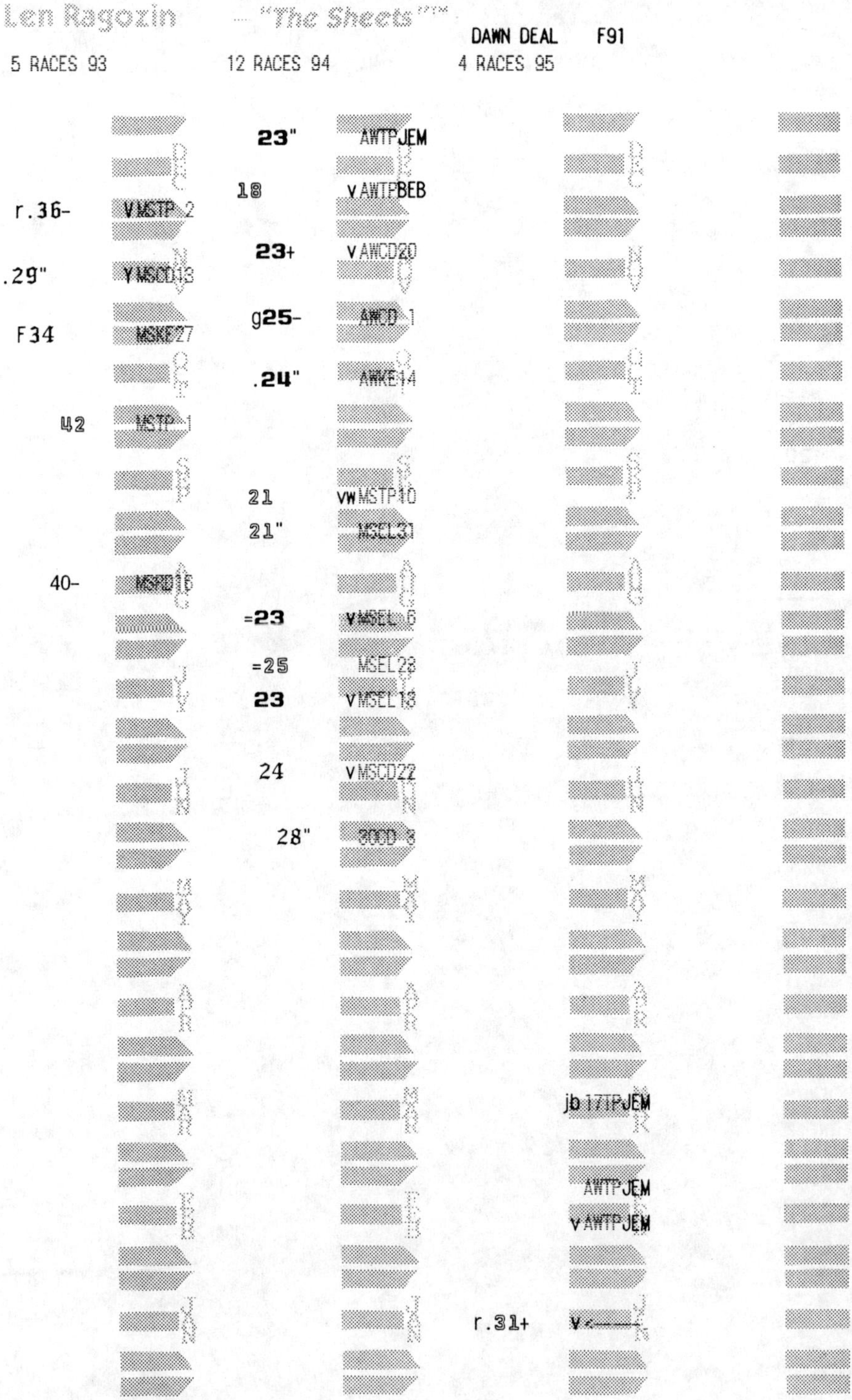

Len Ragozin ... "The Sheets"™

DAWN DEAL F91

5 RACES 93

r.36- VMSTP 2
.29" VMSCD13
F34 MSKE27
42 MSTP 1
40- MSRD16

12 RACES 94

23" AWTPJEM
18 vAWTPBEB
23+ vAWCD20
g25- AWCD 1
.24" AWKE14
21 vwMSTP10
21" MSEL31
=23 vMSEL 6
=25 MSEL28
23 vMSEL13
24 vMSCD22
28" 3OCD 8

4 RACES 95

jb 17TPJEM
AWTPJEM
vAWTPJEM
r.31+ v<——

in her second race back from a layoff had to be eased. She spent another five months on the shelf, then turned up at Turfway — a big drop in class from the Southern California tracks where she'd done her previous racing — and ran unimpressively. The two extended layoffs and that recent poor race strongly suggested there was something seriously wrong with her physically.

Dawn Deal had run an 18 five weeks earlier at Turfway. It was 3 points better than her best previous effort and she had reacted badly in her next race fifteen days later.

Again, the crowd made it easy for Friedman. It made Parrish Queen the 7–10 favorite, a ridiculous price even if you believed she would come close to her two previous good races. Viz, with all the earmarks of a crippled horse, was sent off as the 4–1 second choice. Meanwhile, Blondeintheshower, whose previous consistency stamped her as the filly most likely to run decently, was 12–1.

EIGHTH RACE
Turfway Park
JANUARY 14, 1995

1 MILE. (1.34) ALLOWANCE. Purse $27,900 (includes $9,300 KTDF). Fillies and mares, 4-year-olds and upward, which have not won a race other than maiden, claiming, optional or starter. Weight, 121 lbs. Non-winners of $13,000, allowed 3 lbs. $11,700, 6 lbs. $8,775, 9 lbs. (Races where entered for $25,000 or less not considered in allowances).

alue of Race: $27,900 Winner $18,135; second $5,580; third $2,790; fourth $1,395. Mutuel Pool $67,573.00 Exacta Pool $46,085.00 Trifecta ool $53,570.00

ast Raced	Horse	M/Eqt.	A.	Wt	PP	St	¼	½	¾	Str	Fin	Jockey	Odds $1	
ec94 ^{9}TP^8	Blondeintheshower	Lb	4	113	3	11	$5\frac{1}{2}$	4^2	2^{hd}	2^4	1^2	Kutz D	12.50	4 wide, clear late
an95 ^{9}TP^2	Cheswell	Lf	4	115	5	7	6^{hd}	$7\frac{1}{2}$	$5\frac{1}{2}$	$3\frac{1}{2}$	2^{nk}	Estrella R I	9.30	5 wide rally
Dec94 ^{7}TP^2	Parrish Queen	Lbf	4	121	1	2	1^1	1^{hd}	$1\frac{1}{2}$	1^{hd}	3^3	Allen K K	0.70	Outfinished inside
Dec94 ^{7}TP^3	Phone The Bride	L	4	118	2	1	2^3	$2^{1\frac{1}{2}}$	3^3	4^1	4^2	Bartram B E	8.50	No inside rally
Dec94 ^{5}TP^1	Naval Guardian	Lb	4	114	8	10	4^1	3^{hd}	4^3	5^5	5^5	Bruin J E	16.00	Rail early, outrun
Dec94 ^{7}TP^6	Viz	Lb	4	121	9	8	$10\frac{1}{2}$	$6^{1\frac{1}{2}}$	$6^{1\frac{1}{2}}$	6^5	6^7	D'Amico A J	4.00	Even rally
Dec94 ^{7}TP^6	Regal Export	L	4	112	6	6	$7^{1\frac{1}{2}}$	8^4	7^6	7^3	7^3	Bourque S J	67.70	Lost ground
Dec94 ^{10}TP^3	Grey Ambition		5	108	7	9	$8\frac{1}{2}$	$9\frac{1}{2}$	8^3	8^4	$8^{1\frac{1}{2}}$	Hughes L L^7	37.50	Outrun
Dec94 ^{5}TP^4	Zitkala	Lf	4	112	10	4	11	$10^{1\frac{1}{2}}$	9^1	9^5	9^7	Martinez J R Jr	48.70	Lacked speed
Dec94 ^{7}TP^6	Dawn Deal	L	4	121	11	5	9^{hd}	11	11	10^2	10^{12}	Thompson T J	26.60	Ran wide
an95 ^{7}TP^7	Call Your Raise	Lb	5	115	4	3	3^2	5^2	10^6	11	11	Johnston J A	112.10	Brief speed

OFF AT 4:41 Start Good. Won driving. Time, :23^1, :48, 1:13^2, 1:26^4, 1:41 Track muddy.

$2 Mutuel Prices:			
3-BLONDEINTHESHOWER	27.00	11.40	4.20
5-CHESWELL		10.00	3.60
1-PARRISH QUEEN			2.20

$2 EXACTA 3–5 PAID $170.60 $2 TRIFECTA 3–5–1 PAID $564.60

B. f, by Bates Motel–Randolph Macon, by To the Quick. Trainer Habeeb Donald J. Bred by Jones Brereton C (Ky).

BLONDEINTHESHOWER moved to four wide in the backstretch, rallied hard and ran clear in time. CHESWELL moved to five ide, had a clear run and took second late. PARRISH QUEEN increased her lead briefly into the stretch, then was outfinished. HONE THE BRIDE just outside of PARRISH QUEEN, lacked a rally. NAVAL GUARDIAN moved to the rail early, remained ere to lack a rally. VIZ had an even rally. REGAL EXPORT lost ground. GREY AMBITION was outrun. ZITKALA lacked speed. AWN DEAL ran wide. CALL YOUR RAISE had brief speed inside.

Owners— 1, Greenhill Jeff; 2, Graf Max; 3, Parrish Hill Farm; 4, Jones Brenda; 5, Singer Craig B; 6, Shapiro S & Stark D & Vizvary S; Bradley & Hurst & Patrick; 8, Jackson Helmut S & Moses R J & S D; 9, Nelson James E; 10, Zimmerman George A; 11, Nafzger Larry

Trainers—1, Habeeb Donald J; 2, Metz Lawrence C; 3, Lemieux David; 4, Hauswald M James; 5, Granitz Anthony J; 6, Jumps Kenneth J; Bradley William; 8, Jackson Helmut S; 9, Segretto Joseph; 10, Morgan James E; 11, Nafzger Larry

Corrected weight: Call Your Raise (115) **Overweight:** Blondeintheshower (1), Naval Guardian (2), Grey Ambition (3).

Scratched— Connecting Flight (23Dec94 ^{7}TP^3)

$2 Pick Three (7–4–3) 3 Correct Paid $2,875.40; Pick Three Pool $14,746. $2 Pick Six (1–5–4–7–4–3) 4 Correct Paid $787.00; Pick Six Pool $4,036; Carryover Pool $10,905.

Parrish Queen led early, but Blondeintheshower collared her at the quarter-pole and drew clear late to win by two lengths and pay $27. The slowly improving Cheswell rallied to neck Parrish Queen, producing an exacta payoff of $170.60 and a triple worth $564.60.

Most betting choices won't be so clear-cut. For example, in the Aqueduct race discussed earlier, an argument could have been made before the race that the 21–1 price on the slightly slower Is Sveikatas was more inviting than the 10–1 Paragallo's Hope offered. Ideally, you're looking to play races where one of the betting choices is seriously overbet, creating an overlay somewhere else. Often in those cases there is likely to be more than one horse offering good value.

My father used to draw up his own odds line for each race, and was prepared to bet any and all horses in the race whose odds were longer than his judgment said was correct.

Because he was involved in running a business and there was no OTB prior to 1971, there was just one way to be sure he got the prices he wanted: he would send my mother, Sarra, to the track with the cash and the odds list.

On one occasion, his list included a bet to be made at odds of 5–1 or better. Throughout the betting, the price on this horse — Number 4 — fluctuated between 9–2 and 5–1, leaving my mother hanging on the last flash of the odds. Just before post time, the tote board showed 5–1, and she rushed to the window and placed a $100 bet.

The only problem was, she had become so fixated on the 5–1 price, she shouted "Five!" to the ticket seller and ended up with a bet my father didn't want. When the number five horse won at 23–1, this made for a lively argument at the dinner table — with relatives drawn into the debate. Who was supposed to get the winnings?

For years after that, when the subject of racing came up at family gatherings, my Uncle Al would ask us, "Have you made any good mistakes lately?"

I grew up in an era when the daily double was the only exotic bet. Friedman's rise as a successful bettor, on the other hand, was during the expansion of exotic wagering, under which the same principle of shopping for overlays applies, but with better payoffs.

Friedman's decision to key Paragallo's Hope did not force him to discard Is Sveikatas; he was able to use the two horses together in exactas. Even when a 5–2 shot ran second in the race, his return on his exacta plays was more generous than the 10–1 win odds.

Before exactas were introduced, if I bet a 20–1 shot and it ran second to an 8–5 favorite, my place and show payoffs were going to be very low because so much of the money wagered in those pools was going to be paid out to those who backed the favorite. But an exacta with the favorite winning and the 20–1 shot second might pay $100 on a $2 bet. If that 20–1 shot wins with the 8–5 shot second, the exacta and triple payoffs will not be depressed nearly to the degree that place and show pools will be by the favorite finishing in the money. One of Friedman's largest scores involved a pair of 60–1 shots sandwiched around a 5–2 favorite in a triple race. The favorite sharply cut into the place and show prices on the two bombs, but the triple paid $52,459, the second-largest triple payout in New York thoroughbred history.

Exotic betting plays right into the strength of *The Sheets,* which are much better at telling you who probably *won't* win the race than who will. If enough horses have unfavorable figures or an unfavorable trend, you may be left with only a few for your exotic bet — giving you a big edge over the average bettor.

In fact, the general tendency to overbet the three or four favorites in exactas and triples offers such good value on longshots that you can often spread your play much wider than would seem logical. In the infamous "Lebon" ringer race, Friedman actually keyed a 22–1 shot named Georgetown as well as "Lebon," which was why he had two tickets on the winning triple when Georgetown wound up third. The additional money involved in using Georgetown in triples hardly mattered when weighed against the $60,000 payoff.

Usually if Friedman is crafting a triple bet, he'll look for at least a couple of horses who look so hopeless they can be thrown out completely. But in cases where he's keying a horse who's around 50–1, he'll play even the hopeless horses in $1 combinations to avoid the annoyance of missing a five-figure triple.

In the early years, from 1956 to 1969, when my main income was from my own betting, I had no time to go to the races and shop the odds — I was too busy working on the figures. So I was forced to bet with bookies without knowing the on-track odds — even though overlay odds are vital to success.

My solution was to identify a few horses with such outstanding individual patterns of development that I was confident I would get an unusually big effort from the horse. There was a big built-in overlay. The odds on these jump-ups *had* to be generous. I didn't have to worry about the competition. My horse was supposed to run an effort he rarely ran or perhaps had never run. And if my horse was entered against faster runners, the price was so good that I didn't have to concern myself about these faster horses being likely to beat me. In the long run, the occasional payoffs would be good enough to offset that situation. In the short run, the place or show payoff would keep me afloat.

Of course, these extreme-overlay types of development lines don't pop up too often. I usually handicapped forty or fifty races a day and ended up with two or three bets.

If you're betting a favorite, you'd better be pretty sure he's going to run a strong race that day. If your horse is 30–1, on the other hand, you can take a shot simply based on *The Sheets* showing that the horse once before ran the kind of number that could win this race — or on a subtle trend that shows he could improve to such a number. If you're able to separate 30–1 shots who actually have a chance to win from the others at the same price who don't have a prayer, you'll cash enough bets to make it worthwhile.

Friedman likes to see a horse going off 50 percent higher than he thinks it should be before he makes a bet. Someone less accustomed to making an odds line might want to look for twice what they think a horse's price should be, because most bettors (including Friedman) overestimate their horse's chances.

We'd rather bet a 15–1 shot we think should be 5–1 than an 8–5 shot who should be even money. Legitimate even-money horses will win half the time, and legitimate 5–1 shots win 17 percent of the time, but at 15–1, the odds are so much in your favor that the long-run percentages become excellent. However, if you get severely rattled by losing streaks, you might want to focus more on overlays who are favorites — it's easier on the nerves.

A prime example of overlay betting occurred in the 1994 running of the Hollywood Turf Handicap on Memorial Day. Bien Bien looked like a solid favorite; he had consistently been running 3s and looked ready to run another. But the strong second choice in the race was Arcangues, who seemed to be getting bet more because of his win on dirt in the Breeders' Cup Classic the previous November than his unimpressive turf form since. And the third choice in the race was Misil, a prolific stakes winner in Europe whose first turf race at Hollywood suggested he might not be fast enough to be competitive.

My numbers suggested Grand Flotilla — who had run second to Bien Bien in their previous race five weeks earlier — should be the second choice in the race, but he was going off at 14–1. The real value was in the exactas: with Bien Bien on top of Grand Flotilla, the probable payoff at Belmont Park — to which the race was being simulcast — was $30, and the other way the combination was paying $64. At Hollywood, the exacta with Grand Flotilla on top was paying $54.

It appeared that even running his best, Grand Flotilla would have trouble beating Bien Bien, but at odds of 26–1 or 31–1, depending where you were betting, a strong exacta reverse made sense.

As it turned out, Chris McCarron rode Bien Bien overconfidently, blithely sweeping four-wide around the last turn to reach contention, while Gary Stevens, moving from last with Grand Flotilla, steered him right up the rail around the turn. Taking the more direct path allowed Grand Flotilla to gain the lead shortly after the field straightened for home, and he won by over a length.

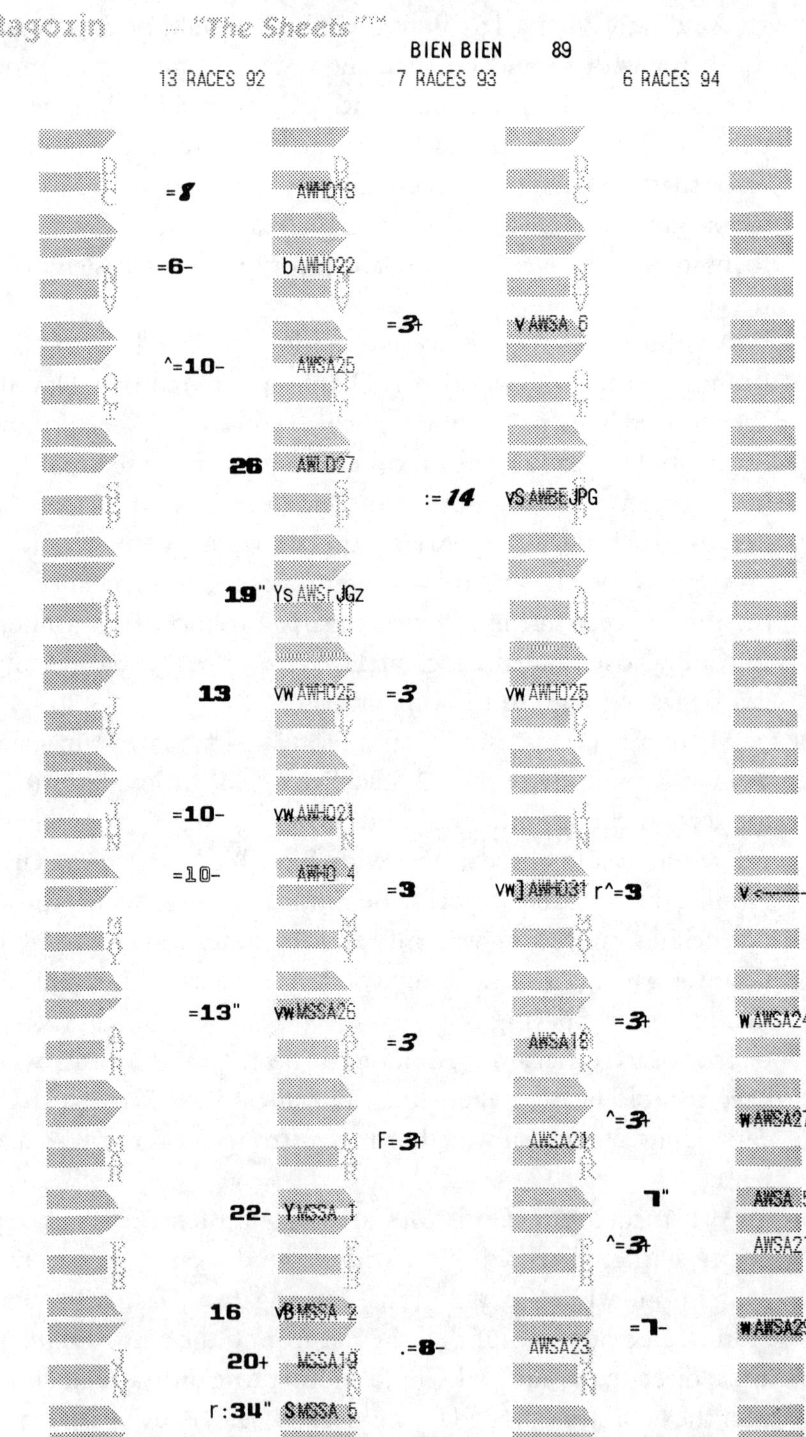
Len Ragozin
"The Sheets"™
BIEN BIEN 89
13 RACES 92
7 RACES 93
6 RACES 94
=6- b AWHO22
=3+ v AWSA 6
^=10- AWSA25
26 AWLD27
:= 14 vS AWBEJPG
19" Ys AWSr JGz
13 vw AWHO25
=3 vw AWHO25
=10- vw AWHO21
=10- AWHO 4
=3 vw] AWHO31
r^=3
=13" vw MSSA26
=3+ w AWSA24
=3 AWSA18
^=3+ w AWSA27
F=3+ AWSA21
7" AWSA 5
22- Y MSSA 1
^=3+ AWSA21
16 vB MSSA 2
=7- w AWSA29
20+ MSSA19
.=8- AWSA23
r:34" S MSSA 5

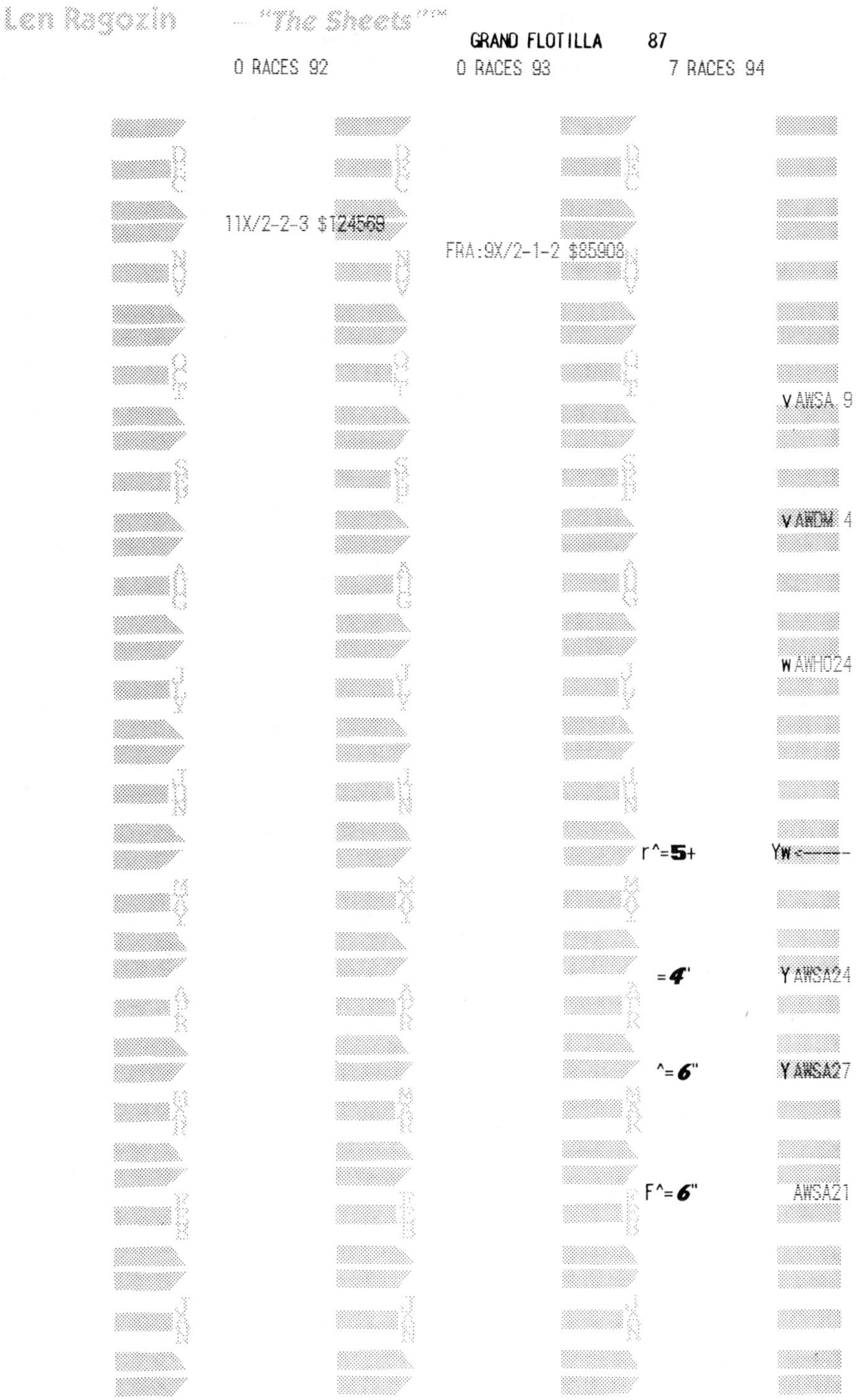

Len Ragozin — "The Sheets"™

GRAND FLOTILLA 87

0 RACES 92 | 0 RACES 93 | 7 RACES 94

11X/2-2-3 $124569

FRA:9X/2-1-2 $85908

VAWSA 9

VAWDM 4

WAWHO24

r^=5+ Yw

=4' YAWSA24

^=6" YAWSA27

F^=6" AWSA21

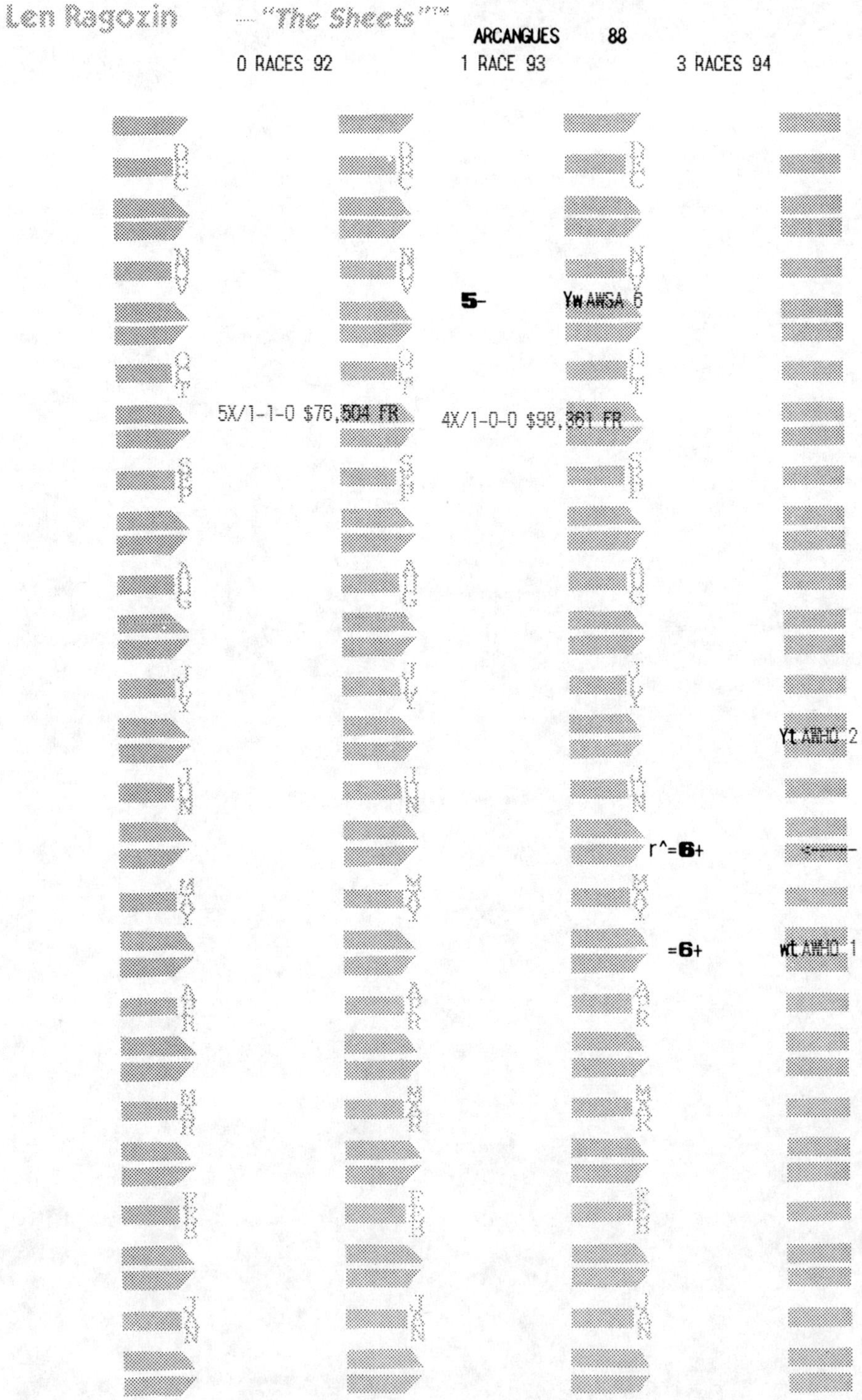

Len Ragozin ... "The Sheets"™

ARCANGUES 88

0 RACES 92 1 RACE 93 3 RACES 94

DEC

NOV

5- YwAWSA 6

OCT

5X/1-1-0 $76,504 FR 4X/1-0-0 $98,361 FR

SEP

AUG

JLY

YtAWHO 2

JUN

r^=6+ <------

MAY

=6+ wtAWHO 1

APR

MAR

FEB

JAN

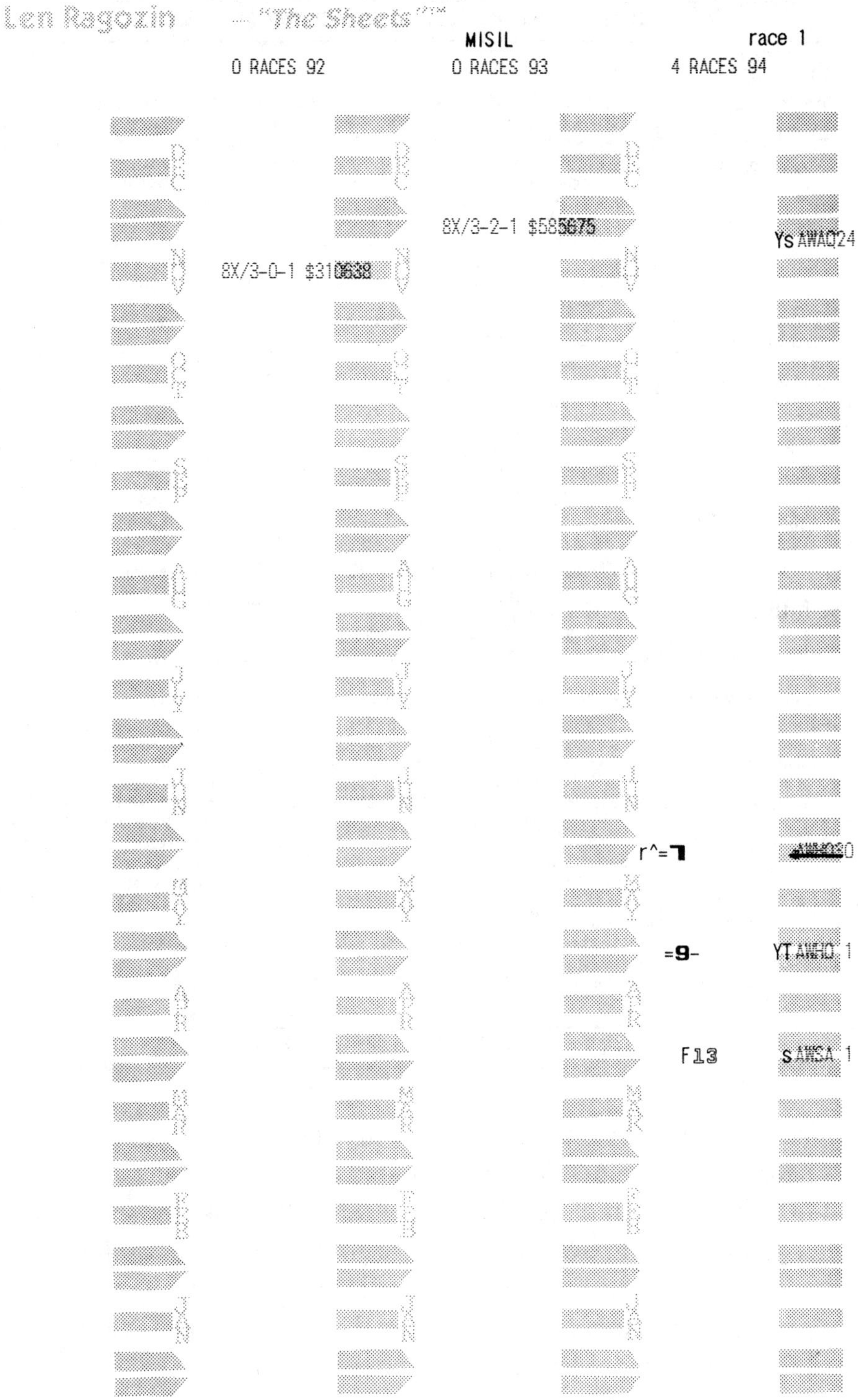

Len Ragozin — *"The Sheets"*™

MISIL race 1

0 RACES 92 | 0 RACES 93 | 4 RACES 94

8X/3-2-1 $585675

Ys AWAQ24

8X/3-0-1 $310638

r^=7 [illegible]0

=9- YT AWHQ 1

F13 s AWSA 1

\$3 Triple (1–10–2) Paid \$2,757.30; Triple Pool \$130,128.

FOURTH RACE
Hollywood
MAY 30, 1994

1¼ MILES. (Turf)(1.57^{3}) 26th Running of THE HOLLYWOOD TURF HANDICAP. Purse \$500,000 Grade I. 3-year-olds and upward. By subscription of \$500 each, which shall accompany the nomination, \$2,500 additional to pass the entry box and \$3,000 additional to start, with \$275,000 to the winner, \$100,000 to second, \$75,000 to third, \$37,500 to fourth and \$12,500 to fifth. Weights Sunday, May 22. Starters to be named through the entry box by closing time of entries. This race will not be divided. The field will be limited to 14 (fourteen) horses. In the event that more then fourteen horses pass the entry box preference will be given to high weights based upon the weight assigned to each horse, adjusted for scale weights and sex allowance (assigned weight). Total earnings in 1994 will be used in determining the preference of horses with equal assigned weight. All fees for entrants that fail to draw into this race will be cancelled. Trophies will be presented to the winning owner, trainer and jockey. Closed Wednesday, May 18, with 13 nominations.

Value of Race: \$500,000 Winner \$275,000; second \$100,000; third \$75,000; fourth \$37,500; fifth \$12,500. Mutuel Pool \$612,141.00 Exacta Pool \$539,260.00 Trifecta Pool \$274,320.00 Quinella Pool \$68,937.00

Last Raced	Horse	M/Eqt.	A.	Wt	PP	¼	½	¾	1	Str	Fin	Jockey	Odds \$1
24Apr94 ^{8}SA^{2}	Grand Flotilla	LB	7	116	1	8	8	$7^{1\frac{1}{2}}$	$4^{1\frac{1}{2}}$	1^{hd}	$1^{1\frac{3}{4}}$	Stevens G L	14.30
24Apr94 ^{8}SA^{1}	Bien Bien	LB	5	124	2	$6^{1\frac{1}{2}}$	6^{2}	5^{1}	3^{hd}	2^{hd}	$2^{1\frac{3}{4}}$	McCarron C J	0.80
14May94 ^{8}GG^{1}	Blues Traveller-IR	LB	4	114	7	2^{hd}	1^{1}	1^{hd}	1^{1}	$3^{1\frac{1}{2}}$	$3^{2\frac{3}{4}}$	Antley C W	14.90
1May94 ^{8}Hol^{2}	Misil	LB	6	119	3	$3^{\frac{1}{2}}$	3^{2}	$3^{1\frac{1}{2}}$	$5^{1\frac{1}{2}}$	5^{2}	4^{3}	Black C A	5.60
1May94 ^{8}Hol^{1}	Arcangues	B	6	124	8	1^{1}	$2^{\frac{1}{2}}$	2^{2}	$2^{\frac{1}{2}}$	4^{2}	$5^{3\frac{1}{2}}$	Delahoussaye E	2.70
11May94 ^{8}Hol^{1}	Navarone	LB	6	118	4	$7^{\frac{1}{2}}$	$7^{\frac{1}{2}}$	8	$7^{1\frac{1}{2}}$	7^{2}	6^{hd}	Valenzuela P A	20.70
28Nov93 ROM^{4}	Mashaallah	B	6	118	6	$4^{1\frac{1}{2}}$	$4^{\frac{1}{2}}$	6^{hd}	8	8	$7^{1\frac{1}{4}}$	Pincay L Jr	21.30
14May94 ^{2}Hol^{1}	The Tender Track	LB	7	114	5	5^{1}	$5^{\frac{1}{2}}$	4^{hd}	$6^{1\frac{1}{2}}$	6^{hd}	8	Solis A	59.20

OFF AT 2:57 Start Good. Won driving. Time, :24^{1}, :47^{4}, 1:11^{3}, 1:35, 1:59^{1} Course firm.

\$2 Mutuel Prices:

1–GRAND FLOTILLA	30.60	6.20	4.20
2–BIEN BIEN		2.80	2.40
7–BLUES TRAVELLER–IR			5.20

\$2 EXACTA 1–2 PAID \$54.00 \$2 TRIFECTA 1–2–7 PAID \$627.20 \$2 QUINELLA 1–2 PAID \$17.40

Ro. h, by Caro–Maurita, by Harbor Prince. Trainer Sahadi Jenine. Bred by Juddmonte Farms (Ky).

GRAND FLOTILLA saved ground off the early pace, moved up inside leaving the backstretch and through the second turn, slipped through inside BLUES TRAVELLER to gain a slim lead in midstretch and kicked clear under urging. BIEN BIEN unhurried outside early, advanced three deep on the second turn and into the stretch, raced even with the winner in midstretch but could not match that rival in the final furlong. BLUES TRAVELLER rank in the run to the first turn, pulled his way to the front from between rivals into that turn, held a slim lead inside ARCANGUES down the backstretch and second turn, edged away from that rival leaving that turn, battled briefly between rivals in midstretch, could not match the top pair but held on well for the show. MISIL steadied in tight quarters into the first turn, came off the rail leaving the second turn and weakened. ARCANGUES assumed the lead in a leisurely first quarter mile, battled outside BLUES TRAVELLER to the second turn but began to weaken leaving that turn. NAVARONE unhurried to the stretch, came wide into the stretch and did not rally. MASHAALLAH not far back outside THE TENDER TRACK to the second turn, gave way. THE TENDER TRACK saved ground just off the pace to the second turn, swung out into the stretch and also gave way.

Owners— 1, Sloan Mike H; 2, McCaffery & Toffan; 3, Tanaka Gary A; 4, Kai Horafuki; 5, Wildenstein Stable; 6, Hibbert R E; 7, Cardemil Jorge; 8, Nakkashian Or Perez Or Roberts

Trainers—1, Sahadi Jenine; 2, Gonzalez J Paco; 3, Rash Rodney; 4, Whittingham Charles; 5, Mandella Richard; 6, Rash Rodney; 7, Frankel Robert; 8, Abrams Barry

\$3 Triple (10–2–1) Paid \$3,306.00; Triple Pool \$96,649.

Because he saved ground and thus ran a shorter distance, and had light weight, Grand Flotilla's rating was a 5¼ — actually 2 points off Bien Bien's. But the payoff certainly justified taking a shot that racing luck might overturn the more likely result. Also, the lighter weight was worth 1.6 points. Even if the finish had been reversed, getting a 14–1 exacta on what loomed before the race as the most logical result would have been a terrific overlay.

There was no way to foretell that Bien Bien would lose far more ground than Grand Flotilla. Both were come-from-behind types, but Bien Bien had shown ability to dash for openings when urged by his jockey, suggesting he was actually *less* likely to have to circle horses to reach contention. The race may have pivoted on McCarron's sense that his horse was so much the best that he could disdain saving ground, while Stevens saw that route as his only chance to win. But no bettor could anticipate all these developments. There is tremendous randomness in racing, which is why you need an approach that deals in probabilities rather than trying to single out a winner.

8

The Bounce, and How to Catch It

EVEN IF YOU INTELLECTUALLY ACCEPT the idea that you should look for a long-run advantageous return on your money, it is very tempting to take short odds on the horse you are convinced is the fastest. The justification is plain: it's better to cash a ticket than to rip one up because you searched for value. In the long run, however, the track takeout on winning bets is so high it will leave a player losing money overall unless he is astute and patient enough to insist on getting the right price for every bet placed.

Let me emphasize that by "right price" I mean good value given the horse's chances of winning the race, not some artificial yardstick like 4–1 or better that some handicappers recommend. There are horses who go off at 2–1 that we'll pounce on because we believe they should be 3–5. My predilection is to bet longshots, but when I was playing seriously, I showed a huge profit when I did bet odds-on favorites. When the horse with by far the best figures in the race also popped up as one of my top condition–development lines, I made my usual bookie bet. These horses went off odds-on and more than 90 percent of them won. But we're talking about one or two dozen bets a year here.

Perhaps the best example of a bad odds-on favorite is a horse who is being bet because of an outstanding race in his last start — a race that departed dramatically from his usual form. I can't emphasize enough the importance of not allowing yourself to be overwhelmed by a horse's most recent race, whether it was terrific or awful. Horses who have just run an exceptionally good race will frequently follow it by reverting to their previous, unexceptional form, or by running worse than their norm, making them good horses to bet against. Conversely, horses who develop in a healthy manner but who run one inexplicably bad race, and who show up to race right on schedule (which tells you their trainers see no physical problem), will often run back to their previous good form. They may even improve upon it, because the last race expended less of their reserves than usual. Their prices are likely to be generous, because the crowd has been scared off by that recent clinker.

There is nothing sinister or even very surprising about most of these reversals. Like human athletes, horses react to the physical strain of competition. A big effort may be what a young horse needs to help him develop enough to compete at a higher level, or it may take so much out of him that it sets him back for a long time, even permanently. The starkest examples that come to mind are two great fillies, Ruffian and Go For Wand, who in races fifteen years apart literally ran themselves to death when they were raced back with insufficient recuperation time after supreme efforts.

Even in cases where the intense effort ultimately lays the ground for a new level for a horse, it is likely to set him back for the short term. That often creates situations in which you have a short-priced favorite who is still feeling the effects of the big race that attracted the crowd's notice. Such horses are a big risk to run poorly.

When we observed this happening often enough, we began to talk about it as "the bounce." Today this word of ours has become part of the generally accepted language of racing.

The likelihood of a horse to bounce off a big effort can vary depending upon his running style, the types of races he runs in, the surfaces over which he runs, how much racing he's done recently, how much time off he got following that strong performance, and the skills of his trainer. Naturally, age is important: an immature horse may have a better top up his sleeve. Sex is also a factor: a filly sprinter is always a good bet to bounce off a big effort.

At different stages of his career, a horse establishes what we call a "top." This is the peak effort the horse is capable of at that point of development. In most cases, two- and three-year-olds run new tops every couple of months if they're developing well. A four-year-old coming to full maturity may be able to establish a couple of additional tops better than his best races at three. By the age of five, many — but not all — horses have begun to decline, and are no longer capable of the best efforts they produced at three and four. It's a matter of judgment — from the look of a horse's lifetime of figures — just when a horse is over the hill. When that conclusion is reached, I would posit that the best number the horse ran within a recent period of three to six months is now his true top, and would gauge future races against that peak rather than considering older races he no longer can approach.

I've found that even younger horses, if they just improved more than 3 points off their most recent top, are likely candidates to bounce in their next start. There will be horses that go against that expectation — three-year-old colts before June are the most likely exceptions, especially if they just made their first real move from something that looks roughly like a longstanding level. But racing is a game of odds and probabilities. My old bookie Ralph never tired of warning me about betting a horse coming off a big improvement that resulted in a longshot win: "You missed the wedding, now you're showing up for the funeral."

There's an inherent logic to the bounce. If you're trying to judge a horse's condition, it's pretty evident that there have to be ebbs and flows, and ebbs by definition stem from a peak. So if you're looking at a horse whose most recent race was a peak, you have a decision to make: Is this really the best the horse can do, or could it be a transitional step to an even higher peak?

Sometimes too much sudden development is a bad sign that can change a young horse from one who figured to steadily improve to one who has, at least temporarily, reached the end of the line. A single big race can knock him off stride for weeks or even months, while also causing his trainer to move him into the kind of elite company in which his routine races don't give him a prayer of winning.

Let's look at Virginia Rapids. The colt's early races were decent if unspectacular, as indicated in the column at the far left of the horse's sheet.

Virginia Rapids made his two-year-old debut over a sloppy track at Saratoga in August 1992, running a 21¼. Two races later, trainer Allen Jerkens moved him to the turf and he ran a 20−, good enough to win the maiden race. An off-race on the turf followed, and Virginia Rapids was given six weeks off. When he returned to the races at Aqueduct, he ran a 14−, 6 points better than his previous top. For a two-year-old, such a jump doesn't have to be a killer. He reacted somewhat in his next race, slipping to a 17−, but followed that with a 14 on Christmas Eve at Calder, showing the new top at Aqueduct had not taken too much out of him.

In his first start as a three-year-old at Gulfstream, Virginia Rapids ran a 12½ (a quote mark on a sheet figure means half a point). The race represented a 1¼-point improvement over his two-year-old top (14− is the same as 13¾), the kind of small move that signals further progress in the near future. In his next start, Virginia Rapids improved to a 12−, a ¾-point gain that again was a positive sign.

Two weeks later, Virginia Rapids reacted slightly, running a 15¼ in his first dirt race around two turns, but this single backing-up effort (which he actually won) would not change our favorable view of his development. The horse was then given a two-month breather to await the start of Belmont's spring meeting.

Len Ragozin — "The Sheets"™

VIRGINIA RAPIDS 90

7 RACES 92	13 RACES 93	10 RACES 94	7 RACES 95
14 s AWCR24	r11- sm AWAQHAJ	=13 vs AWBEHAJ	=13 s AWBEHAJ
.17- vm AWAQHAJ	g- Vsm AWAQHAJ	7- Vm AWBEHAJ	r'6- v[m AWBEHAJ
14- vS] AWAQHAJ	r.10- vsm AWAQHAJ	13- Yst AWSrHAJ	g9 Vm AWAQHAJ
=29- V AWBEHAJ	9- Ys AWBEHAJ	5 wm AWBEHAJ	8- vsm AWAQHAJ
=20- Yw MSBEHAJ	.10 YwsQmu AWBEHAJ	=6 VD AWBEHAJ	9- vsm AWAQHAJ
'24" [MSSrHAJ	9+ mu AWBEHAJ	3" Vsm AWBEHAJ	F17 Y AWGPHAJ
.21+ m MSSrHAJ	7- m AWSrHAJ	3" vwm AWBEHAJ	18" vs AWGPHAJ
	r^12" AWBEHAJ	6 wm AWAQHAJ	
	7+ Yw AWBEHAJ	11 AWGP14	
	'3 vSm AWBEHAJ	=13 v AWGP 8	
	15+ ws AWGP27		
	12- vs AWGP13		
	12" s AWGP13		

In his first start there, the Withers Stakes, the horse produced the explosion foreshadowed by the small forward moves, though it was bigger than we expected. He ran a 3 while finishing a close second to Williamstown. This is the kind of number that will win most Grade 1 stakes.

The problem was, the improvement was so huge that it set Virginia Rapids back for the rest of the year. He bounced to a 7¼ even while winning his next start, then further declined to a 12½ a race later, prompting Jerkens to give him another two months off. The freshening helped a bit — Virginia Rapids ran a 6¾ in his return race at Saratoga, but then he went backward to a 9¼, and his form for the remainder of the year hovered at that level, stamping him as a minor stakes horse who had run one outstanding race, then went way off.

It took him a year to fully recover. With the added maturity of being a four-year-old, he held on somewhat better. Advancing from a 6 (better than anything he had run in his year of bad form), he ran a 3½ to win the Carter Handicap. He then matched that 3½ finishing fourth behind Holy Bull in a very tough Metropolitan Handicap. He managed a few fair efforts — and wins — on his way down from there, but Virginia Rapids's numbers again declined from the dangerous peak.

That sort of decline off an extraordinary effort is generally even more pronounced in horses who have never shown stakes-winning ability and therefore are less likely to be raced only a dozen times a year or to get generous vacations to recover their racing legs.

A horse is a better candidate to bounce if he's been heavily raced. This might mean after eighteen or twenty races in a year, but could also mean just ten races if they've been packed into a three-month period. It used to be you could predict most declines on a seasonal basis, with autumn a more likely time than spring to see them. Year-round racing in many parts of the country, however, has diminished if not obliterated the concept of giving horses a long rest in the winter to freshen up. But there is still some seasonal rhythm, partly based on equine genetics.

Rest of any duration can be a safeguard against horses bouncing. A horse who gets four weeks off after a big improvement is less likely to react sharply than one who's back in the starting gate within two weeks.

Rest is a factor even when you're considering horses who improved just a point or two in their most recent races and thus should not be knocked out. Even these horses, who are still in good condition overall, are more likely to go backward temporarily than to pair up or improve upon the good race unless they are given at least a three-week breather.

That was a key element in handicapping the second race at The Fairgrounds in New Orleans February 25, 1995. It was not hard to throw out horses in the field of twelve maidens running for a $15,000 claiming price: seven of them, all 35–1 or higher, had never run well enough to suggest they could be competitive. Two others had marginal chances: the 12–1 Music's Last had run one race, a 26 the previous December, good enough to make her a contender if she could improve on it by a few lengths, and the 18–1 Mitey Private had just run a 25¼ on the turf, a number that would make her a factor if she could do the same on the dirt.

That left the three prime contenders in the race, Staressentials, Booty's Girl, and Weep No More, who were also the three betting choices.

In her previous race, Staressentials had run a 20½ in finishing second over a sloppy track against $20,000 maiden claimers. That was a point better than the next best number among the competitors, the 21½ run December 20 by Weep No More. Weep No More had also been six lengths in back of Staressentials in the February 17 race, and 7½ lengths behind her in their previous race January 20, and so the bettors made Staressentials 4–5.

The short price was not the only reason to be wary about betting Staressentials. Her last race was more than 3 points better than her previous number. While it represented just a 1½-point jump over her previous career top, immediately after that 22 she had to be sidelined for more than nine months, a sure sign of physical problems. Her racing history combined with her being reentered just eight days after setting a new top argued strongly that she would bounce today.

The second choice in the betting, the 5–2 Booty's Girl, was also coming off a career top, having run a 22½ in finishing second against statebred maidens with a $12,500 claiming tag January 30. After some dismal races as a three-year-old, she had clearly matured during four and a half months on the sidelines, running three straight tops in January. The twenty-six days of rest since her last race made her less likely to bounce, but it's rare for horses, particularly fillies, to improve in four straight races, and Friedman thought she was more likely to back up a bit, though less sharply than Staressentials.

Weep No More's last effort had been 5 points worse than Staressentials's in the same race, but Friedman was inclined to discount it because it had come over a sloppy track. In her first two starts at The Fairgrounds late the previous fall, she had run a 23 and a 21½. About two and a half months had elapsed since Weep No More had run the 21½, making the timing right for her to go forward again. But even if she didn't, getting back to the 23 would probably be good enough to win if Staressentials and Booty's Girl went backward, as Friedman expected. At 6–1, she offered by far the best value among the top contenders.

So Friedman keyed Weep No More on top of Booty's Girl, also making a solid reverse bet in the event that his second choice surprised him with a fourth straight improved effort. He then used Staressentials and Mitey Private underneath in the exotics.

Weep No More ran a 23½, a bit short of her best, but good enough to win the race by a neck over Booty's Girl — who backed up 1½ points to a 24 — and trigger a $47 exacta. Staressentials was two lengths further back, just lasting by a nose over Mitey Private for third and limiting Friedman's profit on his triple bets. The heavy favorite had bounced 4 points, to a 24½.

Clearly, you have to make a fairly sophisticated read of the race to bet Weep No More against Staressentials. The favorite had beaten the other filly decisively in their two recent encounters, and both were being entered back quickly. The difference, aside

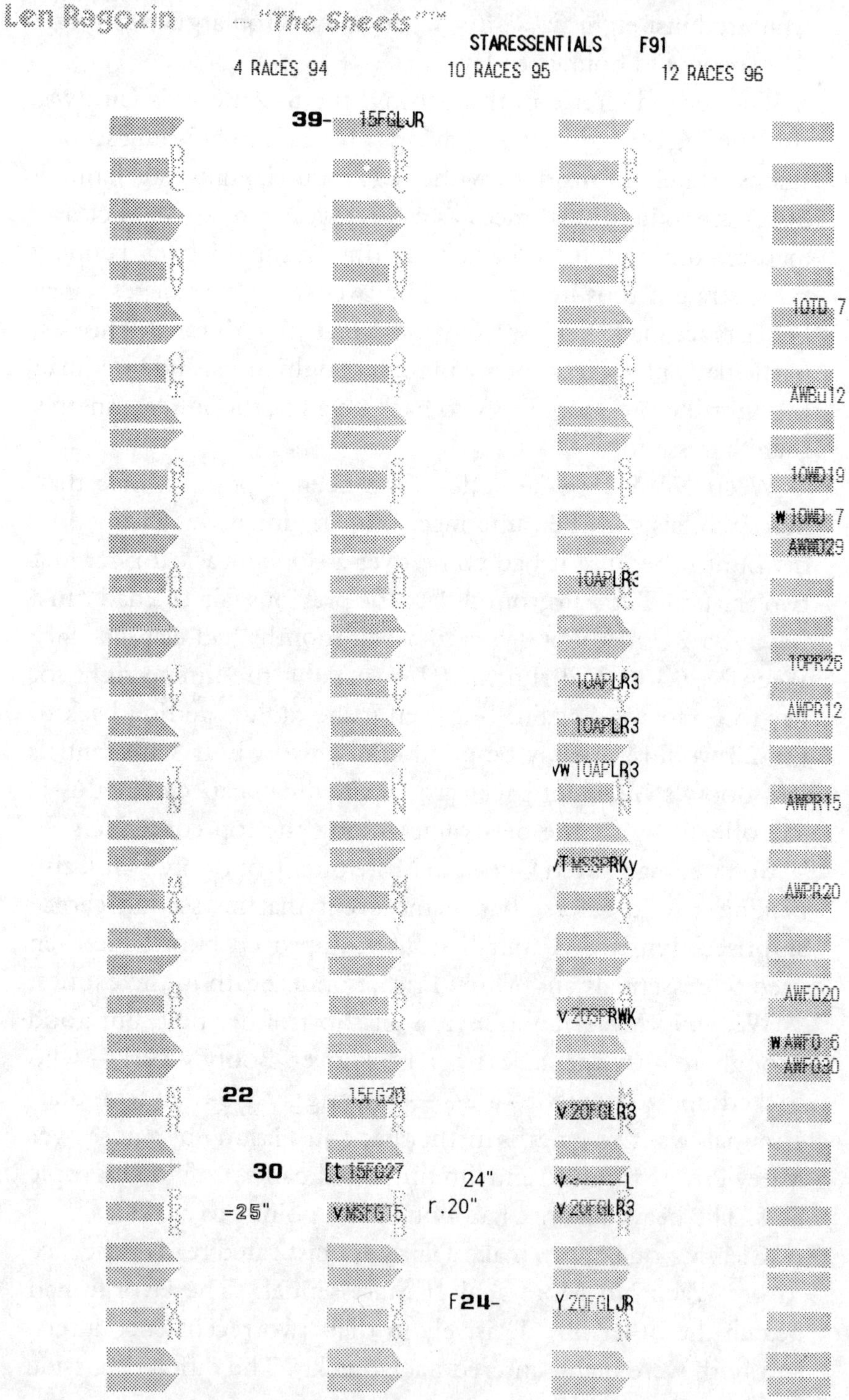

Len Ragozin — "The Sheets"™

STARESSENTIALS F91

4 RACES 94 10 RACES 95 12 RACES 96

39- 15FGLJR

10TD 7

AWBu12

10WD19

w 10WD 7

AWWD29

10APLR3

10PR26

10APLR3

AWPR12

10APLR3

vw 10APLR3

AWPR15

/T MSSPRKy

AWPR20

AWFO20

V 20SPRWK

w AWFO 6

AWFO30

22 15FG20

V 20FGLR3

30 [t 15FG27 24" V------L

=25" vMSFG15 r.20" V 20FGLR3

F24- Y 20FGLJR

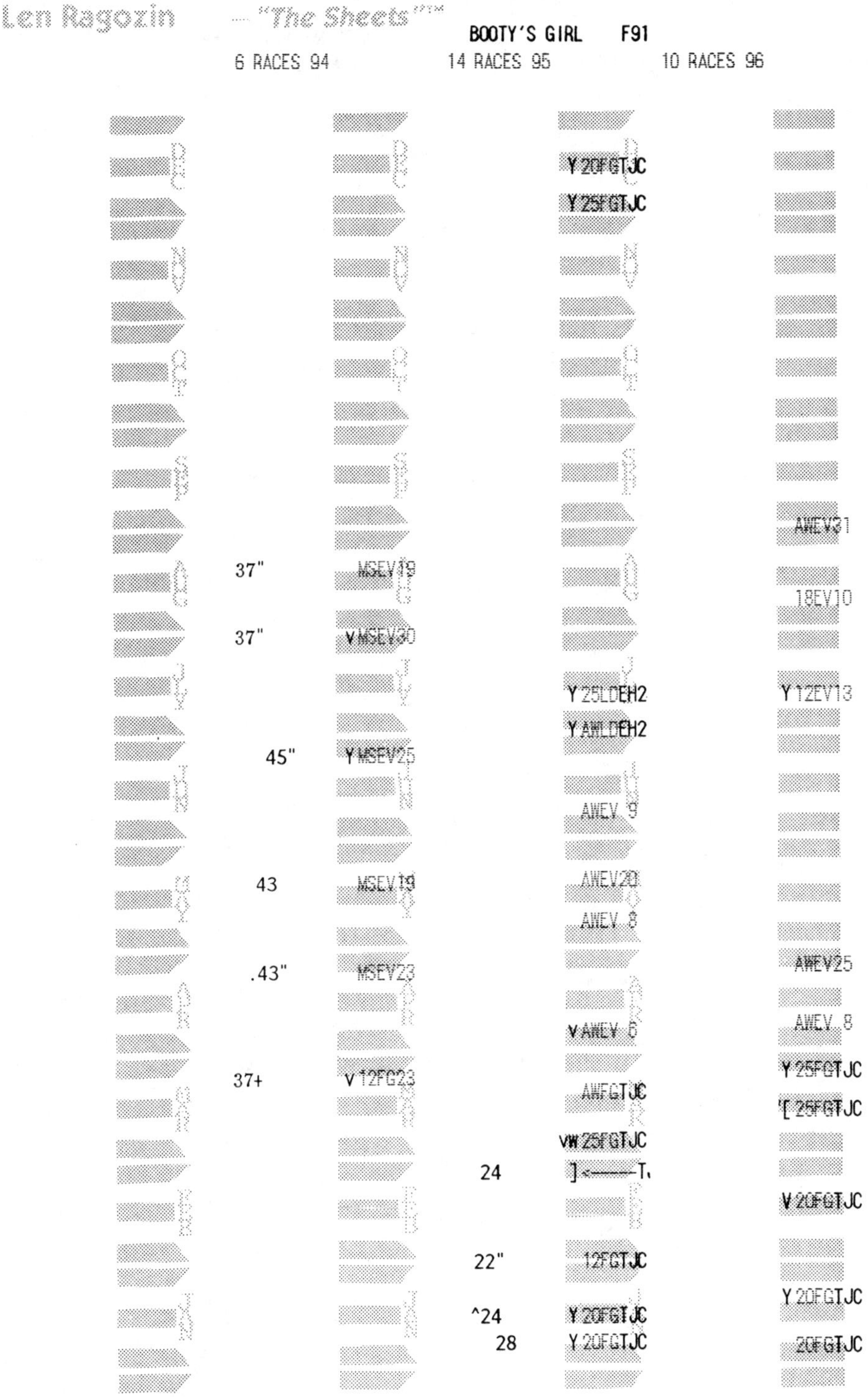

Len Ragozin — "The Sheets"™

BOOTY'S GIRL F91

6 RACES 94

37" MSEV19
37" V MSEV30
45" Y MSEV25
43 MSEV19
.43" MSEV23
37+ V 12FG23

14 RACES 95

Y 20FGTJC
Y 25FGTJC
Y 25LDEH2
Y AWLDEH2
AWEV 9
AWEV20
AWEV 8
V AWEV 6
AWFGTJC
vw 25FGTJC
24]<———T
22" 12FGTJC
^24 Y 20FGTJC
28 Y 20FGTJC

10 RACES 96

AWEV31
18EV10
Y 12EV13
AWEV25
AWEV 8
Y 25FGTJC
'[25FGTJC
V 20FGTJC
Y 20FGTJC
20FGTJC

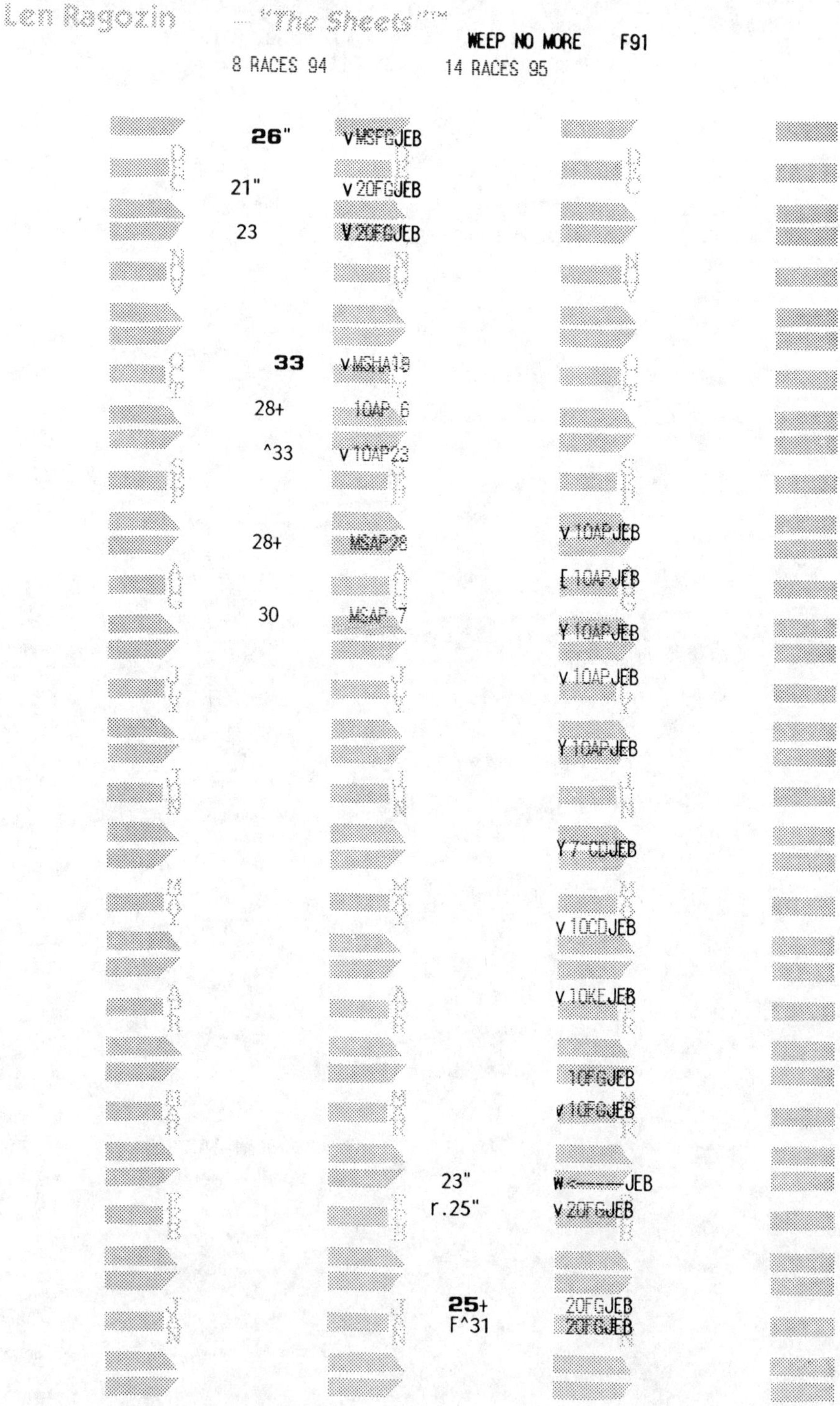

Len Ragozin — "The Sheets"™

WEEP NO MORE F91

8 RACES 94

26" vMSFGJEB
21" v20FGJEB
23 V20FGJEB
33 vMSHA18
28+ 10AP 6
^33 v10AP23
28+ MSAP28
30 MSAP 7

14 RACES 95

v10APJEB
[10APJEB
Y10APJEB
v10APJEB
Y10APJEB
Y7"CDJEB
v10CDJEB
v10KEJEB
10FGJEB
v10FGJEB
23" W<-----JEB
r.25" v20FGJEB
25+ 20FGJEB
F^31 20FGJEB

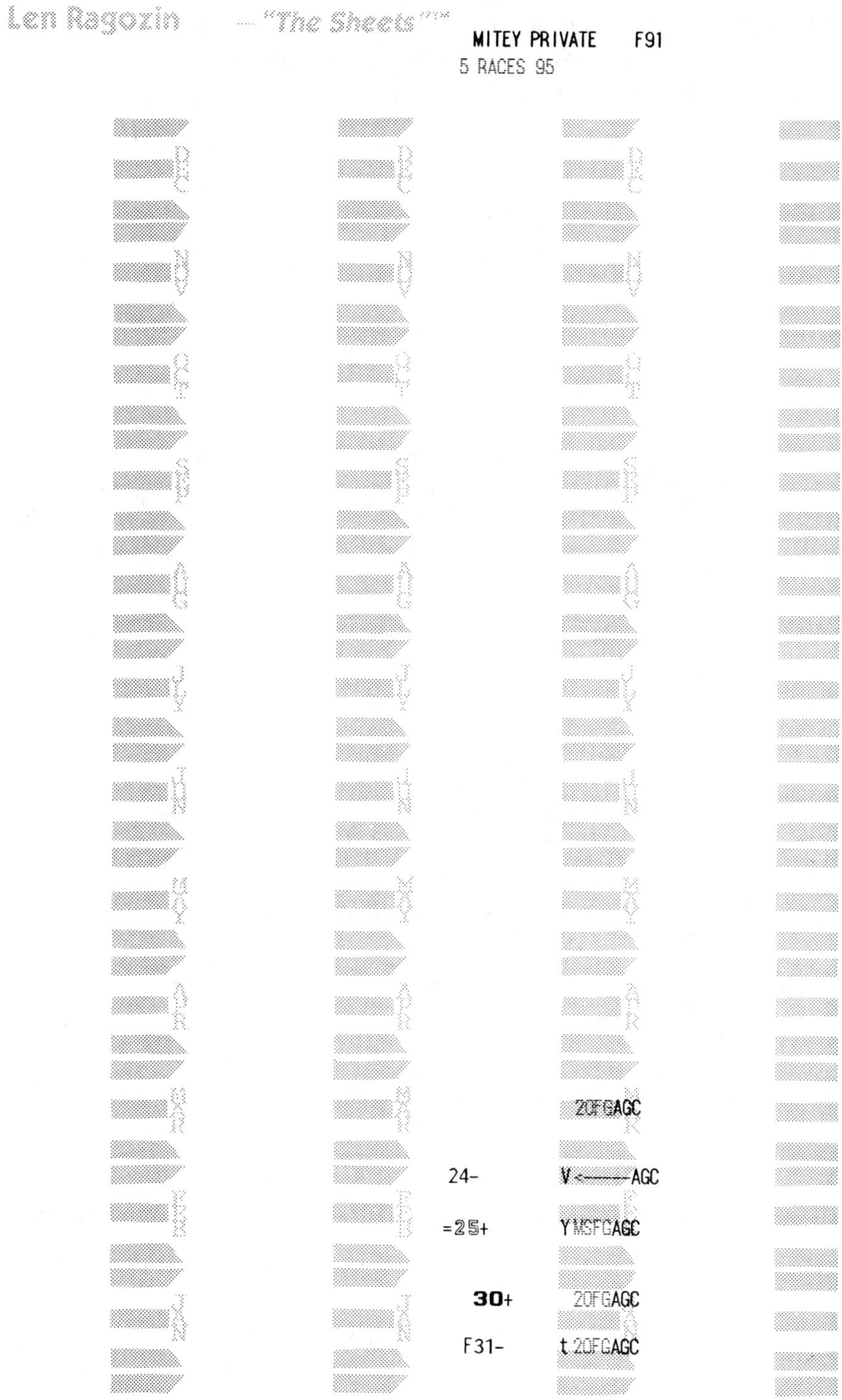

Len Ragozin — "The Sheets"™

MITEY PRIVATE F91
5 RACES 95

20FGAGC

24- V <——— AGC

=25+ YMSFGAGC

30+ 20FGAGC

F31- t 20FGAGC

from the odds on the two, was that Staressentials's pattern virtually dictated a bounce; Weep No More had done her bouncing following the 21½ December 9 and was working her way down toward her better numbers even as she had lost her previous two races against Staressentials. The overall form cycles of horses, particularly cheap ones like these, are going to wax and wane, and that is why it's so important to avoid easy conclusions based only on the most recent race or two.

SECOND RACE **6 FURLONGS. (1.08^{4}) MAIDEN CLAIMING. Purse $7,500. Fillies, 4-year-olds. Weight, 121 lbs. Claiming price $15,000.**

Fair Grounds

FEBRUARY 25, 1995

Value of Race: $7,500 Winner $4,500; second $1,500; third $825; fourth $450; fifth $225. Mutuel Pool $56,776.00 Exacta Pool $52,591.00 Quinella Pool $14,459.00 Trifecta Pool $53,927.00

Last Raced	Horse	M/Eqt.	A.	Wt	PP	St	¼	½	Str	Fin	Jockey	Cl'g Pr	Odds $1	
17Feb95 2FG3	Weep No More	L	4	121	1	5	$3^{1½}$	$3^{3½}$	2^{3}	1^{nk}	Broussard J E III	15000	6.10	4-wd rally, got up
30Jan95 3FG2	Booty's Girl	L	4	118	3	2	$2^{1½}$	$1^{½}$	1^{2}	2^{2}	Perez J L	15000	2.60 *	
17Feb95 2FG2	Staressentials	Lbf	4	121	2	6	6^{hd}	6^{2}	3^{1}	3no	Albarado R J	15000	0.80	Rallied 4-wide
10Feb95 6FG10	Mitey Private	Lf	4	121	11	10	$9^{½}$	8^{2}	5^{3}	4^{nk}	Walls M K	15000	18.20	Imp position 5-wid
14Jan95 2FG9	Music's Last	f	4	116	7	4	$5^{1½}$	5^{1}	4^{1}	$5^{9½}$	Ward J Jr	15000	12.10	Outfinished rail
30Jan95 3FG4	Holly Ridge Pasty	Lf	4	116	4	8	$8^{1½}$	7^{2}	7^{1}	6^{nk}	Fontenot T J	15000	54.40	Outrun
17Feb95 2FG9	Kalye Luck	Lb	4	121	5	12	10^{4}	$9^{2½}$	8^{4}	7^{2}	Patin J W Jr	15000	78.00	No threat
30Jan95 1FG7	Hurry Up Sugar	b	4	121	10	1	1^{2}	$2^{2½}$	6^{3}	$8^{1½}$	Dupas R J	15000	35.00	Led, faltered
6Jan95 4FG10	She's A Woodman	Lb	4	121	6	9	11^{15}	11^{15}	10^{2}	$9^{2½}$	Faul R J	15000	40.40	Outrun
17Feb95 2FG10	Givenalittlenotice	L	4	121	8	7	7^{1}	10^{2}	9^{hd}	10^{5}	Costanzo C J	15000	178.70	Outrun
9Feb94 1FG7	Frosty Spark	b	4	118	9	3	$4^{½}$	$4^{½}$	11^{10}	$11^{8½}$	Martin E M Jr	15000	43.70	Tired
17Feb95 2FG12	Ann Wag	b	4	118	12	11	12	12	12	12	Holassie R K	15000	129.00	Trailed

OFF AT 1:00 Start Good. Won driving. Time, :22, :46^{2}, :59^{1}, 1:12^{2} Track fast.

$2 Mutuel Prices:			
1-WEEP NO MORE	14.20	7.00	2.60
3-BOOTY'S GIRL		4.40	2.20
2-STARESSENTIALS			2.20

$2 EXACTA 1-3 PAID $47.00 $2 QUINELLA 1-3 PAID $19.40 $2 TRIFECTA 1-3-2 PAID $71.60

Dk. b. or br. f, by Buckfinder–Gayage, by Sir Gaylord. Trainer Broussard Joseph E. Bred by Kaufman Walter C (Ky).

WEEP NO MORE saved ground while outsprinted, eased out to rally four wide in upper stretch and got up in the final strides. BOOTY'S GIRL drifted out a bit leaving the gate, was straightened out, bid outside HURRY UP SUGAR around the turn, drew clear and to the rail and just failed to last. STARESSENTIALS lacked a serious rally while four wide. MITEY PRIVATE improved position five wide. HURRY UP SUGAR sprinted clear down the backstretch and faltered once headed.

Owners— 1, Garrett J Melton; 2, Bonura Martin; 3, Roussel Louie J III; 4, Icahn Carl C; 5, Romero Russell L; 6, Richards Corale A; 7, Melancon Francis Jr; 8, Duffau Audrey & Sandra; 9, Stidham James H; 10, Whisenant James; 11, Triplett David; 12, Graham George

Trainers—1, Broussard Joseph E; 2, Cuccia Tony J; 3, Roussel Louie J III; 4, Cohn Alice G; 5, Romero Russell L; 6, Richards Corale A; 7, Melancon Francis Jr; 8, Duffau John; 9, Stidham James H; 10, Whisenant James; 11, Northrup Travis; 12, Graham George

Scratched— Flash Mac Kate (17Feb95 2FG11)

$2 Daily Double (9–1) Paid $40.20; Daily Double Pool $49,489.

Weep No More and Staressentials also illustrate the greater tendency of fillies and mares to bounce than colts and horses, although top-level females are nearly as consistent as good males. Fillies and mares are less inclined than males to pace themselves. Beginning with fast early fractions, their strong races exact a greater physical toll. I'd never bet a filly right off a peak;

Friedman, as he did with Booty's Girl, will use a filly in his combinations if he figures that peak should not produce too sharp a bounce, but he would not make that filly his key horse.

Lack of pacing also is one of the reasons sprinters are more likely to bounce than routers. Sprint races are run strongly from the beginning. If a horse is not setting the fast fractions on the lead, he's still running harder than he would be in a route race. Even if a horse is well back until the last quarter of a sprint, he is making that big late move in the slowest quarter of the race. Usually, while it may not seem that way to the naked eye, that horse was running just as fast earlier to stay close enough to be in contention, so he too was relatively hard-used throughout.

But the main factor creating bigger bounces from sprinters is that trainers tend to put unsound horses in shorter races because they think a long race will aggravate a horse's physical problems. This is especially true of a bleeder, who can get through a sprint with very few breathing cycles and thus spare his vulnerable lung tissue.

Unsound horses are the ones most likely to have sharp performance fluctuations — both forward and backward — depending on how their legs and lungs feel on a particular day.

Routers, on the other hand, need the kind of stamina that virtually assures that they have to be in decent physical condition to run. They also benefit from the fact that distance races tend to have less demanding early fractions.

Turf races tend to have the most evenly run fractions, to the point where it's common for the first quarter of a race to be run as slow as or slower than the final quarter. A rapidly run opening quarter is more likely to leave a horse gasping at the finish, and so the typical turf race is going to be less taxing and less likely to produce big bounces than a dirt sprint.

More important, where turf is concerned, is that grass is a more natural surface for horses to run on, as well as being easier on their legs. I believe horses are less confident that they can stride out on dirt, particularly if it contains a lot of moisture. You certainly see more truly abysmal numbers run by horses over sloppy tracks than you see over soft turf. Whatever the reason, turf lines are less ragged and your bet should be based mostly on ability.

Some handicappers assume that a horse is less likely to bounce off a winning race if he appeared to cross the finish line without strong urging from the jockey. *The Racing Form* uses the comment "driving" to denote cases where a horse was being fully extended under the whip to win a race, and comments like "ridden out," "handily" or "easily" for cases in which the rider used only his hands or appeared to take hold of the reins as he guided the horse through the final yards to the finish.

The evidence offered in *The Sheets* is that such distinctions are not important, either in formulating the horse's figure for that race or deciding whether it makes him likely to bounce in his next start. Horses, unlike human beings, want to continue running even when they've used up their reserve energy. Even after a grueling race a horse will continue running for a quarter of a mile or more past the wire, decelerating very slowly even though the jockey is standing up in the saddle and tugging on the reins. Contrast this with the scene after the finish line in a human track meet's longer races — no running, a lot of staggering.

A horse in a head-to-head battle through the stretch may look to the fans as if he's giving everything he's got and maybe a little beyond. It's less obvious but just as true that runaway winners are doing their best. After studying thousands of "easy" winners and their subsequent performances, my conclusion is that those horses also gave all they had that day, even if the jockey was wrapping up on the horse as they came to the finish. The slight amount of restraint that a jockey begins to exert in the late stages of a runaway win has no effect on the horse's basic effort. Don't give a horse any extra credit for having won easily, and don't believe he is less likely to bounce. The more important factor in trying to predict a bounce is whether that winning effort was a substantial improvement — a figure out of line with his current form or overall potential.

Of course there will be cases where that easy winner repeats his performance next time out. This often occurs with good colts early in their three-year-old season, and you might treat these differently. But I think you're gaining over the long run when you project a horse to bounce if that easy win was a substantial move forward. You're going to get caught when these horses "pair up" a good forward move or even improve on it. But the odds on such horses tend to be low, and the value in that kind of situation usually does not rest in betting the horse who dazzled everybody the last time he raced, but rather in gambling that he will back up from that peak. The only time to consider going the other way is on an early three-year-old colt at decent odds who just made his first improvement of the season and probably needs to improve again to win. But this longshot play is good whether or not the improvement was an easy win. (See example, Frisk Me Now, page 158.)

What about cases where jockeys mistime their move and ask a horse to do his best running too late, or get blocked for much of the stretch run and are unable to find a clear path for their mounts? Such horses seem to burst past the finish line on that unused energy, and look as if they would have run a better figure if they had had a smoother trip. Our follow-up analysis of these horses shows that you will get into more trouble by crediting these horses with extra-good numbers than by ignoring the fast finish. That appearance of a late burst is often more a result of the final fatigue of the competition than of your horse calling on unused energy. Try clocking that horse's final 1⁄16 of a mile. You'll see that it usually wasn't any faster than he ran the previous sixteenth.

There is no uniform answer to the question How badly do you expect a given horse to bounce? A horse might go backward only a point or two, or it might fall off the charts, depending upon how badly that big race affected him. By and large, a sharper improvement means a risk of a bigger bounce, and a filly is riskier than a colt.

If a horse has raced frequently enough, a pattern may have emerged on his sheet. Sunseth, a solid allowance horse racing mainly in New Jersey and Philadelphia, followed his top races by running 4 or 5 points worse in his next start, while Valley Crossing, a stakes-caliber horse who often benefited from rests of four to six weeks between starts, usually bounced only 2 points or less after a top effort.

There are going to be instances where a horse seems likely to bounce 2 points and still run better than his opponents. In such cases, at the right price you'd want to bet that horse. But there are no absolutes in racing, and no guarantee that the bounce will be that small, or that some other horse won't awaken and run so strongly that the bouncer will lose if he declines even slightly. Ultimately, you have to ask yourself whether the odds you're getting on the bounce candidate are good enough that you feel compelled to use him in your betting combinations, or if — at the price — it makes sense to throw him out completely even if you might wind up shredding your tickets after the race. Such losses will inevitably occur, but they should be more than overcome by the situations in which you got terrific returns on your money because you were bold enough to discard a short-priced favorite.

The biggest bounces are likely to come in situations where a big race is completely out of whack with the form that a horse has established as meaningful, unless there's some obvious reason for the wake-up, like the horse being gelded or having an operation to correct a breathing problem or switching to the turf for the first time. The temptation is great to bet any big-improvement horse if you decide he's good enough to win even if he bounces 4 points off that big race. Resist. If the bounce figures to be big, it could as easily be 10 points as 4 points. In a spot like that, I'm not trying to figure whether the horse can wind up in the exacta or triple even with a bounce; I'm looking to find horses who might improve enough to knock him out even if his bounce is less drastic than it could be.

Trainers also enter into the equation. Some trainers will take over a horse and instantly improve his performance, then keep him going forward at a time when you would figure the horse to be bouncing. Either the trainers have gotten better or there's something very effective in the stuff they're using, whether it's drugs or something legal. Whatever the explanation, bounces tend to be less severe and predictable than twenty years ago, which has cut down on the instances in which a bettor can confidently throw out the heavy favorite on the projection that he'll run badly. The overlay situations still exist, but decades ago they were better — just ask my old customers.

Once a still-developing three-year-old produces a bounce on his line, its extent should influence your thinking about his future races. If he has progressed about 5 points from the first tops that really set him back as an immature two-year-old, he is in a gray area — he might have more in reserve and he might not. Here the bounce may give a clue: a large bounce is not a good sign, while one of 2 points or less is often an encouraging tip-off that the big race did not knock out the horse and further improvement will come soon. A routinely developing three-year-old who ran a new top of 12 and then bounced to a 13½ in his next race is a horse to watch: a new top is likely to come shortly. A three-year-old who reacts more severely to the new top may take two months or more before running another peak effort. And if he runs more than one bad race, you might want to see a turn for the better before you consider him favorably.

A look at the eighth race at Laurel on January 6, 1995, makes clear the advantages accurate speed figures give you in analyzing bounces to give you a sense of which way the horse is going based on recent races.

In this race, the crowd made Son of Zora a 2–1 favorite, based on a race seventeen days earlier in which he ran an 11½. Son of Zora looked like a vulnerable favorite for two reasons, however. Throughout his career, he followed top efforts by bouncing; the only exception occurred the previous year when, after running an 11 at Laurel March 8, he had been given fifty-three days' rest before notching an 11½ on April 30. The shorter rest this time around made it likely he would bounce significantly.

In addition, even if he ran another 11, a look at the rest of the field indicated that might not be enough to win this race.

The rail horse, Paddy's Landing, was a developing four-year-

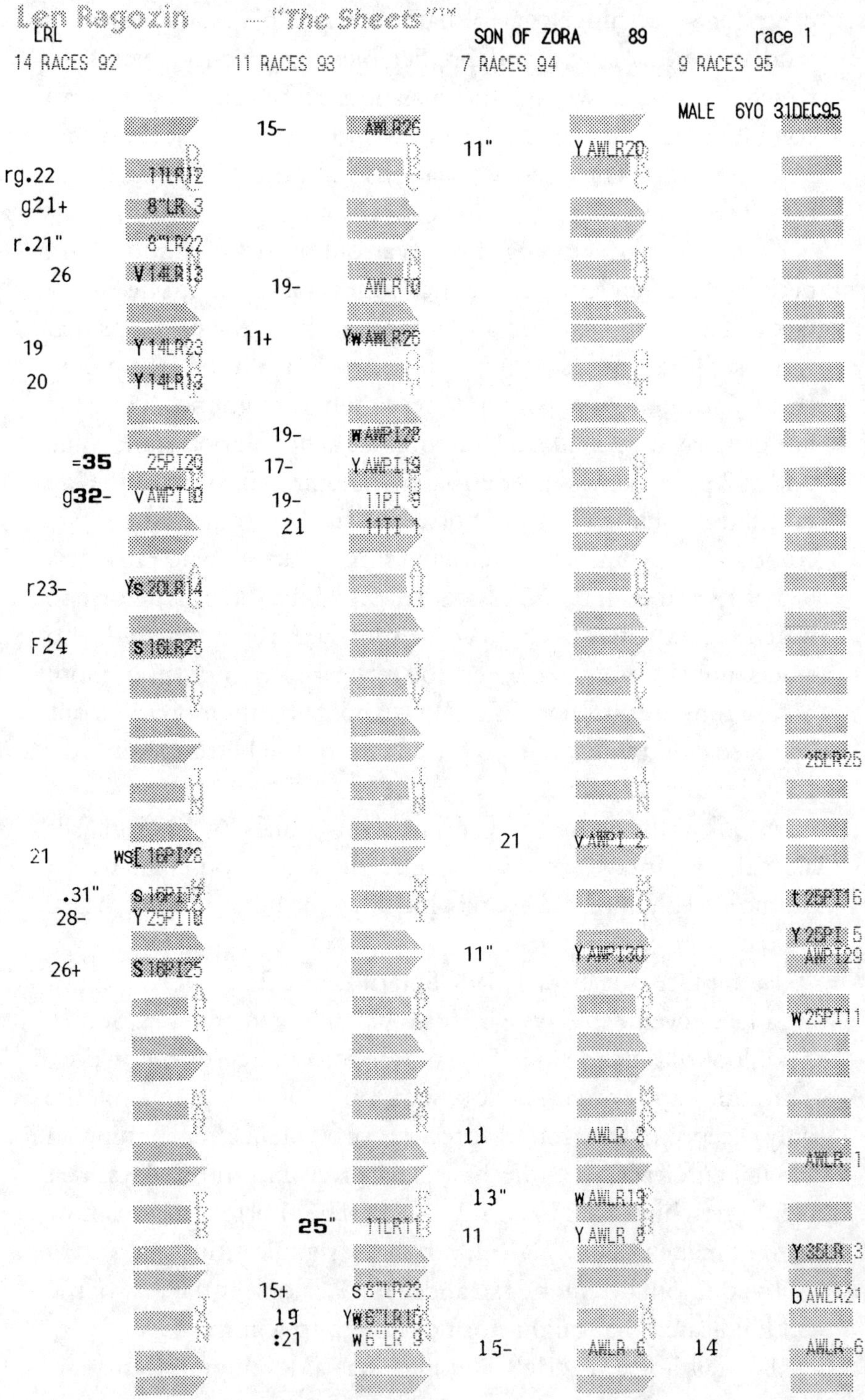

Len Ragozin — "The Sheets"™

LRL SON OF ZORA 89 race 1

MALE 6YO 31DEC95

14 RACES 92

rg.22 11LR12
g21+ 8"LR 3
r.21" 8"LR22
26 V 14LR13
19 Y 14LR23
20 Y 14LR13
=**35** 25PI20
g**32**- V AWPI10
r23- Ys 20LR14
F24 s 16LR25
21 ws[16PI28
.31" s 16PI17
28- Y 25PI10
26+ S 16PI25

11 RACES 93

15- AWLR26
19- AWLR10
11+ Yw AWLR25
19- w AWPI28
17- Y AWPI19
19- 11PI 9
21 11TI 1
25" 11LR11
15+ s 8"LR23
19 Yw 6"LR16
:21 w 6"LR 9

7 RACES 94

11" Y AWLR20
21 v AWPI 2
11" Y AWPI30
11 AWLR 8
13" w AWLR19
11 Y AWLR 8
15- AWLR 6

9 RACES 95

25LR25
t 25PI16
Y 25PI 5
AWPI29
W 25PI11
AWLR 1
Y 35LR 3
b AWLR21
14 AWLR 6

old who at three made a ¾-point breakthrough to a 12½ on November 26, 1994, then backed up only 1 point in his next start. Nearly six weeks had elapsed since that new peak, enough time to give him a good chance of going forward again. He might not be fast enough to win, but his form was good enough to require that he be used in exactas.

Night Spirit a year earlier had made a 3¾-point jump, from a top of 18½ in December 1993 to a 15– on January 2, 1994. The big move clearly set him back: though he didn't bounce that badly in his next start, a race later he was laid off for four months. It was not until mid-August that he was able to match the 15–. On November 20, he had broken through to a 12¼. In his next race, when he figured to bounce, he moved forward again, running an 11¼. But the two consecutive forward moves and the cumulative jump of 3½ points from his early four-year-old top made further improvement less than three weeks after the new peak unlikely, with a much greater chance of a negative reaction.

Tom Tylor looked like a throw-out on several grounds. His best race had been a 12– November 15, 1994, at Philadelphia Park, raising questions as to whether he was fast enough to win. The 12– had also come as the best of a three-race cluster that was far better than anything he had done since early in his three-year-old season. Earlier in the year, running a new top of 12½ in mid-April had triggered a series of ten straight races in which he ran at least 4 points slower than that peak, increasing the chances that his recent off-form would continue today. And the horse had raced thirty-one times in the last fourteen months, never getting more than a month off between starts, making it likely he was a tired horse.

Don's Sho, on the other hand, was a lightly raced horse with an encouraging line. He had run a 15 as a two-year-old, surpassed it in his first start at three, and then, after treading water for four months, made his first significant jump to a 9¾ November 11, more than 4 points better than he had previously run. He didn't back up badly, given the size of the jump and the short rest, when he ran a 14½ nine days later. He came back to

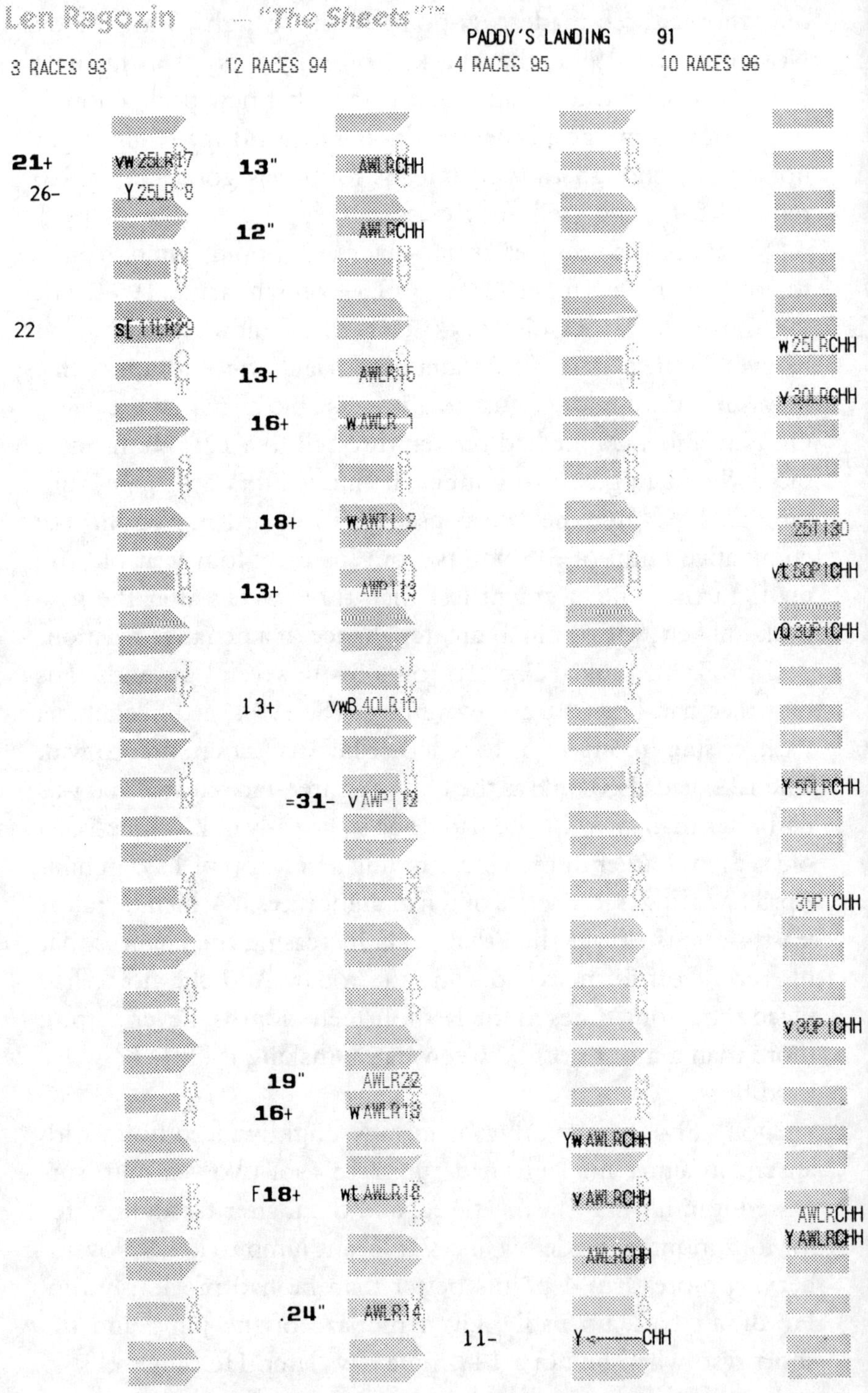

Len Ragozin — "The Sheets"™

PADDY'S LANDING 91

3 RACES 93

21+ vw25LR17
26- Y25LR 8
22 s[11LR29

12 RACES 94

13" AWLRCHH
12" AWLRCHH
13+ AWLR15
16+ wAWLR 1
18+ wAWT1 2
13+ AWP113
13+ vwB40LR10
=31- vAWP112
19" AWLR22
16+ wAWLR13
F18+ wtAWLR18
.24" AWLR14

4 RACES 95

YwAWLRCHH
vAWLRCHH
AWLRCHH
11- Y<———CHH

10 RACES 96

w25LRCHH
v30LRCHH
25T130
vt50P1CHH
vQ30P1CHH
Y50LRCHH
30P1CHH
v30P1CHH
AWLRCHH
YAWLRCHH

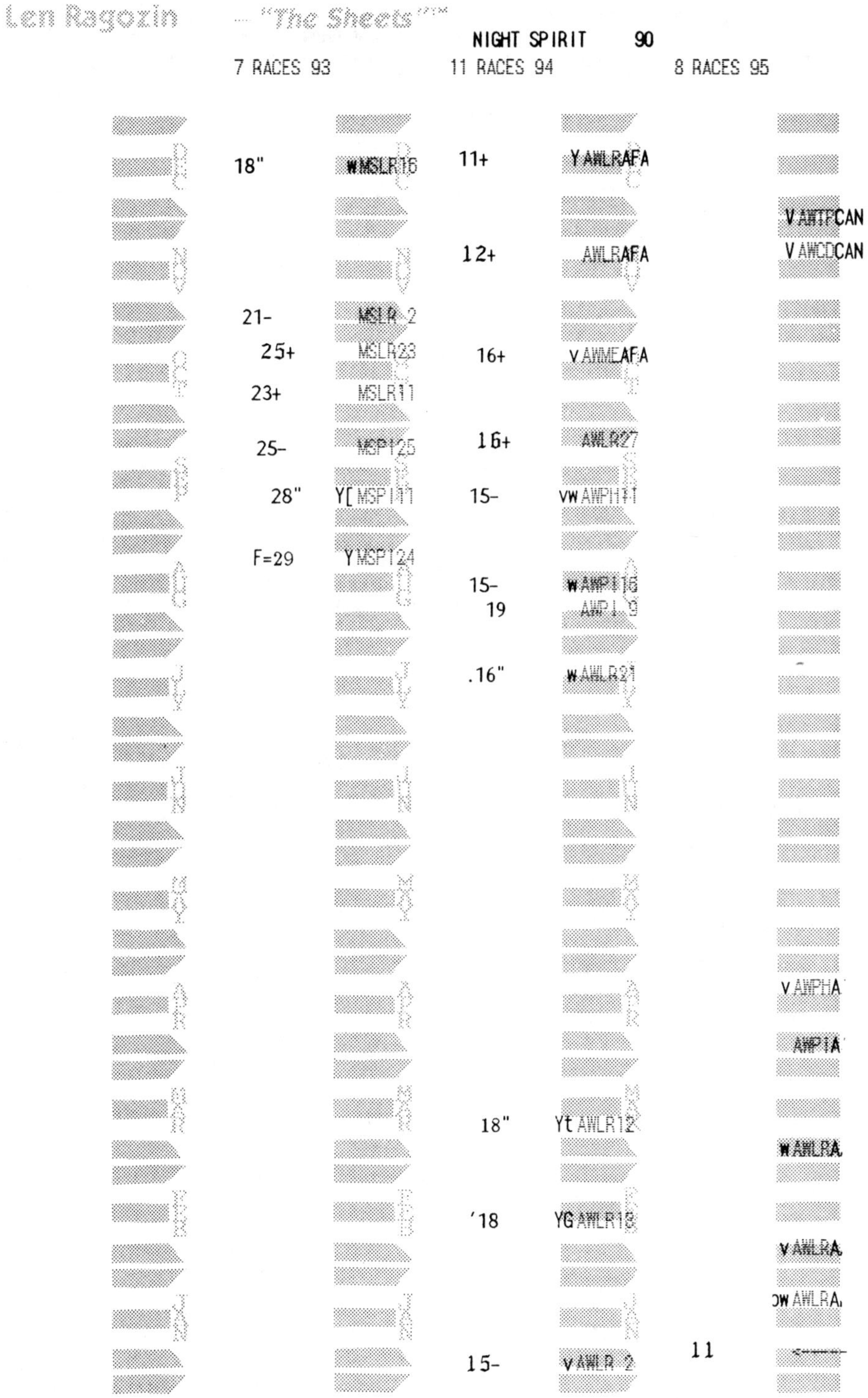

NIGHT SPIRIT 90

7 RACES 93		11 RACES 94		8 RACES 95
18"	WMSLR16	11+	YAWLRAFA	
				VAWTFCAN
		12+	AWLRAFA	VAWCDCAN
21-	MSLR 2			
25+	MSLR23	16+	VAWMEAFA	
23+	MSLR11			
25-	MSP125	16+	AWLR27	
28"	Y[MSP111	15-	vwAWPH11	
F=29	YMSP124			
		15-	wAWP116	
		19	AWPL 9	
		.16"	wAWLR21	
				vAWPHA
				AWPIA
		18"	YtAWLR12	
				wAWLRA
		'18	YGAWLR18	
				vAWLRA
				owAWLRA
		15-	vAWLR 2	11

Len Ragozin — "The Sheets"™

TOM TYLOR 90

16 RACES 92		11 RACES 93		24 RACES 94		4 RACES 95	
/22"	AWPH26	/21+	V AWPH28	17+	25PHDSR		14PH
15–	W AWPH 1	15"	T AWLR17	15	W AWPHDSR		Y 25ME
17–	AWPH21	^18+	AWPH 6	16–	AWMEDSR		
.18–	W 22PH 3	16"	V AWMEDSR	12–	VW 18PH15		
17	W 22PH23	21+	AWMEDSR	g12"	AWPH 6		
F26+	W 15PH20	.30+	V AWPH 6	14–	18DE26		
29"	40CR24	XX	DJ AWPH25	'17	AWPH25		
30–	sR 30CR15	g21+	V 99AQDSR	16+	V AWPH11		
30	Y AWCR 5	^15–	L AWGSDSR	g19–	W 14PH28		
32+	AWCR21	'15	S 75AQDSR	17	14PI20		
r30"	YW 25CR12	^18–	Y AWLR10	21–	Y 14AT 9		
39"	25CR 4			.21–	V 18PH18		
38"	35CR20			=36	20DE25		
42+	Y 25CR 5			22–	Y AWPH11		
35+	vG 30CR22			17–	W AWPH24		
48+	R MSCR16			21+	Y AWPH10		
				20–	t AWPH23		
				17	V AWPH12		
				12"	W 18PH 1		
				26	AWGSDSR		
				^17	W 16GSDSR		
				35–	AWGSDSR		
				g19–	AWPH14		
				s30–	Y AWLR27		
							V 25GSD
						16"	Y ------

run a 13, enough to have him going in the right direction without taking much out of him, and was racing today with eight weeks since his peak, enough of a gap to give him a good chance to run something like that number. The 9¾ was his only top-notch number thus far, but he had just turned four and had raced only sixteen times in his life, making it a reasonable possibility that he could at least match that effort in the near future. And merely getting within a point or two of that number would likely be enough for him to win the race. At 8–1, he looked like an incredible overlay.

The outside horse, Vet Jet, had the best figure of the entrants, a 9 run in the rain at Laurel the previous November 18. But the horse had just run one of his better efforts and almost never put two good ones together, and he too was coming in off a heavy campaign with no extended rest over the past year. He was now five years old, and in forty-one career races had run faster than 11½ only once. The 9 looked more like a knockout number for him than a level he could now sustain.

Don's Sho won the race and paid $19.20, an astonishing price in a six-horse field given his numbers. The other lightly raced four-year-old, Paddy's Landing, finished second, triggering a $96.20 exacta.

As could have been anticipated from their past patterns, both Vet Jet and Son of Zora bounced, with Vet Jet running fourth by five and a quarter lengths and Son of Zora another two and a half lengths behind in fifth. This underscores the fact that a horse doesn't need to run a top to be susceptible to bouncing; an effort close to his peak will often have the same effect, particularly among older horses. I'd advise that any older horse whose last race is at least 4 points better than any of his other recent races — regardless of how close it is to his top — should be bet. He'll be a much better gamble after a bounce.

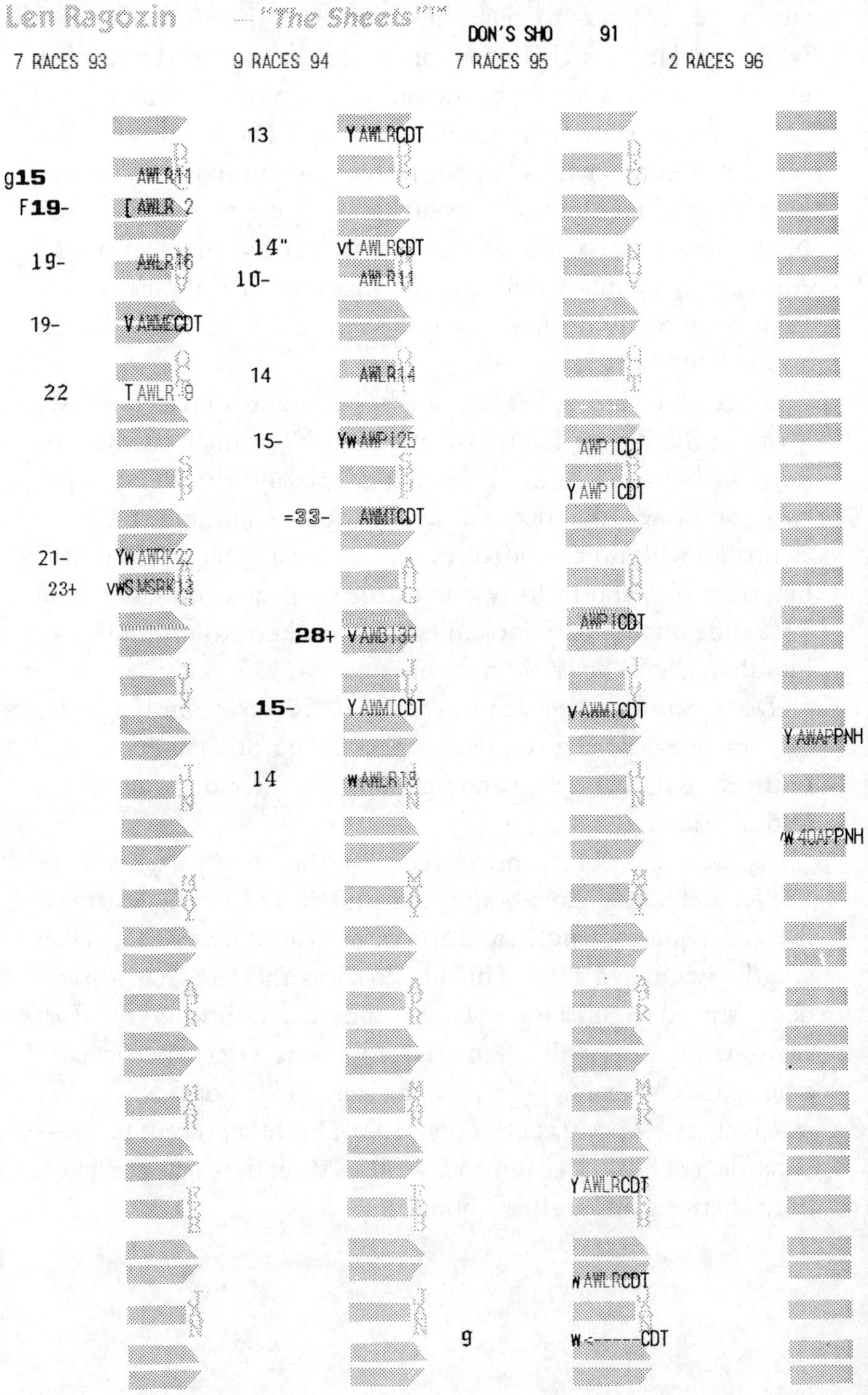

Len Ragozin — *"The Sheets"*™

DON'S SHO 91

7 RACES 93		9 RACES 94		7 RACES 95		2 RACES 96
		13	Y AWLRCDT			
g**15**	AWLR11					
F**19**-	[AWLR 2					
		14"	vt AWLRCDT			
19-	AWLR16	10-	AWLR11			
19-	V AWMECDT					
22	T AWLR 9	14	AWLR14			
		15-	Yw AWP125		AWP CDT	
					Y AWP CDT	
		=33-	AWMTCDT			
21-	Yw AWRK22					
23+	vWS MSRK13					
		28+	v AWB130		AWP CDT	
		15-	Y AWMTCDT		v AWMTCDT	
						Y AWAFPNH
		14	w AWLR18			
						w 40AFPNH
					Y AWLRCDT	
					w AWLRCDT	
				g	w ------CDT	

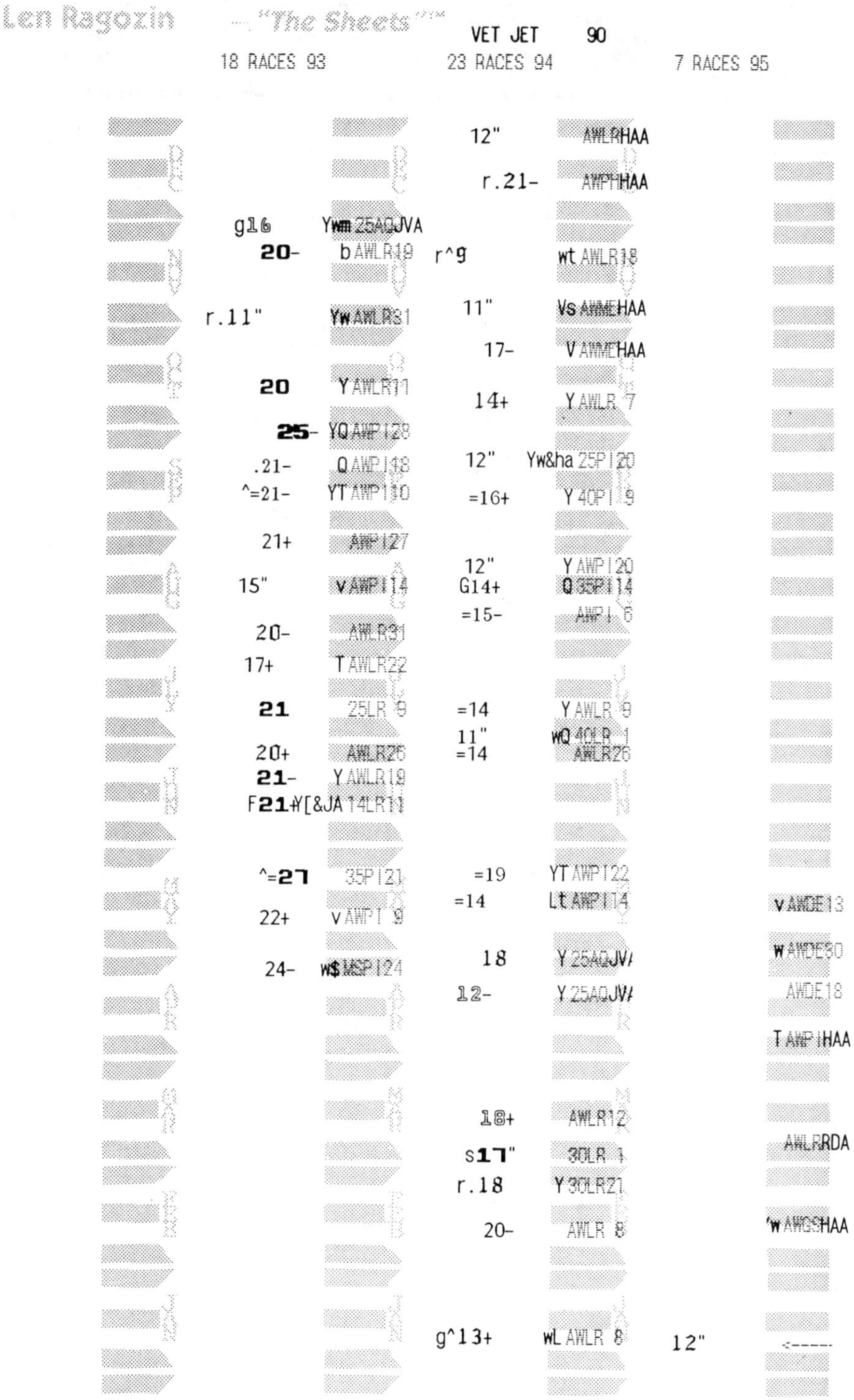

Len Ragozin "The Sheets"™

VET JET 90

18 RACES 93

g16 Ywm 25AQJVA
20- b AWLR19
r.11" Yw AWLR31
20 Y AWLR11
25- YQ AWP I28
.21- Q AWP I18
^=21- YT AWP I10
21+ AWP I27
15" v AWP I14
20- AWLR31
17+ T AWLR22
21 25LR 9
20+ AWLR26
21- Y AWLR19
F21+ Y[&JA 14LR11
^=27 35P I21
22+ v AWP I 9
24- w$ MSP I24

23 RACES 94

12" AWLRHAA
r.21- AWPHHAA
r^g wt AWLR18
11" Vs AWMEHAA
17- V AWMEHAA
14+ Y AWLR 7
12" Yw&ha 25P I20
=16+ Y 40P I 9
12" Y AWP I20
G14+ Q 35P I14
=15- AWP I 6
=14 Y AWLR 9
11" wQ 40LR 1
=14 AWLR26
=19 YT AWP I22
=14 Lt AWP I14
18 Y 25AQJV/
12- Y 25AQJV/
18+ AWLR12
s17" 30LR 1
r.18 Y 30LR21
20- AWLR 8
g^13+ wL AWLR 8

7 RACES 95

v AWDE13
w AWDE30
AWDE18
T AWP IHAA
AWLRRDA
'w AWGSHAA
12" <-----

EIGHTH RACE

Laurel

JANUARY 6, 1995

7 FURLONGS. (1.21²) ALLOWANCE. Purse $22,000. 4-year-olds and upward which have not won four races other than maiden, claiming, starter or hunt meeting. Weight, 122 lbs. Non-winners of two races since December 11, allowed 3 lbs. A race, allowed 5 lbs. (Maiden, claiming and starter races not considered in estimating allowances).

Value of Race: $22,000 Winner $12,540; second $4,620; third $2,420; fourth $1,320; fifth $660; sixth $440. Mutuel Pool $26,889.00 Exacta Pool $48,199.00

Last Raced	Horse	M/Eqt.	A.	Wt	PP	St	¼	½	Str	Fin	Jockey	Odds $1	
23Dec94 8Lrl3	Don's Sho	Lbf	4	117	5	1	2^2	$2^{1\frac{1}{2}}$	1^{hd}	$1^{1\frac{3}{4}}$	Klinger C O	8.60	Driving
15Dec94 8Lrl5	Paddy's Landing	Lbf	4	117	1	2	6	$5^{3\frac{1}{2}}$	$4^{1\frac{1}{2}}$	2^1	Wilson R	3.30	Rallied
18Dec94 9Lrl3	Night Spirit	Lbf	5	117	2	3	$1\frac{1}{2}$	$1\frac{1}{2}$	$2^{2\frac{1}{2}}$	$3^{2\frac{1}{2}}$	Reynolds L C	3.00	Weakened
23Dec94 8Lrl2	Vet Jet	Lbf	5	117	6	4	3^1	$3^{2\frac{1}{2}}$	$3^{1\frac{1}{2}}$	$4^{2\frac{1}{2}}$	Verge M E	4.10	Gave way
20Dec94 8Lrl2	Son of Zora	Lb	6	117	4	5	4^5	$4^{2\frac{1}{2}}$	5^6	$5^{2\frac{1}{2}}$	Johnston M T	2.00	No factor
23Dec94 5Pha4	Tom Tylor	L	5	117	3	6	5^{hd}	6	6	6	Pino M G	8.70	Outrun

OFF AT 3:36 Start Good. Won driving. Time, :23¹, :46², 1:10³, 1:23 Track fast.

$2 Mutuel Prices:			
5-DON'S SHO	19.20	12.40	4.80
2-PADDY'S LANDING		4.80	3.40
3-NIGHT SPIRIT			3.20

$2 EXACTA 5-2 PAID $96.20

B. c, by Don's Choice-Nashoba, by Superbity. Trainer Thrasher Clint D. Bred by Sondra Bender & Howard M. Bender (Md).

DON'S SHO dueled outside NIGHT SPIRIT and drew off in the drive. PADDY'S LANDING circled the turn and rallied. NIGHT SPIRIT saved ground and weakened. VET JET circled and gave way. SON OF ZORA was no factor. TOM TYLOR was outrun.

Owners— 1, C & K Stable; 2, Wallace Helen G; 3, Burning Daylight Farms; 4, Main Line Stable; 5, Stanely Stables; 6, Factor Marvin S

Trainers—1, Thrasher Clint D; 2, Hadry Charles H; 3, Allen A Ferris III; 4, Allen Harold A; 5, Leatherbury King T; 6, Reeder Donald S

Scratched— Owned By Us (26Nov94 9LRL5)

$2 Pick 3 (1-7-5) Paid $458.80; Pick 3 Pool $13,618.

9

Avoiding the Crowd

BETTING OPPORTUNITIES can be created less by the merits of a particular horse than by the drawbacks of another horse who is likely to be overbet. One of the prime scenarios involves horses whose numbers aren't particularly good but are being well bet because they are switching to a distance that superficially would seem to benefit them based on their running style. It doesn't matter whether the horse is moving into a sprint after showing speed and then quitting in distance races, or going long after making late runs in sprints; such horses invariably wind up underlays. If their numbers aren't good enough to win, the change of distance will have little impact.

I would also proceed with caution regarding any horse going in a route race who has never run — or never run well — around two turns. And I wouldn't use good dirt figures as the basis for betting a horse making his first start on grass. I'll have more to say about these situations in chapter 15, "Breeding Counts — Sometimes." But I would be particularly wary of a horse who has raced for two or three years almost exclusively in sprints and is trying to go a route today.

But I would not hesitate to bet a router who has been switched to a sprint if his numbers are good enough to win the race. Most routers at some point early in their careers had success at sprint distances. The overlays you tend to get because the public fears the races are too short for these horses to run their best will compensate for the cases in which the horses don't make a serious effort because the trainer is using the race as a workout to get them ready for longer routes.

There are a couple of other situations in which I like to bet horses because the public's tendency to focus on the most recent race creates overlays on otherwise solid horses.

One involves what we call alternators, which are horses who seem to follow every good effort with a bad one. An alternator's recent line might read 14–19–14–19, or offer a bit of a variation, like 14–19–13–18.

How much you like a horse like this following the most recent off-race depends on two things: whether the good numbers in his pattern could win today's race, and his condition trend. If a horse ran 15–16 in his two races before the alternating 14s or 13s, then his recent good races would not be such a sharp jump as to suggest his form may soon cave in and lead to nothing but off-races for a while. If he was running in the 20s prior to the alternating, however, then the good races are too sharp an improvement to make me comfortable that he'll run well today. I'd also hesitate to bet an alternator whose numbers were declining; for example, a pattern of 15–21–17–24.

I also like to bet horses who are coming off one poor race — particularly if that poor effort came under adverse weather or track conditions — if I believe their overall development before that looked healthy. I would make allowances even for two bad races by a horse I had previously strongly thought was ready to hit or surpass its best previous effort.

A classic example was Owned By Us going into the running of the Northern Dancer Handicap at Laurel October 29, 1994. In his previous start, a minor turf stake, the three-year-old gelding had run a dismal 25½ in finishing twelfth by twenty-seven lengths. A race earlier, he'd run a 16 in finishing fifth by seven and a half lengths in allowance company. Scared away by those two races, the Laurel bettors sent off Owned By Us at 16–1, the second-longest shot in a contentious eight-horse field racing 1⅛ miles.

I would discount both races. The most recent noneffort confirmed a dislike for grass that he hinted at in his previous turf race back in May. The 16 might have represented a meaningful bounce from the 11– a month earlier, but it was very possible that extreme weather conditions were responsible. (The "r" to the left of the number indicates it was raining as the race was run, the "G" denotes a heavily gusting wind, and the dot means the track was sloppy.)

Throw out those two races, and you were looking at a horse who had shown steady rather than extreme development from the time he ran his first decent race — the 16 that broke his maiden at Laurel March 8. The 11– was also more than a point faster than any other horse in the field had run in a two-turn race. Canton River's 9¼ came in a 7-furlong sprint, and his best race in three tries at a mile or more on the dirt had been a 14¼, while Sandman Sims had run his 11½ in a five and a half-furlong sprint. More than two months had passed since Owned By Us had run his peak, enough time to have him ready to go forward — and merely matching that 11– would probably win. Churchbell Chimes, the favorite, was slow.

The mistake of the bettors in dismissing the chances of Owned By Us became obvious when, under a perfect ground-saving ride by Mark Johnston, he sat close to the leaders until the stretch, then spurted clear late to win by over a length and pay $35.20. Justalittleshower, who closed for second to complete a $164 exacta, also had a strong forward-moving condition pattern, having made a ½-point forward move to a 13 in his next to last race. He followed with an excusable off-race in the mud that set him up for a new top of 11 in the Northern Dancer and set us up for a juicy exacta.

I should add that I would feel differently about a horse who had run two poor efforts after a series of encouraging races and then was dropped into a claiming race at a price that begged some other owner to grab him. Usually if they're holding a fire sale, the trainer has some greater insight into those lousy races than I can get from the horse's sheet. Beyond that, a horse taking a major drop in company figures to be bet heavily despite the recent bad races, so where is the value in playing him?

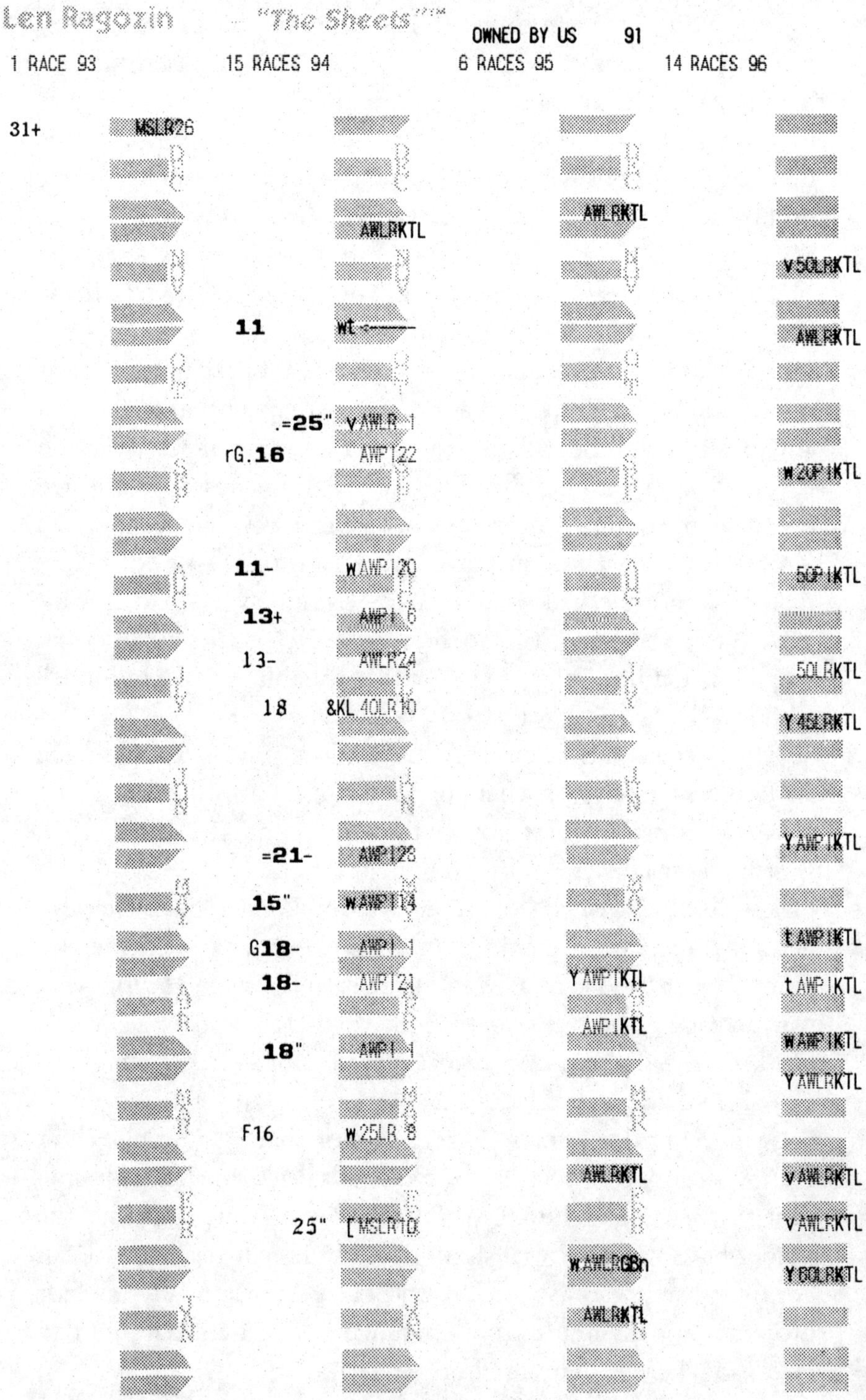

Len Ragozin "The Sheets"™

OWNED BY US 91

	1 RACE 93	15 RACES 94	6 RACES 95	14 RACES 96
	31+ MSLR26			
DEC				
		AWLRKTL	AWLRKTL	
NOV				v50LRKTL
		11 wt ------		AWLRKTL
OCT				
		.=25" vAWLR 1		
		rG.16 AWPI22		
SEP				w20PIKTL
		11- wAWPI20		50PIKTL
AUG				
		13+ AWPI 6		
		13- AWLR24		50LRKTL
JLY		18 &KL 40LR10		Y45LRKTL
JUN				
		=21- AWPI23		YAWPIKTL
MAY		15" wAWPI14		
				tAWPIKTL
		G18- AWPI 1		
APR		18- AWPI21	YAWPIKTL	tAWPIKTL
			AWPIKTL	
				wAWPIKTL
		18" AWPI 1		
				YAWLRKTL
MAR				
		F16 w25LR 8		
			AWLRKTL	vAWLRKTL
FEB		25" [MSLR10		vAWLRKTL
			wAWLRGBn	Y60LRKTL
JAN			AWLRKTL	

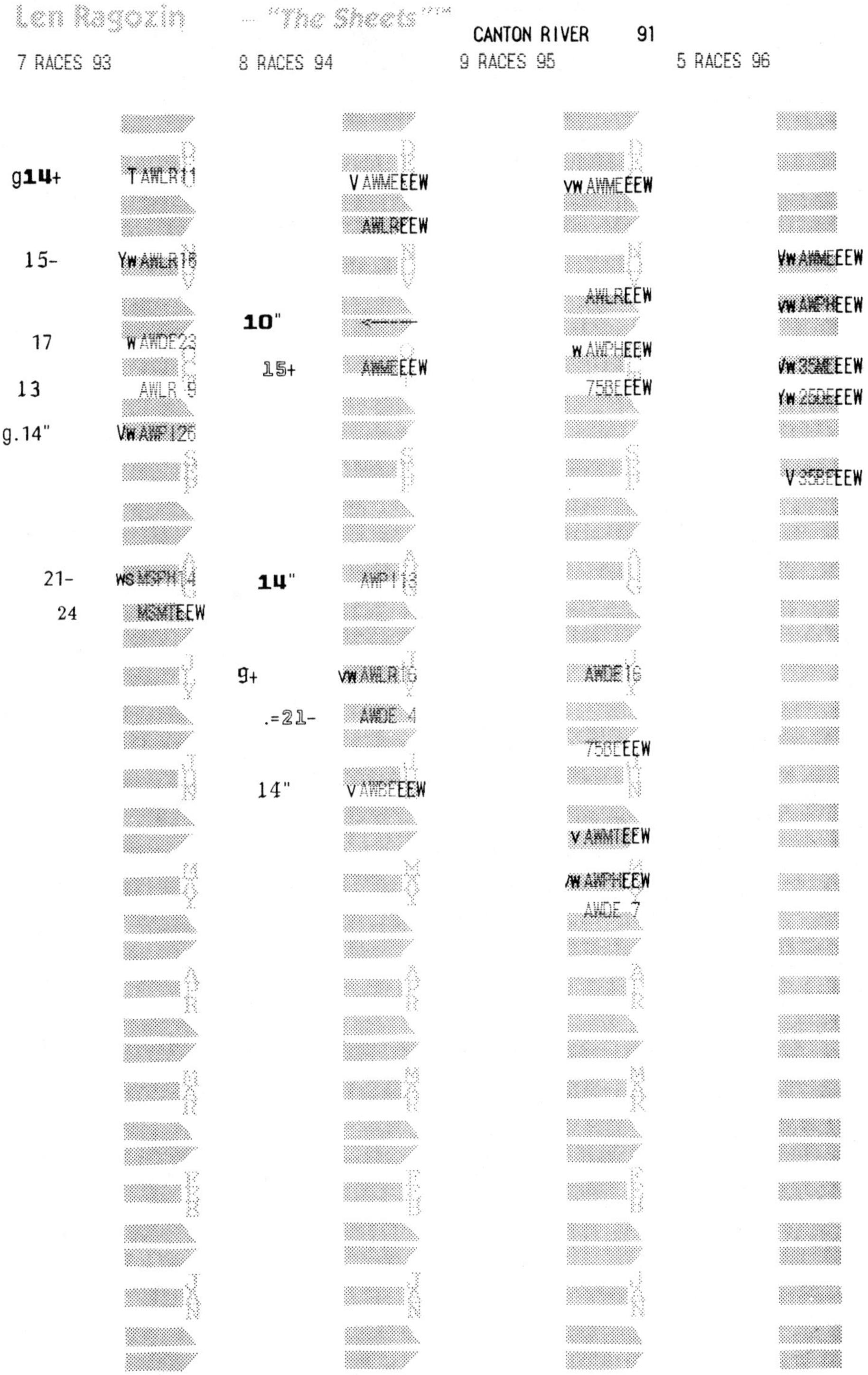

Len Ragozin — "The Sheets"™

CANTON RIVER 91

7 RACES 93

g14+ TAWLR11
15- YwAWLR15
17 wAWDE23
13 AWLR 9
g.14" VwAWF125
21- wsMSPH14
24 MSMTEEW

8 RACES 94

VAWMEEEW
AWLREEW
10"
15+ AWMEEEW
14" AWP113
9+ vwAWLR16
.=21- AWDE 4
14" VAWBEEEW

9 RACES 95

vwAWMEEEW
AWLREEW
wAWPHEEW
75BEEEW
AWDE16
75BEEEW
vAWMTEEW
wAWPHEEW
AWDE 7

5 RACES 96

VwAWMEEEW
vwAWPHEEW
Vw35MEEEW
Yw25DEEEW
V35BEEEW

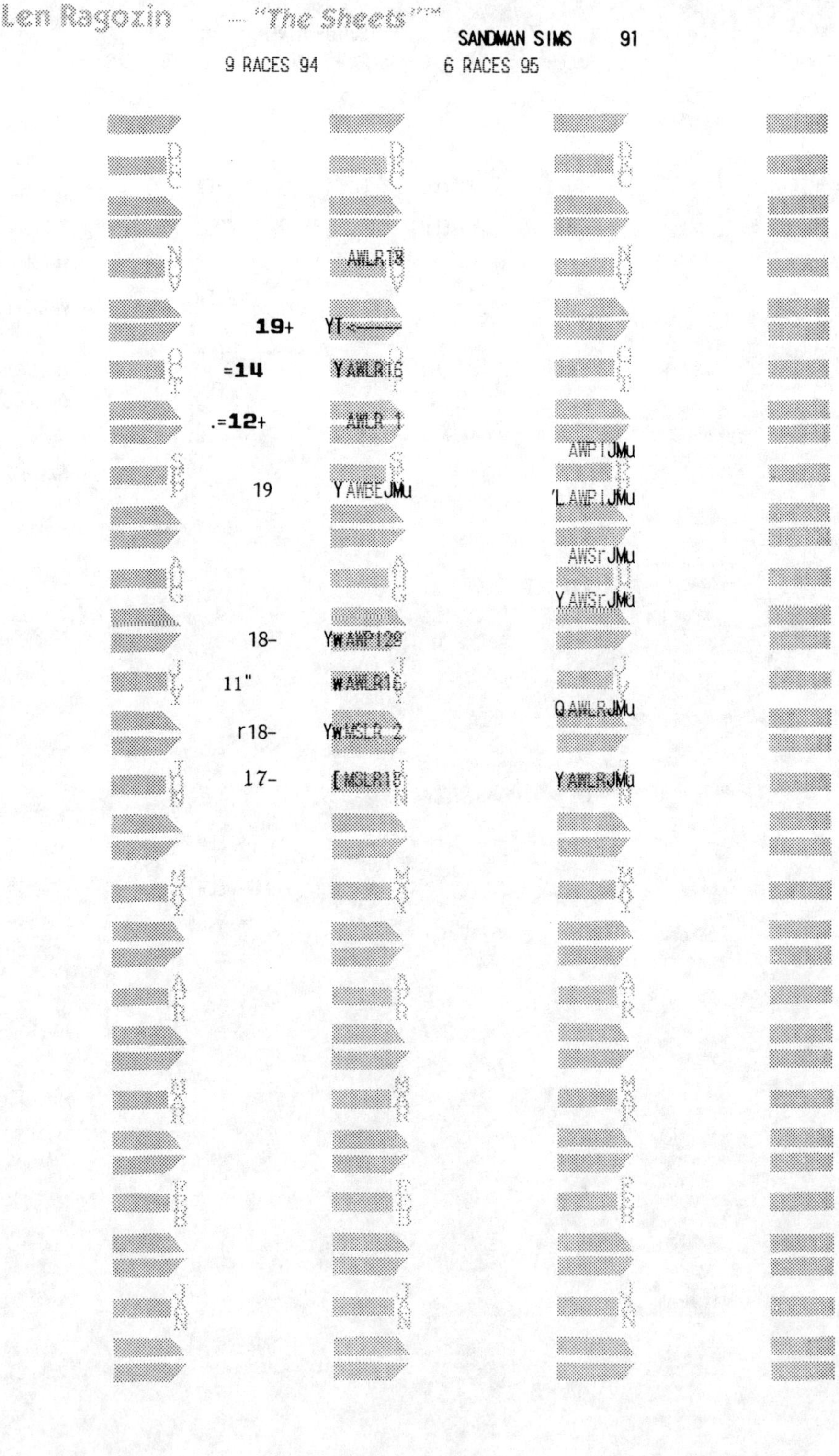

Len Ragozin — "The Sheets"™

SANDMAN SIMS 91

9 RACES 94 6 RACES 95

AWLR18

19+ YT

=14 YAWLR16

.=12+ AWLR 1

AWPTJMu

19 YAWBEJMu

'LAWPIJMu

AWSrJMu

YAWSrJMu

18- YwAWP120

11" wAWLR16

QAWLRJMu

r18- YwMSLR 2

17- [MSLR18

YAWLRJMu

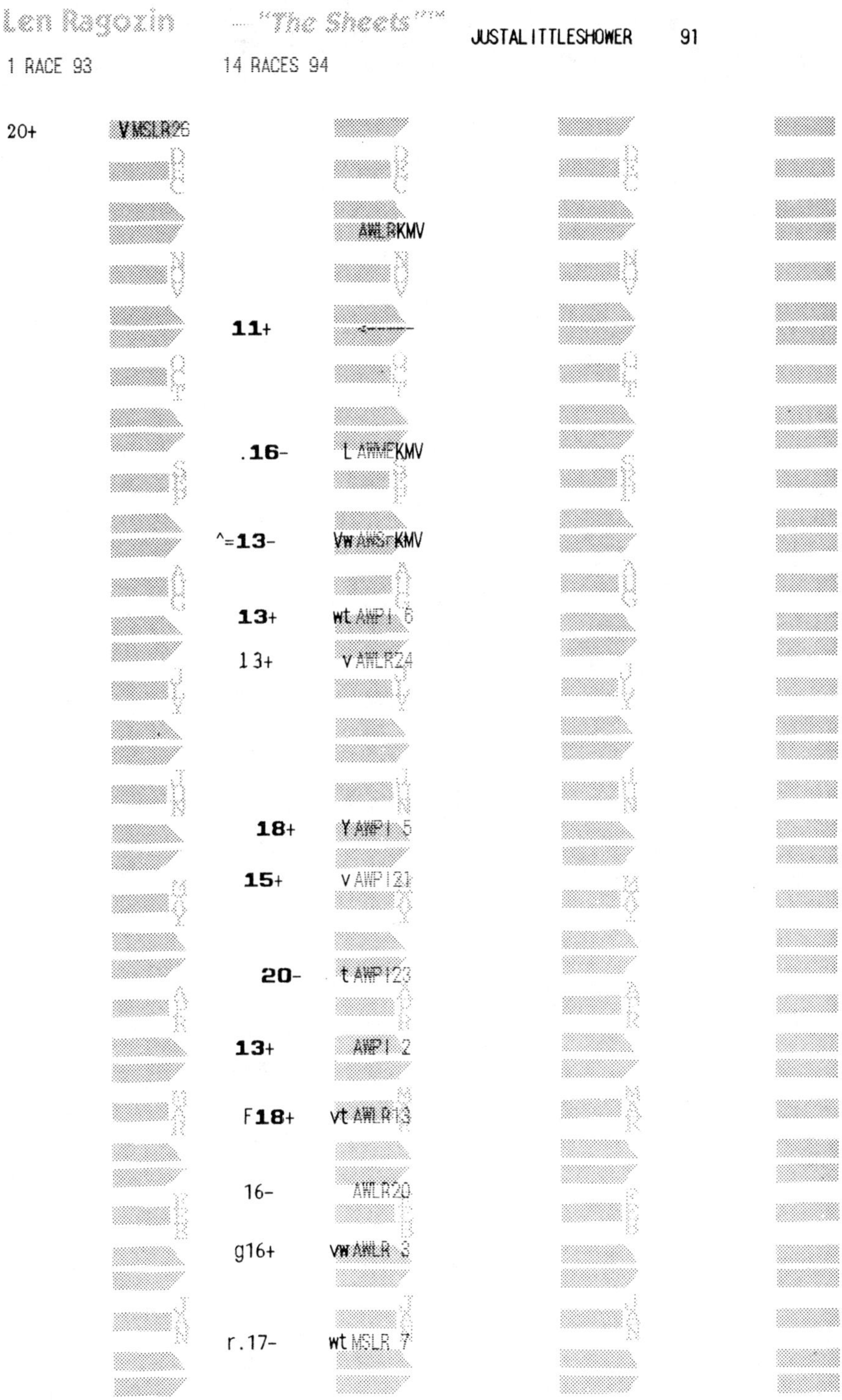

Len Ragozin "The Sheets"™ JUSTALITTLESHOWER 91

1 RACE 93		14 RACES 94	
20+	VMSLR26		
			AWLRKMV
		11+	
		.16-	L AWMEKMV
		^=13-	VwAWSrKMV
		13+	wt AWPI 6
		13+	v AWLR24
		18+	Y AWPI 5
		15+	v AWPI21
		20-	t AWPI23
		13+	AWPI 2
		F18+	vt AWLR13
		16-	AWLR20
		g16+	vw AWLR 3
		r.17-	wt MSLR 7

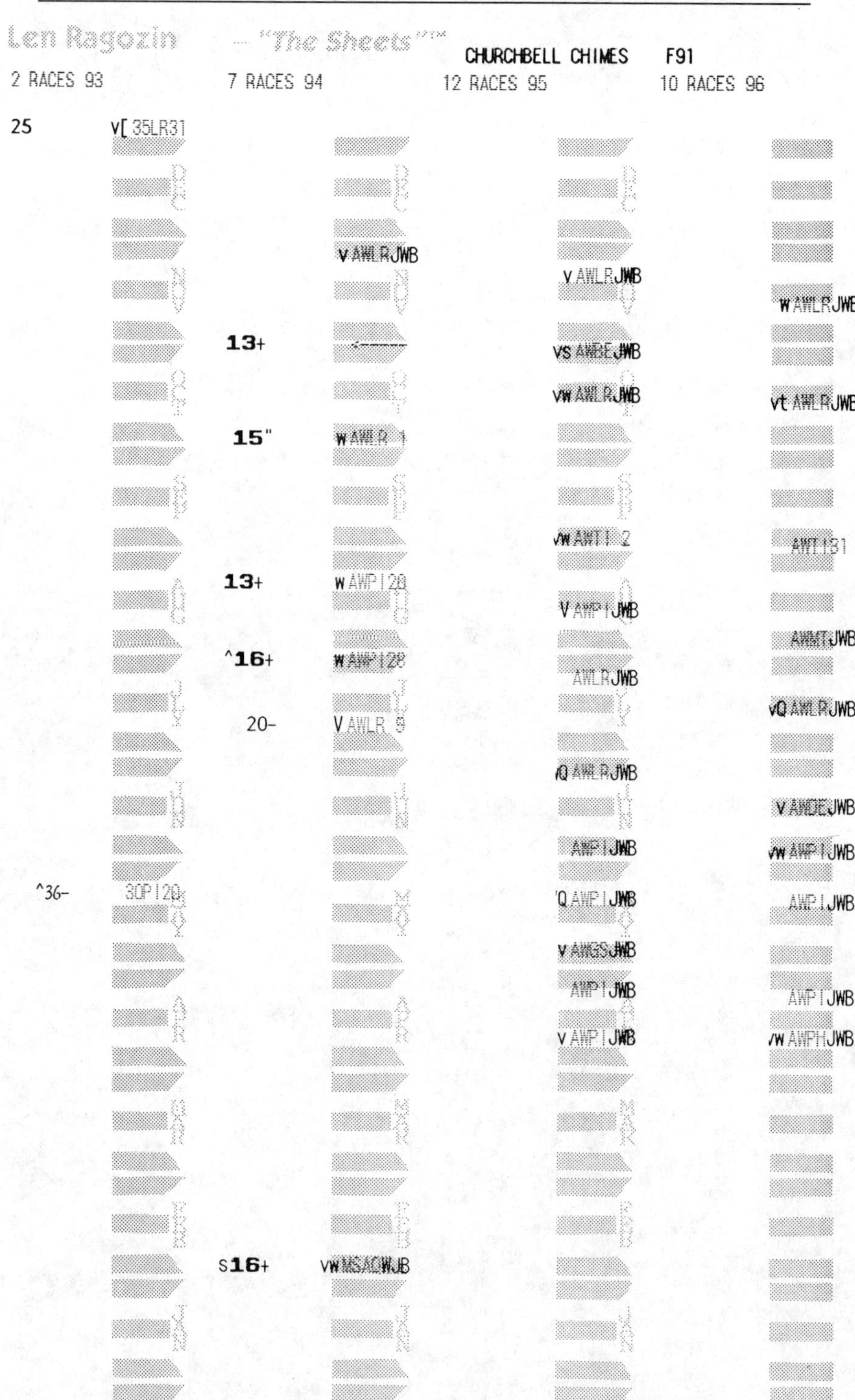
Len Ragozin — "The Sheets"™
CHURCHBELL CHIMES F91
2 RACES 93
7 RACES 94
12 RACES 95
10 RACES 96
25 v[35LR31
VAWLRJWB
VAWLRJWB
WAWLRJWB
13+
vs AWBEJWB
VWAWLRJWB
vt AWLRJWB
15" WAWLR 1
vwAWTI 2
AWTI31
13+ wAWPI20
VAWPIJWB
AWMTJWB
^16+ wAWPI28
AWLRJWB
vQ AWLRJWB
20- VAWLR 9
vQ AWLRJWB
VAWDEJWB
AWPIJWB
vw AWPIJWB
^36- 30PI20
'Q AWPIJWB
AWPIJWB
V AWGSJWB
AWPIJWB
AWPIJWB
VAWPIJWB
vw AWPHJWB
s16+ vwMSACWJB

TENTH RACE
Laurel
OCTOBER 29, 1994

1⅛ MILES. (1.473) 9th Running of THE NORTHERN DANCER. Purse $100,000 guaranteed. 3-year-olds, registered Maryland breds. By subscription of $100 each which should accompany the nomination, $700 to pass the entry box, $700 additional to start, with $100,000 guaranteed, of which 60% of all monies to the winner, 20% to second, 11% to third, 6% to fourth and 3% to fifth. Weight: 122 lbs. Non-winners of a race of $75,000 at one mile or over since January 1, 1994, allowed 3 lbs. Such a race of $50,000 since then, 5 lbs. Such a race of $35,000 since then, 7 lbs. (Maiden or claiming races not considered in estimating allowances). Field will be limited to fourteen (14) starters with preference to fourteen (14) starters with highest career earnings. Six (6) horses may be placed on the also eligible list. Starters to be named through the entry box by the usual time of entry. Trophy to the owner of the winner. Closed Friday, October 7, with 16 nominations.

Value of Race: $100,000 Winner $60,000; second $20,000; third $11,000; fourth $6,000; fifth $3,000. Mutuel Pool $47,322.00 Exacta Pool $60,989.00 Triple Pool $37,366.00

Last Raced	Horse	M/Eqt.	A.	Wt	PP	St	¼	½	¾	Str	Fin	Jockey	Odds $1	
10Oct94 8Lrl12	Owned By Us	Lb	3	116	2	2	3hd	31½	3½	3hd	11½	Johnston M T	16.60	*Jumped shadow 3/4
23Sep94 9Med4	Justalittleshower	L	3	115	3	3	62	61½	63	2½	2no	Pino M G	6.50	Wide
15Oct94 3Med4	Canton River		3	115	7	5	2hd	21	21½	11½	33¾	Molina V H	6.40	Wide early, hung
15Oct94 4Lrl1	Private High	L	3	115	1	6	8	8	8	75	4½	Seefeldt A J	4.00	Passed faders
10Oct94 6Lrl1	Churchbell Chimes	bf	3	116	4	8	41	4hd	52½	44	53½	Delgado A	1.60	Weakened
25Sep94 11AP5	Kahlua Jimmy	b	3	115	6	7	75	78	76	6hd	66¾	Ardoin R	48.30	No factor
16Oct94 10Lrl5	Sandman Sims	b	3	115	8	4	12	12	1½	5hd	7½	Prado E S	9.10	*Ducked out 3/4
15Oct94 4Lrl2	Say Capp	Lb	3	117	5	1	53	53	4hd	8	8	Rocco J	4.40	*Steadied 7/8

OFF AT 5:05 Start Good. Won driving. Time, :242, :481, 1:124, 1:373, 1:50 Track fast.

$2 Mutuel Prices:			
2-OWNED BY US	35.20	10.80	8.20
3-JUSTALITTLESHOWER		7.40	6.40
7-CANTON RIVER			6.20

$2 EXACTA 2-3 PAID $164.00 $2 TRIPLE 2-3-7 PAID $1,747.40

Gr. g, (Mar), by Waquoit-Owned by All, by Mitey Prince. Trainer Leatherbury King T. Bred by Owned By All Stable (Md).

OWNED BY US jumped a shadow inside the three quarters pole, saved ground to the far turn, worked between horses entering the stretch, closed inside rivals and edged clear. JUSTALITTLESHOWER, swung wide entering the stretch, rallied. CANTON RIVER, wide the first turn, circled the far turn and hung between the top pair. PRIVATE HIGH passed tired ones. CHURCHBELL CHIMES reached contention between horses turning for home then weakened. KAHLUA JIMMY was no factor. SANDMAN SIMS, sent to the lead, ducked out when shying form a shadow inside the three quarters pole causing his rider to briefly lose his right iron, showed speed and weakened. SAY CAPP lightyl steadied in traffic on the first turn, gave way in the drive.

Owners— 1, One & Won Stable; 2, Peace & Plenty Farm; 3, Hobbs Andrew G P; 4, Meyerhoff Robert E; 5, Granville Susan Y; 6, Cook Leland; 7, Maloney Sharon A; 8, Goldsmith C Oliver

Trainers—1, Leatherbury King T; 2, Voss Katharine M; 3, Weymouth Eugene E; 4, Small Richard W; 5, Boniface J William; 6, Romero Gerald J; 7, Murphy James W; 8, Cartwright Ronald

Scratched— Looming (16Oct94 10LRL6)

10

Reading Between the Lines

EVEN AS OTHER HANDICAPPERS over the past two decades began to develop speed figures that were at least in the right ballpark, we maintained one unique advantage that resulted from the superior precision of our numbers: the ability to read horses' patterns.

The most extreme cases, of course, involved big forward moves that were likely to be followed by bounces, or an unusually dismal race that made a horse an overlay when he reverted to or improved upon his normal efforts in his next start. But since horses typically are running somewhere between their best and their worst, it is helpful to get clues from these intermediate races and what their trend means to a horse's long-term development. Your basic question remains, When is a recent good performance an indication of better races to come and when is it too much of a good thing? Your answer may be modified by the shape of the intermediate races.

When I began to consider horses in terms of their condition, which begins with looking at how a recent group of races compares with the previous group, I found it was useful to look at a horse's entire racing career to assess how well he had developed, how long it had taken him to reach new plateaus, and whether his recent form suggested he was still developing or had reached the end of the line.

In the late 1950s, I began grouping horses by condition, rating them "A," "B," "C," "D," or "X." I gave another letter for immediate pattern, so a horse off a big jump got "A" for long-term condition but "X" on pattern. Right from the first, horses whom I deemed to be in "AA" condition often beat horses who had superior numbers but whose condition was inferior. I literally became a winning bettor overnight, though I suppose these ideas had been brewing in my subconscious for some time.

Condition increasingly becomes a factor as the racing year progresses. Beginning around mid-September, you'll find a lot of situations in which you're relying not so much on a horse to improve as you are on the rest of the field to decline because most of the horses are worn out. Chances are in the late spring or during the summer most of those horses ran one or more races that represented their peaks, and the price for that is most likely to be paid during the fall. This will sometimes occur even in races involving some of the best horses in training — whose races are usually well spaced to guard against their wearing down — and there can be a path to huge profits when you discern those situations.

The 1990 running of the Meadowlands Cup appeared to be a particularly strong race. The field was headed by Summer Squall, who after winning the Preakness had been given a four and a half–month layoff, then won the Pennsylvania Derby in early September, and was coming into the mid-October race with nearly six weeks' rest.

Mi Selecto, who had won the previous edition of The Meadowlands' richest thoroughbred race, was also entered, along with the California star Beau Genius.

But when heavy rains fell the night of the race, turning the track sloppy, one of my longtime customers, Bernie Wishengrad, looked elsewhere for value. The fact that Summer Squall had not run as strongly in winning the Pennsylvania Derby as he had when he made his three-year-old debut off an even longer layoff raised doubts in Bernie's mind about the toll taken by the Derby and Preakness on the even-money favorite. He thought the other choices in the race looked a bit worn down after hard seasons of racing. Each of them on his best day was capable of running a 3 or 4, but given the shakiness of their condition, Bernie wondered whether they'd come close to peak efforts. It has been our experience that horses in sparkling condition ignore bad track conditions, while a tired horse may seize upon this excuse to chuck it.

Norquestor, going off at 10–1 with Julie Krone riding, did not look as fast as the other horses, but seemed to be in excellent condition, making him less likely to be affected by the adverse weather and track conditions, and Bernie made him his key. Among the horses he used in exactas was Great Normand, a horse who had run 5s on the turf but whose best on dirt was an 8. Still, he had often run dirt figures in line with nearby grass figures, and Great Normand seemed to be in excellent shape — and he was 99–1. At that price, Bernie not only reversed the exacta with Norquestor for $30, he made a $50 win bet on Great Normand.

By early stretch, the result was pretty much decided: Great Normand had a comfortable lead, and Norquestor was splashing home second, with Beau Genius third, and Summer Squall — despite having previously demonstrated he could handle a sloppy track — lagging in sixth. While Great Normand's *Sheet* figure ended up slightly poorer than the two horses he beat, his lighter weight and ground-saving trip gave him the win.

As they neared the wire, Bernie shouted "Score!" and quickly became conscious of the silence all around him. Not wishing to further signal any potential muggers in the crowd, Bernie shut up and walked quietly to the cashing window.

Great Normand paid $364.80 — the highest win price in Meadowlands history — and the exacta came back for more than $1,200, providing him with a total payoff of more than $27,000. Neither Friedman nor any other regular customers of mine had the winner or the exacta — clearly this was a case where the horse's odds rather than his numbers were the main reason to play Great Normand to win and on top of exactas. But the condition

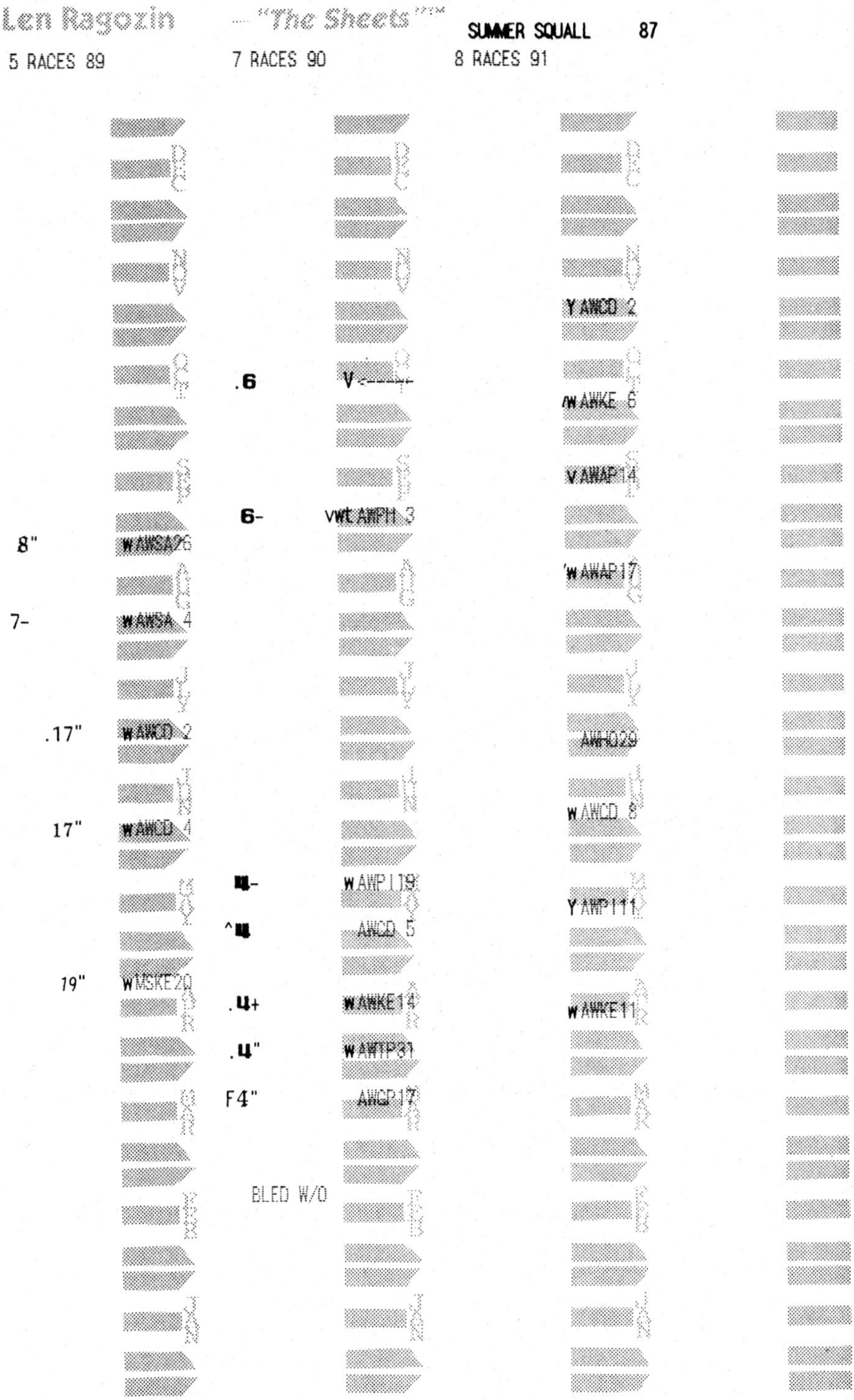

Len Ragozin — "The Sheets"™ SUMMER SQUALL 87

5 RACES 89 | 7 RACES 90 | 8 RACES 91

8" wAWSA26

7- wAWSA 4

.17" wAWCD 2

17" wAWCD 4

19" WMSKE20

.6 V

6- vwt AWPH 3

u- wAWPU19

^u AWCD 5

.u+ wAWKE14

.u" wAWTP31

F4" AWGP17

BLED W/O

Y AWCD 2

/w AWKE 6

v AWAP14

'w AWAP17

AWHO29

w AWCD 8

Y AWP111

w AWKE11

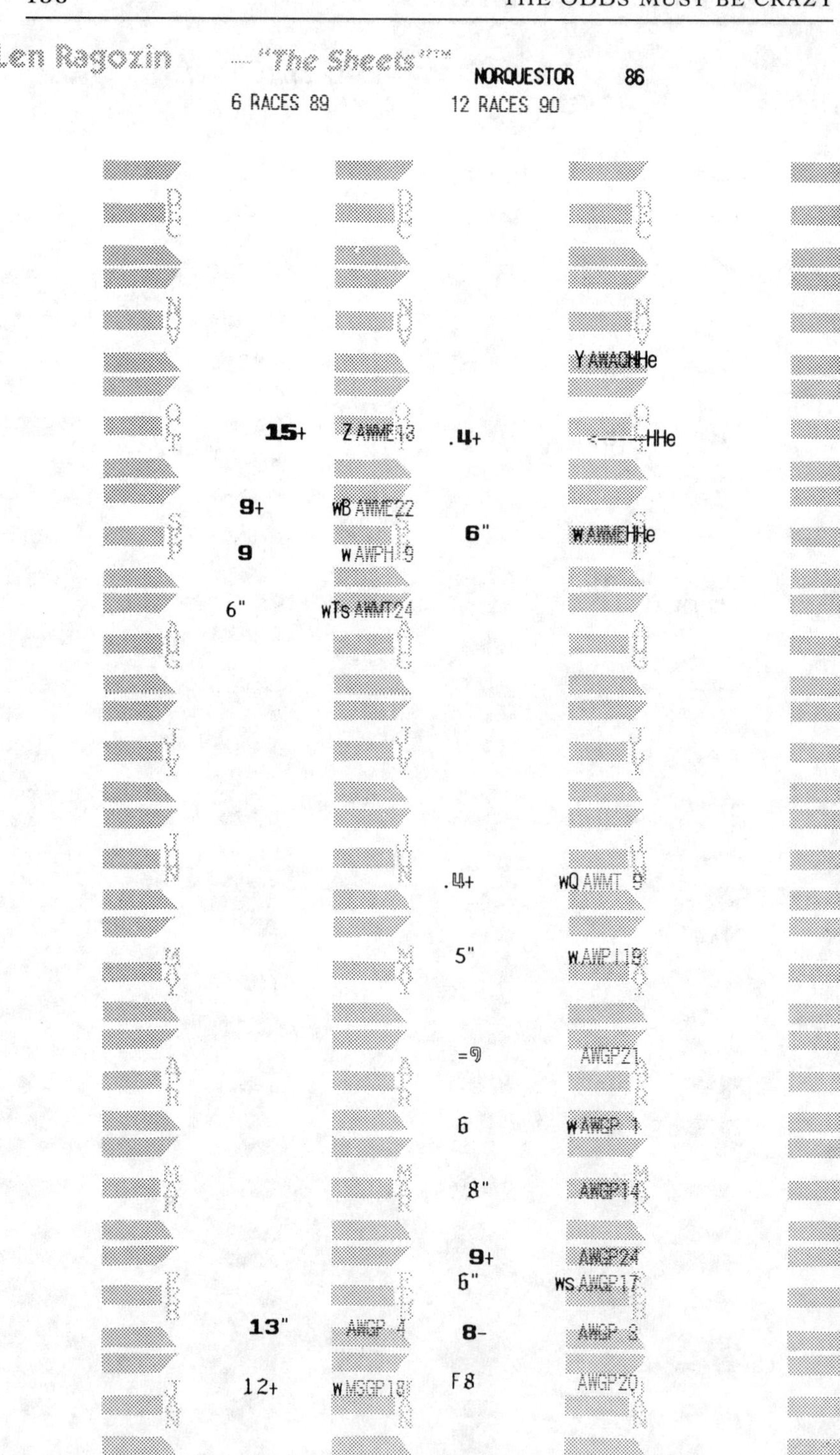
Len Ragozin
"The Sheets"™
NORQUESTOR 86
6 RACES 89
12 RACES 90
Y AWAQHHe
15+ Z AWME13
.4+ <------HHe
9+ wB AWME22
6" w AWMEHHe
9 w AWPH 9
6" wTs AWMT24
.4+ wQ AWMT 9
5" w AWP 19
=9 AWGP21
6 w AWGP 1
8" AWGP14
9+ AWGP24
6" ws AWGP17
13" AWGP 4
8- AWGP 3
12+ w MSGP18
F8 AWGP20

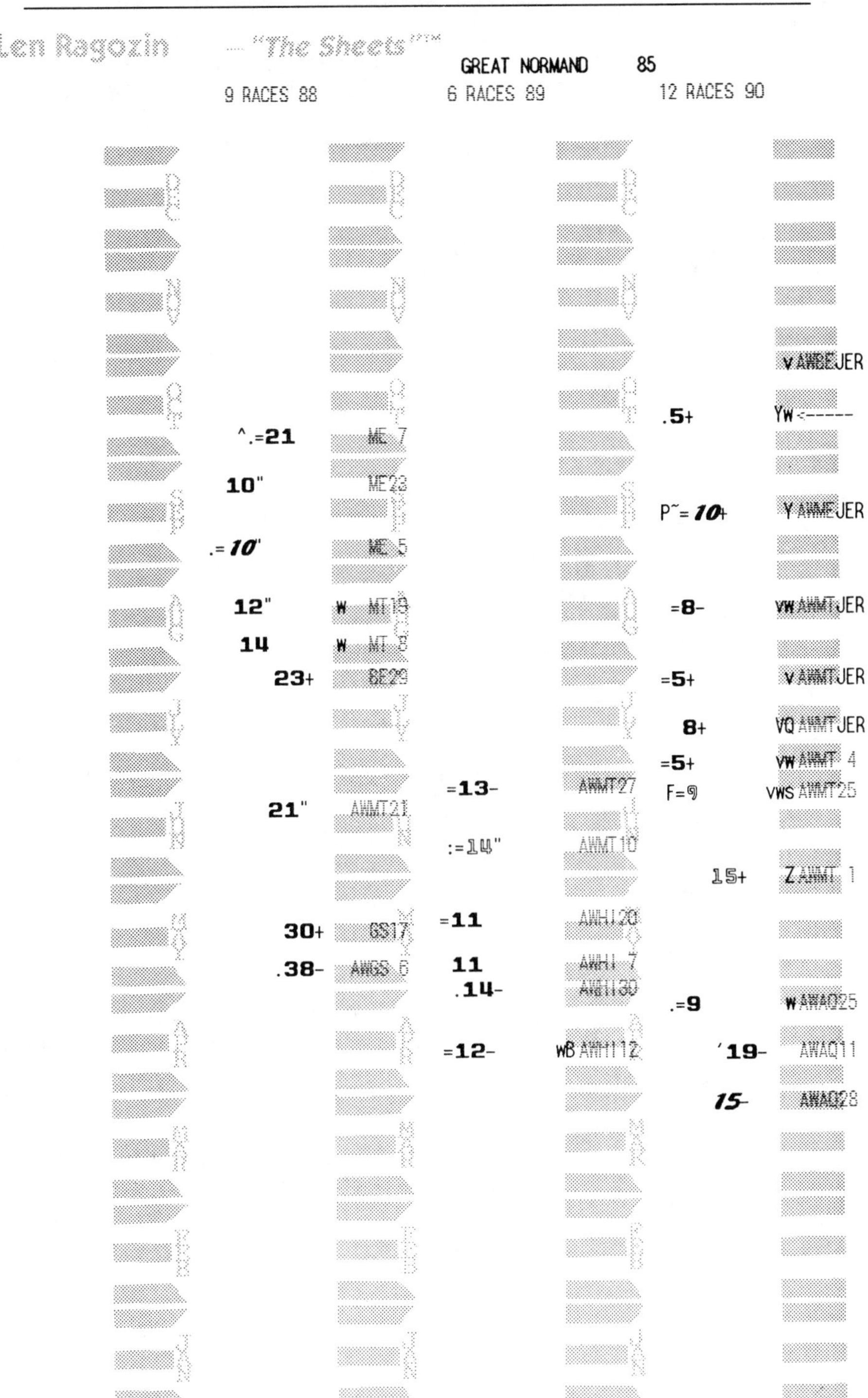
Len Ragozin "The Sheets"™
GREAT NORMAND 85
9 RACES 88
6 RACES 89
12 RACES 90

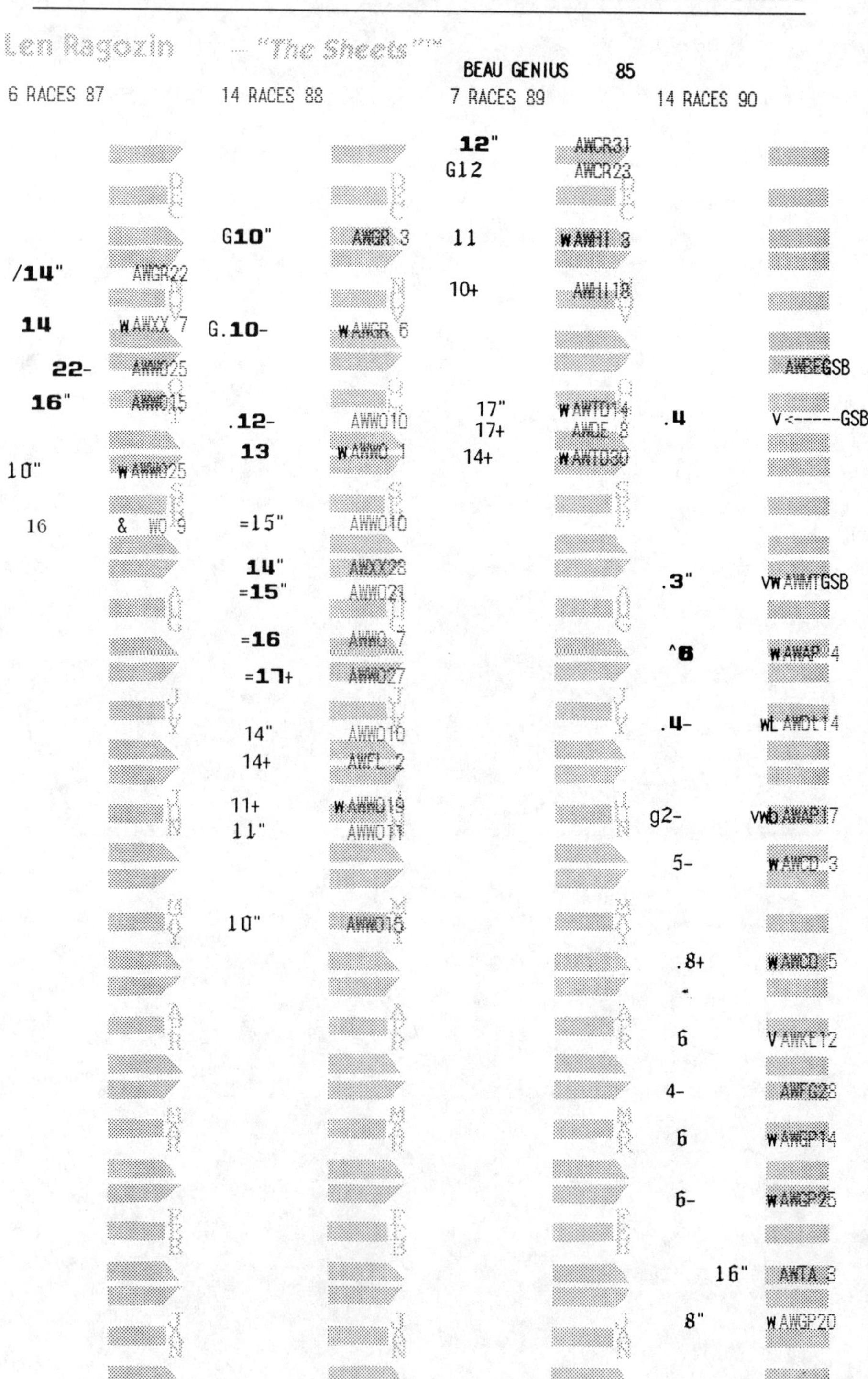
Len Ragozin — "The Sheets"™
BEAU GENIUS 85
6 RACES 87
14 RACES 88
7 RACES 89
14 RACES 90

the horse was in offered precisely the kind of opportunity, given the right odds, on which a creative condition handicapper should look to capitalize.

There are some obvious signs that a horse is healthy and developing nicely or, in the case of a mature animal, maintaining his good form.

Healthy three-year-olds should quickly be able to run a number better than anything they did at two, usually in the first couple of starts of their campaign. The males should be able to run a new top about every two months; in the first five months of the three-year-old year, maybe even every month. Fillies might take a few weeks longer. For both sexes, it's a particularly good sign if many of the intervening races are no worse than 2 or 3 points off the prior peak.

Older, more heavily raced four-year-old horses may take close to three months to recover from a surge and run a new top; late in the year they may never fully recover. Because extensive racing may have begun to wear on them, you have to regard them differently from three-year-olds when they continually run strong efforts. Three consecutive good performances by a younger horse is almost always a positive sign; the one case in which I would be wary is if each of those efforts came on less than two weeks' rest and the horse was entered back quickly again for today's race. If that horse runs badly today, he should still be considered for a bet next time out. I'm inclined to discard bad races on short rest when I believe a horse is developing well.

In a five-year-old, on the other hand, three straight good efforts has to be viewed as a probable prelude to a bad race, simply because the aches and pains that come with age make it more difficult for mature horses to run near their best every time out. A four-year-old is a judgment call: Just how worn out does his overall line indicate he is? Some may be as fresh as three-year-olds. Others have been worn down and are old before their time.

Generally you don't want to bet horses coming off tops. One conspicuous exception, however — assuming the price is decent — is a three-year-old early in the year who just surpassed his two-year-old top, but not by so much that you fear he could be knocked out. Once they've broken through that two-year-old peak, they figure to improve by at least another 4 points somewhere down the line — and sometimes, especially if they're lightly raced, it will happen immediately.

That doesn't mean the sky's the limit. I've found that the best way to measure a young horse's potential is to look at the first number that was strong enough to set him back for at least a couple of months, and figure he can probably run about 7 to 10 points faster than that number sometime later in his development.

Typically, horses will reach their peak somewhere in their four-year-old season, but horses by certain sires — Meadowlake is a prime example — will peak earlier than that, and so will some sprinters with front-running styles, especially fillies. Some horses and their offspring are naturally precocious, and a front-running sprinter is more likely to wear out early in life because of the demands his style places on spindly legs. These horses will rarely develop even 5 points from the first effort that set them back. The 7- to 10-point rule works as an estimated limit, not as a guarantee of development for all horses.

For most male horses, however, the rule holds up pretty well. Cherokee Run, who won the 1994 Breeders' Cup Sprint, was set back for the first time after he ran consecutive 11¼s late in 1992 as a two-year-old, throwing in two off-races before being rested for ten weeks. He eventually peaked with a 1¾ in the summer of his four-year-old season, a 9½-point move from the "setback" efforts.

Kissin Kris ran a 16¾ in his third career start as a two-year-old, then ran two slightly off-races before being rested for three months. He broke through that top in his first race as a three-year-old, an excellent sign. When he ran a 6 in winning the Haskell at Monmouth that summer, it might have seemed that there was plenty more improvement to come. But that race was nearly 11 points better than the initial setback number, and he failed to exceed it later that year or at four.

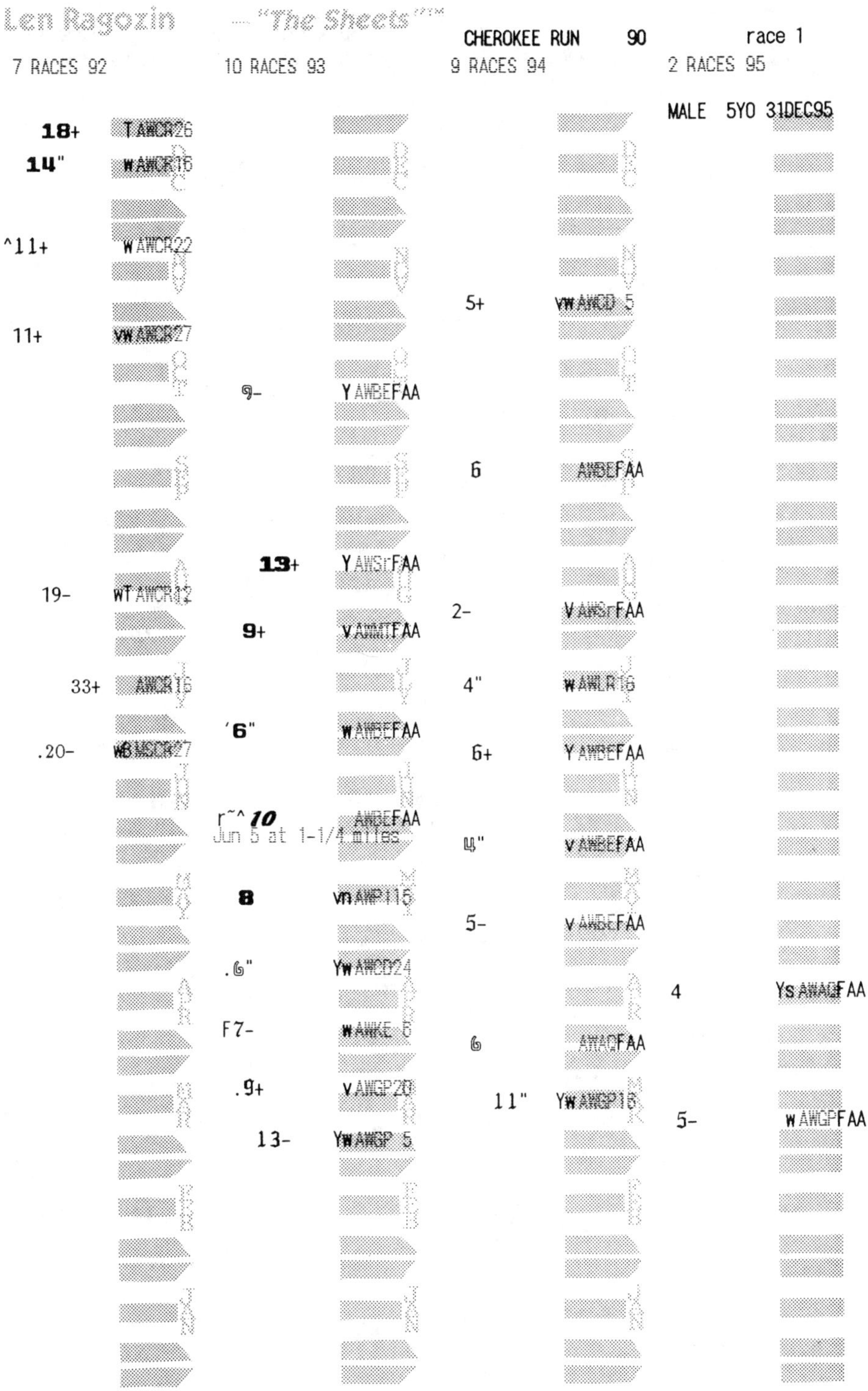

Len Ragozin — "The Sheets"™

CHEROKEE RUN 90 race 1

MALE 5YO 31DEC95

7 RACES 92

18+ TAWCR26
14" wAWCR16
^11+ WAWCR22
11+ vwAWCR27
19- wTAWCR12
33+ AWCR16
.20- wBMSCR27

10 RACES 93

9- YAWBEFAA
13+ YAWSrFAA
9+ vAWMTFAA
'6" wAWBEFAA
r~^10 AWBEFAA
Jun 5 at 1-1/4 miles
8 vnAWP115
.6" YwAWCD24
F7- wAWKE 6
.9+ vAWGP20
13- YwAWGP 5

9 RACES 94

5+ vwAWCD 5
6 AWBEFAA
2- VAWSrFAA
4" wAWLR16
6+ YAWBEFAA
4" vAWBEFAA
5- vAWBEFAA
6 AWACFAA
11" YwAWGP15

2 RACES 95

4 YsAWAQFAA
5- wAWGPFAA

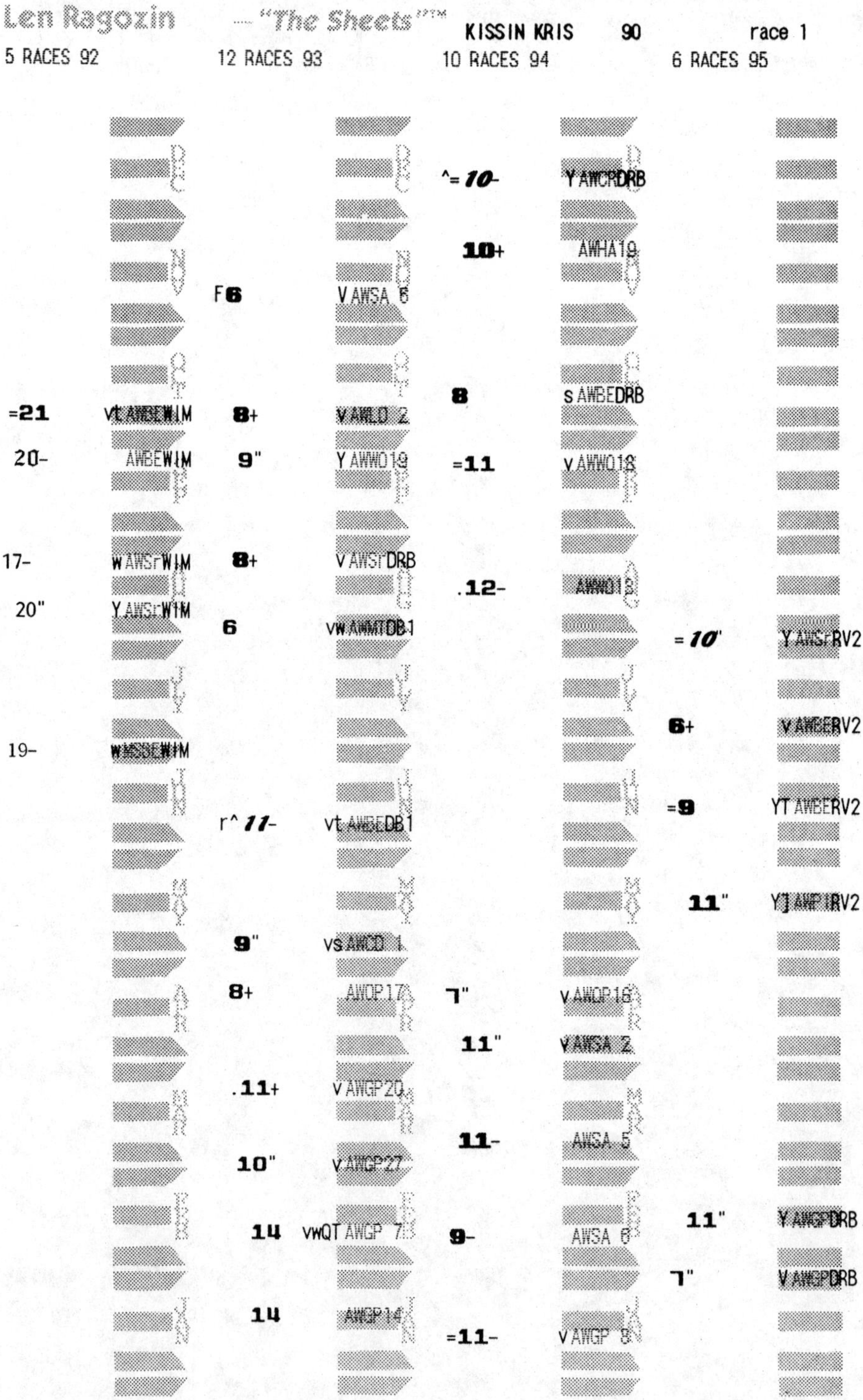

Len Ragozin — "The Sheets"™ KISSIN KRIS 90 race 1

5 RACES 92		12 RACES 93		10 RACES 94		6 RACES 95	
		F6	V AWSA 6	^=10-	Y AWCRDRB	=10"	Y AWSrRV2
=21	vt AWBEWIM	8+	V AWLD 2	10+	AWHA19	6+	V AWBERV2
20-	AWBEWIM	9"	Y AWWO19	8	s AWBEDRB	=9	YT AWBERV2
17-	w AWSrWIM	8+	V AWSrDRB	=11	V AWWO18	11"	Y] AWPIRV2
20"	Y AWSrWIM	6	vw AWMTDB1	.12-	AWWO13	11"	Y AWGPDRB
19-	wMSSEWIM	r^ 11-	vt AWBEDB1	7"	V AWOP16	7"	V AWGPDRB
		9"	vs AWCD 1	11"	V AWSA 2		
		8+	AWOP17	11-	AWSA 5		
		.11+	V AWGP20	9-	AWSA 6		
		10"	V AWGP27	=11-	V AWGP 8		
		14	vwQT AWGP 7				
		14	AWGP14				

Since some horses mature later than others, it's foolish to conclude in a race early in the season that one horse has indisputably established himself as faster or slower than his competition, particularly if the difference amounts to only a couple of points. That's why condition analysis is so important: it will give you the resolve to bet a horse who either looks a touch slow or is coming off a bad race if you like the general direction in which his form is moving.

When I was making my living by betting, if I spotted a horse who looked too slow to win but seemed ready to move forward based on his condition, I'd bet him to win and make a heavier bet to show. I got big odds because of the relatively slow numbers, cashed a lot of $6 show bets, and made maybe two big scores a year.

Friedman uses a different strategy that takes advantage of exotic wagering. If the horse is 15–1 or better, he's likely to make a win bet and then cover himself by using the horse more heavily for second and third in the exotics than on top of his combinations.

This strategy can pay huge dividends even when the "A" condition horse is facing faster animals whose condition is also decent, as was shown when Concern won the 1994 Arkansas Derby and paid $43.40. Going into the race, Concern looked too slow: his lifetime top was 15 and he was running against horses like Silver Goblin, who had run an 8¼ in beating him by twelve lengths two races earlier, and Blumin Affair, who had run a 7¾ as a two-year-old and was coming off a 9¾ in his second start of the year.

In retrospect, looking at those horses' numbers and those of a couple of the other contenders, Friedman wonders whether the 20–1 he got was really an overlay; he figures now that 40–1 might have been a more realistic price. But he was assured of a nice payoff if the horse hit the board, and so in addition to his win bet, he keyed Concern for second and third behind Blumin Affair and Silver Goblin and prayed that the other big-figure horses would bounce.

From the start of his racing career, Concern had displayed precisely the type of development you wanted to see in a young colt. From his second to his fifth start, he had progressed from a 25¼ to a 16½, just what you'd hope for from a healthy two-year-old. Nothing really set him back.

In his first race at three, two months after he ran the 16½, he produced a new top of 15½ in winning a race at Oaklawn Park. About six weeks later, he took another small step forward, to a 15. A new top was looming.

Blumin Affair had run a 7¾ late in his two-year-old campaign. The 9¾ in his most recent race seemed to set him up well for the Arkansas Derby. On the surface, whether you were looking at my numbers or their past-performance charts in *The Racing Form,* it would have seemed there was no way Concern could outrun Blumin Affair. There was, however, some chance that the 9¾ would produce a temporary bounce today from Blumin Affair.

Decades of pattern analysis have taught us that lightly raced horses who make small moves forward, as Concern had, are a threat to make a big jump in the near future. Concern had exactly three weeks between his new top and the Arkansas Derby — around the time we'd want to see elapse before betting that a horse would make that big move. The horse's trainer, Richard Small, was an excellent judge of horses. He wouldn't have entered Concern if he didn't believe he was rounding into top form. And there was a good chance that the favorites in the race would bounce.

Concern made the big move, improving more than 7 points to a 7¾. Blumin Affair actually shaded his two-year-old top by running a 7¼ but lost by a neck (with Silver Goblin third) because he went wider than Concern early. Concern remained on the rail until they turned for home (saving ground on both turns), then angled out in the straightaway and finished just to the outside of the runner-up.

Coming into the Arkansas Derby, Concern was what we call an "explosive" horse — a horse who had made an improvement of 1½ points or less over his two-year-old top and therefore was

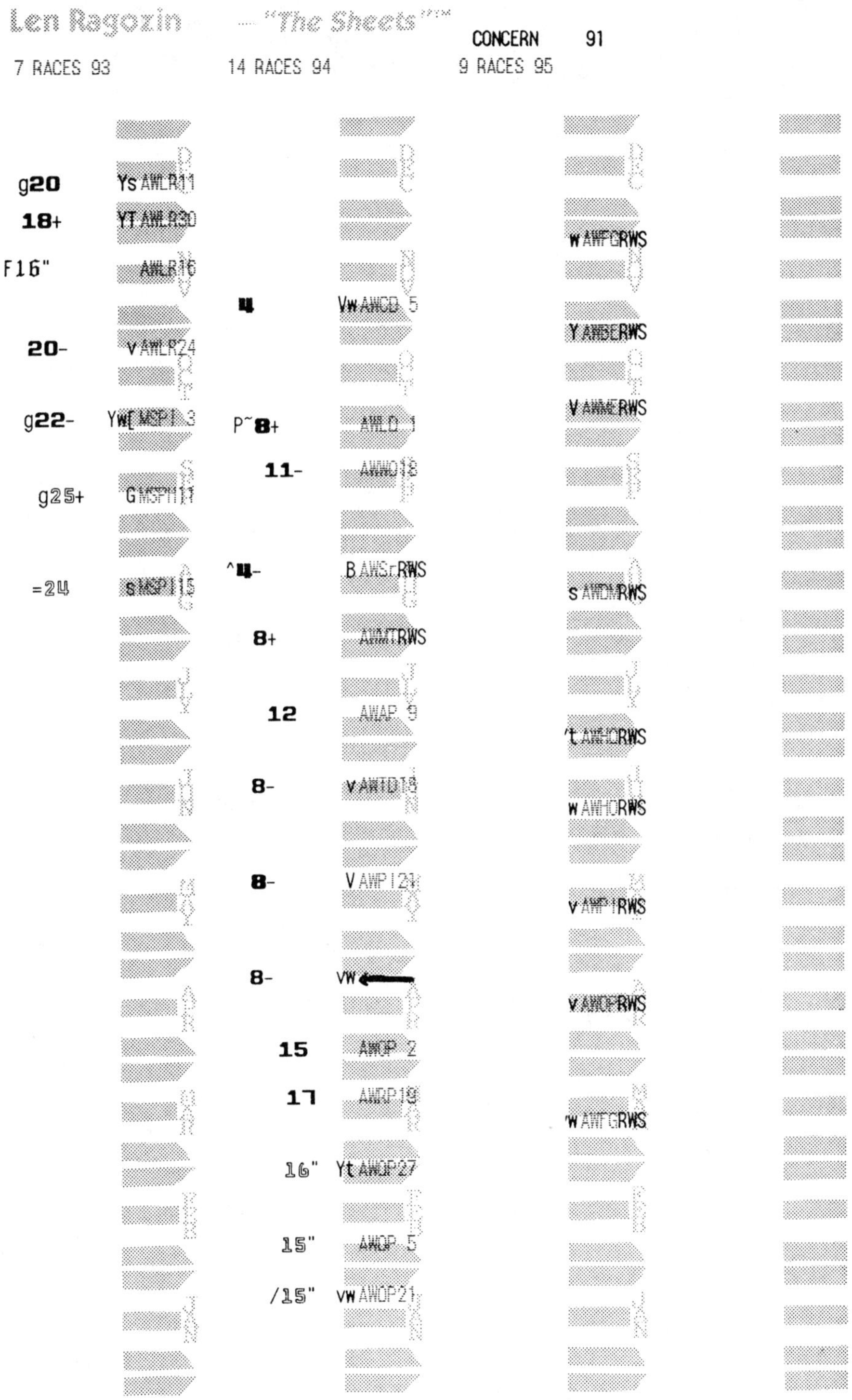

Len Ragozin — "The Sheets"™

CONCERN 91

7 RACES 93

g20 Ys AWLR11

18+ YT AWLR30

F16" AWLR16

20- v AWLR24

g22- Yw[MSP! 3

g25+ G MSPH11

=24 s MSP!15

14 RACES 94

4 Vw AWCD 5

P~8+ AWLD 1

11- AWWO18

^4- B AWSrRWS

8+ AWMTRWS

12 AWAP 9

8- v AWTD15

8- V AWP!21

8- VW

15 AWOP 2

17 AWRP19

16" Yt AWOP27

15" AWOP 5

/15" vw AWOP21

9 RACES 95

w AWFGRWS

Y AWBERWS

V AWMERWS

s AWDMRWS

't AWHORWS

w AWHORWS

v AWP!RWS

v AWOPRWS

'w AWFGRWS

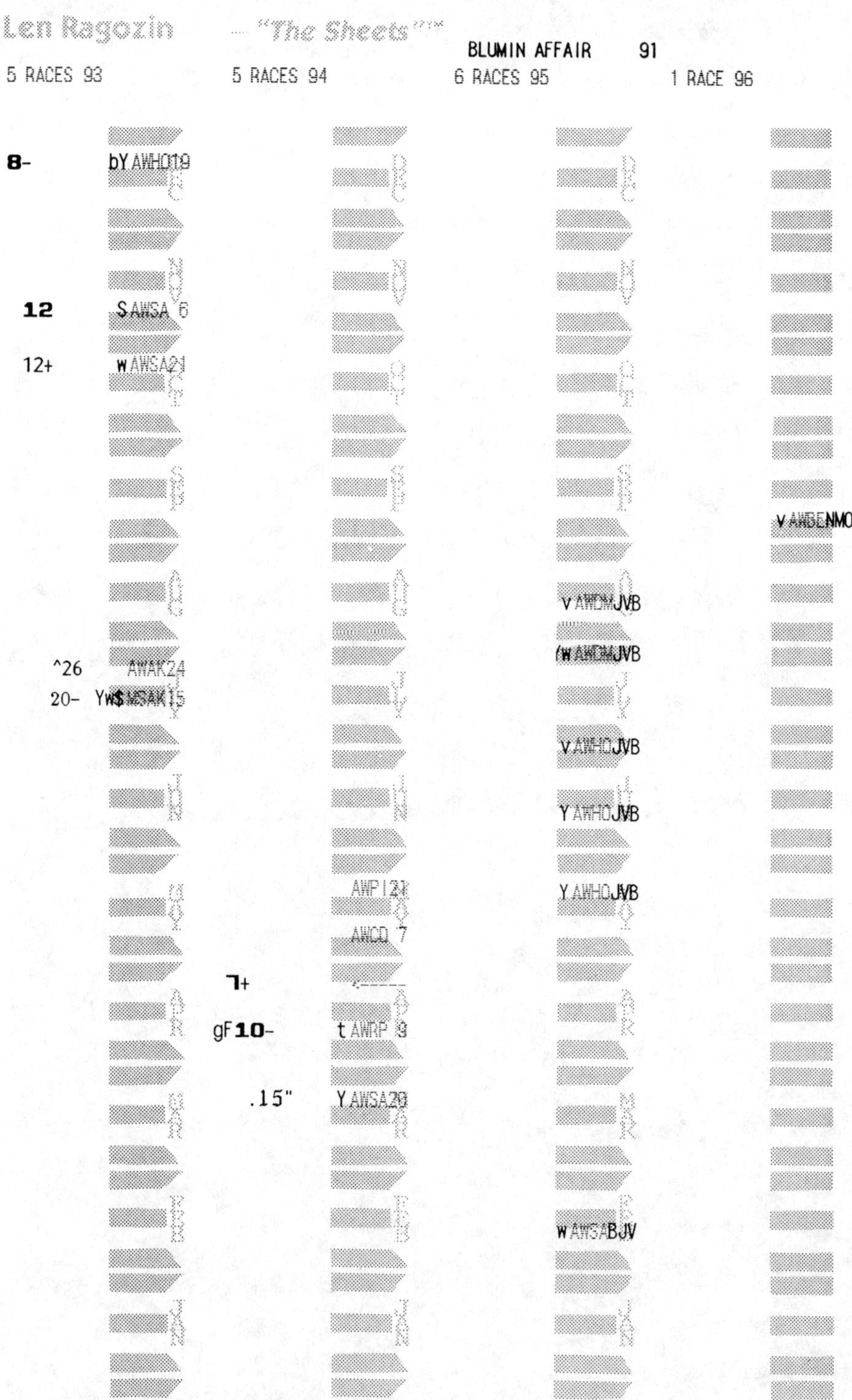
Len Ragozin
"The Sheets"™
BLUMIN AFFAIR 91
5 RACES 93
5 RACES 94
6 RACES 95
1 RACE 96
8- bY AWHO19
12 SAWSA 6
12+ wAWSA21
^26 AWAK24
20- Yw$MSAK15
AWP I21
AWCD 7
7+
gF10- tAWRP 9
.15" YAWSA20
vAWDMJVB
YwAWDMJVB
vAWHOJVB
YAWHOJVB
YAWHOJVB
wAWSABJV
vAWBENMO

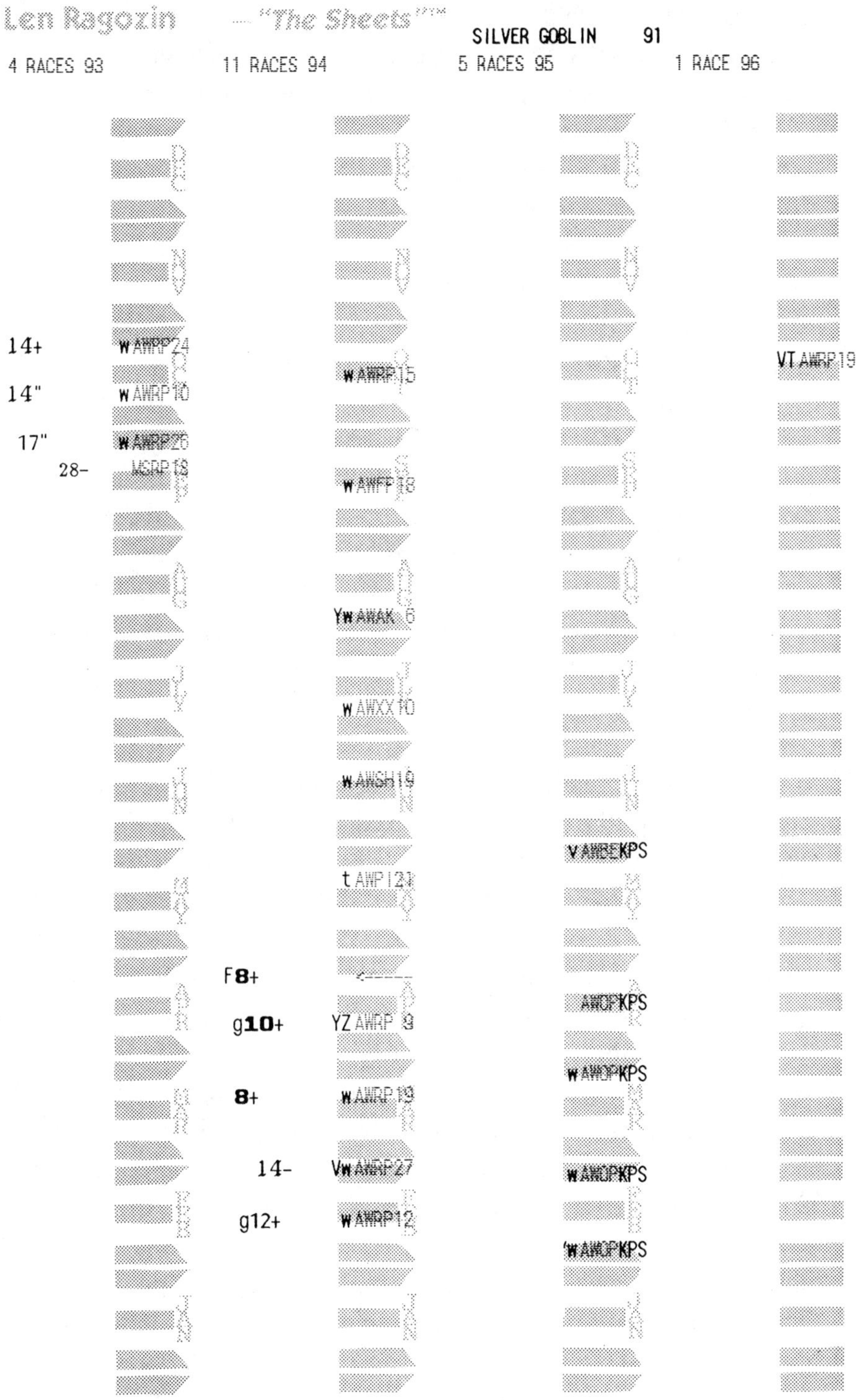

Len Ragozin — "The Sheets"™

SILVER GOBLIN 91

4 RACES 93		11 RACES 94		5 RACES 95	1 RACE 96
14+	w AWRP24				VT AWRP19
			w AWRP15		
14"	w AWRP10				
17"	w AWRP26				
28-	WSRP18		w AWFF18		
			Yw AWAK 6		
			w AWXX10		
			w AWSH19		
				V AWBEKPS	
			t AWP121		
		F8+	<-----		
				AWOPKPS	
		g10+	YZ AWRP 9		
				w AWOPKPS	
		8+	w AWRP19		
		14-	Vw AWRP27	w AWOPKPS	
		g12+	w AWRP12		
				'w AWOPKPS	

likely to make a good move to a new peak sometime in the ensuing two months. Sad to say, this explosion was so good that it put the horse on our "don't bet" list for the near future.

That may sound like a lack of gratitude, but horses' development needs constant reassessment. This kind of big move is a jump that most horses would spread over several races in smaller increments. It's a rare horse that won't react to that strong a move by backing up severely. As it happened, however, Concern took this jump in stride — but this exception doesn't shake our confidence in the general rule.

Lofty Expression and Williamstown are horses of varying ability who nonetheless had similar reactions to making the big move in an "explosive" situation. Lofty Expression became an explosive filly when she ran a 26¾ — a point better than her two-year-old top — in the fourth start of her three-year-old campaign. In her next race she produced the payoff: a 22¼ in winning a cheap allowance race by four lengths at $27.40 at Garden State Park. But the sudden jump clearly took its toll: she bounced to a 30½ in her next race, and remained at that level throughout her next few starts.

Williamstown marked himself as explosive when he ran an 11 in his three-year-old debut at Keeneland, 1¼ points better than his best race of 1992. This time, the big leap forward came two races later, when he ran a 4½ in winning the Withers Stakes (the same race that knocked out Virginia Rapids). He kangarooed to a 16½ in his next start despite having a month to recover, and three and a half months would elapse before he got within 3 points of his peak.

Explosive jumps sometimes represent such huge gains over a horse's prior form that it's unlikely he'll equal such a top in his future races. Duke Rumelius marked himself as explosive when he ran a 16¼ — ½ point better than his previous top — against $20,000 claimers at Golden Gate on June 24, 1994. The explosion came two races later, when he ran a 10½ in a losing effort in allowance company at Bay Meadows, triggering a huge bounce. Three races later, he began a string of races that were better than his old top of 16¼ without coming too close to his new peak.

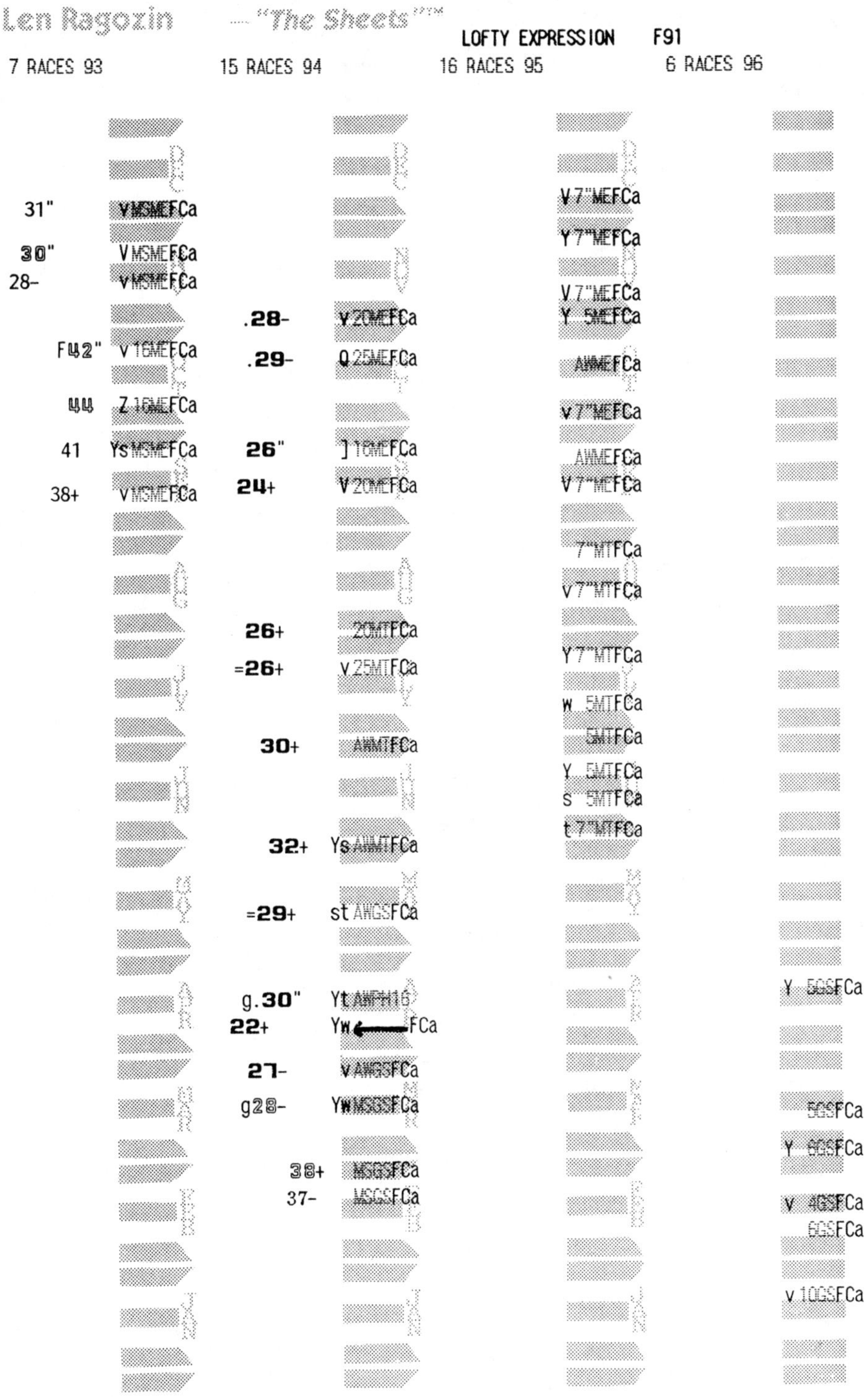

Len Ragozin — "The Sheets"™

LOFTY EXPRESSION F91

7 RACES 93

Figure	Notes
31"	YMSMEFCa
30"	VMSMEFCa
28–	VMSMEFCa
F42"	V16MEFCa
44	Z16MEFCa
41	YsMSMEFCa
38+	VMSMEFCa

15 RACES 94

Figure	Notes
.28–	V20MEFCa
.29–	Q25MEFCa
26"	]16MEFCa
24+	V20MEFCa
26+	20MTFCa
=26+	V25MTFCa
30+	AWMTFCa
32+	YsAWMTFCa
=29+	st AWGSFCa
g.30"	YtAWFH16
22+	Yw ← FCa
27–	VAWGSFCa
g28–	YwMSGSFCa
38+	MSGSFCa
37–	MSGSFCa

16 RACES 95

Figure	Notes
	V7"MEFCa
	Y7"MEFCa
	V7"MEFCa
	Y 5MEFCa
	AWMEFCa
	V7"MEFCa
	AWMEFCa
	V7"MEFCa
	7"MTFCa
	V7"MTFCa
	Y7"MTFCa
	W 5MTFCa
	5MTFCa
	Y 5MTFCa
	s 5MTFCa
	t7"MTFCa

6 RACES 96

Figure	Notes
	Y 5GSFCa
	5GSFCa
	Y 6GSFCa
	V 4GSFCa
	6GSFCa
	V 10GSFCa

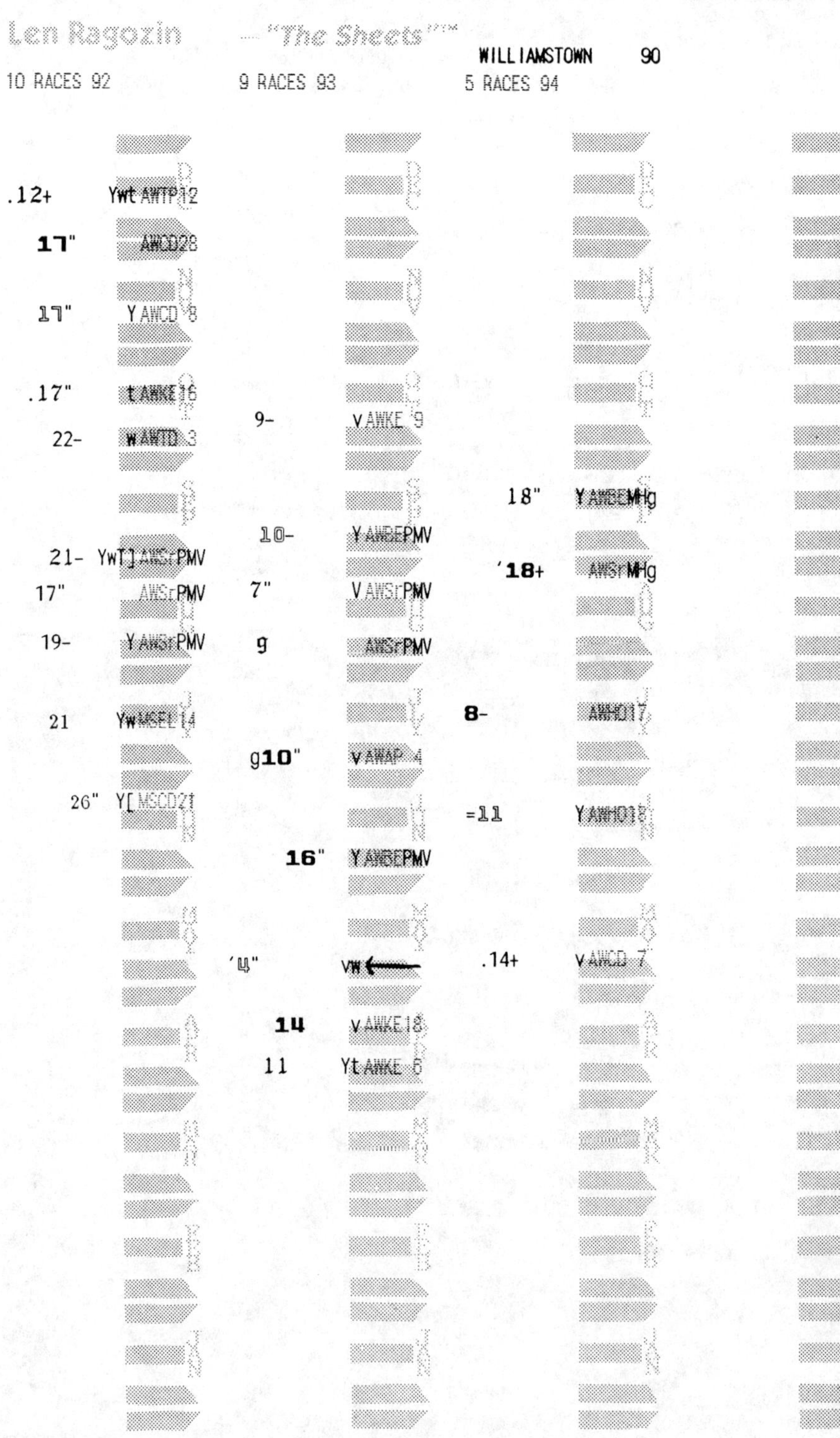
Len Ragozin
"The Sheets"™
WILLIAMSTOWN 90
10 RACES 92
9 RACES 93
5 RACES 94

Len Ragozin — "The Sheets"™

DUKE RUMELIUS 90

5 RACES 92		18 RACES 93		17 RACES 94		8 RACES 95	
^30-	v 40SA30	18+	V 16BM30	15	AWBMREW	XX	K 12BMNH3
26"	Ys 32HO27	21+	Yw 12BM 4	15	v AWBM18	19-	s 12SRNH3
26"	Vs 32HO18	18+	10BM19	15-	AWBM20	16-	b 12SO12
28+	V 32DM31	26-	Y 12BM30	13+	AWBM30	20	V AWGGNH3
F28	S 32DM10	24	V 16BM 9	17+	AWBM 9	17+	vB 15GGREW
		20	Y&ra 10BM26	24"	v 25BM21	.21-	Y 20GGREW
		18"	v 12BM 4	10"	bV ←	=19"	vt AWBMREW
		25+	Yw 12BM14	18-	AWSO16	16+	v AWBMREW
		23	V 12SO28	16+	Y 20GG24		
		17-	12PL11	21	25GG 4		
		18	bv 12GG16	17+	v AWGG21		
		21+	32HO 3	^17+	Y 25GG28		
		21+	32HO 8	17-	Yw AWGG15		
		26"	v 40SA17	=17+	Y AWGG 2		
		23	32SA 2	19-	vT AWGG11		
		22"	Y 32SA17	.21"	v AWGG21		
		21+	40SA 3	^18	w 16BM28		
		21+	v 32SA11				

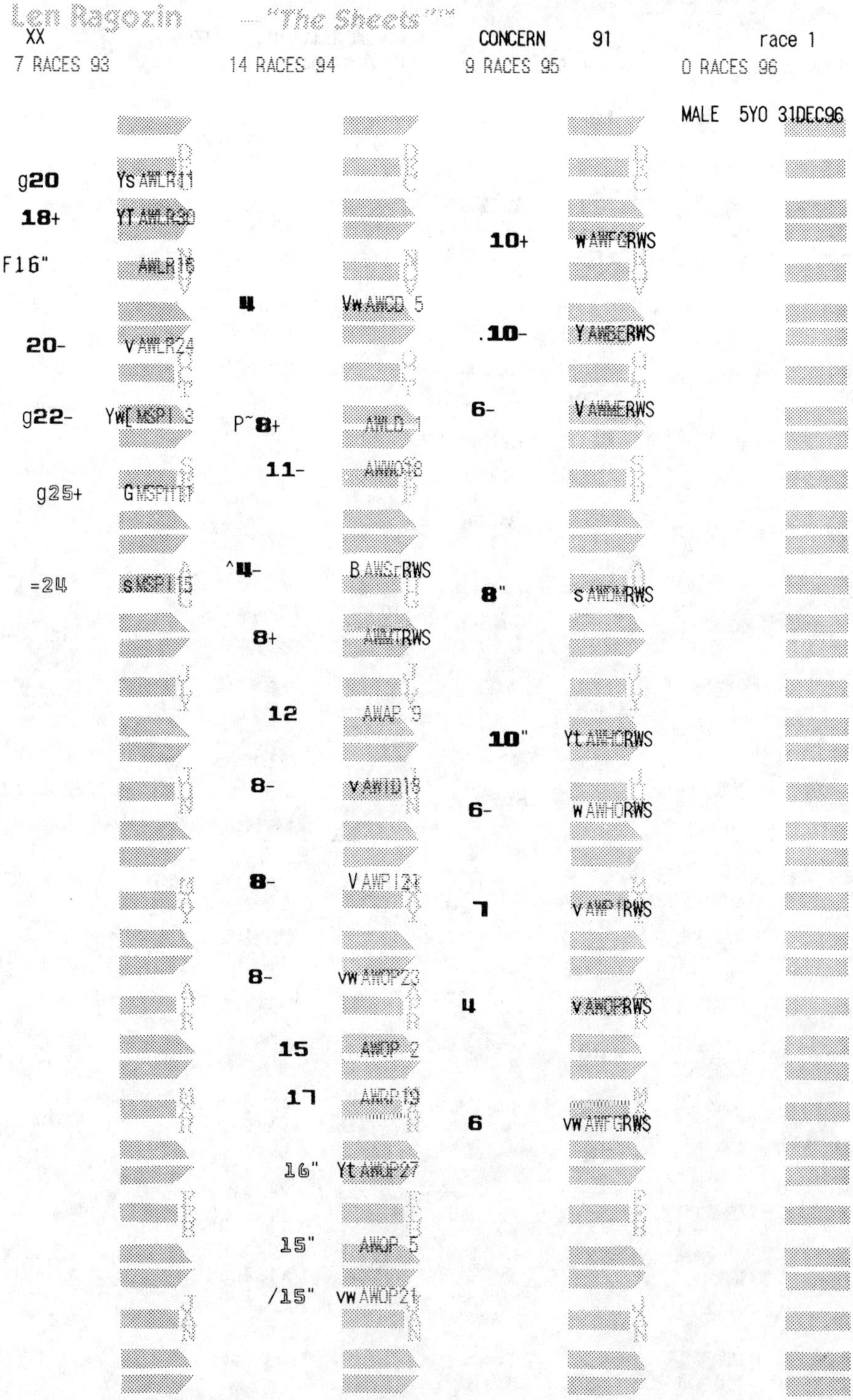

Len Ragozin — *"The Sheets"*™

XX CONCERN 91 race 1

7 RACES 93	14 RACES 94	9 RACES 95	0 RACES 96
g20 YsAWLR11	4 VwAWCD 5	10+ wAWFGRWS	MALE 5YO 31DEC96
18+ YTAWLR30	P~8+ AWLD 1	.10- YAWBERWS	
F16" AWLR16	11- AWWO18	6- VAWMERWS	
20- vAWLR24	^4- BAWSrRWS	8" sAWDMRWS	
g22- Yw[MSP1 3	8+ AWMTRWS	10" YtAWHORWS	
g25+ GMSP1?1	12 AWAP 9	6- wAWHORWS	
=24 sMSP115	8- vAWTD18	7 vAWP1RWS	
	8- VAWP121	4 vAWOFRWS	
	8- vwAWOP23	6 vwAWFGRWS	
	15 AWOP 2		
	17 AWRP19		
	16" YtAWOP27		
	15" AWOP 5		
	/15" vwAWOP21		

Concern, however, showed that he was a hardier horse than most. He repeated the 7¾ in running third in the Preakness. By itself, this wasn't necessarily a good sign, because horses who make a big jump to a new top and then pair it will usually bounce following the pair. But he repeated the number while losing the Ohio Derby, and the third straight big effort was an indication that the top might not be a ceiling but rather a foundation for future development.

After a slightly off-race at Arlington Park, the horse got close to his top running an 8¼ while finishing third behind Holy Bull in the Haskell at Monmouth. Then Concern made a big move forward again by running a 4 while just missing to the same horse in the Travers at Saratoga. He would repeat that 4 in early November in the Breeders' Cup Classic, and with no Holy Bulls in the field, it was good enough to win.

To see that Concern's stakes win at a long price was not a once-in-a-lifetime situation, note that the Fountain of Youth stakes, run at Gulfstream on February 24, 1996, had many similarities. The pattern of numbers on the 143-to-1 winner, Built for Pleasure, was not as strong as that of Concern, but had the extra boost of second-time Lasix. With a long rest followed by a ¼-point move and no real limit to his development as yet established, the horse was certainly a threat to improve a few points. He was getting weight from everybody, and 7 pounds (1½ points) from the favorite, Unbridled's Song. And although the latter by no means had a weak line, and could well be projected to run 6 or better, there was at least some chance of a temporary bounce, considering that he ran a top immediately after a layoff. The second favorite was the other fast horse, Editor's Note, who was much more likely to bounce, having improved a full 2 points in his first Florida start. And even a tiny chance of these bounces was enough, considering the astronomical odds.

Well, as it happened, Unbridled's Song didn't bounce, and Built For Pleasure improved more than you had a right to expect. Victory Speech, whose gradual improvement gave him the best-looking condition line of all, came third in the three-horse photo

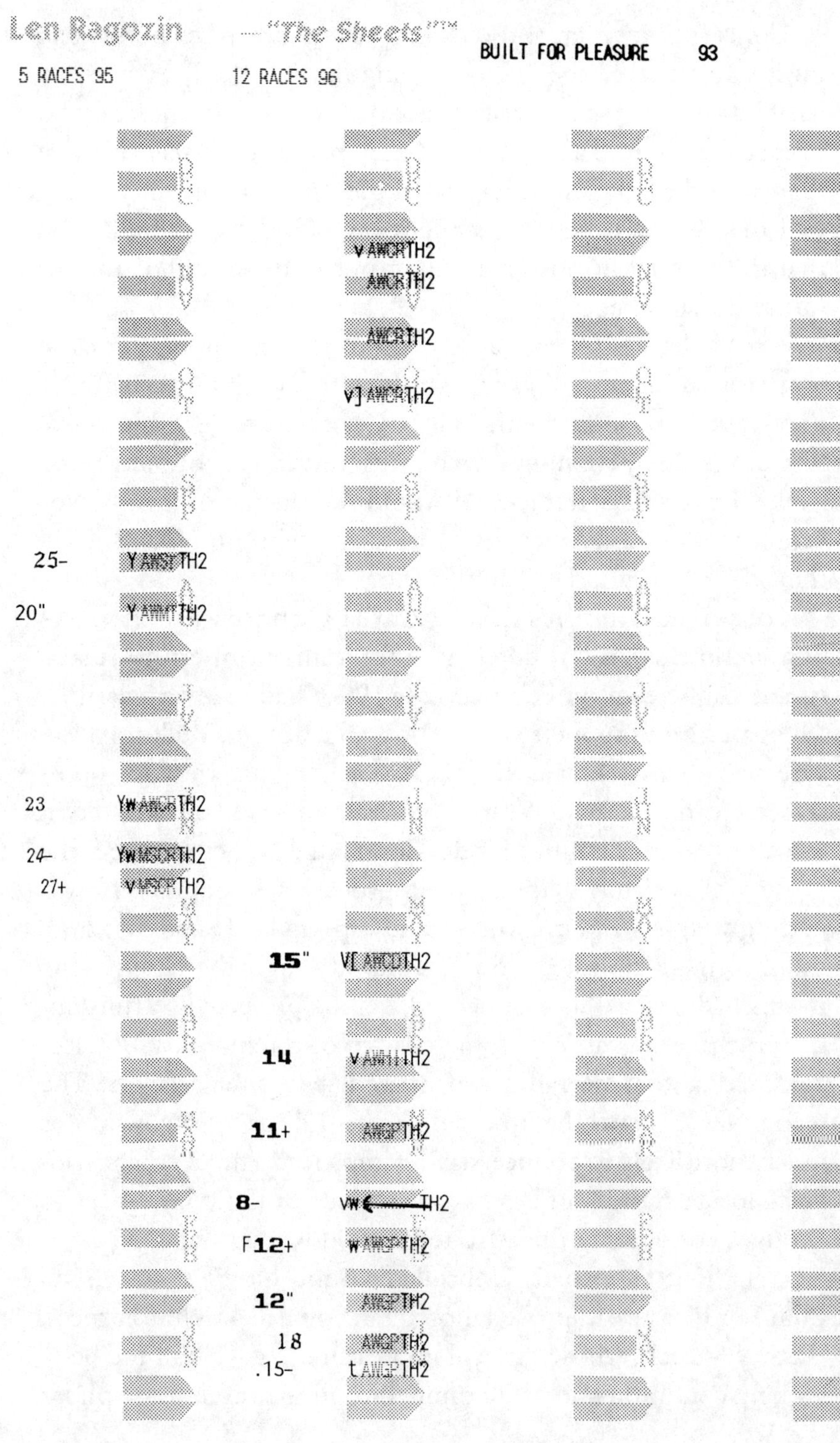
Len Ragozin "The Sheets"™
BUILT FOR PLEASURE 93
5 RACES 95
12 RACES 96
V AWCRTH2
AWCRTH2
AWCRTH2
V] AWCRTH2
25- Y AWSRTH2
20" Y AWMTTH2
23 YW AWCRTH2
24- YW MSCRTH2
27+ V MSCRTH2
15" V[AWCDTH2
14 V AWMITH2
11+ AWGPTH2
8- VW TH2
F12+ W AWGPTH2
12" AWGPTH2
18 AWGPTH2
.15- t AWGPTH2

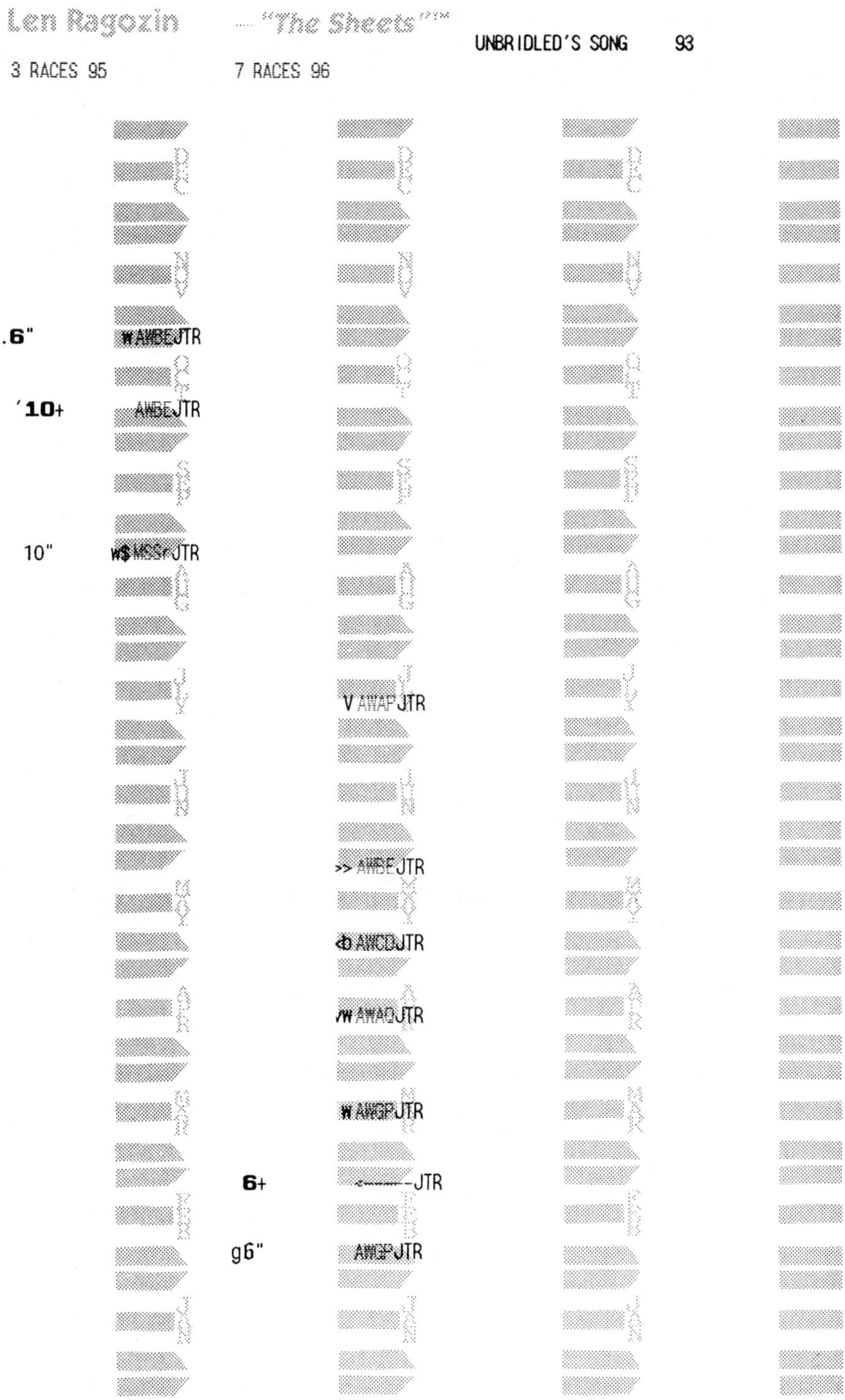

Len Ragozin ..."The Sheets"™

UNBRIDLED'S SONG 93

3 RACES 95		7 RACES 96	
.6"	AWBEJTR		
'10+	AWBEJTR		
10"	w$ MSSrJTR		
			V AWAPJTR
			>> AWBEJTR
			AWCDJTR
			/W AWAQJTR
			W AWGPJTR
		6+	-JTR
		g6"	AWGPJTR

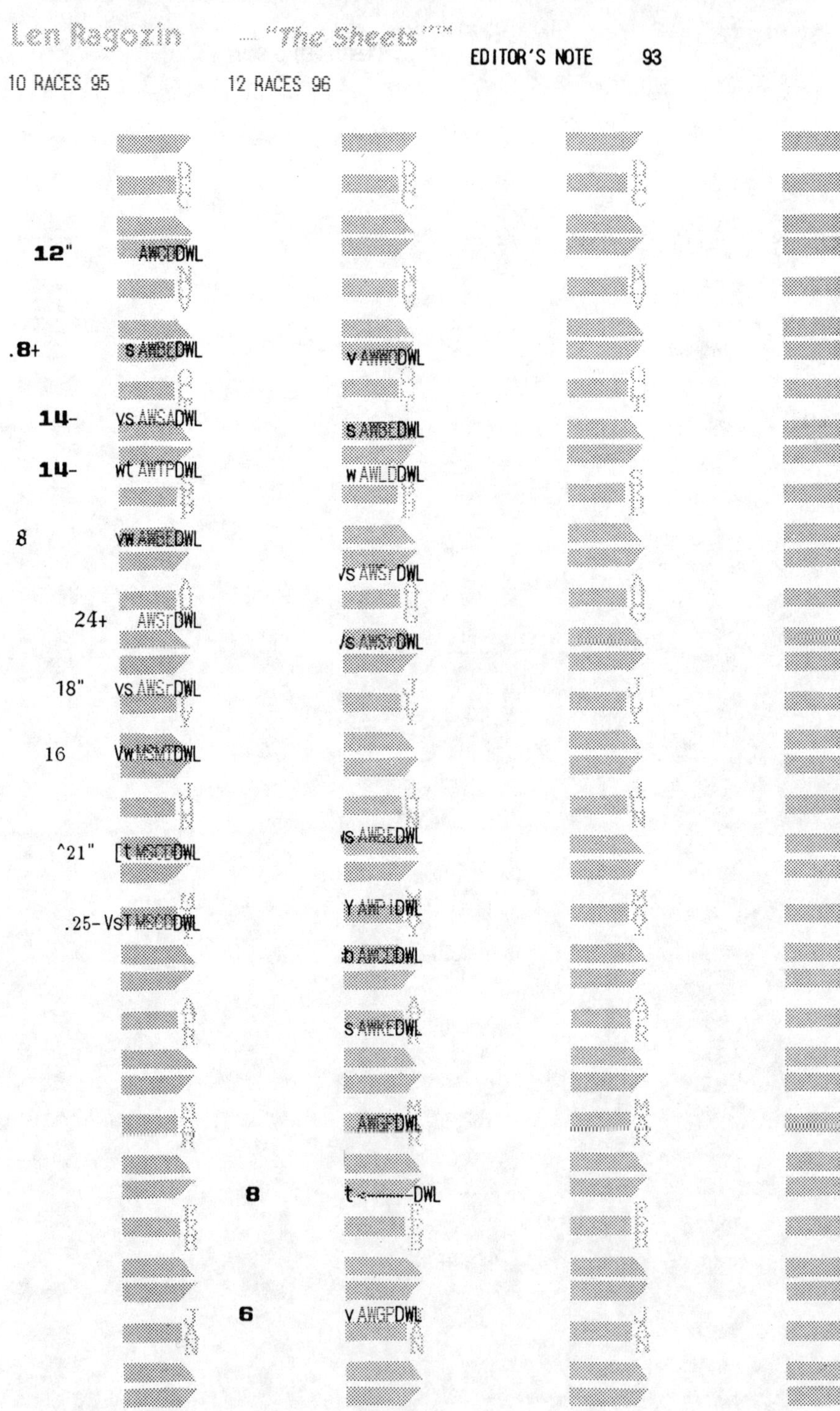
Len Ragozin "The Sheets"™
EDITOR'S NOTE 93
10 RACES 95
12 RACES 96
12" AWCDDWL
.8+ s AWBEDWL
14- vs AWSADWL
14- wt AWTPDWL
8 vw AWBEDWL
24+ AWSrDWL
18" vs AWSrDWL
16 Vw MSMTDWL
^21" [t MSCDDWL
.25- VsT MSCDDWL
v AWWODWL
s AWBEDWL
w AWLDDWL
vs AWSrDWL
/s AWSrDWL
vs AWBEDWL
Y AWPIDWL
b AWCDDWL
s AWKEDWL
AWGPDWL
8 t DWL
6 v AWGPDWL

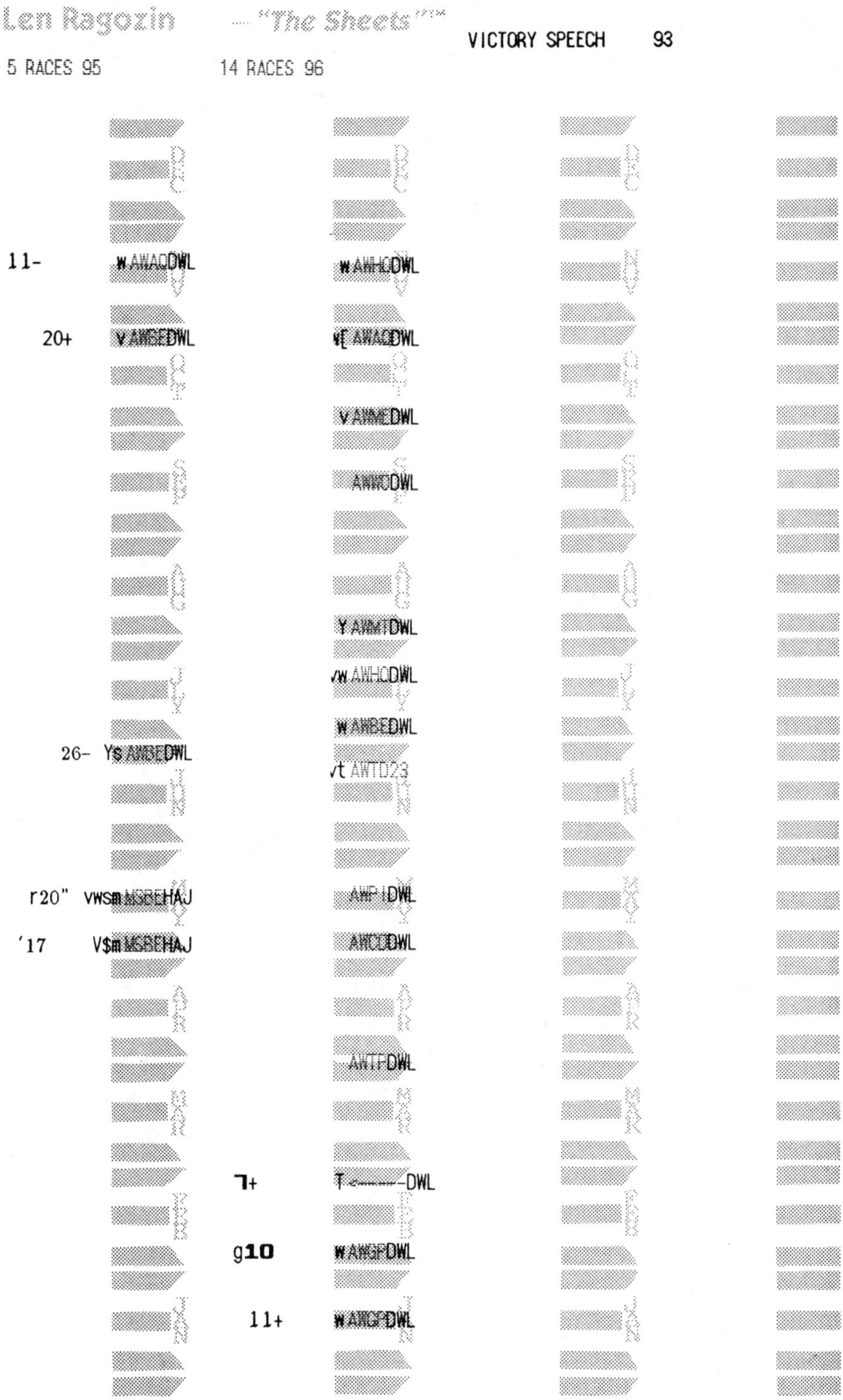

Len Ragozin — "The Sheets"™

VICTORY SPEECH 93

5 RACES 95

14 RACES 96

5 RACES 95		14 RACES 96	
11-	wAWAQDWL		wAWHQDWL
20+	vAWBEDWL		v[AWAQDWL
			vAWMEDWL
			AWWCDWL
			YAWMTDWL
			vw AWHQDWL
			wAWBEDWL
26-	Y$ AWBEDWL		vt AWTD23
r20"	vwsm MSBEHAJ		AWP DWL
'17	V$m MSBEHAJ		AWCDDWL
			AWTFDWL
		7+	T<------DWL
		g10	wAWGPDWL
		11+	wAWGPDWL

at 6–1 for a triple of $4,086. And there were two other horses in the race who weren't really throw-outs. The right play was some triples and exactas with Built For Pleasure on the bottom, I suppose. But, just as happened with Blumin Affair/Concern, racing luck intervened and Built For Pleasure won the photo over Unbridled's Song for a $288 payoff, with a $663 exacta. Not a winner you really *should* have, perhaps, but an illustration that some high-odds winners don't come from as far out of the blue as you might think from looking in the *Racing Form*.

The best time to bet a horse right off a new top is, of course, when you're dealing with an immature three-year-old male, as in the two examples just discussed. In 1997, the first of Gulfstream Park's series of races for horses with Derby aspirations, the Hutcheson Stakes, saw another super-payoff — this time, more than $200 — on a horse who was distinctly eligible to explode.

Both the favorite, Confide, and the extreme outsider, Frisk Me Now, had just made the small move to a slight new top, which we like so much. They were both eligible to go forward, and they both did. But whether such a horse will make a modest improvement or explode down to something near his ultimate potential in one dramatic leap is really not predictable.

Confide was ready to improve over his 11¼ — and he moved almost 2 points, to a 9½. Frisk Me Now, like Concern, was ready to improve from a 15–; but he took a 5¼-point leap and won the race, paying $213.80 — an amazing price in an eight-horse field.

Friedman overlooked this one. But his ex-wife, Orly, who had taken a little holiday and accompanied him to Gulfstream Park to help him with his seminar, rubbed salt in the wound. She bet her usual $20 unit on Frisk Me Now. When the horse came home she thought for a moment that she had won about $200. She lacked experience in winning at 100–1 odds.

Once again, this is not the sort of thing that becomes a bedrock of your handicapping success. But once again it shows that some "impossible" upsets really aren't.

Most horses make their improvements in small increments over the course of their career, going forward a point or two far

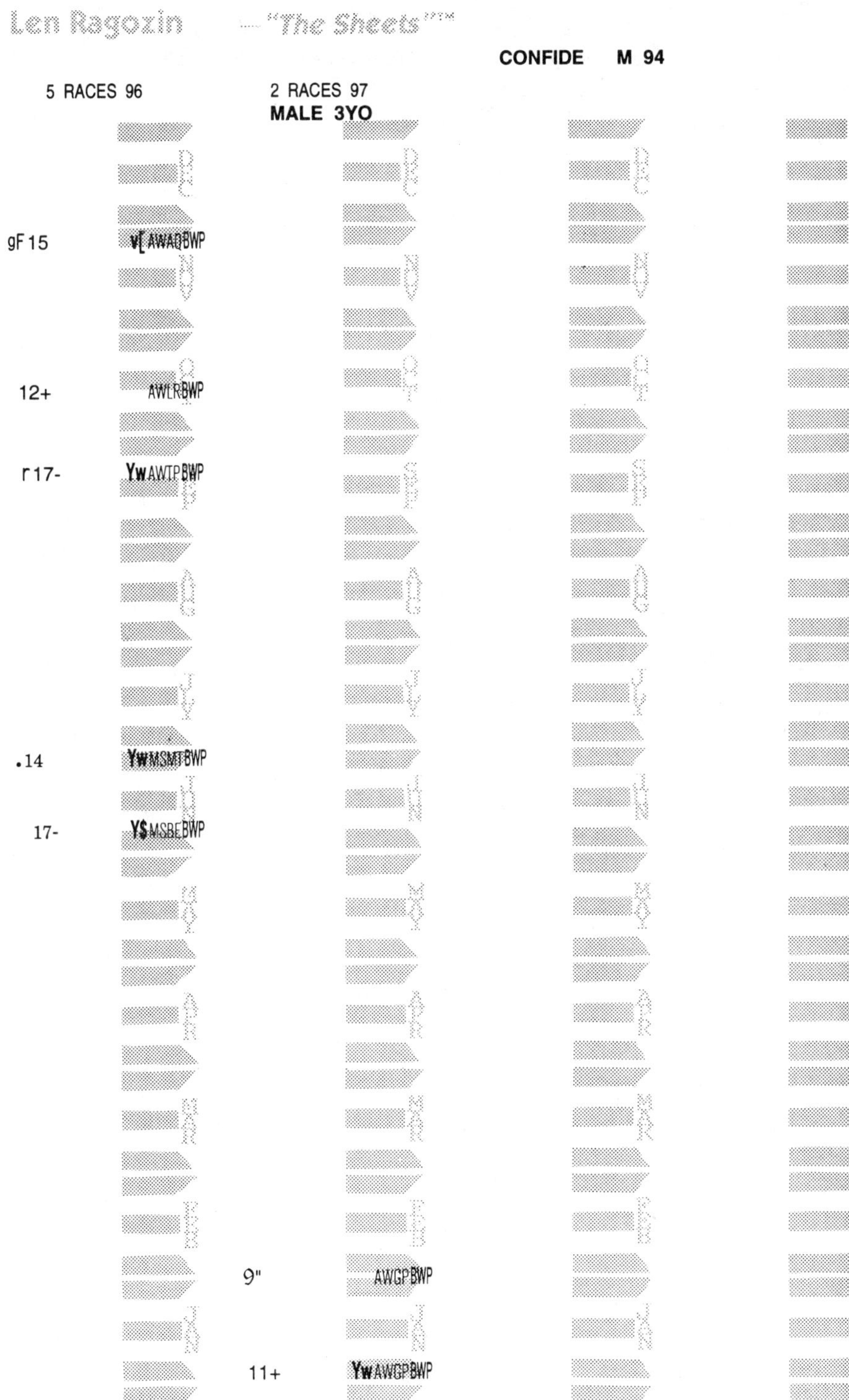
Len Ragozin "The Sheets"™
CONFIDE M 94
5 RACES 96
2 RACES 97
MALE 3YO
gF15
12+
r17-
.14
17-
9"
11+

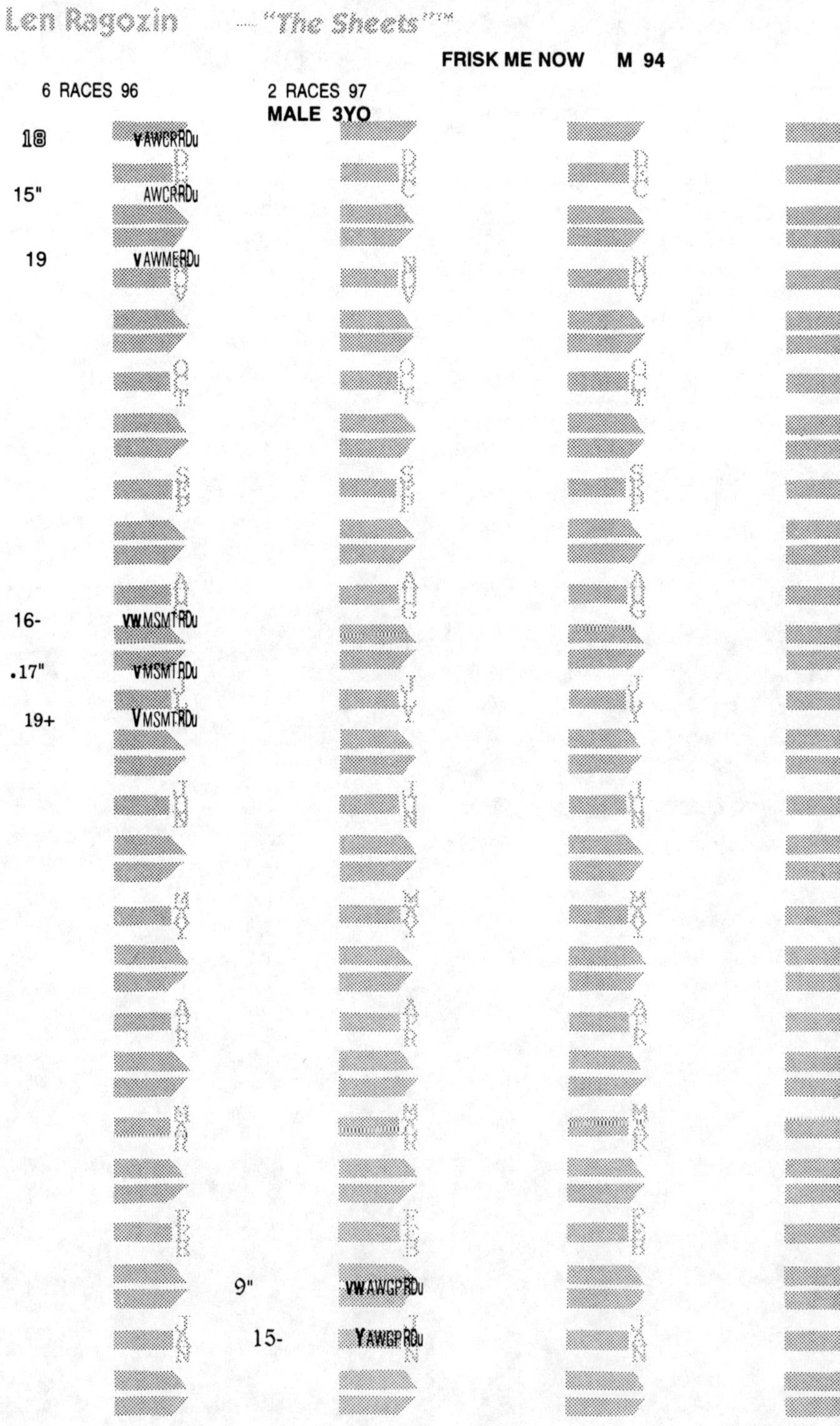
Len Ragozin "The Sheets"™
FRISK ME NOW M 94
6 RACES 96
2 RACES 97
MALE 3YO
18 VAWCRRDu
15" AWCRRDu
19 VAWMERDu
16- VWMSMTRDu
.17" VMSMTRDu
19+ VMSMTRDu
9" VWAWGPRDu
15- YAWGPRDu

more often than they make a 4- or 5-point jump. Except for three-year-olds who have just moved past their two-year-old top, you aren't going to want to bet them immediately off those peak races, because the chances are they'll go backward and at short odds.

That brings us to a new question: What are you going to do in a horse's second start off a peak? My decisions are going to be influenced by two considerations: what the horse ran in the intermediate race, and whether I believe that peak was good or bad for the horse in terms of future development.

If the peak represented a big jump in the horse's form, I'm going to be wary of betting him two races later, regardless of whether the intermediate race produced an effort equal to or slightly better than that top, one a couple of points worse, or a significant bounce. My feeling would be different, however, if the peak was just a small move forward. Here you look for reasons to be optimistic.

A very frequent development for horses who run a new peak is that they follow it with an effort in the range of 2 points worse. If that peak was a big improvement, or if the horse is heavily raced and shows gaps of three months or more between its top efforts, the following near-peak effort may have exhausted the horse. The next race in the sequence has a good chance to accelerate the backward trend and to be at least 5 points worse than the peak.

If the peak was just a small move forward, however, the 2-point reaction (it could be 1½ points or 2½ points and I'd feel the same) can be read as a good sign — handling the peak without disintegrating. It is likely to be followed by a race matching or improving upon the top.

I realize this seems contradictory. But if a horse has made a big jump that you feel for the short term is likely to be harmful to his development, then a subsequent race just 2 points off that peak figures to further deplete him. You'd actually prefer that he bounced by 6 points, because the noneffort would probably take less out of him and you'd be getting a much better price on him if you thought he could rebound at least to a near-top today.

Conversely, if you thought the small move to a peak was an indication of better things to come, the small regression can be read as a positive sign that he could be ready to make a new move today rather than later. And the "small" move could be larger without changing my feeling if it comes from a three-year-old colt who has not yet reached his limits of development (7 to 10 points from the first peak that really set him back).

There's a temptation to read too much into the exact extent of bounces, particularly early in a horse's career. Young horses' form will often fluctuate significantly as they gain experience and are introduced to different aspects of racing that include running at longer distances, racing on turf or in the slop, even getting dirt kicked in their faces or having to race in between horses. Concentrate on an overall look at the horse's history. Thus, if a two-year-old bounces by 2 points after its first good race, then by 4 points following its subsequent peak, you should not read that as a negative sign or as a tipoff that the next bounce following a peak will be even higher. More important is how the levels reached in his series of surges compare: smooth development, or a sharp break. This should indicate his ability to handle — or be hurt by — the recent peak.

When looking at two horses who have improved not as three-year-olds but as four- or five-year-olds, I am even stronger in preferring the one whose new top represents a less startling jump from what he was able to run earlier in his career. A horse who has improved 6 or 7 points in his four-year-old season alone is much more likely to have reached the end of the line than one who has moved just a point or two from his three-year-old season. A five-year-old has even less leeway.

A good illustration is the contrast between Soviet Problem and King Ruckus going into the 1994 Breeders' Cup Sprint. Soviet Problem as a three-year-old had run a 7½ in winning a sprint race in early spring at Golden Gate. The race clearly knocked her out, but in her fourth start as a four-year-old, she was able to surpass it, running a 7 in a losing effort April 16 at Golden Gate. This time she bounced in her next race, but followed that with two straight 7s and then an encouraging 6¾ on the turf at Hollywood Park. Again she reacted a bit and ran a 10 even while winning a stakes race at Del Mar, but over her next two races she worked her way back to a 7.

King Ruckus's best number at three had been a 10¼ in winning a race at Woodbine. He broke through that top in his first race at four, running a 6 in a win at Aqueduct in February. He bounced slightly, and then righted himself in July, eventually hitting a new top of 3¾ September 10 while winning a sprint stake at Philadelphia Park.

With Soviet Problem going off as one of the favorites in the betting throughout the country and King Ruckus going off in the vicinity of 30–1, on the surface it would have appeared as though King Ruckus was much the better bet of the two. After all, his peak was 3 points faster than the best race Soviet Problem had ever run, and following his previous peak — the 6 at Aqueduct — he had bounced by less than 2 points. A further look back at his career showed that his peak efforts at three were followed by bounces of 2½ points or less. There was a temptation to conclude that even with a bounce — and that possibility was reduced by the eight-week layoff he'd had since setting the new peak — he could outrun Soviet Problem, and at a tremendous overlay.

But in our seminar on the Breeders' Cup, we did not push this horse as an attractive longshot. King Ruckus had improved 6½ points already over his three-year-old top. And his new top was an awfully low number. All this made it likely he had reached the end of his development, and that the reaction today would be sharper than after his previous peaks.

Soviet Problem, on the other hand, had maintained good, steady form throughout the year, while only improving by ¾ of a point over her best race as a three-year-old. She was too short a price to want to bet her, but her chances of doing enough to outrun King Ruckus looked awfully good even considering the 3-point gap in their best numbers.

Thus, it was no big surprise when Soviet Problem ran a new

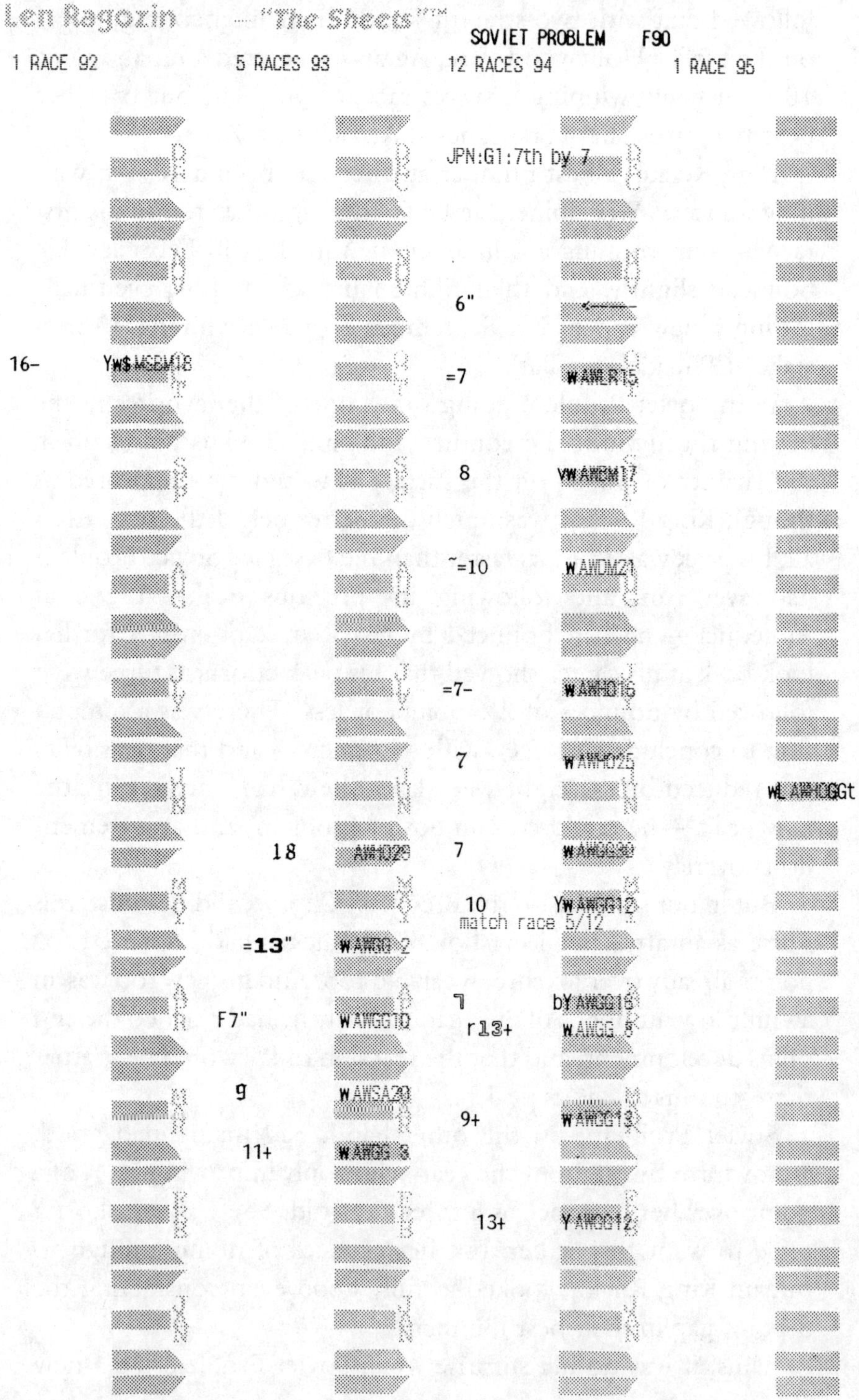

Len Ragozin — *"The Sheets"*™

SOVIET PROBLEM F90

1 RACE 92		5 RACES 93		12 RACES 94		1 RACE 95
				JPN:G1:7th by 7		
				6"		
16–	Yw$MSBM18			=7	wAWLR15	
				8	vwAWBM17	
				~=10	wAWDM21	
				=7–	wAWHO16	
				7	wAWHO25	wL AWHGGt
		18	AWHO28	7	wAWGG30	
				10	YwAWGG12	
				match race 5/12		
		=13"	wAWGG 2			
				7	bYAWGG16	
		F7"	wAWGG10	r13+	wAWGG 8	
		9	wAWSA20	9+	wAWGG13	
		11+	wAWGG 3			
				13+	YAWGG12	

Len Ragozin —"The Sheets"™

KING RUCKUS 90

	9 RACES 92	14 RACES 93	10 RACES 94	10 RACES 95
DEC				Y AWFGD
	gF/31- Y AWGR 6			
				AWFGD
NOV		G15- Y AWGR21		
	21 AWGR 7		10" V [arrow] 5	
	24" AWWO25	15" Yw AWGR27		
OCT	g.18+ w MSWO16	.15+ vm AWWO17		V AWWOD
	19+ Y MSWO 1	13- V AWWO 8		
SEP			4- vw AWPH10	
		.10+ vwBm AWWO 3		w AWWOD
AUG		^=19" AWWO21		
	^24+ Y AWWO16	16- V AWWO12		
			7- w AWWO 7	
	23" MSWO 2			
				vw AWWOD
JLY	^23+ MSWO19			
			7- Vw AWWO10	
				V AWFL 4
JUN				v AWSUD
			=12- AWFE 5	
MAY			8+ V AWWO21	v AWWOD
	.24+ [MSWO25		G13 AWWO24	v AWWOD
APR		21" Y AWGR18		
			8+ w AWWO10	Y AWWOD
		^14- AWGR 4		
MAR		11" wm AWAQMCS		
		11+ sm AWAQMCS	g.8- vm AWAQMEH	
FEB		12+ bvsTm 50AQMCS	6 vw AWAQMEH	
		14" bw 35AQMCS		
JAN		38 Ym 50AQMCS		

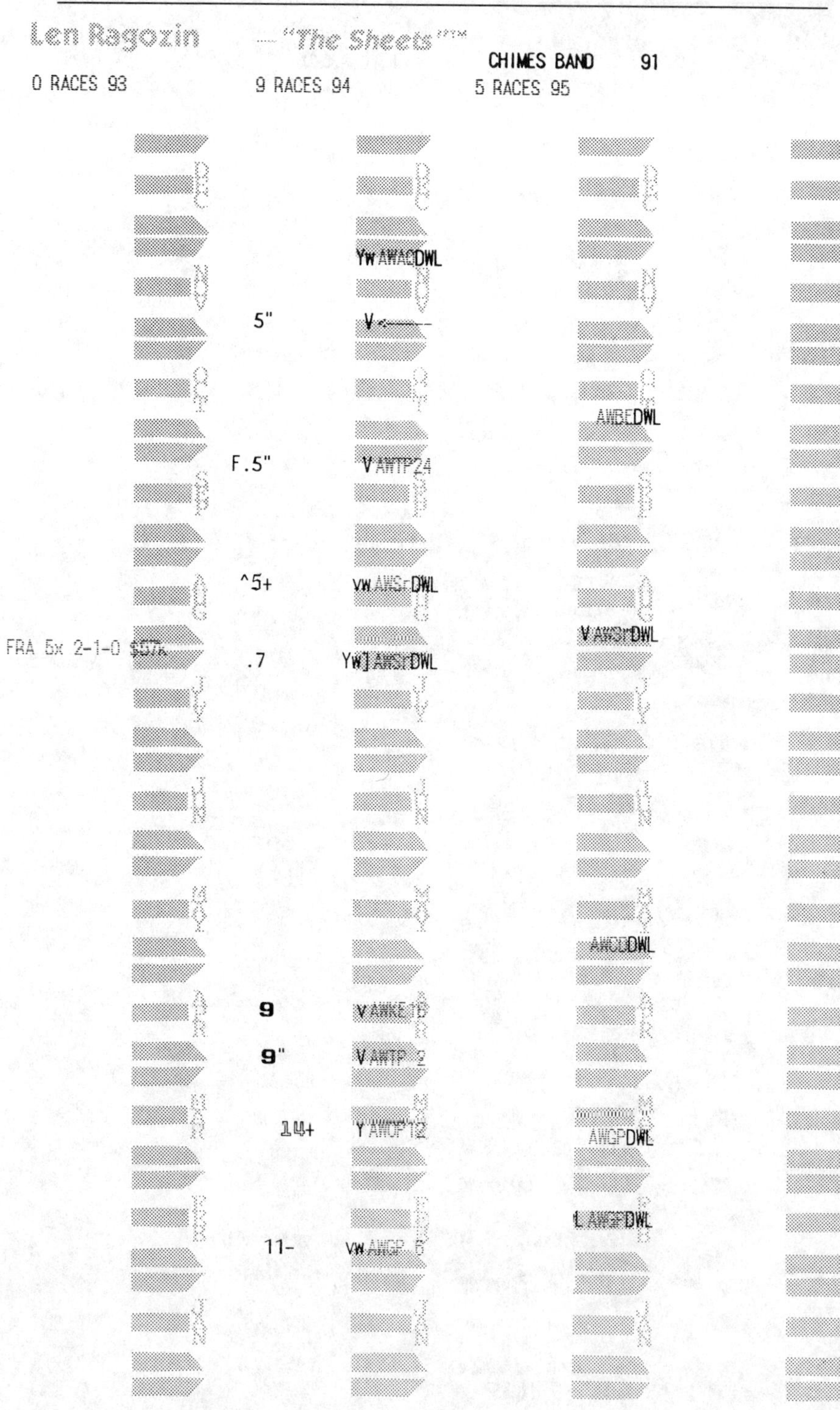
Len Ragozin — "The Sheets"™
CHIMES BAND 91
0 RACES 93
9 RACES 94
5 RACES 95
FRA 5x 2-1-0 $57k
5"
F.5"
^5+
.7
9
9"
14+
11-
YwAWAQDWL
V
VAWTP24
vwAWSrDWL
Yw]AWSrDWL
vAWKE15
VAWTP 2
YAWOP12
vwAWGP 6
AWBEDWL
VAWSrDWL
AWCDDWL
AWGPDWL
LAWGPDWL

top of 6½ in finishing a close second to Cherokee Run while King Ruckus finished up the track while bouncing almost 7 points to a 10½. (The value play in the race was actually the three-year-old Chimes Band, who went off around 20–1. The colt was stuck in Post 14, however, which, despite his reasonable early speed, assured that he would have to go wide around the turn. This probably cost him the race. He lost by one and three quarter lengths, finishing fourth while running a 5½.)

On the whole, small is better when it comes to improvements. Please note, however, that a horse who in this campaign has established a top of, say, 16, who then runs a 12 followed quickly by an 11 is not to be considered as having made only a 1-point improvement: the 12–11 is really the end of a 5-point movement from the level of 16.

Horses with greater consistency are often better bets than horses who can occasionally run numbers a couple of points faster. A horse consistently running within 2 or 3 points of his established top, just like the developing horse not bouncing badly immediately after a top, is demonstrating that his peak has not set him back significantly and he can probably improve further. A horse who is frequently running 4 or 5 points — or more — worse than his peak is telling you the opposite.

As much faith as Friedman and I have in the power of condition handicapping, occasionally we are reminded that when the value is there, you have to remember that this is a game built on identifying the horses with the best numbers relative to the odds you're getting on them. We got a rude reminder of that in the 1995 Kentucky Derby.

As a general rule, picking the Derby comes down to figuring out which horse is ready on the first Saturday in May to deliver his peak effort to that point in his young life. This is complicated by the fact that some trainers wind up getting that peak in a race before the Derby, which they enter just to convince themselves that their horse is good enough to run for the roses. Before he avoided this mistake with Winning Colors in the 1988 Derby, D. Wayne Lukas had become almost legendary for his knack for getting a peak so strong a race or two before the Derby that his horses were bound to bounce at Churchill Downs.

At our 1995 Derby seminar, Friedman told the audience that he liked two of Lukas's horses, Timber Country and Serena's Song. Since he wasn't thrilled with their probable odds, his value selection was Tejano Run.

The third Lukas horse, Thunder Gulch, was running uncoupled, and he was the one Friedman thought fit D. Wayne's old pattern: he badmouthed the horse as a Lukas "peak-out" who was gradually declining and who was unlikely to improve on his recent off-race in the Blue Grass Stakes.

What troubled Friedman was the big development Thunder Gulch had from the end of his two-year-old campaign into his first start as a three-year-old, followed by two backward moves. The 5– the horse ran in winning the Fountain of Youth was a big jump from his best race at two. The reaction to a 6½ while winning the Florida Derby was inevitable and forgivable, but the off-race in the Blue Grass, coming after it appeared Thunder Gulch had had enough time to recover, soured Friedman on his chances.

Had he known the horse would go off as one of the longshots in the race, Friedman probably would have hedged his opinion. But as the winner of the biggest three-year-old race in Florida and the beaten favorite in the Blue Grass, Thunder Gulch figured to be a short enough price in the Derby that the value would lie in going against him.

Then, on Derby Day, one of our associates, Eric Connell, was betting in New York and noticed that Thunder Gulch was going off at 28–1. Eric knows all about condition handicapping and reading a horse's line. But as he said after the race, "If it's five-to-two, I hate the line; if it's twenty-to-one, I like the line."

There were three horses in the race who had run their best numbers late in their two-year-old campaigns or early at three, then had gone slowly backward: Thunder Gulch, Suave Prospect, and Afternoon Delites. But throughout their careers Thunder Gulch had always been running a tick or so better than Suave

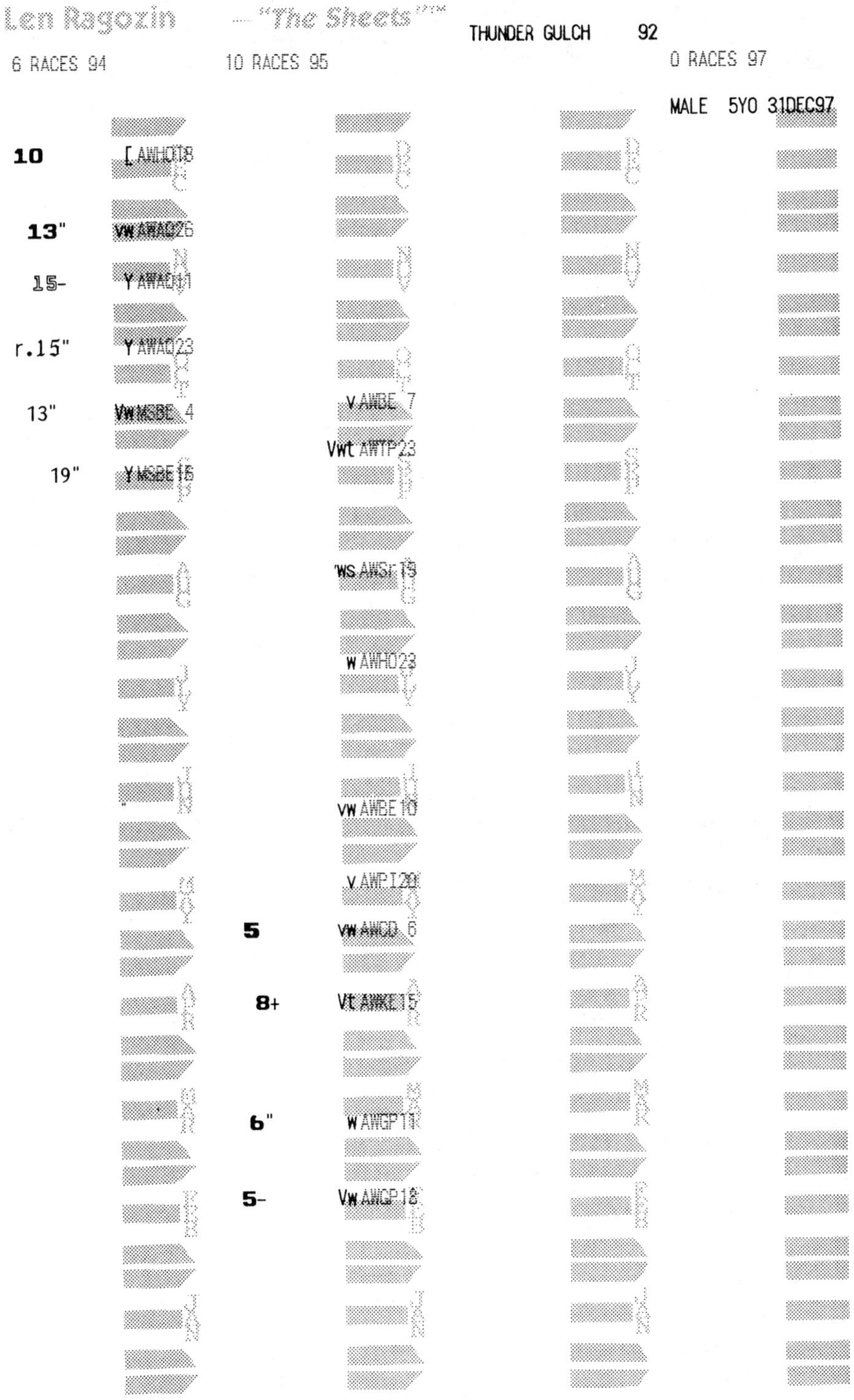

Len Ragozin — "The Sheets"™ THUNDER GULCH 92

6 RACES 94	10 RACES 95	0 RACES 97
		MALE 5YO 31DEC97
10 [AWHO18		
13" VW AWAQ26		
15- Y AWAQ11		
r.15" Y AWAQ23		
13" VW MSBE 4	V AWBE 7	
19" Y MSBE16	Vwt AWTP23	
	ws AWSr13	
	w AWHO23	
	vw AWBE10	
	v AWPI20	
	5 vw AWCD 6	
	8+ Vt AWKE15	
	6" w AWGP11	
	5- Vw AWGP18	

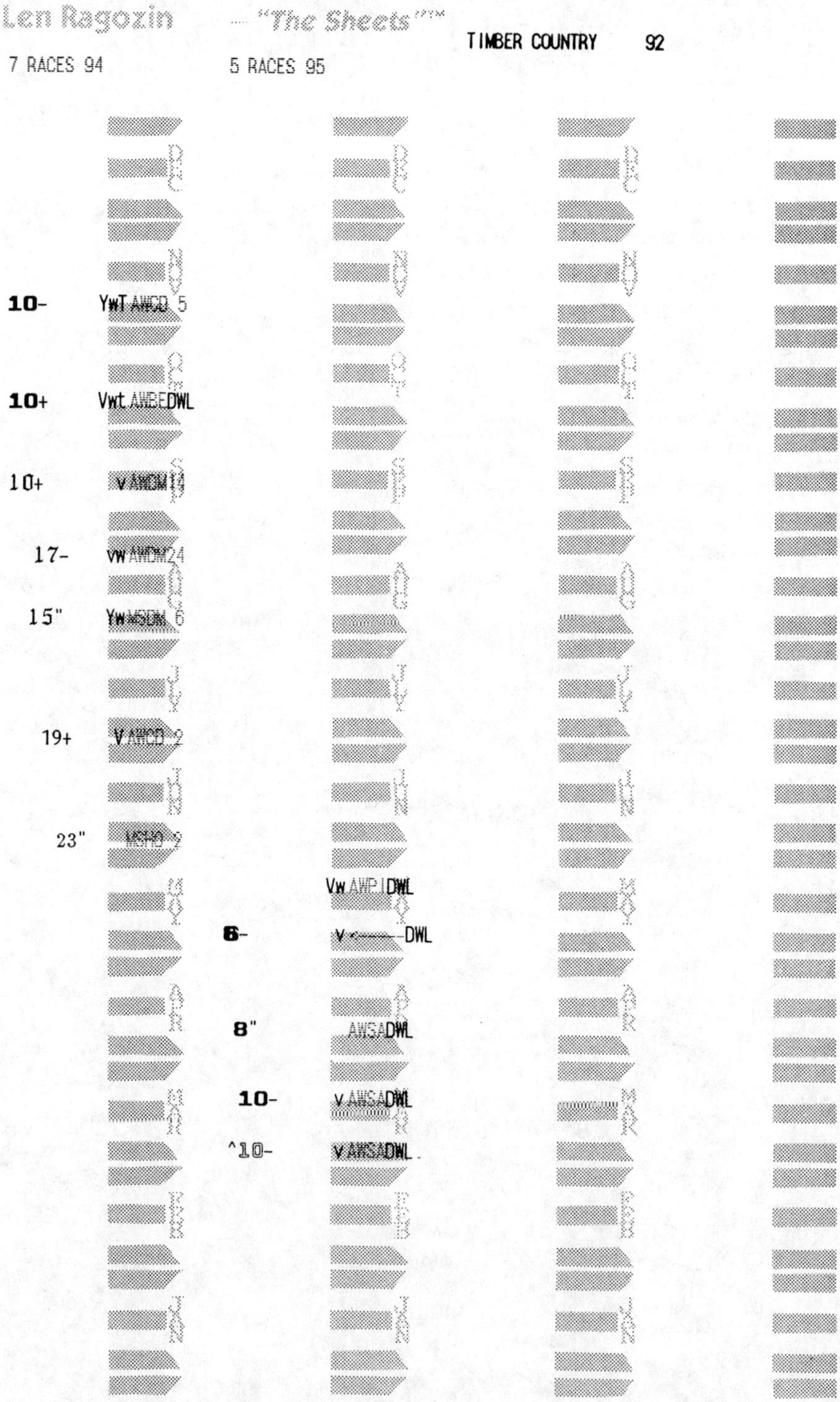

Len Ragozin — "The Sheets"™

TIMBER COUNTRY 92

7 RACES 94

5 RACES 95

10- YwT AWCD 5

10+ Vwt AWBEDWL

10+ v AWDM14

17- vw AWDM24

15" Yw MSDM 6

19+ V AWCD 2

23" MSHO 2

Vw AWPIDWL

6- v<------DWL

8" AWSADWL

10- v AWSADWL

^10- v AWSADWL

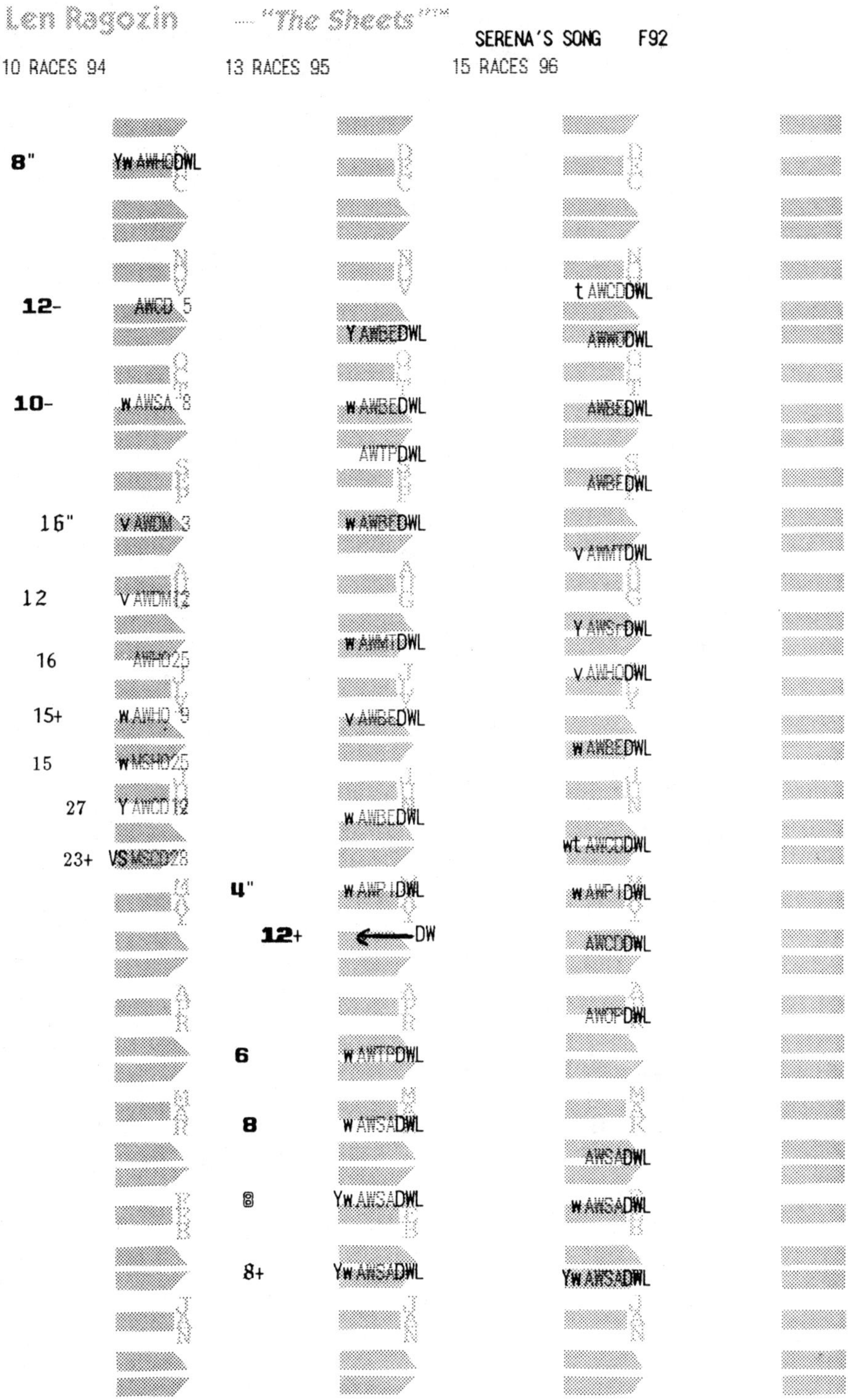

Len Ragozin "The Sheets"™

SERENA'S SONG F92

10 RACES 94 | 13 RACES 95 | 15 RACES 96

10 RACES 94

8" YwAWHQDWL
12- AWCD 5
10- wAWSA 8
16" vAWDM 3
12 vAWDM12
16 AWHO25
15+ wAWHO 9
15 wMSHO25
27 YAWCD12
23+ VSMSCD28

13 RACES 95

YAWBEDWL
wAWBEDWL
AWTPDWL
wAWBEDWL
wAWMTDWL
vAWBEDWL
wAWBEDWL
4" wAWP IDWL
12+ ← DW
6 wAWTPDWL
8 wAWSADWL
8 YwAWSADWL
8+ YwAWSADWL

15 RACES 96

tAWCDDWL
AWWODWL
AWBEDWL
AWBEDWL
vAWMTDWL
YAWSrDWL
vAWHODWL
wAWBEDWL
wtAWCDDWL
wAWP IDWL
AWCDDWL
AWOPDWL
AWSADWL
wAWSADWL
YwAWSADWL

Len Ragozin "The Sheets"™

SUAVE PROSPECT 92

10 RACES 94		11 RACES 95		7 RACES 96
11+	vwAWCRLAS			
=18	YAWCRLAS			
				YmAWAQNPZ
14+	vwAWCR 3			
				YAWWONPZ
			AWCRLAS	
17+	AWCR15			
				YAWBENPZ
17+	vAWCR24		AWTPNPZ	
				vmAWBENPZ
.21"	YAWCR10			
			vAWBENPZ	
				YmAWSrNPZ
22	TAWCR20			
F24	YwTMSCR30		vmAWMTNPZ	vAWSrNPZ
				mAWBENPZ
			LmAWMTNPZ	
.20+	vMSCR15			
20+	$ 10CR 2			
			AWBENPZ	
		8	V<------NPZ	
		8	vAWKENPZ	
		8-	YAWGPNPZ	
		5"	vAWGPNPZ	
		7+	vwAWGPNPZ	

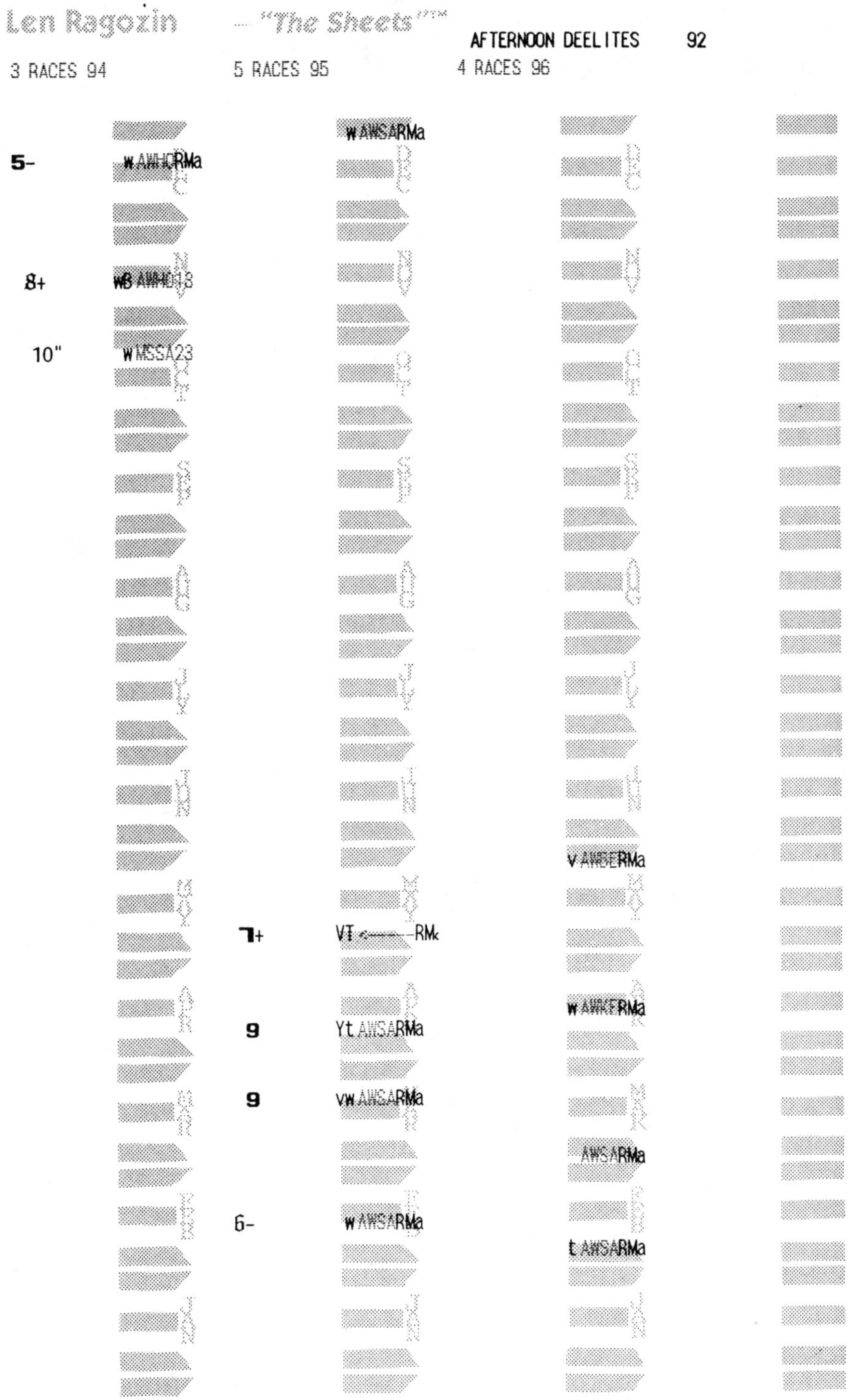

Len Ragozin — "The Sheets"™

AFTERNOON DEELITES 92

3 RACES 94		5 RACES 95		4 RACES 96
			wAWSARMa	
5-	wAWHCRMa			
8+	wB AWHC13			
10"	WMSSA23			
				v AWSERMa
		7+	VT ←——RMk	
				w AWKERMa
		9	Yt AWSARMa	
		9	vw AWSARMa	
				AWSARMa
		6-	wAWSARMa	
				t AWSARMa

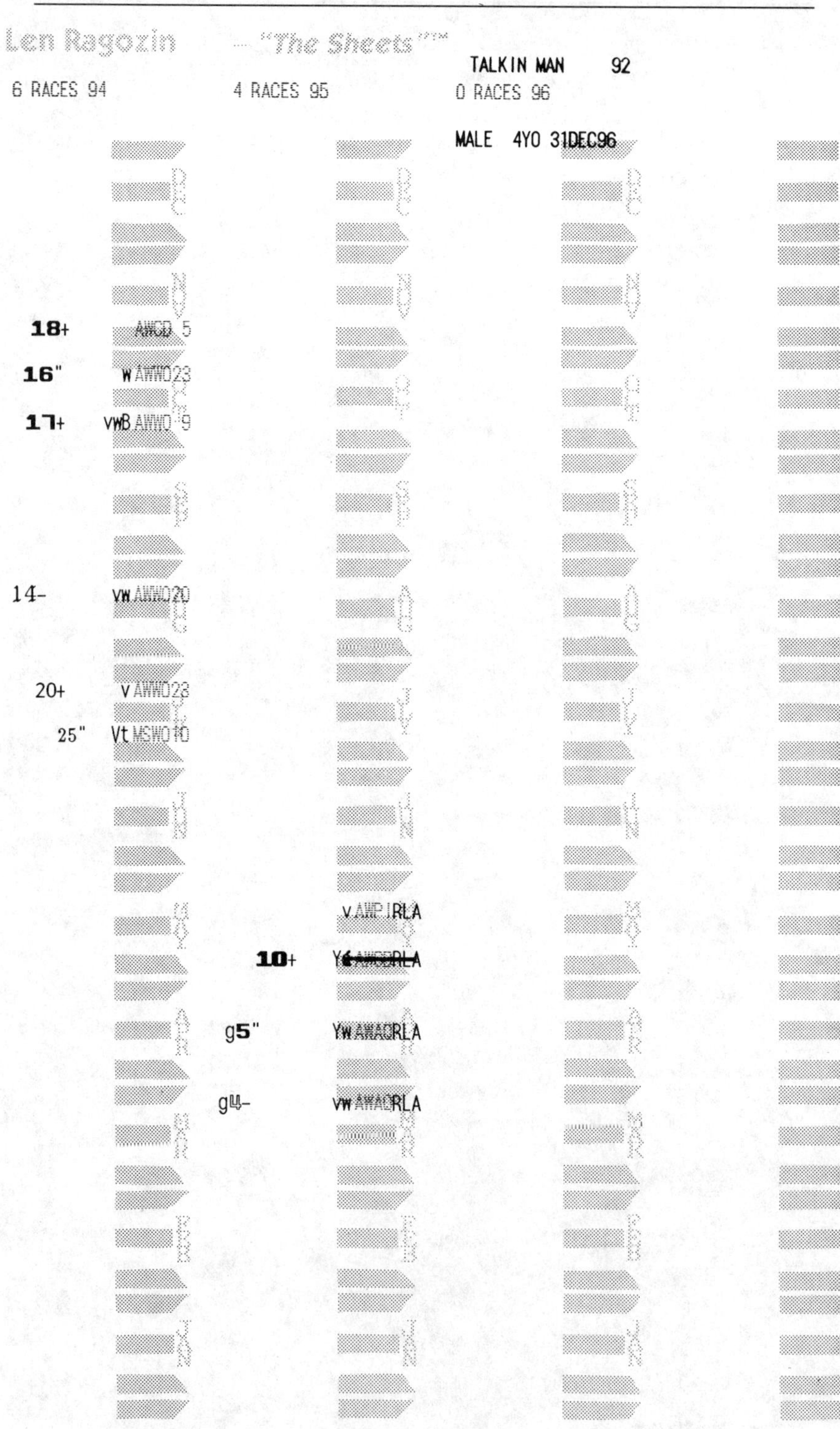
Len Ragozin "The Sheets"™
TALKIN MAN 92
6 RACES 94
4 RACES 95
0 RACES 96
MALE 4YO 31DEC96
18+ AWCD 5
16" wAWWO23
17+ vwBAWWO 9
14- vwAWWO20
20+ vAWWO23
25" VtMSWO10
vAWP RLA
10+ RLA
g5" YwAWACRLA
g4- vwAWACRLA

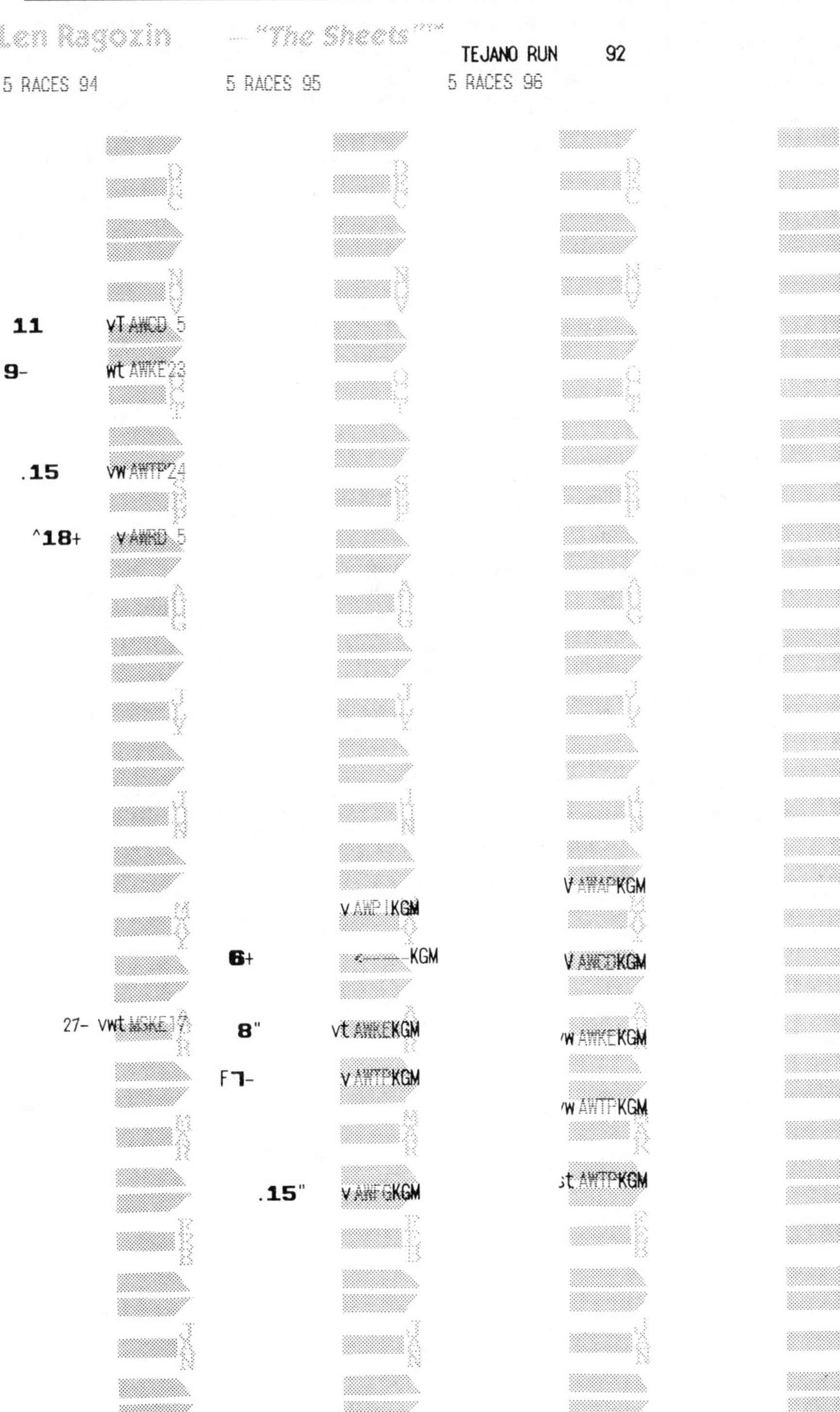

Len Ragozin "The Sheets"™
TEJANO RUN 92
5 RACES 94
5 RACES 95
5 RACES 96
11 vT AWCD 5
9- wt AWKE23
.15 vw AWTP24
^18+ v AWRD 5
27- vwt WSKE17
6+ v AWPJKGM
KGM
8" vt AWKEKGM
F7- v AWTPKGM
.15" v AWFGKGM
V AWAPKGM
V AWCDKGM
vw AWKEKGM
vw AWTPKGM
st AWTPKGM

Value of Race: $957,400 Winner $707,400; second $145,000; third $70,000; fourth $35,000. Mutuel Pool $12,851,173.00 Exacta Pool $5,476,539.00 Trifecta Pool $3,921,394.00

Last Raced	Horse	M/Eqt.	A.	Wt	PP	¼	½	¾	1	Str	Fin	Jockey	Odds $1	
15Apr95 ^{7}Kee^{4}	Thunder Gulch	b	3	126	16	$6^{1\frac{1}{2}}$	$5^{\frac{1}{2}}$	$5^{\frac{1}{2}}$	$3^{1\frac{1}{2}}$	$1^{1\frac{1}{2}}$	$1^{2\frac{1}{4}}$	Stevens G L	24.50	4-wide, stiff drive
15Apr95 ^{7}Kee^{3}	Tejano Run	L	3	126	14	13^{hd}	12^{1}	10^{hd}	6^{hd}	3^{hd}	2^{hd}	Bailey J D	8.60	*
8Apr95 ^{5}SA^{4}	Timber Country		3	126	15	$14^{\frac{1}{2}}$	13^{hd}	12^{hd}	11^{hd}	10^{hd}	$3^{\frac{3}{4}}$	Day P	b-3.40	*
8Apr95 ^{5}SA^{3}	Jumron-GB	L	3	126	10	8^{hd}	$9^{1\frac{1}{2}}$	$9^{1\frac{1}{2}}$	$4^{\frac{1}{2}}$	$5^{\frac{1}{2}}$	4^{hd}	Almeida G F	5.60	*
23Apr95 ^{11}Hia^{2}	Mecke	Lb	3	126	18	$16^{\frac{1}{2}}$	$16^{1\frac{1}{2}}$	19	$13^{1\frac{1}{2}}$	$8^{\frac{1}{2}}$	$5^{\frac{1}{2}}$	Davis R G	f-11.60	Mild rally inside
20Apr95 New^{3}	Eltish		3	126	7	10^{1}	10^{hd}	11^{hd}	9^{2}	$6^{\frac{1}{2}}$	6^{3}	Delahoussaye E	10.90	*
15Apr95 ^{9}Aqu^{2}	Knockadoon		3	126	2	19	19	18^{hd}	$14^{\frac{1}{2}}$	$12^{\frac{1}{2}}$	7^{nk}	McCarron C J	f-11.60	*Slow start, bumped
8Apr95 ^{5}SA^{2}	Afternoon Deelites		3	126	12	7^{hd}	6^{hd}	$6^{\frac{1}{2}}$	5^{hd}	7^{hd}	8^{nk}	Desormeaux K J	8.70	*
19Apr95 New^{3}	Citadeed	L	3	126	19	$3^{\frac{1}{2}}$	$7^{\frac{1}{2}}$	2^{hd}	$7^{\frac{1}{2}}$	$9^{\frac{1}{2}}$	$9^{\frac{3}{4}}$	Maple E	f-11.60	Bid far turn, tired
8Apr95 ^{5}SA^{6}	In Character-GB	L	3	126	9	17^{1}	15^{hd}	17^{hd}	$12^{1\frac{1}{2}}$	13^{2}	$10^{\frac{1}{2}}$	Antley C W	f-11.60	*
15Apr95 ^{7}Kee^{2}	Suave Prospect	L	3	126	6	$9^{1\frac{1}{2}}$	11^{4}	14^{1}	$8^{\frac{1}{2}}$	$11^{\frac{1}{2}}$	$11^{\frac{1}{2}}$	Krone J A	13.10	*
15Apr95 ^{9}Aqu^{1}	Talkin Man		3	126	11	$4^{1\frac{1}{2}}$	3^{hd}	4^{hd}	2^{hd}	2^{1}	$12^{\frac{1}{2}}$	Smith M E	4.00	*
22Apr95 ^{9}OP^{1}	Dazzling Falls	Lb	3	126	1	12^{hd}	$14^{\frac{1}{2}}$	$13^{1\frac{1}{2}}$	19	15^{1}	13^{nk}	Gomez G K	27.60	*
5Feb95 KYO^{1}	Ski Captain	f	3	126	17	$18^{\frac{1}{2}}$	17^{hd}	16^{1}	$15^{1\frac{1}{2}}$	14^{1}	$14^{1\frac{1}{2}}$	Take Y	f-11.60	*Off slowly
15Apr95 ^{7}Kee^{5}	Jambalaya Jazz	f	3	126	5	$15^{\frac{1}{2}}$	$18^{1\frac{1}{2}}$	15^{hd}	16^{hd}	16^{2}	15^{nk}	Perret C	a-18.00	*
1Apr95 ^{11}TP^{1}	Serena's Song		3	121	13	1^{hd}	$1^{1\frac{1}{2}}$	$1^{\frac{1}{2}}$	1^{hd}	4^{1}	$16^{1\frac{1}{2}}$	Nakatani C S	b-3.40	*
1Apr95 ^{10}Hia^{1}	Pyramid Peak		3	126	3	5^{1}	8^{hd}	8^{hd}	17^{1}	17^{6}	17^{6}	McCauley W H	a-18.00	Gave way
8Apr95 ^{5}SA^{5}	Lake George		3	126	8	11^{1}	4^{1}	7^{1}	10^{hd}	18^{12}	18^{21}	Sellers S J	f-11.60	*
15Apr95 ^{7}Kee^{1}	Wild Syn	Lf	3	126	4	$2^{\frac{1}{2}}$	$2^{1\frac{1}{2}}$	$3^{\frac{1}{2}}$	$18^{\frac{1}{2}}$	19	19	Romero R P	18.80	*

a-Coupled: Jambalaya Jazz and Pyramid Peak.
b-Coupled: Timber Country and Serena's Song.
f-Mutuel Field: Mecke and Knockadoon and Citadeed and In Character-GB and Ski Captain and Lake George.

OFF AT 5:33 Start Good. Won driving. Time, :22^{2}, :45^{4}, 1:10^{1}, 1:35^{3}, 2:01^{1} Track fast.

$2 Mutuel Prices:			
11–THUNDER GULCH	51.00	24.20	12.20
10–TEJANO RUN		10.20	6.80
2B–TIMBER COUNTRY (b–entry)			3.80

$2 EXACTA 11–10 PAID $480.00 $2 TRIFECTA 11–10–2 PAID $2,099.20

Ch. c, (May), by Gulch–Line of Thunder, by Storm Bird. Trainer Lukas D Wayne. Bred by Brant Peter M (Ky).

THUNDER GULCH, away in good order, was reserved while within easy striking distance until near the end of the backstretch, made a run four wide approaching the stretch and, after putting TALKIN MAN away with a furlong remaining, was kept to pressure to increase his advantage. TEJANO RUN, unhurried while outrun early, rallied between horses racing into the far turn, came out to continue his bid approaching the stretch and continued on with good energy to gain the place. TIMBER COUNTRY, outrun into the backstretch, dropped back after moving up along the inside at the far turn, came out looking for room through the upper stretch and finished gamely while angling in between horses. JUMRON brushed with AFTERNOON DEELITES early, raced five wide while advancing nearing the stretch but failed to sustain his bid in a long drive. MECKE, outrun to the far turn, moved up inside horses around the far turn and into the stretch and continued on with good energy. ELTISH, in close after the start, rallied from between horses nearing the stretch, came out for the drive but hung under pressure. KNOCKADOON, bumped after breaking slowly, raced between horses to the stretch and failed to seriously menace after angling inside for the drive. AFTERNOON DEELITES appeared to try and savage JUMRON after brushing with that rival near the eighth–pole the first time, reached an easy striking position outside horses at the first turn, continued five wide while between horses to the stretch and weakened during the drive. CITADEED, close up early, made a run between horses approaching the far turn but tired through the drive. IN CHARACTER, in close after the start, angled out approaching the stretch but failed to reach serious contention. SUAVE PROSPECT saved ground to the backstretch, angled out seven wide after going a half, continued very wide while remaining within striking distance for a mile and gave way. TALKIN MAN, close up early while saving ground, caught SERENA'S SONG from the inside leaving the far turn, held on well to midstretch and tired. DAZZLING FALLS bumped KNOCKADOON after the start, saved ground into the backstretch, then passed tired horses after angling out very wide for the drive. SKI CAPTAIN, off slowly, was never close. JAMBALAYA JAZZ, always outrun, was checked between horses on the far turn. SERENA'S SONG, away alertly, was pressed while showing speed in the three path to the backstretch, held on well for a mile while continuing out from the rail and tired badly. PYRAMID PEAK saved ground for six furlongs and had nothing left. LAKE GEORGE, in close after the start, moved up six wide down the backstretch but was finished before reaching the stretch. WILD SYN showed good early foot along the inside, came out between horses when unable to stay with SERENA'S SONG around the first turn, raced forwardly to the turn, stopped suddenly and was eased.

Prospect. Afternoon Delites was the only horse in the Derby field with a number as good as Thunder Gulch's peak going two turns. (Talkin Man's 4− came in a one-turn mile.) I could argue that there were reasons to like Thunder Gulch better than Afternoon Delites, but even if you decided to bet both horses, the odds steered you toward Thunder Gulch.

If you did a simple analysis of who was best by the numbers going into the race, without the more sophisticated condition-theory approach, you had yourself a $58 winner in the Kentucky Derby. When the numbers can point out that kind of overlay, there's no reason to get too theoretical in how you interpret horses' lines.

11

Comebacks and Throw-outs

HORSES TEND TO RUN more bad efforts than good ones, with the exception of stakes horses, whose trainers usually give them enough time between races to let them run near their best. Both good and bad races are often run in clusters. This presents another aspect of condition handicapping: trying to pinpoint when a horse will recover from a period of bad form.

A recovery line is the term we use to describe horses who went off form but whose most recent races suggest they're ready to start climbing back to a peak. The typical recovery horse is one who went bad right after a peak, and then gradually righted himself, often after a layoff. Once again, it is best if the turn-the-corner improvement comes gradually rather than in a big jump.

A recent example of a classic recovery line play was Summer Ensign in the 1995 Seneca Handicap at Saratoga. Summer Ensign ran a top of 8– on turf shortly before he laid off early in his five-year-old campaign. After a year off, he ran a 12½ in his first start back. For two months after that effort, he ran races between 13½ and 15. Then on July 26 he ran a 12–, ¾ of a point better than his initial outing as a six-year-old.

Our analysis has long been that when a horse returns to, or

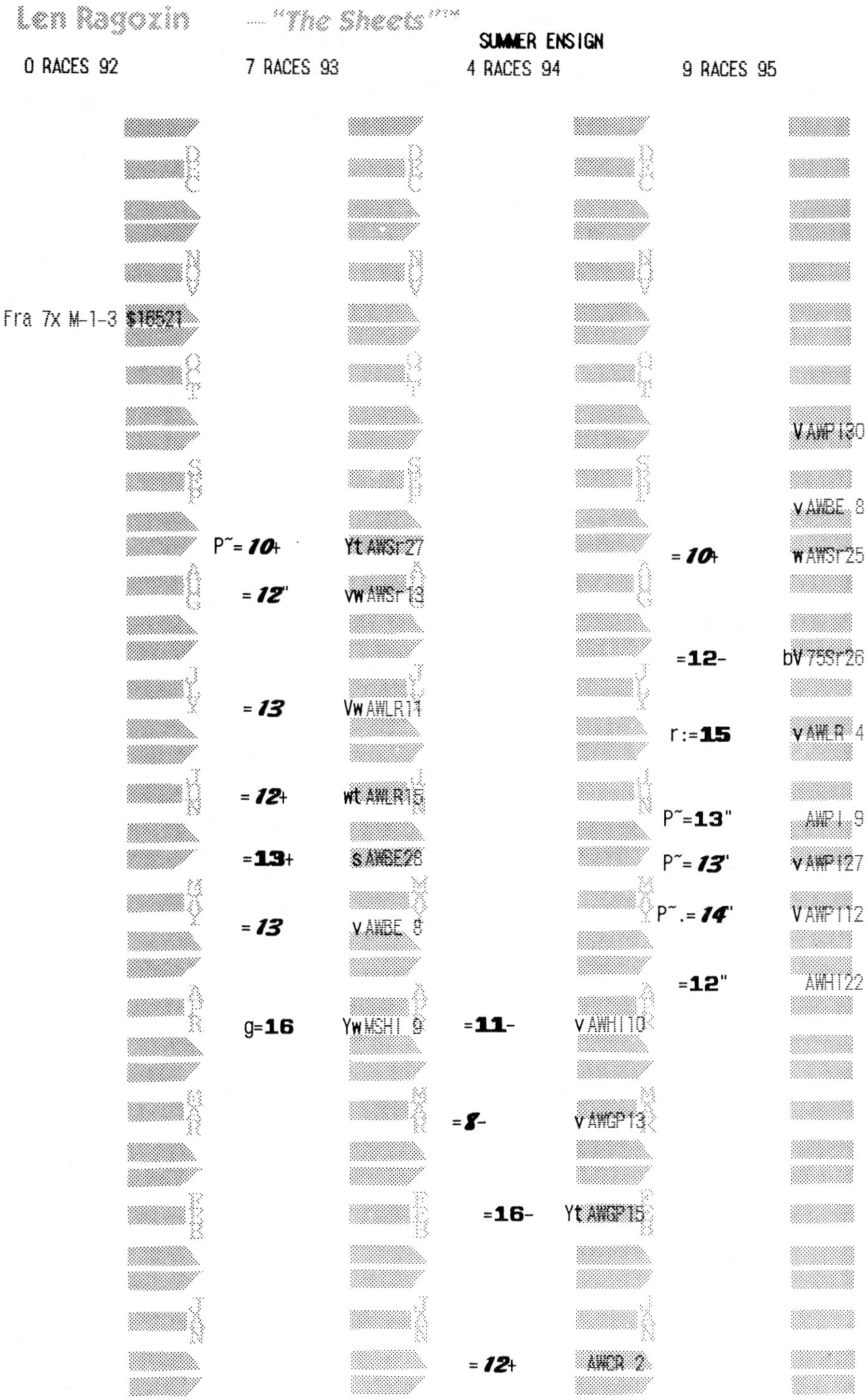

Len Ragozin — "The Sheets"™

SUMMER ENSIGN

0 RACES 92	7 RACES 93		4 RACES 94		9 RACES 95	
						VAWP130
						vAWBE 8
	P~=10+	YtAWSr27			=10+	wAWSr25
	=12"	vwAWSr13				
					=12-	bV75Sr26
	=13	VwAWLR11				
					r:=15	vAWLR 4
	=12+	wtAWLR15				
					P~=13"	AWPL 9
	=13+	sAWBE28			P~=13'	vAWP127
					P~.=14'	VAWP112
	=13	vAWBE 8				
					=12"	AWH122
	g=16	YwMSHI 9	=11-	vAWHI10		
			=8-	vAWGP13		
			=16-	YtAWGP15		
			=12+	AWCR 2		

Fra 7x M-1-3 $16521

DEC NOV OCT SEP AUG JLY JUN MAY APR MAR FEB JAN

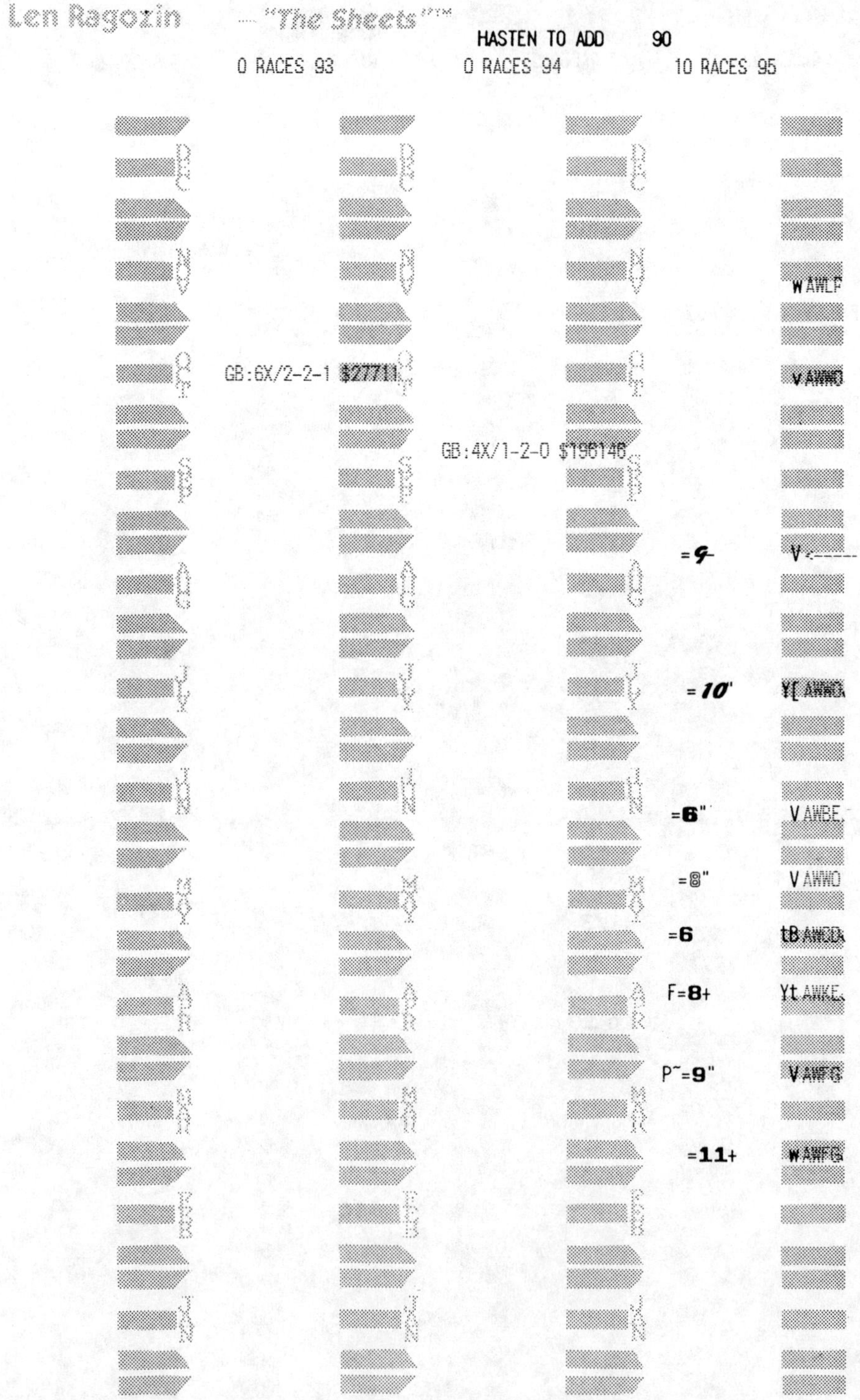

Len Ragozin "The Sheets"™

HASTEN TO ADD 90

0 RACES 93 0 RACES 94 10 RACES 95

GB:6X/2-2-1 $27711

GB:4X/1-2-0 $196146

=9 V

=10 Y[AWWO

=6" V AWBE

=8" V AWWO

=6 tB AWCD

F=8+ Yt AWKE

P~=9" V AWFG

=11+ w AWFG

w AWLF

v AWWO

improves slightly on, his first or second effort after a layoff, one of his next two efforts more than likely will be a nice forward move to his best race of this campaign.

Because none of his recent efforts figured to be good enough to win the Seneca, Summer Ensign went off at over 19–1 odds, even though he was part of a coupled entry (by himself he would probably have been over 40–1). Carrying light weight and getting a ground-saving rail trip, Summer Ensign eked out a nose win over the solid fast horse on our sheets, Hasten to Add. This was another example of the accuracy of the numbers (a ¾-point move) paying off big.

But this subtle development didn't matter to a lot of our customers. In fact, several of our "purist" condition handicappers, including Len Friedman, resented the fact that many *Sheet* players hit the $258 exacta in the race by keying on the second-place finisher, Hasten to Add, at 4–1 and throwing in Summer Ensign rather randomly among others in their exacta play!

Another type of recovery line is a horse that has been in continuous training and is circling back to a previous peak effort. Here is one who came up as a bet during my two-month public trial of *The Sheets* in October–November 1996.

Hongkong Lady is a good example of this type of "recovery." She had a very solid pattern since her last peak effort of 21+ in June. Her numbers went back gradually to the 26 level and then gradually improved to a 23. The only race out of line was her last effort of a 30, and our betting approach has always been to forgive any single off effort by a horse with an otherwise solid pattern. The 23 she ran was the kind of small forward move from her previous form that is subtle enough that, when combined with the subsequent off effort, produces — in many cases — a big overlay.

Hongkong Lady paid $27.40 to win in a race where only one other horse, the 8–5 favorite American Boots, had a recent effort better than 22 — and that horse spotted Hongkong Lady two pounds in weight, was several post positions further outside, and figured to be tired from recent tops.

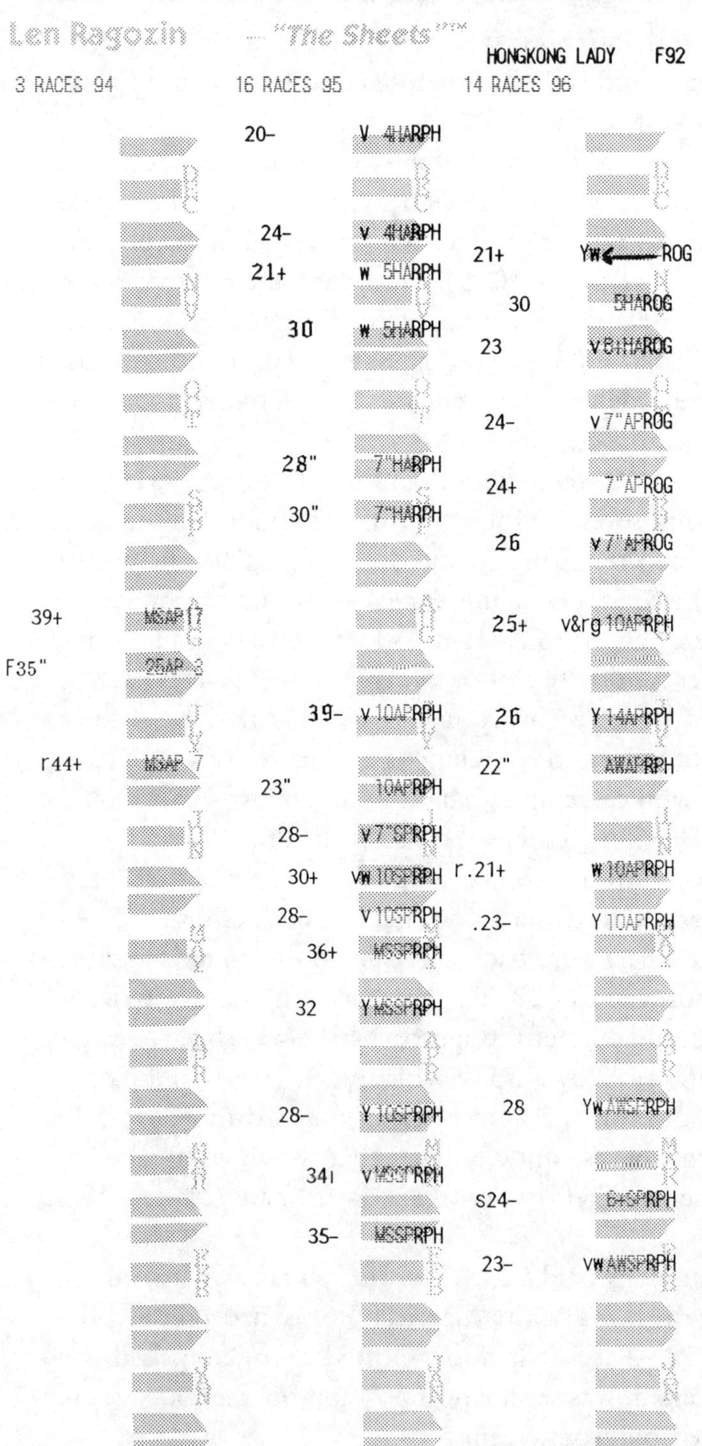
Len Ragozin — "The Sheets"™
HONGKONG LADY F92
3 RACES 94
16 RACES 95
14 RACES 96
20- V 4HARPH
24- V 4HARPH
21+ W 5HARPH
30 W 5HARPH
28" 7"HARPH
30" 7"HARPH
39- V 10APRPH
23" 10APRPH
28- V7"SPRPH
30+ VW 10SPRPH
28- V 10SPRPH
36+ MSSPRPH
32 YMSSPRPH
28- Y 10SPRPH
34I VMSSPRPH
35- MSSPRPH
21+ YW ROG
30 5HAROG
23 V 8HAROG
24- V 7"APROG
24+ 7"APROG
26 V 7"APROG
25+ V&rg 10APRPH
26 Y 14APRPH
22" AWAPRPH
r.21+ W 10APRPH
.23- Y 10APRPH
28 YW AWSPRPH
s24- B+SPRPH
23- VW AWSPRPH
39+ MSAP 17
F35" 25AP 3
r44+ MSAP 7

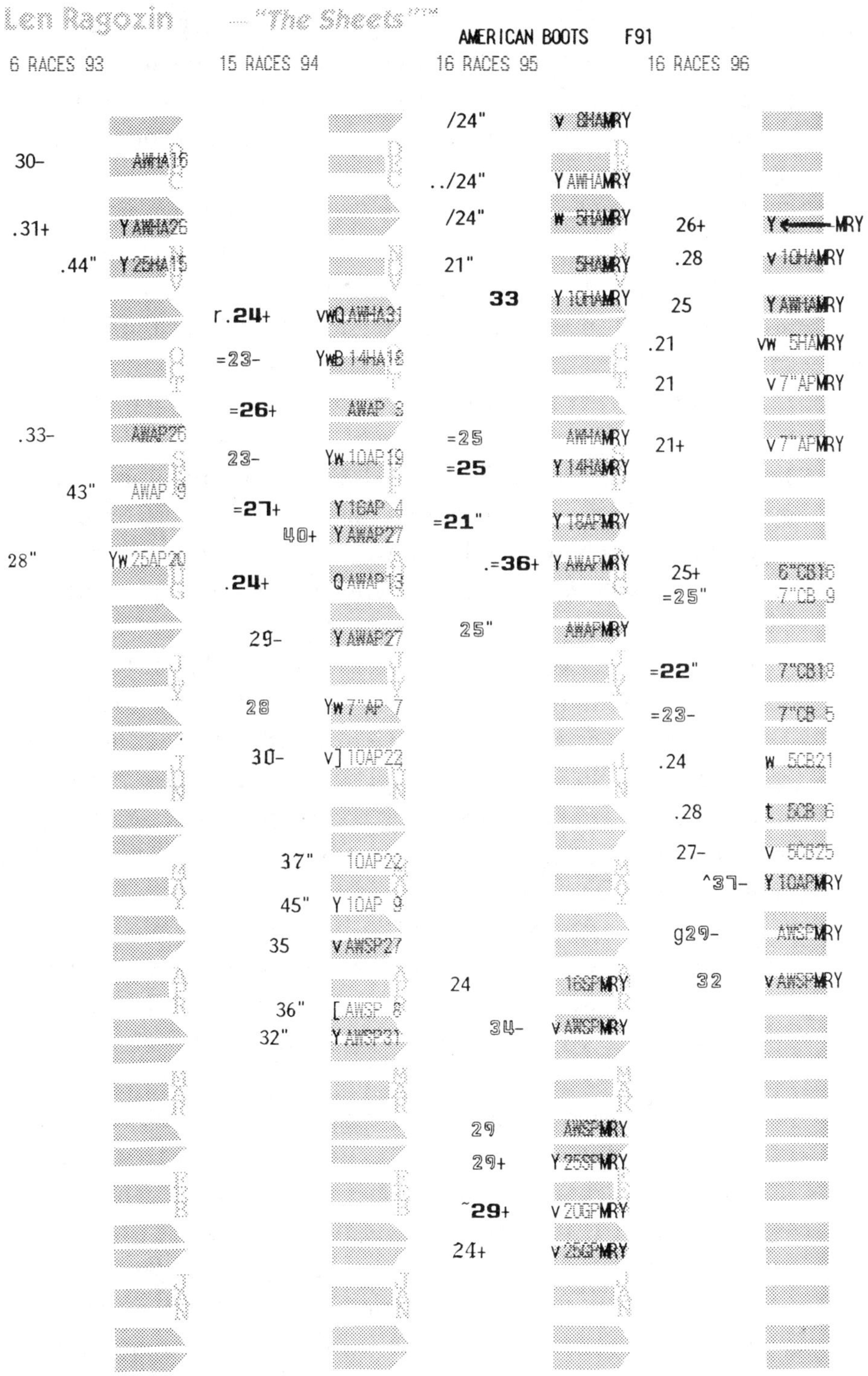

Len Ragozin — "The Sheets"™

AMERICAN BOOTS F91

6 RACES 93		15 RACES 94		16 RACES 95		16 RACES 96	
30–	AWHA16	r.24+	vwQ AWHA31	/24"	v 8HAMRY	26+	Y ←— MRY
.31+	Y AWHA26	=23-	YwB 14HA18	../24"	Y AWHAMRY	.28	v 10HAMRY
.44"	Y 25HA15	=26+	AWAP 8	/24"	w 5HAMRY	25	Y AWHAMRY
.33-	AWAP25	23-	Yw 10AP19	21"	5HAMRY	.21	vw 5HAMRY
43"	AWAP 9	=27+	Y 16AP 4	33	Y 10HAMRY	21	v 7"APMRY
28"	Yw 25AP20	40+	Y AWAP27	=25	AWHAMRY	21+	v 7"APMRY
		.24+	Q AWAP13	=25	Y 14HAMRY	25+	6"CB16
		29-	Y AWAP27	=21"	Y 18APMRY	=25"	7"CB 9
		28	Yw 7"AP 7	.=36+	Y AWAPMRY	=22"	7"CB18
		30-	v] 10AP22	25"	AWAPMRY	=23-	7"CB 5
		37"	10AP22	24	16SPMRY	.24	w 5CB21
		45"	Y 10AP 9	34-	v AWSPMRY	.28	t 5CB 6
		35	v AWSP27	29	AWSPMRY	27-	v 5CB25
		36"	[AWSP 8	29+	Y 25SPMRY	^37-	Y 10APMRY
		32"	Y AWSP31	˜29+	v 20GPMRY	g29-	AWSPMRY
				24+	v 25GPMRY	32	v AWSPMRY

Our next example, Pucker, shows two recovery lines on his sheet. The first line is a type that is usually better for betting purposes, except that in his case it took a lot longer than it normally would to cash a bet. The second line is less typical, but it produced a stream of wins.

Pucker showed sudden improvement in his first two starts as a four-year-old, running consecutive 17s, then six races later advanced ¼ of a point to a 17–. At that point, his form caved in, and after six straight miserable races, he was sidelined for the last five months of 1992.

His first start at five produced a 19–. That number was distinctly better than his most recent races and stamped him as a potential recovery horse. The only drawback was that the sudden appearance of a number so close to his top might cause a temporary setback. This sort of horse will often run well not immediately after that first strong effort after a layoff but in a month or two — or following three or four subsequent races.

Pucker actually won his next start, although he slipped to a 20¼. The race that indicated to me he was ready to do some good running came two starts later, when he repeated the 19–. He now had overcome any minor setback caused by coming so close to his top right off the layoff. That made him a good proposition in his upcoming starts to equal or even — considering that he was well rested and not too old — exceed his top.

In this case, Pucker remained in solid form, running a 19– twice and an 18– among his next five starts, but he didn't produce the breakthrough I'd anticipated until four races after that, when he ran a 15½ in beating a field of $6,500 claimers at Pimlico.

That new top was followed by a bounce to a 26¼ in his next start on the turf, and Pucker, who had been racing every two weeks on average, now went to the sidelines for five weeks. He came back, crammed six races into fifty-one days, and although he won a race against $5,000 claimers, was not approaching his new top.

Then, off what must have seemed to him a lengthy layoff — eighteen days between races — he ran an 18¼ in beating another

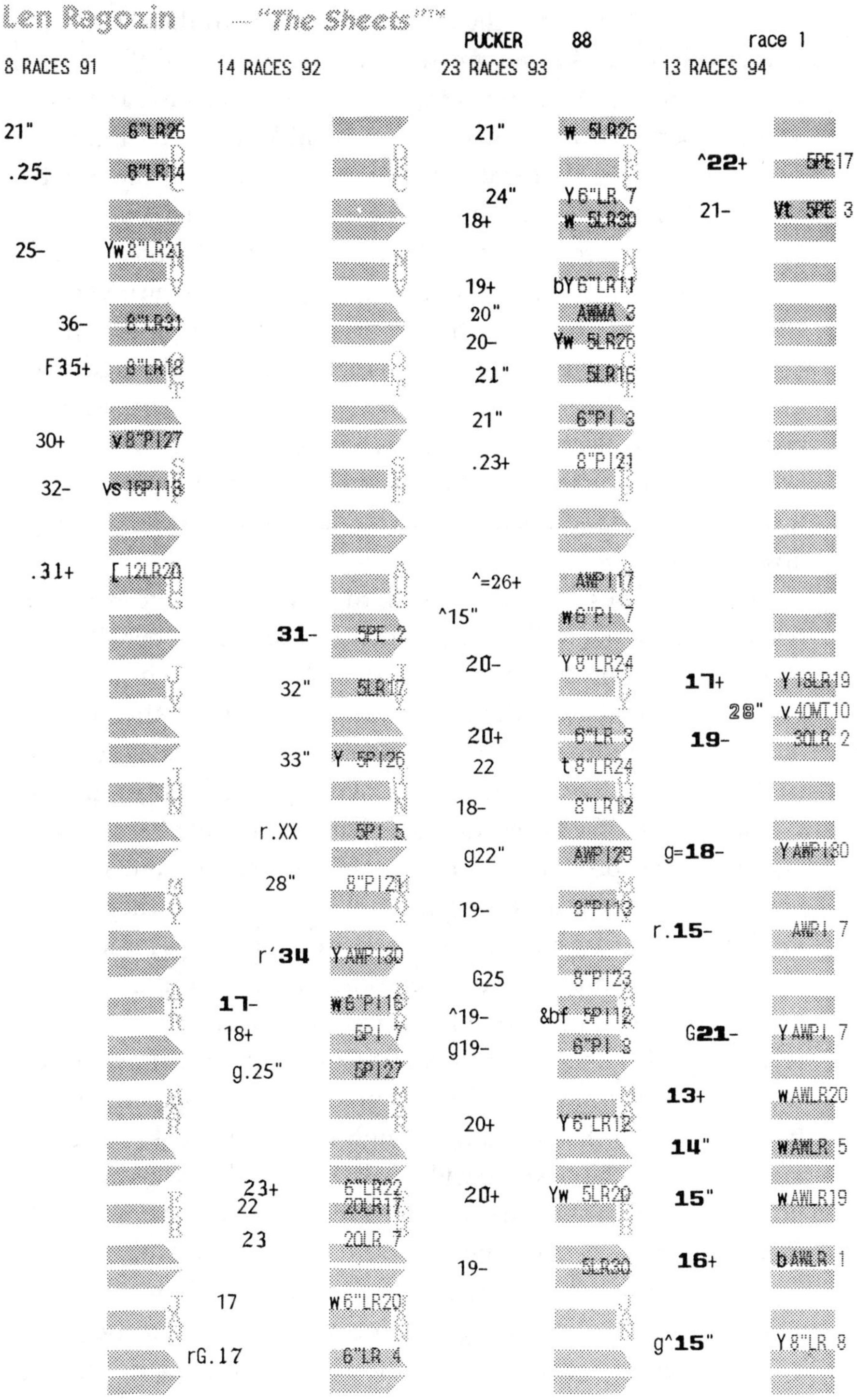

Len Ragozin — "The Sheets"™

PUCKER 88 race 1

8 RACES 91

Figure	Race
21"	6"LR26
.25-	8"LR14
25-	Yw8"LR21
36-	8"LR31
F35+	8"LR18
30+	v8"PI27
32-	vs16PI18
.31+	[12LR20

14 RACES 92

Figure	Race
31-	5PE 2
32"	5LR17
33"	Y 5PI26
r.XX	5PI 5
28"	8"PI21
r'34	YAWPI30
17-	w6"PI16
18+	5PI 7
g.25"	5PI27
23+	6"LR22
22	20LR17
23	20LR 7
17	w6"LR20
rG.17	6"LR 4

23 RACES 93

Figure	Race
21"	w 5LR26
24"	Y6"LR 7
18+	w 5LR30
19+	bY6"LR11
20"	AWMA 3
20-	Yw 5LR26
21"	5LR16
21"	6"PI 3
.23+	8"PI21
^=26+	AWPI17
^15"	w6"PI 7
20-	Y8"LR24
20+	6"LR 3
22	t8"LR24
18-	8"LR12
g22"	AWPI29
19-	8"PI13
G25	8"PI23
^19-	&bf 5PI12
g19-	6"PI 8
20+	Y6"LR12
20+	Yw 5LR20
19-	5LR30

13 RACES 94

Figure	Race
^**22**+	5PE17
21-	Vt 5PE 3
17+	Y18LR19
28"	v40MT10
19-	30LR 2
g=**18**-	YAWPI30
r.**15**-	AWPI 7
G**21**-	YAWPI 7
13+	wAWLR20
14"	wAWLR 5
15"	wAWLR19
16+	bAWLR 1
g^**15**"	Y8"LR 8

field of $5,000 claimers, the closest he'd come to that 15½ top. This race signaled another possible recovery.

Pucker bounced on short rest, which was no surprise, and then beat another field of $5,000 horses and paid $8.60 even while running only a 21½. He turned six before his next race, January 8, 1994, and in this, his third start since that forward-signaling 18¼, made the jump to equal his top. But the end of this second recovery line — reaching his top — was now the beginning of the best cluster of races of his career. It is the sort of line you find in horses that I describe as "forging." It usually happens at an earlier age; but Pucker really hadn't developed a lot despite being six years old. The first peak that really set him back was a 17; so reaching 13½ wasn't exceptional. Two races later he launched a string of three straight wins in allowance company, twice setting new tops while working down to a 13¼.

Forging horses, both in working their way back to tops and in setting new peaks, will do it in small increments. When Pucker broke through his four-year-old top of 17–, he did it in a 1¼-point move, to a 15½; when he finally broke through that top, he did it by 1 point, running a 14½, then made a 1¼-point advance to the 13¼. With this type of horse, you are less likely to get the big surge, often at a generous price, that a less mature "explosive" line will often produce. If you are an owner, however, forging horses are better claims than explosive ones. When they are in good form, you are likely to get a series of good races rather than one spectacular one that sets the horse back for months.

It's not uncommon for a horse that makes an explosive move relatively early in his career to later become a forging horse. Since there are likely to be only 7 to 10 points of development after a horse's first top that's strong enough to set him back, there are going to be few horses who will break through their tops by 3 or 4 points more than once after their first season. Their later improvement is more likely to come in increments of a point or so.

Going back to the topic of recovery: In cases where a horse is older than five, a forward-going recovery move in consecutive races may be less reliable as an indicator of future improvement, because his effective top figures to get worse with age. That means that if a horse's top as a six-year-old was 17, you would not regard his running a 21 in his debut at seven and a 20 in his second start as necessarily positive. At seven, the horse's effective top might be no better than 19, in which case the 20 is too close to his peak and is likely to set him back. If the first two races were a 23 followed by a 22, however, there's enough of a gap between the second number and the likely peak the horse is capable of to be optimistic about his next race.

A different situation is presented by a seven-year-old with a 17 top at age six, who runs a 20 very soon after a layoff, then, after some poorer efforts, comes back to the 20 — or does slightly better — within a month or two. This horse would be a good play to go forward to 17. The quick return to an early number after a layoff confirms that the layoff was physically beneficial, and should be taken to indicate that the horse still has a forward move left in him. If he bounces off this line, play him right back.

There are going to be situations in which horses are good bets right off a layoff without waiting for a recovery pattern to emerge. The best examples are horses about whom the trainer is showing optimism: horses who were laid up for more than a couple of months following a series of bad races who are not taking a substantial drop in class for their return.

A look at the sheet for Sue's Huntress illustrates this. In her first three races as a four-year-old, she advanced quickly down to a new top of 16 racing on the turf at Belmont. But that peak clearly hurt her: she bounced to a 34½, then ran 20¼ twice and had to take another month off, then ran three more bad races on turf. Her trainer, Jim Crupi, was forced to drop her out of the allowance ranks and into a $7,500 claimer at the Meadowlands to win a race, and she did it running a subpar 24. Sue's Huntress then was put on the shelf for six and a half months.

There are two reasons any horse with this type of line is a good bet off that kind of layoff. One is that the horse has been given a clearly needed breather. (Any concern that the layoff seems so long that there is something drastically wrong with the horse would not apply in this particular case because a grass specialist like Sue's Huntress wouldn't be running during the early part of the year, when there's no turf racing in the northeast.)

The second reason is that if a horse continues running even when its form has deteriorated, it is usually because the trainer has not yet figured out what is wrong. From personal experience I know that even excellent trainers are sometimes at a loss to explain why a horse veers sharply off-form. I can recall three cases when I asked my trainers, Preston and Everett King, to unload horses because I was concerned at how their numbers were slipping. Neither the trainers nor the track veterinarian could identify a physical problem and the horses were still running well enough to bring back checks, so the Kings persuaded other clients of theirs to buy the horses from me. But the numbers were right: none of the three horses did any useful running for their new owners, and one actually died of a rare illness.

Sue's Huntress came back in the same barn when she returned from the extended layoff, which made it likely that Crupi was running her because he finally had detected the problem and corrected it. There were two other positive signs: she was not in a claimer but returning to the allowance ranks in this race at Garden State, and despite having lost her past three turf races by a combined fifty-seven lengths, she was only 5–1 in the betting. Sure enough, she won the race, and two starts later, ran a new peak of 15¾. Sue's Huntress could have been expected to work her way down to that level as a five-year-old since her three- and four-year-old campaigns showed a similar pattern of development.

There is a different type of horse that can be bet first or second race after a layoff but whose line displays the earmarks of a cripple. Such horses will usually run fewer than ten races every year and do it in compressed periods of time, in contrast to top-stakes horses who might start that infrequently but usually space their races over a period of six to nine months. Bunched races and long absences suggest that a horse has serious physical problems that can only temporarily be corrected. Rather than racing themselves into shape, these horses are prone to run their

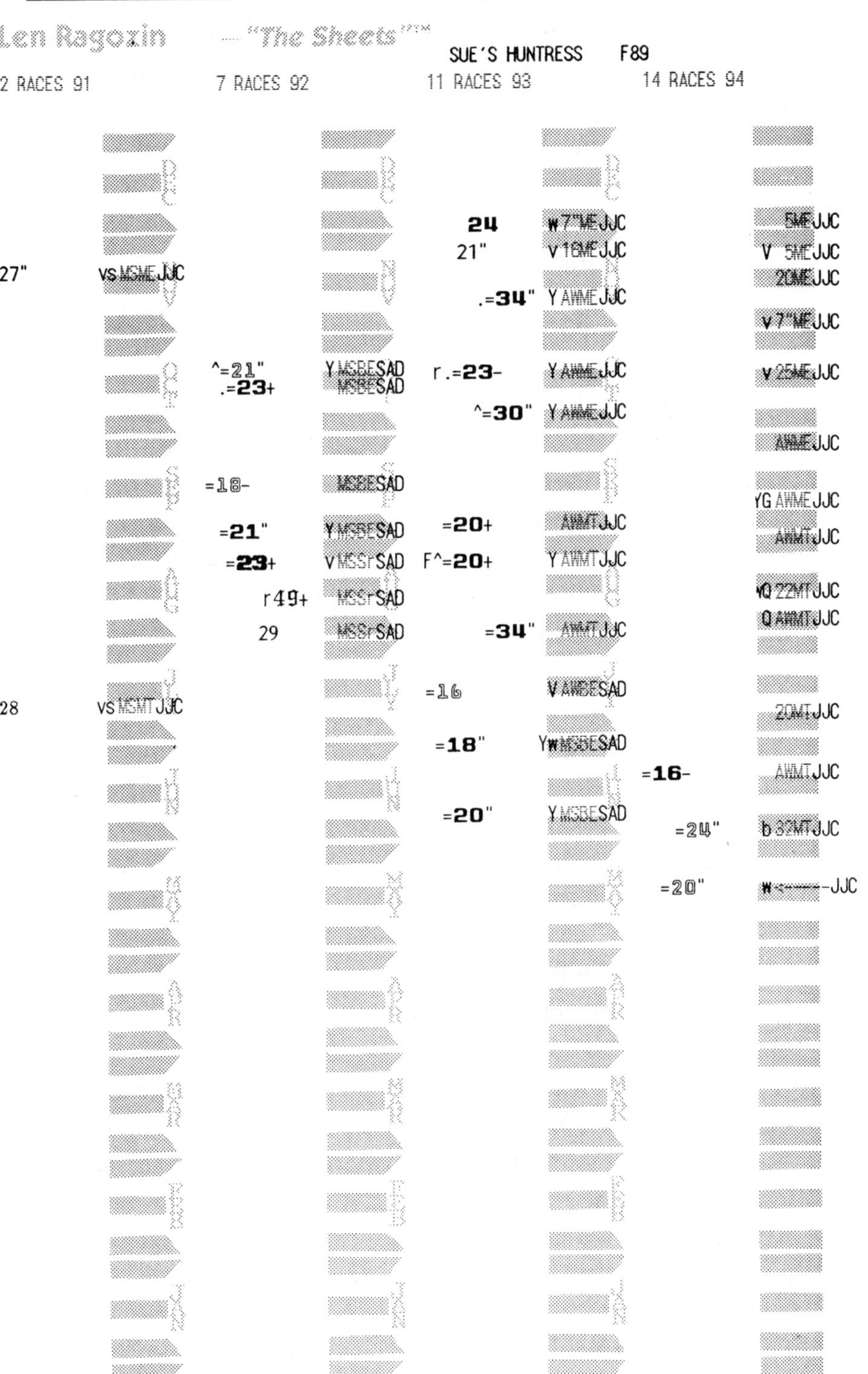
Len Ragozin — "The Sheets"™
SUE'S HUNTRESS F89
2 RACES 91
7 RACES 92
11 RACES 93
14 RACES 94
27" vs MSME JJC
28 vs MSMT JJC
^=21" YMSBESAD
.=23+ MSBESAD
=18- MSBESAD
=21" YMSBESAD
=23+ VMSSrSAD
r49+ MSSrSAD
29 MSSrSAD
24 w7"MEJJC
21" v16MEJJC
.=34" YAWMEJJC
r.=23- YAWMEJJC
^=30" YAWMEJJC
=20+ AWMTJJC
F^=20+ YAWMTJJC
=34" AWMTJJC
=16 VAWBESAD
=18" YwMSBESAD
=20" YMSBESAD
5MEJJC
V 5MEJJC
20MEJJC
v7"MEJJC
v25MEJJC
AWMEJJC
YG AWMEJJC
AWMTJJC
wQ22MTJJC
Q AWMTJJC
20MTJJC
=16- AWMTJJC
=24" b32MTJJC
=20" w------JJC

best numbers in their first races back from a layoff and then go backward as the physical problems recur, usually due to the stresses of racing.

Gold Chill is one example of this kind of horse. In the second race of his three-year-old campaign in 1991, he ran a 13½, a 6¾-point jump over his previous best, and his numbers began an irregular march backward until he was sidelined after running a 24 on the turf at Atlantic City in early August.

He returned five months later and nearly equaled his top, running a 13¾ in a $35,000 claimer at Aqueduct. But his next three races were all at least 5 points worse, and after a recovery to a 15¼, he bounced and had to be sidelined again, this time for nearly a year. He displayed a similar pattern as a five-year-old, but this time his first-out number was significantly worse, even though it would be the best of his abbreviated campaign. It was a similar story for Gold Chill at six. You actually could have cashed a win bet on him at $45.20 when he ran the 18¾ in his third start of the year, but he lost each of his four subsequent races by at least thirteen lengths even as his trainer dropped him down the claiming scale.

Southern Justice is a starker example of the kind of "ouchy" horse you want to avoid. As a two-year-old, he showed promise in two starts, with a decent top of 15½, but then missed his entire three-year-old season. He returned to the races with a thunderclap, running a 5½ in winning at Santa Anita January 2, 1992. But a bounce to an 18 four weeks later followed by a layoff of nearly four months made clear that the horse was not over his physical problems.

He got back to the races with a win at Golden Gate May 25, but his second straight strong effort, when he set the pace and tired to run fifth in the True North Handicap at Belmont, was the last good running he would do. He was beaten a total of thirty-two lengths in two subsequent stakes races at Laurel and Del Mar, and then got another six-month vacation.

Southern Justice resurfaced at Golden Gate in a minor stake February 13, 1993, was made the 9–10 favorite, and tired late

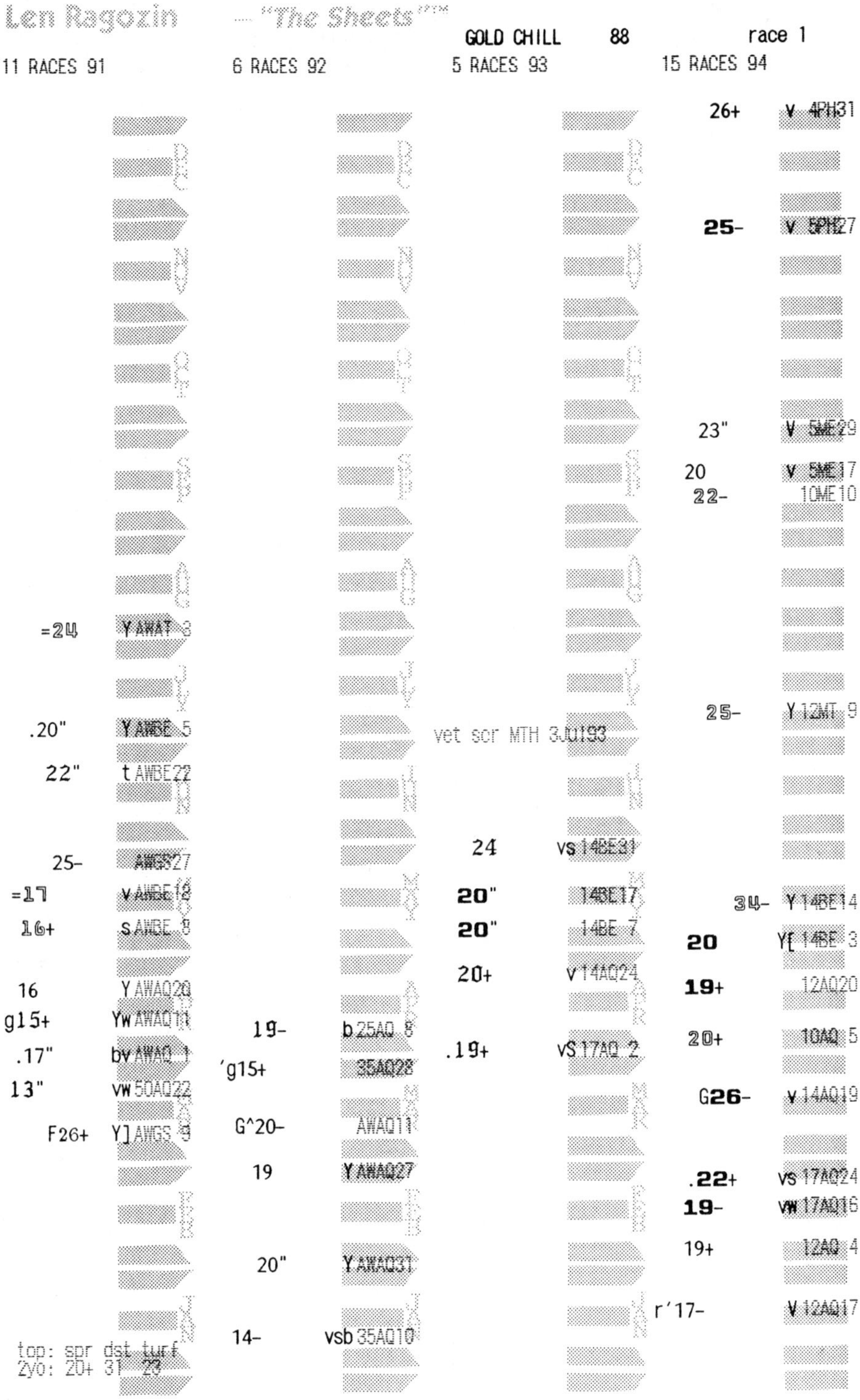

Len Ragozin — "The Sheets"™

GOLD CHILL 88 race 1

11 RACES 91

=24 Y AWAT 3
.20" Y AWBE 5
22" t AWBE22
25- AWGS27
=17 v AWBE12
16+ s AWBE 8
16 Y AWAQ20
g15+ Yw AWAQ11
.17" bv AWAQ 1
13" vw 50AQ22
F26+ Y] AWGS 9

top: spr dst turf
2yo: 20+ 31 23

6 RACES 92

19- b 25AQ 8
'g15+ 35AQ28
G^20- AWAQ11
19 Y AWAQ27
20" Y AWAQ31
14- vsb 35AQ10

5 RACES 93

vet scr MTH 3JU193
24 vs 14BE31
20" 14BE17
20" 14BE 7
20+ v 14AQ24
.19+ vS 17AQ 2

15 RACES 94

26+ v 4PH31
25- v 5PH27
23" V 5ME29
20 V 5ME17
22- 10ME10
25- Y 12MT 9
34- Y 14BE14
20 Y[14BE 3
19+ 12AQ20
20+ 10AQ 5
G26- v 14AQ19
.22+ vs 17AQ24
19- vw 17AQ16
19+ 12AQ 4
r'17- V 12AQ17

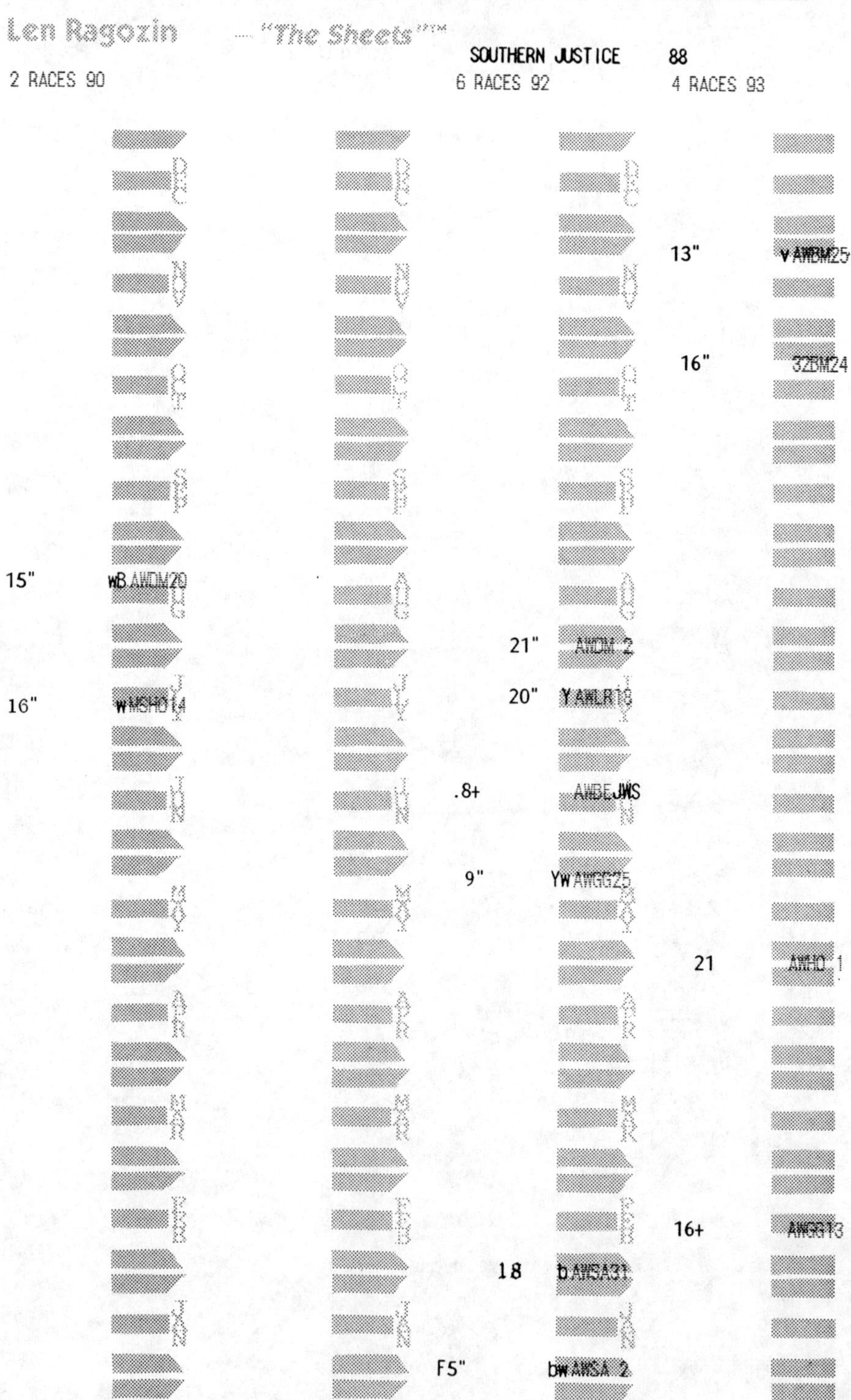
Len Ragozin
"The Sheets"™
SOUTHERN JUSTICE 88
2 RACES 90
6 RACES 92
4 RACES 93
DEC
NOV
OCT
SEP
AUG
JLY
JUN
MAY
APR
MAR
FEB
JAN
13" YAWBM25
16" 3ZBM24
15" wB.AWDM20
21" AWDM 2
16" wMSHO14
20" YAWLR18
.8+ AWBEJWS
9" YwAWGG25
21 AWHO 1
16+ AWGG13
18 bAWSA31
F5" bwAWSA 2

while running a 16¼. Long periods of rest followed, as well as a drop into $32,000 claimers. Still he continued to run far worse than his best efforts at four and still he continued to burn the public's money.

This type of horse, who runs a big top, never gets close to it again, and wraps bad races around his better recovery numbers, should be regarded as damaged goods even if he doesn't have the big gaps of white space that denote extensive layoffs.

12

Training, or Chemistry?

IN JUNE 1954, I began going to the races steadily. Two months later, I'd built my $300 stake into $6,000 and was considering my future to be assured. My father had also been doing quite well, and the next logical step was a full-scale assault on Saratoga.

Driving there from New York City, we buoyantly discussed the figures. We decided the *Racing Form* charts weren't good enough for us. Clocking, too, was pretty crude. In this era before television tapes, we figured we could solve these problems by creating color films of each race. Cost was no object, as far as we were concerned, because our recent success had convinced us we were prospective millionaires. By the time we reached Saratoga, we were agreed that absolutely our only remaining problem as handicappers was whether there was a laboratory in the area that could process the film fast enough.

It turned out, however, that we had other problems. Within a week at Saratoga, I blew about half my capital, and my father was about $20,000 lighter. Saratoga had given us an expensive lesson about the importance of trainers' intentions in pointing their horses for certain "class" meetings.

Nothing particularly shady occurred that August at Saratoga.

There were no fixed races or cases where you could be sure horses' form reversals were so suspicious that they must have been stiffed in their previous starts to set up a big price. But it became clear that certain trainers primed their horses for Saratoga.

Priming for a meet is a practice that occurs to some extent on nearly every racing circuit in the country. Trainers will use a race meeting at one track to get some horses ready for another track. They'll get their share of winners at the "prep" track (often one with smaller purses), but when they switch locales the entire barn seems to be running its best.

This phenomenon is most prominent at "prestige" tracks like Saratoga and Del Mar in the summer and Gulfstream in January, in part because some of the sport's biggest owners schedule their social calendars around these race meetings. At Oaklawn in early spring the tendency is even more pronounced.

At the beginning of these meets (Oaklawn especially), you want to bet horses that have been off for between one and three months. They've been given a breather and trained up to a peak effort, giving them an edge over horses who have been to the post every ten days or so and compiled steady numbers.

Stables that deal primarily in claiming and low-grade allowance horses have difficulty winning at Saratoga or Del Mar because those tracks emphasize races for two-year-olds, turf horses, and stakes-caliber animals. Trainers of cheaper horses use the prestige meetings largely as training grounds to get their horses ready for later campaigns, when there are more races available for their stock and the level of competition falls off. Some of those stables will rest their horses during the summer and early fall, then try to maximize their profits from November through March, when most top horses are on the sidelines.

Some stables are geared to winning races at Gulfstream early in the year, when their owners are wintering nearby. Others use races in Florida to get horses ready for spring and summer assaults on tracks that are their home bases.

All these strategies are intended primarily to impress owners or win purses, not to cash tricky bets. One obvious case I can think of occurred during the early 1980s at Belmont, when the Marlboro Cup was still being run. There was a horse in the first race of the day with dubious recent form who was 4–1 virtually throughout the betting. He drew clear in the stretch and won pretty easily. It was tough to figure the low odds, unless you noted that the owner was Jack Landry, the Philip Morris executive who was the firm's liaison to the track. Philip Morris always had a large delegation on hand for the Marlboro, and Landry's trainer, Lefty Nickerson, clearly understood that if the boss had a winner that day, it was the next best thing to taking the Cup itself. It may have been Nickerson and his help who accounted for the low odds, but my guess is he was getting his biggest payoff through the good will the win earned him from Landry.

This is not to say that trainers don't go to the windows when they like their horses' chances. But most trainers are not spending most of their time manipulating the form of their horses to make a killing, and the ones that do are not terribly successful. Unless you're a really desperate character, there are too many risks involved. Cranking a horse too tight to win a bet could mean he gets hurt, and any reputable trainer — whether it's Shug McGaughey handling the Phipps family operation or a smaller guy dealing with less blueblooded owners and horses — doesn't want to pay that price.

The fact is, trainers are not as larcenous as people think they are, and I say that based on two decades of dealing with a number of trainers whom most people regarded as very sharp and therefore assumed were serious bettors. Most of them get a lot more enjoyment out of giving out their winning first-time starter to thirty or forty friends than they do cashing their own bet.

On the other hand, there are guys like the man I'll call Jerry The Needle. He was a very amply built character who rang my bell one day in the mid-1970s, at a time when I owned quite a few horses. I buzzed him inside my apartment, which was on the fourth floor of a building in Greenwich Village that had no elevator. I opened the door, and heard a man clumping up the stairs, sounding like an elephant who had just run a marathon.

Finally he made it to my floor, came inside, parked his 280 pounds and panted for ten minutes. When he caught his breath, his first words were, "How would you like to be the next Dan Lasater?"

I knew what he meant. Lasater was running dozens of horses — mainly in Philadelphia — and winning with a tremendous percentage. The lines of his horses on our sheets were anti-theory — they jumped to a good figure and just stayed there. It looked like drugs. Jerry explained that he knew what was being used and how to get it, and if I threw in with him I'd win a bundle of races.

I told him I wasn't interested. Belligerently, he asked whether I doubted his ability to do what he said. I told him that wasn't the point — we got our satisfaction from beating the races with brainpower. Using drugs to beat them would hold no enjoyment. He actually understood me, believed me, and was impressed with my attitude. For some years after this he swapped betting information with us — telling us about a proposed coup in return for our evaluation of how to play the exotics. Eventually, he was indicted and convicted.

Well, the truth is, over the past twenty years, drugs — legal and illegal — have increasingly played a role in horses' performance. Most states allow horses to run on Lasix and Butazolidin, and in the states where medication can't be used just prior to a horse's racing, there are ways to mask the drugs. It was well known for a long time that there was a laboratory in Mexico devoted entirely to manufacturing performance-enhancing drugs for horses. Some trainers have prospered nicely through skillful use of these drugs. But in considering the question Leroy Jolley asked in a silly commercial from the late 1970s — "Am I a trainer or am I a trainer?" — my answer for these guys would be, Not really.

While testing methods have grown more sophisticated, some trainers have stayed a step ahead of the testers for years. Probably the most notorious was the late Oscar Barrera, who was the leading trainer in New York — a state where all race-day medication used to be banned — from 1983 to 1986. Rival trainers howled that the performance improvements Oscar was engineering could only occur through the use of drugs or voodoo, and they made needles the morning-line favorite over pins. After intensive scrutiny of Oscar, in 1988 several of his horses tested positive for steroids. He was suspended for months, then returned and saddled 130 straight losers. He was never again a serious factor.

He wasn't the only New York trainer who for a while found a way to escape detection. One trainer still active in New York abruptly became one of the top three trainers on the circuit one year in the mid-1980s. Then he shipped to Florida for the winter and fifteen of his horses tested positive for Sublimaze, the banned drug that was the probable key to the success of Lasater's stable as well. When the trainer returned to New York, his magic touch was gone, and his winners for the year could have been counted on one hand.

Actually, New York's longtime rule against Lasix was silly, because it just meant trainers there wound up going through a back door. It provided a windfall for veterinarians operating in the state, who were paid by the trainers to either administer Lasix so that it wouldn't show up in the testing or use some other drug that had a similar effect and was not being screened for by the state laboratory. You saw so many cases of horses from other states who began running their eyeballs out once they got Lasix, then came to New York and kept running strongly. Obviously their trainers weren't worried by New York's ban.

Lasix, officially known as Furosemide, is a diuretic that by draining a horse's system is supposed to curb bleeding by reducing blood pressure and fluid in the horse's lungs. Some lab researchers say it doesn't necessarily stop bleeding and theorize that in those cases any improvements in performance may occur because of some other drug in a horse's system that Lasix's diuretic effect will help conceal. My personal experience as an owner has been that it can legitimately help a bleeder. As a handicapper, I think that it may push forward the development of a healthy horse, bringing it to its peak more rapidly.

Lasix is permitted in most states only after a horse has bled during a race or a workout. When Lasix first became widely used during the 1970s, there was no question that horses were running strongly the first time they raced with it in their systems, and "first-time Lasix" emerged as a big betting angle.

But by the mid-1980s, Friedman and I found that betting horses the second or third time they ran on Lasix was much more profitable. There were fewer cases where horses were running big races their first time on the stuff, and when they did they offered little value because the public was following this angle strongly enough to sharply cut into the prices on first-Lasix horses.

Bettors become suspicious with experience, and so some handicappers assumed that trainers were stiffing their horses in the first race on Lasix to set up a price in subsequent races. Perhaps so; but the one time we decided we'd make a strong bet on one of our own horses the second time he raced with Lasix, the horse ruined the idea by winning his first time on the drug at 20–1.

Our guess is that a change in rules accounts for horses winning less frequently the first time they get Lasix. Early on, horses were not permitted to race for three weeks or more — depending on the jurisdiction — after they suffered the bleeding that justified the use of Lasix. Those horses were therefore getting what was often much-needed rest along with the medication to treat whatever ailed them, and the combination figured to spell improvement in their first race back. Those rules have since been scrapped, and it's common to see horses racing on Lasix just a week or so after they bled. Without rest, a bad race on first Lasix is not uncommon.

There will still be horses who improve in their first race on Lasix. But if a horse has a decent running line just prior to getting the drug, he's probably going to be overbet in proportion to how much improvement he's likely to make. Betting a horse first-time Lasix makes sense only if his recent form has been horrible but somewhere in the past he ran significantly better numbers, the kind that could win today's race if the Lasix relieved his problems enough to allow him to come close to his best form. And if you're not getting fairly big odds, it's probably not worth it to make a bet that requires you to project a substantial improvement.

Playing horses running on Lasix for the second or third time gives you two advantages: if a horse did not sharply improve in his first start on the drug, that could be enough to scare away other bettors; and, that race gives you some sense of the condition the horse is in. If the horse was not on short rest and ran terribly in his first Lasix start, and particularly if he was laid off for any period of time before that, it's a good indication that what's wrong with him won't be cured with a drug. A horse who improved slightly on his pre-Lasix form — or even one who ran about the same — has shown he is not irreparably damaged, and he is likely to start moving forward toward the better numbers he ran before the problems that led to his bleeding. I'd bet that type of horse to make a good move forward in his second start on Lasix, and if that race produces a good number — but not one within 2 points of a prior top — I'd expect him to go forward in his third start as well.

There are sometimes cases of horses with solid form having to go on Lasix and running badly their first time with the drug. I would not be discouraged; that type of horse will often improve on the solid form in its subsequent starts. When that occurs, though, particularly if they put together a sustained stretch of good efforts, you have to wonder how serious the initial bleeding was and whether the problem wouldn't have cleared up simply by giving the horse some rest.

Two-year-olds and young three-year-olds, who rarely ran on Lasix twenty years ago, now use it routinely. Here the effect is often to shorten the time required for a horse's full development to the top that truly tires him out.

A good trainer will know how to administer drugs judiciously in the same way that he knows every other part of his operation, and do it so you couldn't even be sure if he was doing something illegal. And there are things you can do that are perfectly legal that often produce solid improvement in a horse that you claim.

Shoeing is a very important aspect. There is no question that on deep racetracks like Aqueduct's inner track, mud caulks — and the since-banned turndown shoes — help horses run better by offering greater traction. But trainers strain credulity when they try to explain all unreasonable improvement in recently claimed stock by saying, "It must be the shoes." To buy that, you'd have to believe that all the guys they were competing against knew nothing about shoeing.

Back in the 1970s, Frank Martin constantly made solid long-run improvements in horses he claimed and there was nothing funny or mysterious attached to it. He gave his horses the best nutrition, and he paid his help far better than most trainers. That created good morale around the barn and his workers were more conscientious. As a result, the smallest problem with a horse was going to be quickly reported by the grooms, and catching it early made a big difference.

I don't get the impression that most of the top claiming trainers today, whether in New York or California, run their operations quite as cleanly. They're more likely to have a gimmick.

One of the big questions regarding trainers' impact concerns how much they're likely to improve a horse they've claimed. If a horse has been running steadily for a trainer not known for getting dramatic improvement from his stock and is claimed by a better trainer, there's a good chance that horse will improve by 3 to 5 points pretty quickly. That surge usually won't last, and you might eventually have gotten the same move forward over a longer period if the horse had stayed with its previous trainer, but its first or second start is likely to be a good spot for a bet. (On *The Sheets,* we identify claims by move-up trainers, capitalizing their initials.)

I should add that, in cases where trainers have already developed a reputation for instant improvement off claims, the law of diminishing returns again comes into play. The best example involves our old friend Oscar Barrera. In 1983, horses claimed by Oscar won nearly 50 percent of the time in their first two starts, often at double-digit prices. A year later, as this angle became increasingly well known, his success rate remained high, but the average win prices dropped sharply. By 1985, the public had become so plugged into the angle that, as his percentage of winners shortly after a claim fell from astonishing to merely respectable, betting every such situation would have cost you about $1 for every $2 wagered.

There was nothing subtle about Oscar's methods. He was running horses immediately after the claims, before a change of training regimen figured to have any real effect. A big part of the Barrera-off-the-claim theory involved betting horses running less than a week after the claim. Oscar took this to new heights when he claimed a horse out of the first race one Thanksgiving, when Aqueduct starts its racing at 11 A.M. At that point, the entries for Saturday's races hadn't yet closed, and Oscar saw a spot he liked, so he entered the horse to run on one day's rest without even having had time to take a good look at the newest soldier in his army. He won, of course.

A top trainer won't stop a horse in good form from bouncing, but he's able to postpone the decline, getting horses to follow a big effort with one or even two similar performances before fatigue takes over.

Certain trainers have a knack for getting horses to improve the first time they run on the grass. I mean an improvement that couldn't be expected merely based on how much their pedigrees suited them for turf racing. Eddie Kelly in New York was probably the best I've seen in that regard—all his horses jumped up significantly, whether they won or not. Gary Sciacca among the modern crop of trainers sticks out as someone with that same talent. Willard Freeman, a Kelly contemporary who's still active, also produced major move-ups on turf, and bettors got better prices on his horses because he had less of a reputation for doing it. Undoubtedly there are others at tracks I am less familiar with.

Conversely, a lot of the hot-shot claiming trainers are bad bets when their horses switch to the grass, because whatever the secret is behind their jump-ups on dirt, it doesn't translate to turf.

Sometimes a trainer without a big reputation has to be watched for a more subtle reason. That was a lesson we learned from a trainer named Pedro Briones. Briones was a Maryland-based trainer who back in 1973 brought a South American horse to New York for its American debut in a bottom-level claimer. The horse opened high in the betting and was at 40–1 until a minute before post time, when he abruptly dropped to 20–1 in a single flash of the tote board. In those days, you didn't have triple and exacta and daily double betting in the same race, as you do today. No race had more than one exotic wager, and so the win pools in New York had heavy action, meaning a price drop of this magnitude required a play of thousands of dollars. When the horse romped, Friedman made mental notes regarding Mr. Briones.

He was not seen in New York again until the following year, when he turned up at Aqueduct in June with a six-year-old Argentine horse named Dreyfus II in an $8,000 claiming race. Dreyfus II had not run for nine months, and showed a series of nondescript workouts in Maryland, but Friedman went to the track that day with an eye toward whether the horse would get the same kind of late betting action as Briones's previous bomb. The horse was going off 20–1 or so, and again a late flash drove it down to 11–1. This was in the days when betting windows were set up by dollar amount and sellers punched tickets with that dollar amount one at a time. Friedman, who was standing on the $10 line, told the clerk to just keep punching, but he only got $130 worth of win tickets before the bell rang and the race was off. Sure enough, Dreyfus II won by a length and a half. He paid $25 to win and an unusually high $17.20 to place, and the triple came back an astonishing $9,649.

The place and triple payoffs were what you would have expected from a horse going off at 20–1 or better, and convinced Friedman that Briones or whoever was betting for him was only hitting the win pool, leaving a big opportunity in the triple.

Four months later, a horse named Sacador, who had last raced thirteen months earlier at Arlington, turned up in a $7,500 claimer at Aqueduct. Sacador was sitting at 40–1 in the betting, and since it took Friedman more than fifteen minutes to put in his complicated triple plays on the old mechanical, single-ticket machines, he had to bet out of faith that Pedro would again work his magic rather than because of any signs from the early action on the tote board. When the big downward flash in Sacador's odds finally materialized in the last minute of wagering, Friedman breathed a $3,000 sigh of relief. Sacador won, paid the usual out-of-whack $39 to win, $34 to place, and the triple came back at a bit over $12,000, giving Friedman a profit of better than $30,000 on the race.

A few months passed, and Mr. Briones turned up in the entries again. While it seemed by this time as though form wasn't all that relevant when he shipped a horse to New York, this race shaped up as a very tough one, and Friedman sat it out because he was uncertain the horse could beat a couple of the others in the field. There was the usual late money cascading in, and sure enough, this race was more of a struggle, but Briones's horse won a photo finish. Suddenly the inquiry sign went on and the horse's number started blinking, and he was disqualified for a foul that Friedman wasn't sure actually occurred. It seemed to us that maybe the New York stewards were trying to tell Pedro that these put-overs with huge late bets were giving them indigestion, and they especially weren't appreciated when an out-of-towner was responsible.

That was the last time we saw Briones in New York, but he turned up one day in the entries at Monmouth with a first-time starter in a $6,500 maiden claiming race. Since they ran similar races regularly in Maryland, his presence on the Jersey shore sounded the betting alarms.

The horse was running in the second race, and since Briones never seemed to bet exotics, Friedman decided he might as well wade into the daily-double pool, using three horses in the first with Pedro's first-timer. One of the three won the race at 6–1 odds, and Friedman was holding a $250 ticket, with two other sheet players who accompanied him each having $50 tickets, on a

$300-plus double that would have given them over $50,000 if Briones's horse had won.

Near the end of the betting on the second, the horse was sitting at 30–1, with no sign of a change as they began loading the field into the starting gate. Then came the magic flash, the horse dropped to 13–1, and Friedman and the other two guys stood up and began whooping like the race was already over. The horse bounded out of the gate, opened a big early lead, and coasted home about fifteen lengths in front. Then came disaster: the inquiry sign lit up, and a few minutes later they disqualified the horse, supposedly for bearing in as it came out of the gate. It looked like word about Mr. Briones had traveled down the Garden State Parkway from New York, and Monmouth was giving him the same message. A racetrack doesn't have to prove a guy did anything wrong to make him feel unwelcome. It can disqualify a trainer for phantom fouls or refuse to give him stall space and he may have no recourse.

We never came across other Briones horses running in New York or New Jersey after that second disqualification. Maybe he began hiding behind someone else's name. But I like to think that he took his winnings and retired to a life of luxury.

13

A Different Kind of "Money" Jockey

ASK MOST RACING PEOPLE to name a "money" jockey, the person they want riding in a race that really matters, and they'll give you the names of the most famous riders in the sport: Arcaro, Hartack, Baeza, Cordero, Shoemaker, Pincay, Delahoussaye, Day, Stevens, Bailey.

My own hall of fame features riders most people have never heard of or long ago forgot: Gene Ho, Tommy Wallis, Lee Moon, Kevin Bowie, Brian Peck. They are apprentice riders I used with success on my own horses. Friedman and I made some of our biggest scores betting on them, even in races they didn't win.

Riders can make a difference. An inexperienced apprentice can get into trouble that a top jockey would have anticipated and avoided, and sometimes that will be the difference between winning a race and finishing up the track. But in most situations, having a top rider means only that a horse has a bit more chance to run his best figure that day. If you own claiming horses, this doesn't necessarily help your purse income, because if a horse runs a top one day he won't run it the next. Meanwhile, if he runs — because of the less competent rider — an irrelevant poor race, you can drop him into a cheaper claimer next time and have a much better chance to win.

I won't change my betting opinion about how well a horse will run depending upon who's riding. I don't think a rider is going to make a significant difference on a horse that looks ready to bounce — and that includes someone like Pat Day, whose patience and determination to save ground when possible allows many horses to win without a peak effort.

Now, if you're a trainer or owner who's running his horse in six-figure stakes races and giving him six-week layoffs between races, you should get the best jockey you can, because that rider can make the difference between getting the winner's share of a $500,000 purse or running third and getting a couple hundred thousand less. He'll get that little extra out of a horse and, riding for that kind of money, he'll risk going through a small hole that another rider wouldn't have seen until it was too late.

But in more modest races, tomorrow is another day, and the rider can hardly hurt you. Certainly from a betting standpoint, a less well regarded rider is an advantage: most of the crowd is looking to bet the hot riders. What little you lose in the horse's performance will be more than made up for in the odds you get.

You'll find some cases where a good rider replacing a mediocre one can bring horses to life. But there are probably more cases in which the good rider can't do anything more than the jock he replaced. Remember the hundreds of cases when Angel Cordero was booed because he lost after his presence on a horse with a nondescript record led to that horse being made the betting favorite.

Following the hot jock is going to turn out to be a losing proposition in most situations, unless you were somehow prescient enough to figure out who the hot rider was going to be before it happened. For instance, after forty-five days of the 1994 Monmouth Park meeting, Joe Bravo was winning with an outstanding 31 percent of his mounts. But since Bravo for several years had been the leader of the New Jersey jockey colony, his horses were being bet heavily from the outset. The average win price on his mounts was $6.22. A $2 bet on each of his 303 mounts to that point in the meeting would have netted a loss of $21.

There are indeed cases in which a switch to a top rider is a sign that a horse is ready to run well. Jerry Bailey and Day are almost always going to be riding horses that are dead fit, because they can be choosy. Their agents won't accept mounts unless the trainer assures them the horse is in shape — and he'd better be right if he wants to maintain good relations. But my feeling is if a horse they're riding is ready to run well, that should already be apparent to me looking at the horse's sheet.

The main exception would be a case where a trainer has tapped a joint. This is a process of draining fluid that builds up in some horses' legs. Tapping allows them to run better, but it can be done only occasionally, or the joint will be ruined. The sheet unfortunately won't signal this operation.

There will be nebulous situations where the presence of a top rider on a horse it's tough to figure might lead me to pass a race. One example would be a young horse who hasn't raced in four or five months and gets Day or his equivalent aboard: the horse figures to improve because he's had time off to mature, and the presence of a rider like that could mean the barn is looking to get that big improvement first race back. But it also means the horse will probably be overbet.

Apprentices, at least until they suddenly become "hot" in the eyes of the crowd, are going to get you good value on horses that are in shape. Some of the biggest betting scores Friedman and I have made over the years involved cases in which an apprentice ran second or third at a huge price and triggered a big payoff on an exacta or triple. The weight off for using an apprentice was worth at least as much as having a top rider up, and the prices were far greater than they should have been because of the public's reluctance to bet unknown riders, particularly if they're not riding a horse who's an obvious contender. I should caution that unless the apprentice he's using is in a hot streak, I'd be hesitant if the trainer has a record of never using apprentices when his horses are really ready.

For one stable that Friedman managed, he used apprentices almost all the time. There were two cases in which he put Jorge Velasquez on horses to get that extra edge. Velasquez won both races, but the horses were never able to come close to their winning efforts after that. A top rider like Velasquez is sometimes going to coax a real peak effort from a horse, maybe more than that horse can reasonably run without being knocked out. A race-weary claiming horse may have been surviving by refusing to run that big effort. Exceeding his limits will only hasten his decline — and now you're stuck with an impending collapse. Apprentices aren't strong enough to push the horses to that knockout effort. This may benefit the stable in the long run.

Steve Cauthen won his first stakes race in New York riding one of my horses, Frampton Delight, while he was an apprentice in 1976. Stables we've run or advised made heavy use of Julie Krone, Robbie Davis, and Richard Migliore when they were apprentices, and we also had success riding apprentices whom other people were scared to use.

One example was Victor Molina, who today is one of the better riders on the Pennsylvania circuit. When he began riding for some of the clients we advised, Molina didn't know how to switch hands with the whip or how to whip the horse with one hand while guiding him with the other. But horses ran for him; before he knew much about craft, he had the kind of touch to get horses to respond. We saw on *The Sheets* that his mounts were running figures which were as good as you could expect, and his lack of winners was only because the horses weren't good enough.

Long before the arrival of Julie Krone, whom we helped with some coaching, we had no prejudice against women riders. There was a day in June 1975 in which I had a filly who under the conditions of the race was to carry 106 pounds — eight less than any other entrant. She was in against horses with better figures, and I decided to look for a really big weight advantage by naming a seven-pound apprentice — one who has yet to win thirty-five races — to ride. It wasn't that easy finding a rider who weighed ninety-nine pounds or less, but there was a teenage girl from Maryland named Kevin Bowie who was light enough to fit. (Our trainer, Everett King, was fooled by the name and called her agent and said, "I hear you have a boy that can make ninety-nine pounds." Ev turned out to be half right.)

Actually, Bowie had ridden the filly, Rumson Reach, several times already, because the breeder was the trainer who held her apprentice contract. This familiarity figured to help.

When we met Bowie the afternoon of the race, we were a bit taken aback. She looked even younger than she was and lighter than her ninety-two-pound riding weight. It was also her first trip to New York, and she seemed stagestruck, nodding mutely as King gave her riding instructions. Then he extended his hands and hoisted her up into the saddle, and did it with enough force that suddenly he was reaching out to catch her as if he was afraid she would sail right over the horse.

But when the race began, Bowie made clear she knew what she was doing. Rumson Reach, who was 24–1 because other bettors didn't give her the six-length credit she deserved for the fifteen-pound weight edge at the distance, broke well and Kevin moved her right to the lead without extending her against this field of $13,000 to $15,000 claimers. She held the lead for the first mile of the 1¼-mile turf race, and then Eddie Maple ranged up to challenge her on an old mare named Wing Flutter. Bowie had saved enough horse so that as Wing Flutter began to pass her, Rumson Reach was able to fight back and poke her head in front again in midstretch. When our filly was headed and came back again, Maple called out something that sounded like "You get that filly's nose in front one more time and I'm gonna help you fall off." Maybe he figured his grim joke would break her concentration, but she kept riding.

At the wire, Rumson Reach yielded enough to lose by a neck to Wing Flutter, who picked that advanced stage of her career to run back to a lifetime top she set in her youth. But Bowie's ride was skillful enough to earn her a short feature story in the next day's

New York Times. Not bad for a teenager on her first visit to the big city. Quite good for us, also: the triple paid $1,446 and we made a major score.

Incidentally, our apprentices were often verbally threatened by veteran riders, especially when they rode to our instructions and moved up on the rail. "You move inside me again and you'll end up eating grass in the infield," was the way one longtime superstar rider put it one day after we beat him out.

Gene Ho was a little-used apprentice in the early 1970s when we began riding him to get the ten-pound weight concession given to riders who have yet to win five races. There was one cheap three-year-old I claimed and ran against older horses in allowance company with Ho riding. Between the horse's age allowance and Ho's ten-pound weight break, we would get almost twenty pounds from these fields. Running in 1⅛-mile races at Aqueduct that started in front of the stands, Ho lacked the strength to control the horse going into the first turn and sometimes the animal would head for the Belt Parkway before he could be straightened out. But the horse consistently finished in the money. I wasn't even sure I wanted to win with him, because we were earning nice money running against these nonwinners of one, and a win would force the horse into tougher company. But one day he got stuck inside the other horses and he won the race — and we sold him to a guy from California for $35,000.

This was not an unusual phenomenon — a number of owners bought or claimed horses from us figuring if those horses were running decently for awful jockeys, they could clean up simply by putting big-name riders in the saddle. The man from California took the horse back to the coast and had no success at all, largely because the horse couldn't compete against animals worth more than $8,000 without the big weight concession we got.

There are other advantages to using "bug" riders, who got that nickname because of the asterisks that used to appear on the track program next to the weight listed for any horse carrying an apprentice. One is that their very lack of experience, and their desire to prove their ability, will make them more inclined to take chances than veteran riders, whose bodies bear the scars that illustrate the dangers of thoroughbred racing.

Angel Cordero, as tough and nervy a rider as you'll ever see, was seriously injured often enough that later in his career he would not risk going through a tight hole between horses or between another horse and the rail unless winning that particular race was going to add something to his stature.

Mike Smith, one of the two best riders in New York during the 1990s, draws criticism from some bettors because when riding from off the pace he prefers the big outside sweep on the last turn rather than staying inside. But of course the inside route carries physical risks to rider and horse. The "balcony move" looks powerful, makes some owners happy, and you keep the horse and yourself out of harm's way. But the ground lost is lamentable, at least if you're betting Smith and his horse loses a close one.

There are apprentices who are reluctant to ride in tight quarters also, but there are others who have not yet gained the healthy fear that comes after a bad spill or two and are foolhardy enough to go into even the smallest hole to win a race. Chuckie Lopez, who's now one of the top journeyman riders in New Jersey, as a ten-pound apprentice riding for some of our clients was daring enough to thread those needles. His father, Carlos, is also a solid rider in Jersey, and you might figure he'd have imparted some cautious words to his son about this practice. But Chuckie would go into holes his father would see only in his nightmares.

Chuckie would also ride to instructions, another trait you're far more likely to find in good young apprentices than in more experienced riders. I was much more insistent than most owners about how I wanted my horses ridden, and Friedman is the same way when managing stables.

There are cases where a jockey will keep a horse outside on instructions. Maybe the trainer doesn't want the horse getting dirt kicked in his face or he's reluctant to have the horse snatched up if it gets into trouble trying to go through a hole that closes abruptly. Sometimes, as in the case of Alydar, the trainer has made a mysterious decision that his horse just will not run on the inside.

But staying inside and saving as much ground as possible was what mattered most to us, and we were sure to convey that to both trainers and riders. I drew up a jockey instruction sheet, complete with diagram, and printed it in English and Spanish. If the horse was off the pace, we didn't want him asked for maximum effort until he was at least two-thirds of the way around the final turn, because we didn't want a major ground loss. We wanted the wide move postponed until the straightaway, where it cost little distance.

Friedman and I would tell jockeys to start moving horses toward the rail as soon as they could — be it toward the front of the field or the back. The reasoning was simple: if the horse later got blocked trying to move through inside, it might cost him the race because he couldn't run to his good numbers, but you could still get the good race next time. If he swung wide early for clear racing and then lost too much ground and got beaten in a close finish, you wasted a peak effort. It might be two or three months before he'd run that well again, and you'd have to keep paying for his expenses all that time.

There are handicappers and horsemen who argue that if a horse has to be checked sharply during the stretch run because the rider stayed inside looking for a hole, that's enough to discourage a horse from giving his best the rest of the race. But early in my handicapping days, I made a point of looking at horses ridden by Bill Hartack who were blocked, often several times, because of his determination to stay on the rail. On *The Sheets*, the horses were running precisely the numbers you would have expected, regardless of having been checked.

Hartack had an outstanding win percentage. He was not a smooth or natural rider. His wins didn't come because horses gave him their best. There was no question in my mind that Hartack was winning races other riders wouldn't have won because of the ground he saved.

One famous illustration of the importance of ground lost is the Affirmed/Alydar rivalry. Alydar earned better figures than Affirmed in each leg of the 1978 Triple Crown: 3¼ in the Derby to

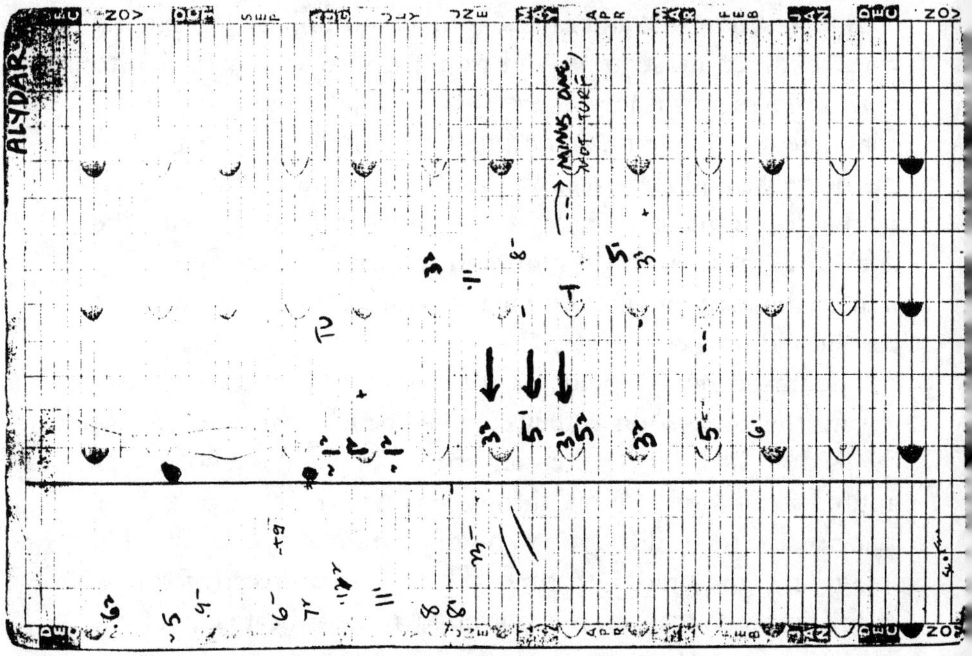

ALYDAR

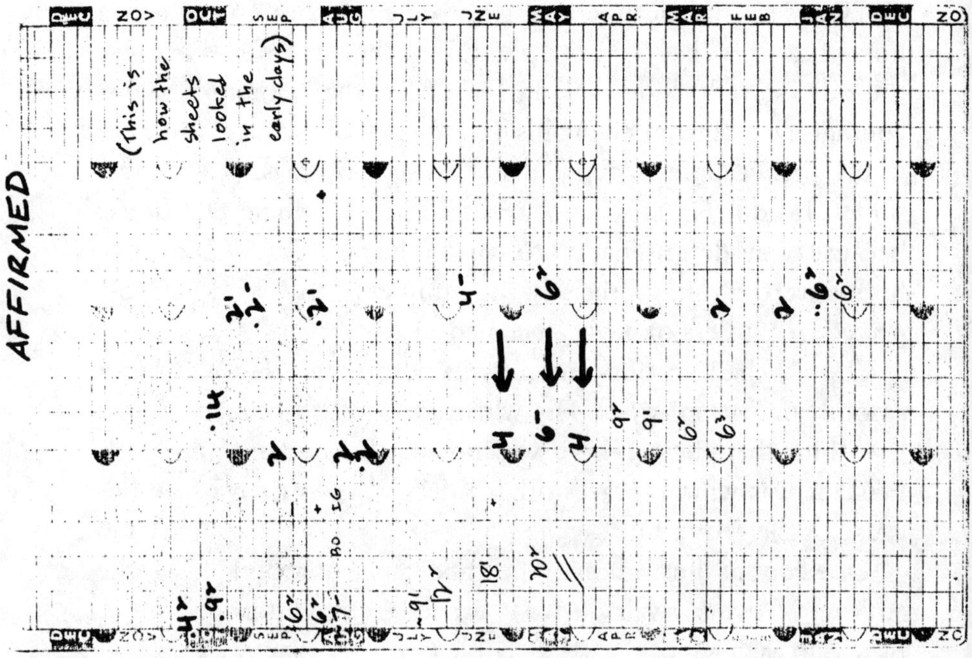

AFFIRMED

(This is how the sheets looked in the early days)

Affirmed's 4; 5¼ compared to 5¾ in the Preakness; and 3½ compared to 4 in the Belmont. After losing bets on Alydar in the Derby and the Preakness, we were drooling over the chance to get even in the Belmont, where the small field and his good post position meant Alydar couldn't lose much ground, so the better figure would surely prevail. But on the trainer's orders, Alydar was taken up and to the outside on the first turn, giving his inside position to Affirmed, and it was the same old story — victory on the sheet, defeat at the betting window.

Of all the riders to whom we preached the gospel of saving ground, none listened better than Lee Moon, a young apprentice rider perhaps best known for being the first Korean jockey to ride in New York. Moon used to come back with a white streak on his left pants leg from scraping the paint off the rail as he rode, which greatly endeared him to me. The ride I remember most was aboard a horse named Admiral Auteuil, whom I claimed out of a bottom-class maiden race December 18, 1973.

The last racing day of the year in New York, December 29, there was a race for cheap claimers who had already won races. It figured to come up weak enough to give Admiral Auteuil a shot to win, maiden or no. I entered him for the bottom price of $9,000, which along with Moon's apprentice allowance meant the Admiral would only have to carry 101 pounds.

I wasn't betting seriously anymore, but I contacted Friedman down in Florida. In those days he always ran south at the first forecast of a snowstorm, playing the horses down there until the weather turned warm. I shipped him a copy of *The Sheets* for Aqueduct a day in advance, and he flew up the next day to join us out at the track. When I asked how much he'd put on the horse in win and triple betting, Friedman said, "I emptied out" — and his pockets ran deep.

Admiral Auteuil was running in the ninth and final race, which at that time of year in New York is run at about 4:30 as twilight gives way to darkness. They broke from the gate directly in front of us, but the thickening darkness swallowed up the field midway on the clubhouse turn.

Down the backstretch, the track announcer also lost sight of the field, leaving us both literally and figuratively in the dark as the horses hit the final turn and entered the stretch of the 1⅛-mile race.

But since we had Lee Moon riding, I decided to concentrate on the rail and see whether any horse came charging up along the inside of the track. Sure enough, here came a horse closing furiously up the rail as the blurs to the outside of him drew closer to the wire. For us, the finish was surreal. Just as the inside horse surged to the front, the light surrounding the finish line parted the gloom to show us it really was the Admiral and Lee Moon getting up to win by a half-length.

The horse paid $24.20. The triple — with a 14–1 shot second — came back at $2,742, and Friedman, his pockets bulging with cash, left the track by cab bound for Kennedy Airport. He caught the next plane back to Florida, a richer man for having chosen, if only for one day, Moon over Miami.

14

Class Won't Tell

IT'S UNDERSTANDABLE why the old-money, upper-class lords of racing would love the theory that class — once established by a horse — is the measure of performance above all others. That so many handicappers used to subscribe to such nonsense is hard to fathom, but I probably shouldn't complain, since in our early days there was a fortune to be made both at the betting windows and through the claiming game by taking advantage of this misconception. In fact, I think I've done more to eliminate class as a handicapping factor through my claiming than through our betting.

My father started a small stable of claiming horses in the 1960s, using my interpretation of our speed figures to determine which horses were moving toward improvements in form that would make them worth owning. After some modest successes, we claimed a horse named Sunny and Mild for $15,000 at Monmouth Park in July 1972.

The horse at that time was trained by Melvin "Sunshine" Calvert, one of the top trainers in New Jersey, for Frances Genter, who eighteen years later won the Kentucky Derby with Unbridled. Some owners and trainers are reluctant to claim from good trainers, figuring they have already gotten a horse to run his best. But I liked Sunny and Mild's line, which had no sharp edges, and was confident that he had plenty of room to improve as he went further into his three-year-old season.

Preston King, my father's trainer, wasn't even present at Monmouth the day we claimed Sunny and Mild. But when the horse got good, he — like all our subsequent trainers in similar situations — had plenty to say to the press about what had caught his eye and led him to claim this fine animal!

We asked Preston to enter the horse in an allowance race on the turf at Monmouth. Rain forced the race to be switched to the main track, and Sunny and Mild won it at 4–1.

Over the next month, we ran Sunny and Mild in three allowance races, two of them on turf, and the horse finished out of the money each time. We gave him a couple of weeks off, then dropped him into a claimer at Belmont for a price of $22,500, and the horse romped, paying 3–1. We then moved him into a $45,000 claimer on turf, and Sunny and Mild ran last in a field of five.

Conventional wisdom would have held that after six races in our barn, Sunny and Mild had established his class: his only winning efforts had come in a medium claimer and an allowance race whose caliber was suspect because he had defeated horses on dirt who were turf-intended. But I could see his numbers slowly improving, with no sharp jump yet, and I had hopes he would pay bigger dividends. At that time we hadn't developed the concept of young horses generally developing 7 to 10 points from their first serious efforts, but even then I could see that Sunny and Mild hadn't yet improved dangerously far from his early form.

My father moved him off the turf to race some pretty good allowance horses 1⅟16 miles, and Sunny and Mild won at 5–1. Running six furlongs nine days later, he again beat allowance horses, this time at 7–2. By now we had been offered $80,000 for the horse, which I wanted to consider. My father, in seventh heaven, said no.

We gave him a couple of weeks off and then aimed high, entering him in the Jerome Handicap, a prestigious mile race at

Belmont for three-year-olds. Sunny and Mild failed his first big test, running seventh at 9–2. We took a step back at the end of October, placing him in an allowance race, where he ran third. But his numbers were still forging forward.

November was the time when most good horses began their winter vacations. *The Sheets* said Sunny and Mild was reaching the point in his development where it made sense to make a run at Aqueduct's weakened late-year stakes. So we entered him in the Stuyvesant Handicap going one mile, and his failure a month earlier in the Jerome led bettors to dismiss him at 11–1. Sunny and Mild ran second behind the only real stakes horse in the race, Icecapade, and it was clear that he could run in these stakes.

Here is where *The Sheets* doubly guided us. We were already running a cheap horse in stakes. Now we decided, after looking at the opposition, that he would have a better chance of winning a stakes race if we ran him in handicaps against older horses instead of the presumably easier spots limited to three-year-olds only.

We entered him a week later in the Queens County Handicap as part of an entry with another horse trained by Pres King, and the entry ran 1–2, with Sunny and Mild winning by half a length and actually setting a track record for the rarely run distance of 1$\frac{3}{16}$ miles. By now he was running 9s on *The Sheets,* 9 points better than when we claimed him. Today I understand this figured to be his ultimate peak; at that time I wasn't sure.

A week later, we ran him back in the Roamer Handicap at the same distance, and his effort to go wire-to-wire barely failed when he was nailed by the stretch-running True Knight. Two weeks later, using an allowance race as a prep, we saw him finish second to the tough Forage, and the week after that, Sunny and Mild ran third in the 2¼-mile Display Handicap. By now we were offered $200,000 for the horse. The figures said he wasn't worth more than that, and the soft-race season was over — but Harry wouldn't sell. I should have pushed him harder. Soon he was retired with injuries, and his stud career was a failure.

In a five-week period, a horse whom in September we had run for a sale price of $22,500 — with no takers — had won one stakes race and finished in the money in three others. It suggested class was not the factor most people had always supposed, and that speed and current physical condition should be the overriding consideration when weighing the chances of a horse when he took on tougher competition.

Sunny and Mild's success was my entrée into the ranks of ownership. My father until then had been paying me just $50 a week to maintain the figures for him, and my own betting off the figures had given me a living but not much of a bank account. My father gave me one-third of the profits from Sunny and Mild's fall success. Len Friedman dug up a partner for me, a Brooklyn lumberyard owner named Lou Esposito, and we pooled our money and began claiming horses.

Our first claim showed that *Sheet* analysis could provoke trainers' rage. We claimed a horse that, going by *The Racing Form,* was not worth taking. The horse's trainer, José Martin, cursed us roundly and claimed him back at a higher price in his first start for us. The horse ran second. So, we were off to a profitable start.

Over the next few years we did very nicely, even winning some minor stakes races. A lot of our success came from a sort of arbitrage: we operated in four different states and used *The Sheets* to spot horses who would do better elsewhere. We claimed a New York–bred in New Jersey and won three big purses when we ran him against state-breds in New York. We took a high-priced two-year-old claimer — Corporate Headache — in New York and without improving he won the Benjamin Franklin Handicap for three-year-olds in New Jersey. We took fillies from Maryland — where the filly claiming races were strong — and brought them to New Jersey and New York to run for bigger purses against weaker fields. Most notable was Campaign Donation, who won eight races for us as a three-year-old and was claimed away for four times her original price just as she peaked out.

My first New York stakes win came after I claimed a three-year-old named Frampton Delight for $22,500 from Frank Martin in 1975. He had developed enough to run a 13¾ followed by a 13½ late in the summer, and I claimed him from his next start, figuring more improvement would be coming late in the year. He bounced that day, and his next three races were also off his top form, but then he repeated the 13½ and improved slightly to a 13¼. I was still optimistic.

But then the horse became ill. Sidelining him for two months forced us to skip the late-fall campaign that had worked so well for Sunny and Mild. When we brought him back, it took Frampton Delight five races to get into shape before delivering another 13½. Although he was healthy, this time I deliberately decided to give him the entire summer off to gear up for the fall races, when other horses figured to be tiring.

We began racing him in September, and the horse slowly worked his way forward without ever matching his best races of the previous fall. I tried him in a couple of stakes races, and his performance was uninspired enough that, if I believed the class theory, I would have abandoned my notion of going after any New York stakes. But I didn't believe; I knew those stakes would come up relatively soft, and if he could work his way back to his best three-year-old numbers, he was going to have a shot at winning them.

He loomed as a longshot in the Gallant Fox Handicap December 11, 1976. Of course he was assigned a low weight, which limited my choice of jockeys. Steve Cauthen had arrived in New York a couple of weeks earlier, a five-pound apprentice fresh from a small track in Ohio. On *The Sheets* it looked like horses were running well for him, and I decided to use him even though no weight allowance for apprentices is granted in stakes races. Neither Cauthen nor the horse impressed the bettors much: Frampton Delight was sent off at 19–1.

The 3–2 betting favorite, Appassionato, took a long lead early in the race. I had instructed Cauthen to stay on the rail as long as possible and then make one sustained move during the final ¼-mile. He sat sixth with Frampton Delight most of the way. He moved outside a bit sooner than I would have liked, but the horse rallied through the stretch to win and pay $40.80. By my figures,

Frampton Delight had run another 13½, which earlier in the year might not have won an allowance race. Now it was enough to set a track record for 1⅝ miles — another example of a bad track record — and win a Grade 2 New York stakes.

I didn't bet Frampton Delight that afternoon. I believed he had a shot to win the race but figured the purse was enough of a payoff. And when we entered him in the Display Handicap two weeks later, I certainly wouldn't have considered him as a bet — he was almost five years old and would probably bounce. Furthermore, considering he just recently had run in claimers, they put much too high a weight on him — 119 pounds — possibly from annoyance that we upstarts had won a New York stakes race. The only optimistic note came from our trainer and from Friedman's racing-stable partner, Arthur Berg, who has a good eye for horseflesh. They both said the horse was acting unbelievably frisky. So maybe 13 — which, after all, he had run many times — wasn't his final top.

The Display was a race packed with plodding horses, the type trainers figured could win a stakes race only by living longer than the competition. At 2¼ miles, the Display was the longest race run in New York; eventually it would be cut back to 1⅝ miles because there weren't enough real marathoners around.

Frampton Delight was also a plodder, and he had drawn an inside post. If he sat well off the pace as usual, he'd probably have to maneuver to the outside of a big field to make his move, costing him precious ground in a spot where, at his weight, he couldn't afford to lose it.

The challenge became finding a way to save ground — a practice that too often is neglected in marathon races. It seemed to me this could be accomplished if the horse was hustled away from the gate just enough to stay inside all the other plodders. I told this to the horse's new rider, Jean Cruguet, and emphasized that this was our only chance to win.

He followed instructions perfectly, and we were on the inside of the plodders' phalanx. Cruguet added a flourish of his own: as the field made its way around the track the first time, he moved around single horses several times and each time he got clear he guided Frampton Delight back to the rail to avoid losing ground.

By the time they turned for home during the final stretch run, Frampton Delight was moving to the lead and Cunning Trick, the 5–2 favorite, was just outside him with Cordero ready to do battle. Angel steered his horse as far inside as possible, hoping to crowd Frampton Delight into the rail and inhibit Cruguet's ability to whip right-handed, and he flailed his left elbow about in a further attempt to intimidate our horse. Those tactics seemed to work: Cunning Trick got a half-length in front at the wire. But then the inquiry sign lit up.

I figured we had no hope because Ogden Phipps, a power on the New York Racing Association board, owned Cunning Trick. The box-seat ushers gathered around and rooted loudly for me because they disliked Phipps, who was their boss. The stewards, maybe just because it was the right call, disqualified Cunning Trick and awarded the race to Frampton. My horse, who paid $27.60 to win, had run an 11½, the best race of his career. But without all the ground saving by Cruguet, per my instructions, he would not have been in position to force Cordero to strong-arm him in the stretch.

Neither Sunny and Mild nor Frampton Delight would subsequently remind racing people of Stymie, who was claimed early in his career for $1,500 and went on to win nearly $1 million during the 1940s. They were not Cinderella horses like John Henry, who was once sold for $1,100 and became a champion while earning $6.5 million. But they proved conclusively that horses in prime condition could step way above their supposed class and not only compete but win.

There are reasons why the notion that class will tell dies hard. It is based on the frequent cases where a horse steps up off a big race and doesn't run well against better horses. Of course I look at this phenomenon in light of the bounce factor; if a horse is coming off a peak performance, it should not be surprising that he reacts negatively. Trainers and owners who don't consider this aspect of the off-performance simply conclude their horses can't compete against better company and don't take the shot a second time. This fuels the class theory. But there are a lot of high-priced claimers in New York and California who could compete in stakes, especially if shipped to lesser tracks.

There are going to be situations in which a horse moving up the ladder in claiming races or from maiden special weight to allowance and then stakes races will encounter problems he didn't have in beating weaker horses, but not because of the myth about class. He may be a front-runner who is used to shaking off an early challenge and then being alone and clear on the rail during the middle part of the race; now he finds the horse doing the early challenging keeps right on pressing him. He might be a midpack horse accustomed to grabbing the lead with a big surge on the turn. Now he discovers that surge is not enough to pass the early leaders and so he winds up very wide throughout the final turn.

But all that means is that it's harder to win a race if there are more good horses in it. There are situations where a horse off a winning race runs against tougher company and finishes sixth, beaten many lengths, and actually improves to a better number on *The Sheets.* We've seen someone else's speed figures occasionally edited to make a winning race look better than a losing performance; we stick to our data.

In 1992, A.P. Indy was a well-beaten third in the Jockey Club Gold Cup behind Pleasant Tap, then was a decisive winner of the Breeders' Cup Classic. But by my numbers he ran 2½ points better — 3¾ to 6¼ — in the Jockey Club than in the Breeders' Cup. In the earlier race, he stumbled badly leaving the gate and was forced to go extremely wide around Belmont's final turn simply to reach contention, while Pleasant Tap had a relatively smooth trip. In the Breeders' Cup, A.P. Indy benefited from a rail trip until midway on the final turn, when Eddie Delahoussaye urged him through a small opening between horses and quickly seized an insurmountable lead while Pleasant Tap, who was compromised by a bad post way outside, was forced to be further back than usual early and by the time he got rolling could only run an unthreatening second as he bounced 5 points from a 1¼.

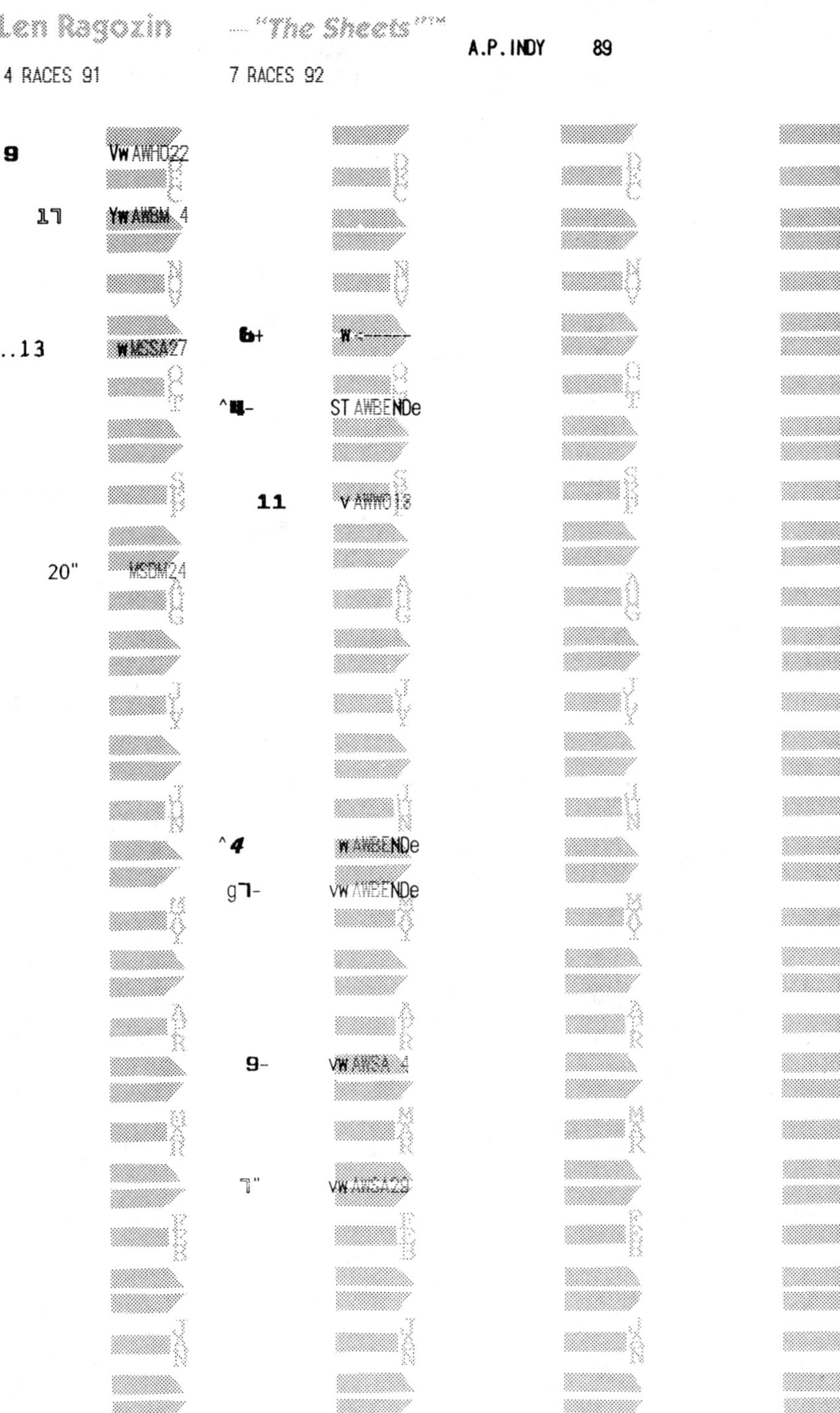
Len Ragozin
"The Sheets"™
A.P. INDY 89
4 RACES 91
7 RACES 92
9 VwAWHO22
17 YwAWBM 4
..13 wMSSA27
6+
ST AWBENDe
11 vAWWO13
20" MSDM24
^4 wAWBENDe
g7- VWAWBENDe
9- vWAWSA 4
7" vWAWSA23

Len Ragozin ..."The Sheets"™

PLEASANT TAP 87

5 RACES 89		9 RACES 90		8 RACES 91		10 RACES 92	
		6	VwAWSA26				
=12-	[tAWH025	8-	AWHD 1	=9+	YAWHD30		
12-	AWGP 4	^=12	VAWBERRP	5-	VAWCD 2	6	←
9-	WAWSA 4	g8-	WAWBERRP	9+	AWSA12	^1+	WAWBECSt
		10"	AWMERRP			2"	VAWBECSt
15+	MSDM 9			10	VWAWDM 7		
16"	sMSDM19						
						5"	YWAWBECSt
						.4	STAWBECSt
						4"	VAWBECSt
		^8-	AWCD 5			8"	WAWCD 2
		9-	AWKE24				
						8	WAWKE12
				6	VAWSA30		
		15+	VAWSA18				
				8-	VAWSA 9		
						6-	b]AWSA20
				12	tAWSA10		
		^16-	YWAWSA 4				
				10	VAWSA19		
						7"	YSAWSA11

Regardless of whether the numbers they run are good enough to win when they step up in company, horses are going to run the race they're in condition to run. A sound horse that ran one year exclusively in claimers and the following year solely in allowances would run the same percentage of good numbers each year. The only difference would be the number of times those good efforts translated into wins.

A corollary of the class theory is that there are some horses that "don't like to win," an assessment that is made by looking at a horse's record and seeing far more second- and third-place finishes than wins. Such animals are also referred to as "sucker horses" because they consistently run well enough to attract betting support but rarely reward their backers.

It might seem to make sense that an occasional horse will have such a strong competitive spirit that he will win more than his share of close photos, but my figures at certain tracks are accurate to a few inches, and I don't see any horses who run a little better in photo finishes. Certainly I would have a hard time believing that there is some genetic defect that causes some horses to deliberately allow others to pass them right at the wire.

When Friedman claimed him during the 1970s, Laddy's Luck had been branded a chronic loser, based on a record of one win in thirty-nine starts. He embodied several racetrack old wives' tales: people said he didn't like to win, that he needed a strong rider to run well, and that he hated to run inside other horses. We thought so much of those last two criticisms that we used apprentice riders exclusively and instructed them not to leave the rail with him until the stretch. Laddy's Luck won seven of his next fifteen races for us, then was claimed away and prospered for several other trainers. Whatever problems he had in winning were cured by entering him in the right races, using apprentices to get weight off, and saving ground.

I gave up my ownership of horses in the late 1970s and began managing stables for owners with more capital. By around 1990, when I was in my early sixties, this became too much of an effort for me. But Friedman until 1996 claimed horses for and advised

Charles and Elaine Bassford — who for years owned Maryland's most successful claiming stable — and Lou Donato, whose stable is based in Canada. In 1996, Friedman became one of four partners in an operation known as the New Top Stable. Starting with $350,000 in capital, a year later they were over $500,000 in the black. He works under the same principles I used for my stable: look for good health and an improving trend, look for hidden value, and put horses at the level where their numbers suggest they will hold their own against the competition. It's the numbers that define them, not some ephemeral quality that's mistaken for class.

The results we've had over the past twenty years bear that out. Perhaps the best-known claim made on our recommendation was Parochial, a fragile colt whom three of my clients sought at his $50,000 price, with Glenn Lane winning the shake in August 1987. In his first three starts for Lane later that year, Parochial won the Fairmount Derby, ran a close third to Alysheba in the Louisiana Super Derby, and then captured Aqueduct's Discovery Handicap, earning $295,000 in purses. I recommended the claim so strongly because the horse in previous nonstakes efforts had frequently run 9s — numbers that suggested he already had the ability of a stakes horse — even as a series of unlucky circumstances caused him to lose those races.

More recently, Friedman had a terrific success with Ginny Lynn, a filly whom he and his partners in New Top bought for $100,000 from Mr. and Mrs. Felty J. Yoder three races into her career. In her first nine starts for New Top, Ginny Lynn won four races — three of them stakes — ran second in three stakes and third in two others and won over $300,000.

Nothing about Ginny Lynn's breeding was that exciting — her father, Texas City, never made it to the races and became a sire only because he was a son of Mr. Prospector. Friedman recommended the purchase strictly on the numbers she ran in her first three starts. Ginny Lynn won her debut race, a $50,000 maiden claimer at Churchill Downs November 19, 1995, running a 14–, a powerful number for a two-year-old filly. She moved into

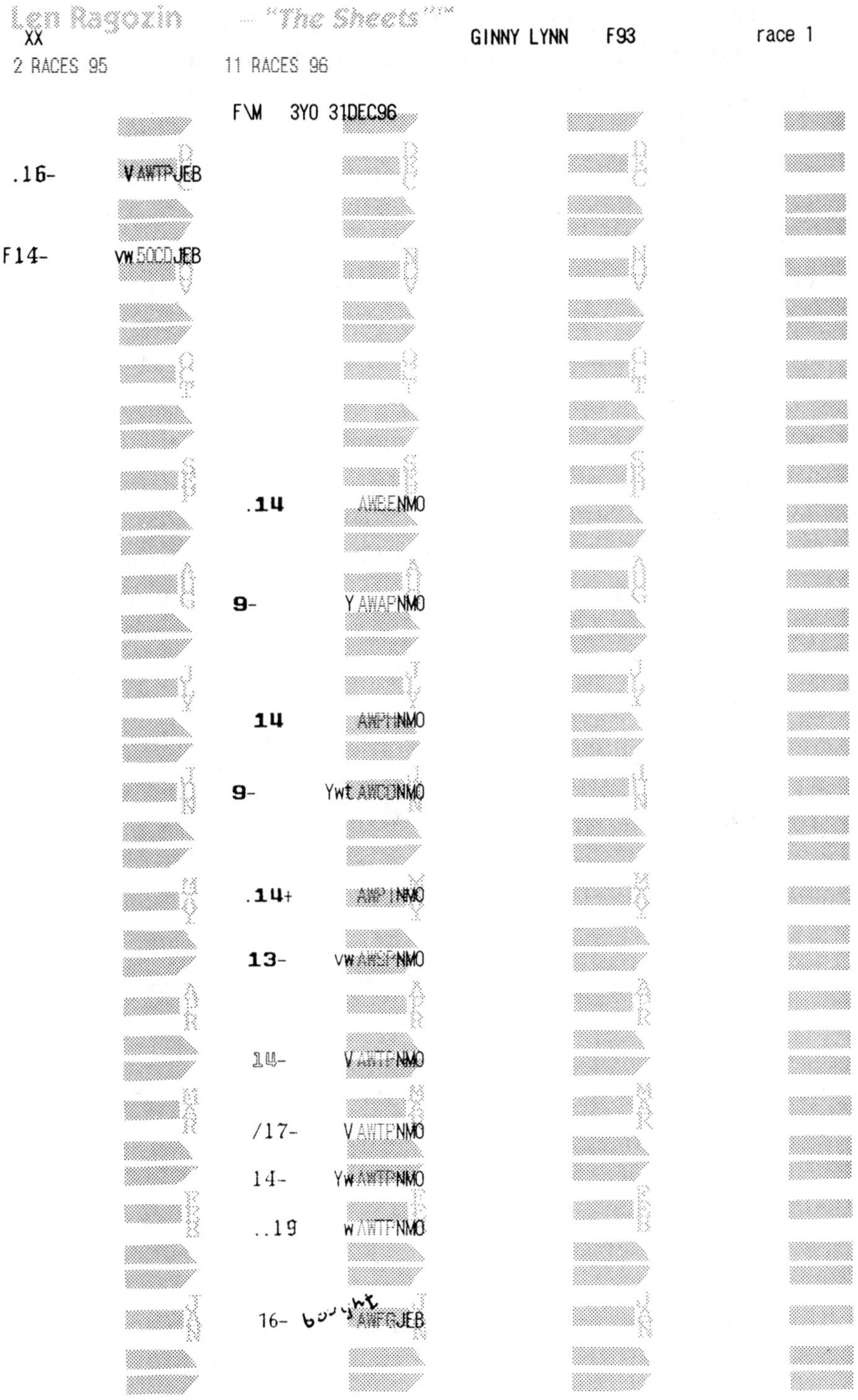

Len Ragozin — "The Sheets"™

XX

GINNY LYNN F93 race 1

2 RACES 95

11 RACES 96

F\M 3YO 31DEC96

.16- V AWTPJEB

F14- vw 50CDJEB

.14 AWBENMO

9- Y AWAPNMO

14 AWPHNMO

9- Ywt AWCDNMO

.14+ AWPINMO

13- vw AWSPNMO

14- V AWTPNMO

/17- V AWTPNMO

14- Yw AWTPNMO

..19 w AWTPNMO

16- bought AWFGJEB

allowance company for a race at Turfway three and a half weeks later and understandably reacted a bit, running a 16– while finishing second.

A month later, beginning her three-year-old season in a minor sprint stake at The Fairgrounds, Ginny Lynn paired the 16– while again finishing second. The fact that she didn't go backward in this race convinced Friedman that her strong maiden win hadn't taken anything out of her. He also liked the fact that the maiden win, which came at seven furlongs, was the longest of the three races she had run, suggesting that she would get better as she stretched out. And our nationwide figures would tell him where to enter her for the best financial results.

Although she backed up to a 19 in her first race for New Top — winning a minor stake at Turfway over a very dull track — Ginny Lynn soon justified Friedman's confidence. She matched her earlier 14– winning an allowance sprint at Turfway, matched it again two races later, and then moved forward to a 13– in winning a $150,000 stakes race at Sportsman's Park April 28, 1996. After running third in the Grade 2 Black-Eyed Susan Stakes at Pimlico, Ginny Lynn broke through to a 9– in winning the Dogwood Handicap at Churchill Downs, then paired it running second in the Arlington Heights Oaks that August. Finally New Top sold her for a half-million.

More than two dozen horses who were claimed or purchased relatively cheaply on our advice over the years became stakes winners who, while their success was less sudden and spectacular than Parochial and Ginny Lynn, showed generous profits.

Main Stem had breeding that was distinctly not Main Line: he was by the unheralded Clem out of an equally obscure mare named Whale Tail.

But in his fourth start as a two-year-old in the fall of 1980, he ran a 10½ in an allowance route at the Meadowlands. He bounced for two races, but then ran a 10¼. Both of those races were what we call "buried" efforts, meaning that they were far better than they looked in *The Racing Form*. Usually, buried efforts occur because other horses in the race surpass their average race. Main Stem's buried efforts were stakes-caliber performances by a horse who had yet to win beyond the maiden ranks.

Friedman also liked the fact that the horse's mother had been amazingly sturdy: she raced 128 times in her career. But those two-year-old numbers were good enough to make us want Main Stem even if we had no reason to expect him to be durable.

After the 10¼, we purchased the horse privately for $60,000. Friedman had visions of Main Stem developing into a Kentucky Derby starter, but illness early in his three-year-old campaign ended that dream. Main Stem never matched that 10¼ during 1981 and seemed to be doing his best running at shorter distances, so we ran him primarily as a sprinter after that.

In his first race at four he broke through to a new top of 7¾ while winning the Coaltown at six furlongs over Aqueduct's inner track; at five he won the Gravesend Handicap and lowered his peak by a ¼ point; at the advanced age of six he surged to a new top of 4½ and won the Paumonok and Toboggan Handicaps at Aqueduct, and at seven he was still good enough to run five straight sprint numbers of 7¼ or better. All told, he started 134 times and earned $521,000.

In 1987, when I was advising Gold-N-Oats Stable on claims, my first strong recommendation to them was a $35,000 claimer named Summer Tale. He had not gotten to the races until midway through his three-year-old year the previous June, but his ten races on dirt over the next seven months displayed steady but incremental improvement with no serious setbacks between tops.

Summer Tale looked like a horse who might really take off at four, especially considering how little he had raced. His best number, a 13¼, was a concealed effort, since he ran it while losing by thirteen lengths in a New York–bred stakes race in his last start of 1986. That performance on the surface looked poor enough to persuade his owner to drop him into claimers. But we liked this fractional advance on his earliest form. It encouraged us to grab him for $35,000, wait for four-year-old development, and point for similar New York–bred stakes.

Summer Tale ran a new top of 11 in the race from which Gold-

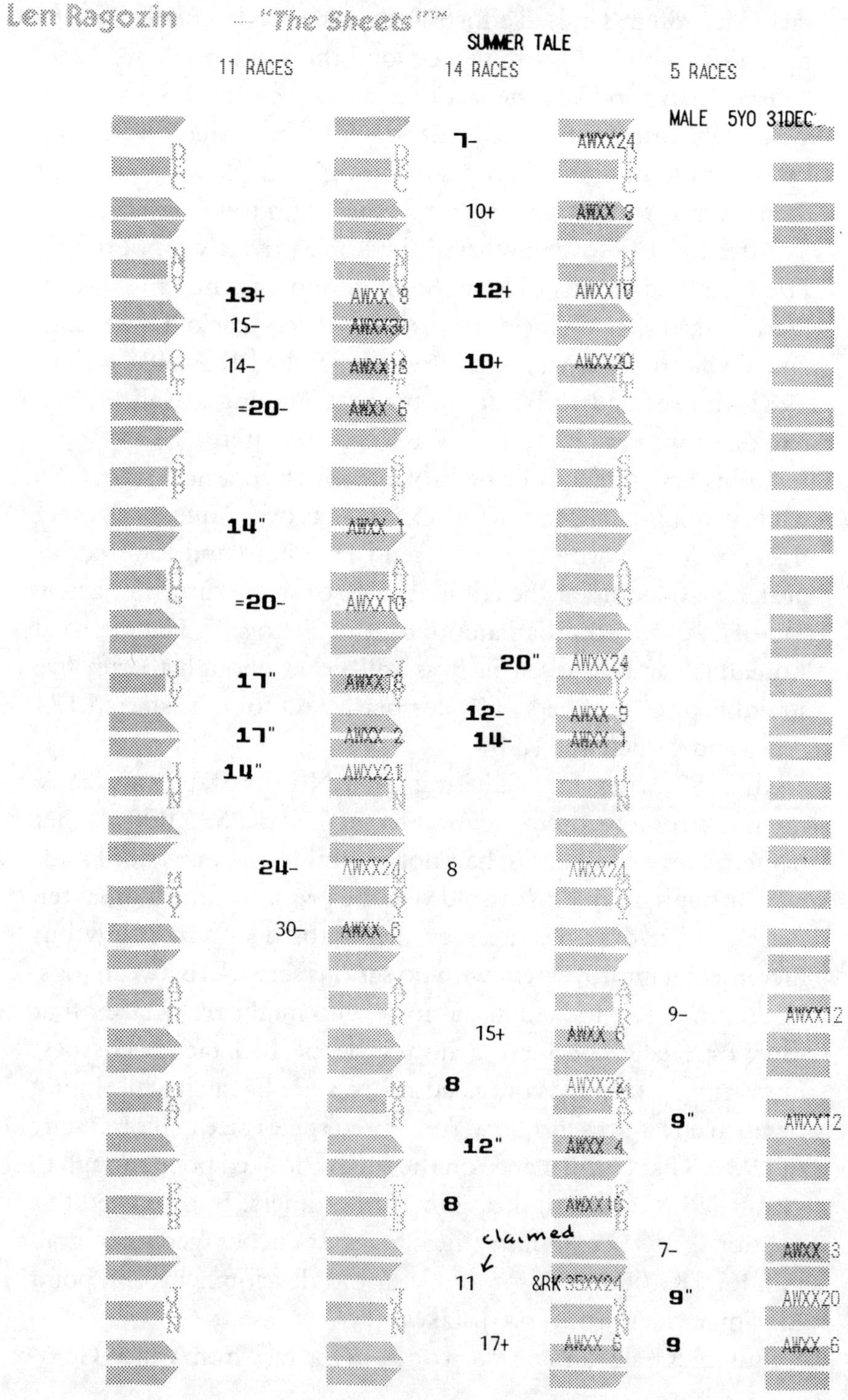

Len Ragozin —"*The Sheets*"™

SUMMER TALE

11 RACES	
13+	AWXX 8
15–	AWXX30
14–	AWXX18
=20–	AWXX 6
14"	AWXX 1
=20–	AWXX10
17"	AWXX18
17"	AWXX 2
14"	AWXX21
24–	AWXX24
30–	AWXX 6

14 RACES	
7–	AWXX24
10+	AWXX 3
12+	AWXX10
10+	AWXX20
20"	AWXX24
12–	AWXX 9
14–	AWXX 1
8	AWXX24
15+	AWXX 6
8	AWXX22
12"	AWXX 4
8	AWXX16
11 (claimed)	&RK 35XX24
17+	AWXX 6

5 RACES	
MALE 5YO 31DEC	
9–	AWXX12
9"	AWXX12
7–	AWXX 3
9"	AWXX20
9	AWXX 6

N-Oats claimed him, and he followed that with an 8 in winning an allowance race. By the end of the year, he set a new top of 6¾ while winning a New York–bred stakes race, and over a fourteen-month period he earned $170,000 for Gold-N-Oats.

In April 1987, the Bassfords claimed a four-year-old filly named Pretty Tricky for $40,000 on Friedman's recommendation. Two races earlier, Pretty Tricky had made a 1½-point move to a new top of 12, which reinforced Friedman's belief that she was still developing and remained in good condition. After she finished out of the money in an allowance field, her owner dropped her claiming price by $10,000 and the Bassfords grabbed her.

King Leatherbury, based on Friedman's enthusiasm about Pretty Tricky's prospects, decided her first race out of that $40,000 claimer should be a minor stake, and she finished second by a neck. In ten starts for the Bassfords, Pretty Tricky won three stakes races and finished second in four others, earning over $160,000 in ten months before she was retired to become a broodmare.

A year after Pretty Tricky was claimed, Gold-N-Oats grabbed a three-year-old gelding named Pappas Swing at my urging. His early three-year-old top was only 17½, but in ten races prior to the day he first tried the turf, Pappas Swing had improved in steady surges without ever backing up much from his top form at that moment. This indicated soundness and potential.

In that turf debut, he made a 3-point jump to a lifetime peak of 14–, but the quality of the race was obscured by his fifth-place finish. This buried effort led his owner to decide the only way to get a purse was to drop him into a $30,000 claimer. He paired the 14–, won the race, and moved into Gold-N-Oats's barn.

If the first 14– had been on dirt, I might have worried that he was at the end of the line. But a sharp jump in his first grass race allowed me to hope he might be a new horse on turf, especially since he had never bounced to high numbers from any of his peaks.

The stable ran Pappas Swing in a $75,000 claimer at Belmont

Len Ragozin — *"The Sheets"*™

PAPPAS SWING 85 race 1

3 RACES 87	
26"	AWH123
23-	wAWH117
23"	AWH128

18 RACES 88	
=11+	wAWFG17
=16	AWLA15
sold	
=14"	AWXX25
=8+	wAWSU 8
=13+	AWRK14
:=14-	wAWHA16
=11+	wAWSU 2
=11+	wAWRK18
=20	BE30
claimed	
=14-	w CR24
=14-	CR16
G20"	CR22
17-	wAWCR 8
20	AWGP27
20"	AWGP20
21"	AWGP 6
20"	AWGP26
F20+	AWGP 9

16 RACES 89	
=12+	50CR10
=15-	AWCD18
=13-	AWCD 4
=14	AWLA23
=22+	AWAP 4
.18	Q AWAP11
17	Q AWAP31
=12"	AWAP14
=16	AWAP 4
=15"	AWHA10
=13"	AWCD20
=11-	AWCD10
.=11-	AWKE27
=11"	AWFG 2
=15+	AWFG 4
=12-	AWFG21

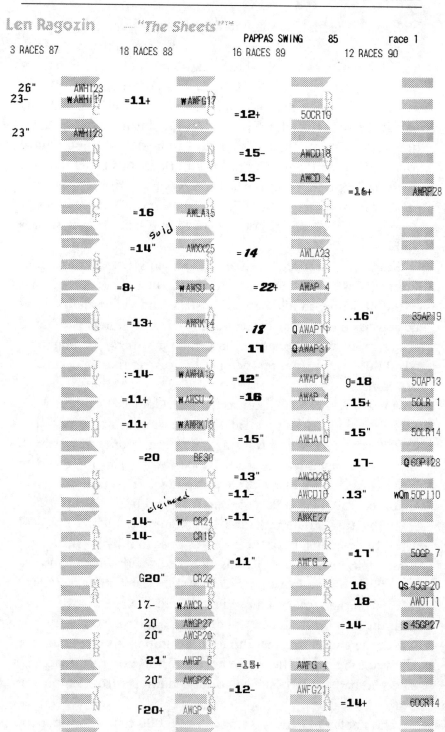

12 RACES 90	
=16+	AWRP28
..16"	35AP19
g=18	50AP13
.15+	50LR 1
=15"	50LR14
17-	Q 60PI28
.13"	wQm 50PI10
=17"	50GP 7
16	Qs 45GP20
18-	AWOT11
=14-	s 45GP27
=14+	60CR14

and the horse backed up to a 20, but in that race he bled severely — too severely for "New York Lasix." We had him shipped up to Rockingham, where — on Lasix — he won an allowance race while breaking through to an 11¼.

One reason I liked Pappas Swing as a claim after his solid turf debut was that *The Sheets* showed me that there were few legitimate stakes-caliber three-year-old turf horses that year. The lack of quality among that group was particularly evident outside the New York area, and so after Pappas Swing ran another 11¼ to win a minor turf stake at Suffolk, we had him shipped to Illinois to run in the Grade 3 Hawthorne Derby on July 16, 1988. My generalship was confirmed when Pappas Swing bounced to a 14– over a soft grass course and still won the race and paid $15.

Two races later, the gelding won another stakes race at Suffolk and ran an 8¼ in doing so, pushing his earnings in the four and a half months since the claim above $150,000. It was becoming unlikely that the horse would improve further, and so Gold-N-Oats sold him for nearly $200,000. Pappas Swing remained a consistent, hard-hitting horse, but he never ran better than a 10¾ after he was sold, and was forced to compete in minor allowance races and then in claimers.

In May 1989, I persuaded Gold-N-Oats to claim another gelding, Passing Ships, for $72,500 at Belmont. Unlike most of our other claims, Passing Ships was a proven commodity rather than a promising horse I hoped would improve. He had already earned $170,000, and the previous fall, as a four-year-old, had run 5¾ in consecutive sprint races in New York. But there are so many killers in the high-priced sprint ranks in New York that his *Racing Form* lines for those races didn't look that special.

That pairing, with a month between the two efforts, convinced me that the gelding took the initial big effort pretty much in stride and would continue to run strongly at age five. It was just a matter of finding the right spots in which to race him. Specifically, this meant getting out of those murderous sprints.

He was slow coming around as a five-year-old, so in late September Gold-N-Oats risked losing him for $70,000 at

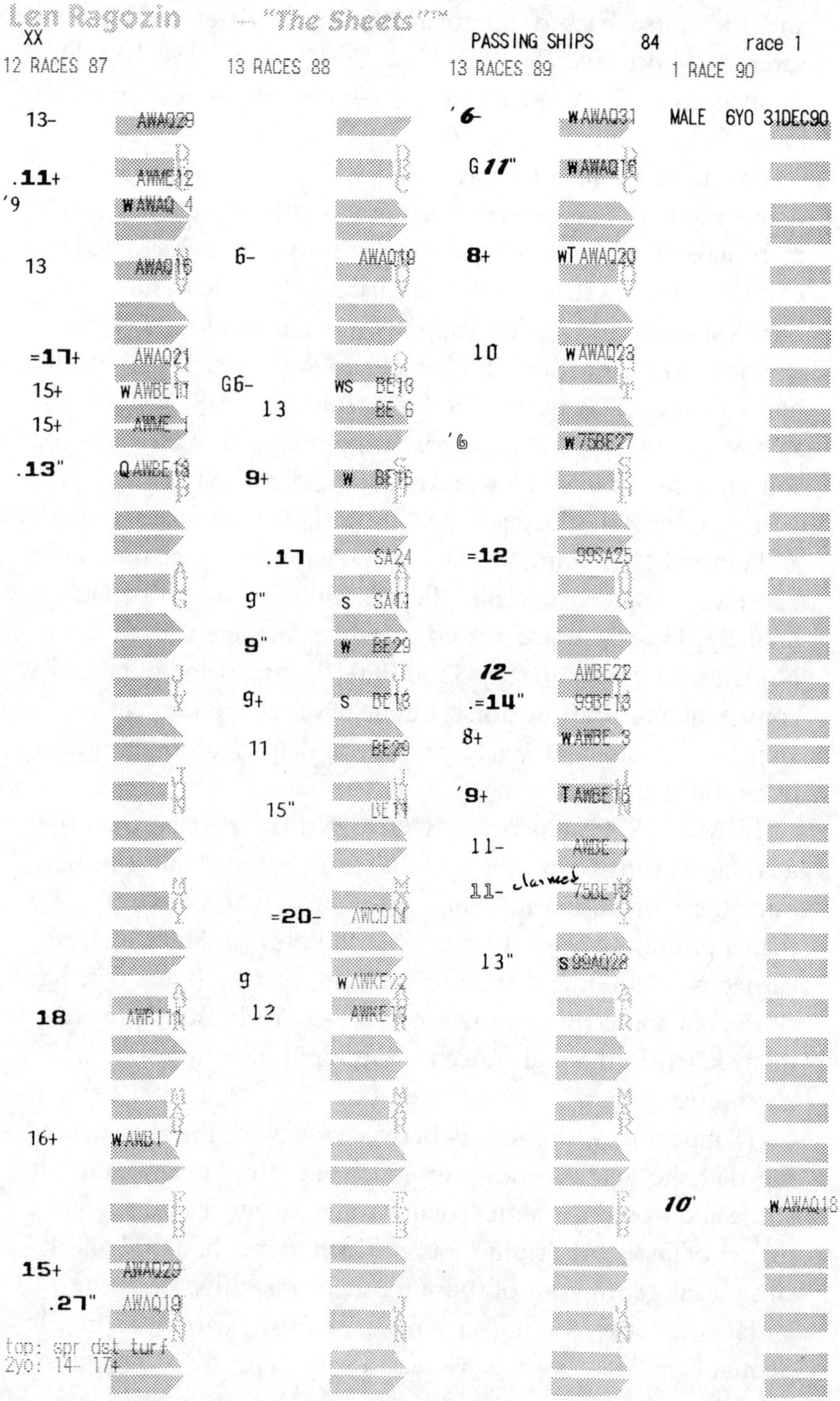

Len Ragozin — "The Sheets"™

XX

PASSING SHIPS 84 race 1

MALE 6YO 31DEC90

12 RACES 87

13- AWAQ29
.11+ AWME12
'9 W AWAQ 4
13 AWAQ16
=17+ AWAQ21
15+ W AWBE11
15+ AWME 1
.13" Q AWBE13
18 AWB11
16+ W AWBI 7
15+ AWAQ23
.27" AWAQ18

top: spr dst turf
2yo: 14- 17+

13 RACES 88

6- AWAQ19
G6- WS BE13
13 BE 6
9+ W BE15
.17 SA24
9" S SA11
9" W BE29
9+ S BE13
11 BE29
15" BE11
=20- AWCD11
9 W AWKF7
12 AWKE13

13 RACES 89

'6- W AWAQ31
G 11" W AWAQ16
8+ WT AWAQ20
10 W AWAQ23
'6 W 75BE27
=12 99SA25
12- AWBE22
.=14" 99BE13
8+ W AWBE 3
'9+ T AWBE15
11- AWBE 1
11- claimed 75BE19
13" S 99AQ28

1 RACE 90

10" W AWAQ18

Belmont but there were no takers. He suddenly popped a 6 while winning this mile race by six and one quarter lengths. Two more wins in allowance company followed, and there was a distinct feeling of déjà vu as the Gallant Fox and Display Handicaps — the two races I'd won with Frampton Delight thirteen years earlier — loomed on the horizon.

As is so often the case, it didn't even take a top effort to win the Gallant Fox. Passing Ships bounced to an 11½ and won by a head. In the Display, despite the marathon distance of 2 miles, he matched his sprint figures, running a 5¾, and won by 17½ lengths. Gold-N-Oats gave him a six-week breather, and then he won another marathon handicap race over Aqueduct's inner track. Having earned $270,000 in nine months with Passing Ships, Gold-N-Oats sold him now for $280,000 to an Arab big shot who intended the gelding as a gift to one of the ten Saudi Arabian princes who ante up $100,000 every year and match horses in a marathon. Cordero went over to Saudi Arabia to ride him, and Passing Ships romped home. We should have held out for a percentage of the purse!

At the end of 1989, Friedman persuaded the Bassfords to claim a three-year-old filly named Double Artemis for $25,000. She had run decently in her debut that June, but followed that with three months of lackluster racing. When she ran a 20¼ in early October, Friedman began to consider her but was wary that she would react with another string of bad races. But after a bounce, she improved to an 18¾, did not back up badly in her subsequent start, and then moved to a 17½, the kind of steady development that suggested she was sound and would improve further.

Her owners moved her from that race for $45,000 claimers into an allowance race, but when she bounced, they ran her back in a claimer with her price cut by $20,000. Nick Bassford claimed her, and she exploded to a new top of 12 while winning by six lengths. We were concerned that this jump would knock her out for an extended period, but four weeks later she began a string of four straight wins that culminated with a victory in a $60,000

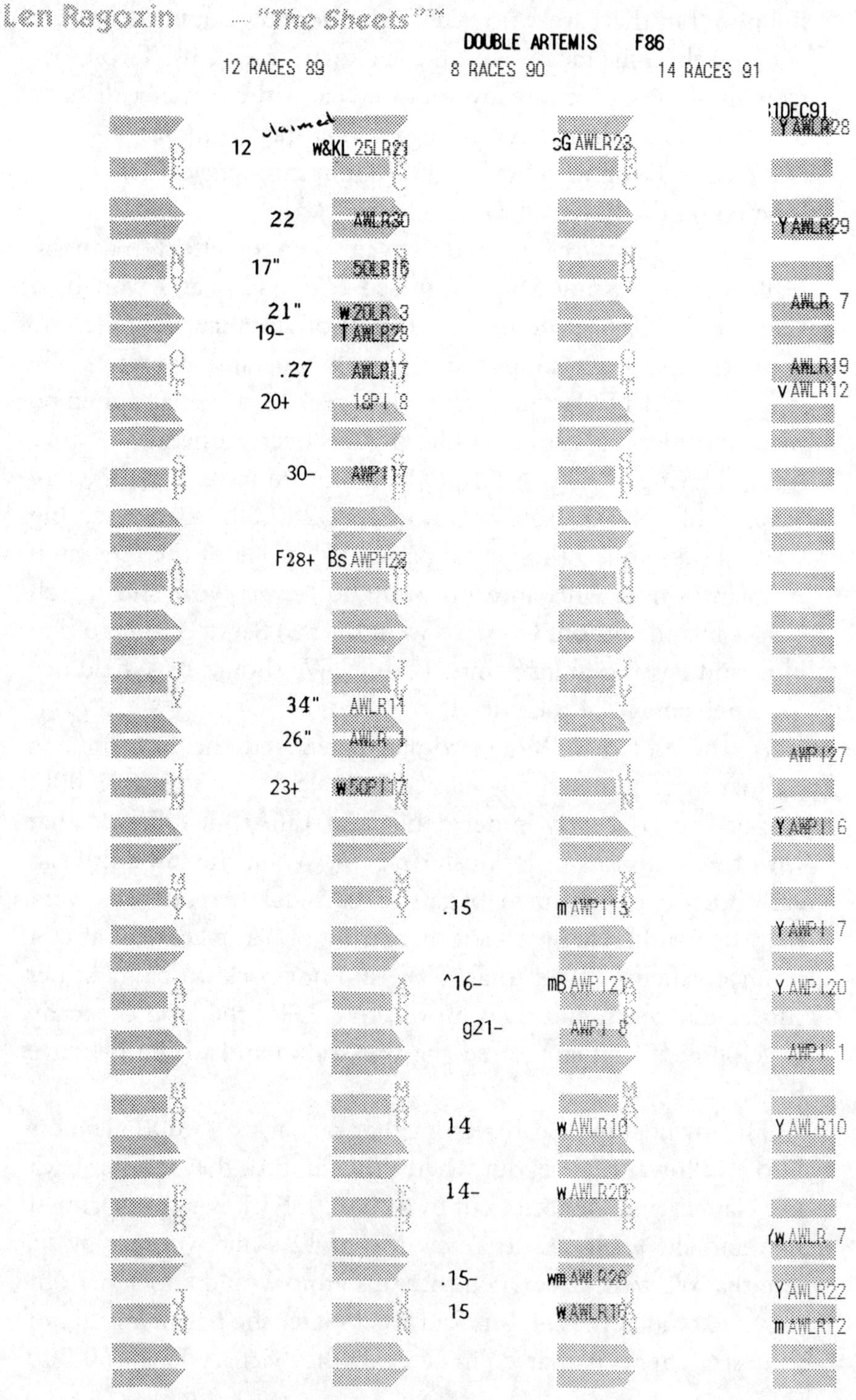

Len Ragozin — "The Sheets"™

DOUBLE ARTEMIS F86

12 RACES 89

12 [claimed] W&KL 25LR21
22 AWLR30
17" 5OLR15
21" w2OLR 3
19- TAWLR28
.27 AWLR17
20+ 18PI 8
30- AWPI17
F28+ BsAWPH28
34" AWLR11
26" AWLR 1
23+ w5OPI17

8 RACES 90

cG AWLR23
.15 mAWPI13
^16- mBAWPI21
g21- AWPI 8
14 wAWLR10
14- wAWLR20
.15- wmAWLR28
15 wAWLR16

14 RACES 91

31DEC91
YAWLR28
YAWLR29
AWLR 7
AWLR19
vAWLR12
AWPI27
YAWPI 6
YAWPI 7
YAWPI20
AWPI 1
YAWLR10
YwAWLR 7
YAWLR22
mAWLR12

Len Ragozin — "The Sheets"™

WAIT FOR THE LADY F87

19 RACES 90

s15" wAWLR27
13+ VsAWLR14
'18+ AWLR23
18+ YAWLR 2
19" YsAWLR 2
g15- vws35PI15
13+ w35PI 3
20+ wAWPI27
=56+ AWLR 7
=**19** AWLR28
'16" w25LR15
claimed
G'25+ &KL35PI11
F21 AWPI19
g19- AWPI 5
g25+ AWPI23
15- AWLR27
25- wB AWLR 9
19" w]50LR20
26" sMSLR 6

12 RACES 91

.20- vAWLR14
10- AWLR28
13" wAWME 9
16 AWLR14
16- YAWME 4
.XX AWDE13
13- vAWMT 6
25- AWDE 2
31- YAWSP 4
.12 wm AWPI23
10- wAWLR18
15" wAWLR26

8 RACES 92

24" YAWPI20
=**32+** YAWPI23
15 VsAWGS25
G**13"** AWPI28
12- wAWLR22
r.20- AWLR15
13" AWLR25
20 vAWLR11

stakes sprint, earning $70,000 in the first two months the Bassfords owned her.

Three months later, in May 1990, the Bassfords claimed Wait For The Lady for $35,000. Friedman had become enthused about her after she made a big jump to a 14¾ in her fourth career start. She was out of a dam who had produced several decent horses, none of whom had run well until their four-year-old seasons, which suggested to Friedman that a filly this fast at three might be something special; certainly that number was awfully good for a still-maturing filly available for $35,000.

As a result, he went against our usual rule of waiting for a horse to get close enough to its initial big number to suggest it hadn't been a knockout race. After a big bounce to a 25¼, Wait For The Lady made a partial recovery to an 18¾, slipped a bit to a 21, and on the day the Bassfords claimed her, regressed to another 25¼. But Friedman's faith that she would start moving forward again was quickly justified when, after giving her a five-week rest, the Bassfords gambled by dropping her in for a $25,000 tag, found no takers, and Wait For The Lady rebounded by winning the race while running a 16½. Four races later, she ran a new top of 13¼.

Like her older siblings, she saved her best running for her four-year-old season, winning four stakes, including the Grade 2 Long Look and the Grade 3 Snow Goose.

At the end of his two-year-old season in 1991, Ameri Valay advanced in successive races from a 26 to a 21½ to an 18 to a 17. The steady development, as well as the numbers themselves, made him seem like a bargain when he began his three-year-old season in a $35,000 claimer. Evidently his connections didn't think much of his undistinguished breeding. The Bassfords claimed him as he won the race while pairing the 17, and he captured two of his next three races while reaching a new peak of 13¼. Ameri Valay has earned over $600,000 since Bassford claimed him, winning eight stakes — among them the 1994 and 1995 runnings of the Grade 3 John B. Campbell Handicap — and finishing in the money in nine others.

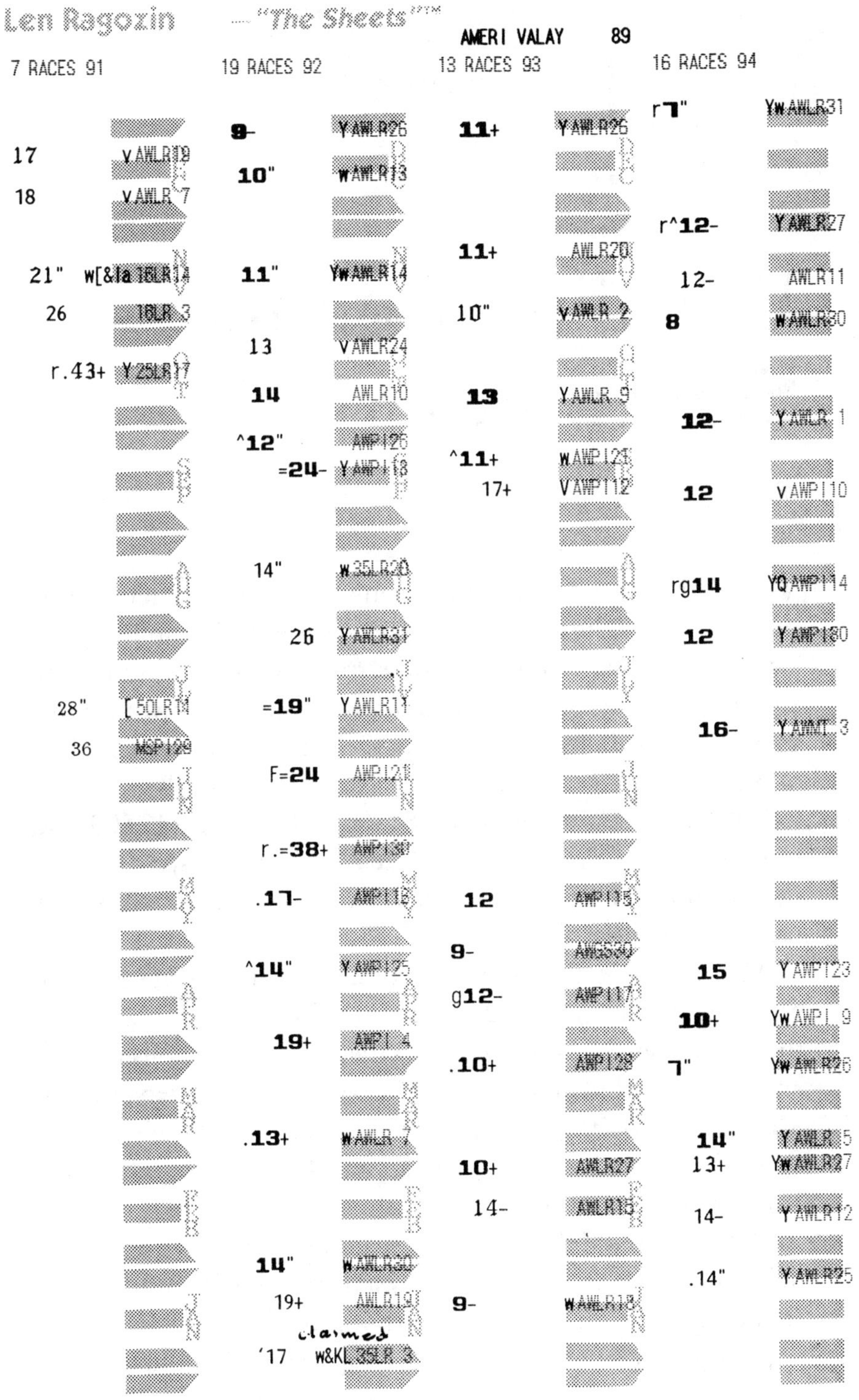

Len Ragozin — "The Sheets"™

AMERI VALAY 89

7 RACES 91

- 17 VAWLR19
- 18 VAWLR 7
- 21" w[&la 18LR14
- 26 18LR 3
- r.43+ Y25LR17
- 28" [50LR14
- 36 MSP129

19 RACES 92

- 9- YAWLR26
- 10" wAWLR13
- 11" YwAWLR14
- 13 VAWLR24
- 14 AWLR10
- ^12" AWP125
- =24- YAWP113
- 14" w35LR20
- 26 YAWLR31
- =19" YAWLR11
- F=24 AWP121
- r.=38+ AWP130
- .17- AWP115
- ^14" YAWP125
- 19+ AWP1 4
- .13+ wAWLR 7
- 14" wAWLR30
- 19+ AWLR19
- claimed
- '17 w&KL 35LR 3

13 RACES 93

- 11+ YAWLR26
- 11+ AWLR20
- 10" YAWLR 2
- 13 YAWLR 9
- ^11+ wAWP121
- 17+ VAWP112
- 12 AWP115
- 9- AWG530
- g12- AWP117
- .10+ AWP128
- 10+ AWLR27
- 14- AWLR15
- 9- wAWLR18

16 RACES 94

- r7" YwAWLR31
- r^12- YAWLR27
- 12- AWLR11
- 8 wAWLR30
- 12- YAWLR 1
- 12 vAWP110
- rg14 YQAWP114
- 12 YAWP130
- 16- YAWMT 3
- 15 YAWP123
- 10+ YwAWP1 9
- 7" YwAWLR26
- 14" YAWLR 5
- 13+ YwAWLR27
- 14- YAWLR12
- .14" YAWLR25

15

Breeding Counts — Sometimes

I CLAIMED HORSES for many years without looking at breeding. All that interested me was a horse's numbers, not his parents. Most champions come from good stock, but there are bottom-level claiming races littered with horses who never showed much ability despite being the children or grandchildren of Northern Dancer and Alydar and Mr. Prospector. By the same token, Seattle Slew was bought as a yearling for $17,500 and Holy Bull's breeding lines suggested an ability to sprint or run on turf, not to beat the best horses of his generation in distance races on the dirt.

My reliance on the numbers produced an interesting result in claims made for myself and for several of our clients: we acquired the best horses ever produced by otherwise undistinguished parents. Those included horses who became stakes winners, such as Main Stem, Wait For The Lady (a daughter of Believe The Queen); Corporate Headache (a son of Catullus); and Ameri Valay (out of Carnivalay).

But there certainly are some situations where sires or broodmares pass down traits to many of their children. With a dirt runner, it's nice to see relatives who moved up on grass. More important, today we always inspect ancestors for soundness or sound offspring, fearing a fragility that will limit the careers of our well-patterned acquisition.

I got this lesson the hard way in the mid-1970s with a horse called Goat Grabber, who was a son of Minnesota Mac, a leading turf sire. Goat Grabber did not race as a two-year-old, but at three quickly showed promise, and after seven races made his turf debut in May and ran an 11¾, a terrific performance for a three-year-old in his first grass race, although he didn't win.

Goat Grabber bounced to a 20¼ in his second turf race, then ran a 16¼ and repeated the 11¾, again without winning. He was running 1⅜ miles on the grass in most of these turf allowance races, and I thought he not only had a real future but could pay a quick dividend if I was able to buy him. I offered the owner $30,000 and was rebuffed, then upped the offer in increments of $10,000 until he finally agreed to sell for $60,000.

That was virtually all the cash our stable had at the time, but I was certain the investment would pay off. I called King Leatherbury, my Maryland trainer, and told him, "I just bought you the winner of the Donald P. Ross Handicap," then one of the bigger turf stakes in Maryland. The purse was $50,000, and I thought we could get the winner's share if — under light weight — Goat Grabber merely repeated his best efforts.

It didn't work out exactly as I planned. First, Golden Don, then the leading grass horse in the country, was entered, something I hadn't anticipated because I figured the purse was half what his connections liked to go after. He didn't belong, but there he was, and Goat Grabber ran well but finished second. Worse, he came out of the race with a fractured sesamoid that forced us to sideline him for more than a year. He never fully recovered, and we retired him after one race as a four-year-old. I subsequently learned that offspring of Minnesota Mac frequently developed sesamoid problems. If I had been more tuned in to breeding, I might have avoided this disaster; then again, Goat Grabber had already run 1⅜ miles many times and showed no bad signs.

There are going to be other cases where breeding should

affect betting or claiming decisions. Lost Code was a champion during the 1980s who became notorious for avoiding big races in New York because Lasix was banned there and nobody explained to his trainer that you could beat the testing. He sires horses who also seem unable to run well until they're given Lasix for the first time. The children of Meadowlake share his precocity and his unsoundness — many run their lifetime best races at two and go downhill at three. Meadow Flight is perhaps one exception — although he peaked out in his sixth race as a three-year-old.

But my emphasis is always on a horse's numbers. Generally, there are only two situations in which breeding should be a major consideration for a bettor: a horse making its debut on grass, or a horse going long — two turns and over a mile — for the first time.

We have a breeding category called "turf move-ups" covering horses whom we project to run races on grass at least 5 points better than those they've been running on dirt, even with no pattern to suggest improvement from their dirt numbers. Sometimes everybody expects these move-ups because the horses are the offspring of turf champions. But there are other cases in which the sire or broodmare was nothing special but ran far better on turf than dirt and passed that quality along. Ten or fifteen years ago there were quite a few of these "concealed sires" whose children offered tremendous value the first time they raced on turf. Handicapping research has gotten better and more intensive, though, and today you can get 30–1 on these horses only if their dirt form is so abysmal that even the well-informed bettors decide to pass despite the switch in racing surface.

Because the first race on turf may be the one real opportunity to get good value on horses with grass in their bloodlines, it's almost always correct to bet them at the right price. It's different with a horse staying on dirt but stretching out for the first time. These should be approached with extreme caution, for several reasons.

One is that most bettors don't attach enough weight to the

difficulty of stretching from, say, seven furlongs to nine furlongs, and so a horse running impressively at the shorter distances will be overbet considering the new challenge he's confronting. Even horses who are bred to get better with added distance often need to go long once to get the hang of it.

I would bet a horse going long for the first time only if his line showed such strong condition that I thought he would almost insist on running well come rain, mud, gales, or the extra furlongs. Friedman's general advice is not to bet horses the first time they're going long unless the odds are generous, and he says he has the losing tickets to prove the folly of ignoring his own counsel.

Sometimes this means not playing a race because the horse you like is an unknown quantity at the distance. But in other cases that horse will be so overbet by the rest of the public based on his form at shorter distances that some other horse who does not seem as fast but has established ability at the longer route offers enough value to make it worth wagering that the fast horse won't run well going long.

The race that attracts the greatest focus on breeding and the ability to go long is the Kentucky Derby, since entrants are almost always running at least one furlong further than they've gone to that point. Breeding experts have made a cottage industry of what is known as the dosage theory, which traces horses' bloodlines back several generations to determine whether they have the necessary mix of speed and stamina in their genes to win the Derby.

The theory is controversial, partly because its rules were concocted "backwards" in the early 1980s to match previous Derby winners; partly because horses who failed to meet the dosage criteria and lost the Derby often went on to win the Travers at the same distance or the Belmont Stakes going ¼ mile longer; and partly because when one horse who didn't meet the criteria, Strike the Gold, won the 1991 Derby, the dosage creators retroactively "qualified" him by granting chef de race status to one of his ancestors. Bold Forbes, the 1976 Derby winner, also got a retroactive boost.

I don't make any bets based on dosage theory, and I couldn't tell you which Derby winners qualified. I'm looking at horses based on what they've done and evaluating their performance in light of how closely their racing pattern conforms to what has been successful in the past. In recent years, I've looked for a horse that the trainer has brought along slowly enough to run that big number for the first time — or repeat a recent improvement — on Derby Day. Slightly overraced horses that throw in too big a race a few months earlier — with an occasional exception like Thunder Gulch — don't win the Derby. But this is all about analyzing patterns, not studying dosage, which frankly holds no interest for me.

16

You Got the Horse Right Where?

YOU MAY HAVE SEEN the old *Honeymooners* episode in which Ralph Kramden, needing a quick $200 to replace lost dues from the Raccoon Lodge, goes to the track to bet $10 on a hot tip on a horse named Cigar Box. When the horse's price drops below 20–1, Ralph hits on a scheme to boost the odds by touting bettors on another longshot, Happy Feet. His own phony tip travels around the racetrack, comes back with some convincing embellishments added by his buddy Ed Norton, and sweeps him along. He puts his money on his own fairy tale.

That routine, lifted by Jackie Gleason from a movie featuring an old-time stuttering comic named Joe Frisco, shows — with only minor exaggeration — how the typical bettor loves a well-told story dressed up as "inside information." Another piece of our folklore, Damon Runyon's wonderful tale "A Story Goes With It," covers the same theme.

Most inside information at the track isn't deliberately wrong — far from it. Nonetheless, Friedman used to have a standing offer to people we knew: if they had inside information on a race, he would pay them $10 to *not* tell him what it was. While there may be a bit of good inside information available, it won't offset all the bad tips you'll get.

Most inside information comes from owners, passing on wisdom from their trainers. Naturally, any horse loses most of the time — and it is in the trainer's interest to produce an epic saga of the battles he is carrying on against the horse's bad habits, minor ailments, bad luck, and mishandling by idiot jockeys. Every now and then all these problems are reported as under control, and a day of great expectations — the "high" an owner really lives for — is created. Naturally, the trainer hopes to win, and the horse probably has a little better chance to run well on this day than another. But rest assured that if he loses this race, the trainer will have another story to explain it.

Even assuming the trainer and owner are able to objectively assess the shape their horse is in, they aren't necessarily good enough handicappers to know whether he can outrun his competition. We have been confidants in cases where a trainer or jockey agent insisted they'd been stiffing some horse for six months to set up a price and this was payday — but they wanted to borrow money to make their bet. Well, that's not the healthiest sign that these guys know what they're doing. As often as not, they'd get their money down and some horse they hadn't figured on would jump up and beat them.

For every Pedro Briones who can pick his spots and cash in big, there's a dozen guys like Jerry the Needle, the operator who wanted me to be his partner in doping horses for profit. This great fixer was always broke. Some time after I'd declined his big offer, Jerry came to me because he knew we dealt with a guy I'll call Ralph Atlas — a bookie who would handle large bets without killing the odds. Jerry asked if I could get down a $2,000 bet for him on a cheap filly running in a claiming race down in Philadelphia. I looked at her figures; she had been running 29s and 30s and I thought even on drugs she wasn't likely to run much better than mid-20s. Jerry had her in the right spot — a $3,000 filly claimer, where a horse running a 26 would usually win. But in a very unusual and unlucky circumstance, the race had attracted three cheap fillies who all looked primed for their absolute top effort — about a 23. We told Jerry this. I guess if he had tried to get back to the owner and change the plan, he might have destroyed his miracle-man aura. At any rate, Jerry pressed me to put in the bet anyway. Ralph Atlas handled the bet, but the filly went off at 5–2 on-track anyhow, probably because her owner couldn't keep his mouth shut. She ran fourth.

Ten days later, Jerry returned with $200, told us it was all he could scrape together, and asked us to bet her again. Presumably the owner had lost faith. This time she drew the usual cheap opposition and won and paid $25. So here you had really good inside information, and the chief plotter more or less broke even.

With a two-year-old race at Saratoga filled with first-time starters, it's not that unusual to hear what's supposed to be inside information on six of the eight horses. It should be pretty clear this is not useful.

Now, if you're talking about a horse that hasn't run in six months after going off form, is coming back with lackluster workouts, but his lifetime top is 10 and he's 4–1 when his *Racing Form* line suggests he'd be 20–1, I'm going to take that money very seriously. If my original plan was to bet a horse I thought could run a 15 today, I may reconsider. But my decision ultimately is going to lean heavily on the horse's sheet: if his past record shows he needs a race or two to get ready, I'm going to disregard the heavy betting action, unless the horse is now being handled by a trainer who specializes in winning with layoff horses. I'd feel the same way if the horse was not being bet strongly but showed several excellent workouts. I won't bet if traditionally he — or his trainer — hasn't done his best off layoffs in the past.

As for trainer tips on a horse who has been running regularly — I'd rather read *The Sheets.* Many a time, trainers of my own horses would suggest that today was a good day for a bet. Often I would tell them that although I agreed that the horse was in good shape, today looked like a day for a temporary bounce. I was right often enough so that it became embarrassing for them.

For the past two decades, as I built up *The Sheets* to cover an increasing number of tracks, I did very little betting, leaving that part of our operation to Friedman. But when I was betting regularly and seriously, I couldn't have told you anything about which trainer was good first start off a layoff, or any other trainer tendencies. I was looking only for the very strongest patterns on a horse's sheet and relying on these to give me such a strong overlay that I had an edge in spite of maneuvers by the trainers of his competitors.

All that being said, the kind of painstaking analysis we do has meant, ironically, that when we ourselves are the sources of the inside information, it's generally pretty good.

One time, I inadvertently ruined a small bookmaker-runner who was feasting on the blue-collar workers at Con Edison's plant on East 14th Street in Manhattan.

My then father-in-law, George Buhagiar, an utterly solid, hard-working, save-your-money master mechanic, worked there. He disapproved of his fellow workers' gambling and didn't hesitate to lecture them about a cold old age being in store for their sins. (Fortunately George worshiped his daughter and took her word that the man she married wasn't essentially a gambler.) But during a visit with him one Sunday, his daughter mentioned casually that my horse Stagecraft seemed to have a good chance the next day and she wanted to bet $10 on it but was going out of town early that morning. George volunteered to make the bet with the bookie who hung around the Con Ed plant.

Now here is a guy who has never made a bet in thirty years, and all the blue collars know it. They see him putting $10 on a horse. Some knew why, some didn't, but the word swept the yard: Old George is betting a horse! When the smoke cleared, that little runner was holding almost $5,000 in bets on Stagecraft, who paid $12.60. I hope his boss accepted his explanations.

The hardest I ever worked to find a tip for someone ended up with her netting about $11. When I worked at *Newsweek* as a writer-researcher, my immediate boss was a wonderful older gal named Olga Barbi. After I left under a political cloud, she remained ready to do me an occasional favor, even including interviewing friends of mine for jobs. One day years later I was chatting with her and said, "I guess you know I own horses these days. I know you ladies make a little bet now and then. Should I get in touch if I think I have something good?" Of course she said yes.

Well, for Olga I wanted the best. Almost a year later a situation came up in which my filly and my father's filly were running as a betting entry. Both had super condition lines, and the price figured to be reasonable. So I advised Olga to bet. "How much should I play?" she asked.

"How do I know?" I replied. "You could bet two hundred dollars, or twenty dollars, or" — kiddingly — "two dollars."

She thought for a while. "Tell you what — give me six dollars — two dollars across the board."

Here was a tip from the world's greatest handicapper — whether she knew it or not — and a tip he had spent a year to dig up, and on a horse (actually, two horses) whose trainer was vouching for physical condition as well. Little did she know that there were gamblers who would put down thousands for me if I gave them such tips. I put in her $6, and when they ran 1–2 I had to spend two hours delivering her $11.20 profit.

Of course even our own information is not foolproof, and there are plenty of pitfalls in planning any maneuver. Actually, although we often bet on our own horses, there were only two cases (out of tens of thousands) in which we entered horses specifically with the idea of cashing a bet.

Seatrain, before we owned him, had certified that he was a pretty bad four-year-old horse by the time his trainer entered him in his first race on turf, a $5,000 claimer at Atlantic City, on September 25, 1976. He finished out of the money, and didn't seem to have any excuses.

When I analyzed the race, however, it became clear that many in the field had run much better than usual, and Seatrain's effort was superior to what you'd expect from a $5,000 claimer. It was another example of a concealed or "buried" race: the quality of his effort was obscured by other horses' atypical performances.

The problem was, Friedman and I knew that on grass the horse had run many lengths better than his career best on dirt, but his trainer couldn't know that. He switched him back onto the dirt. There was only one way to assure that he got another chance on turf: claim him ourselves.

So we did. But soon after Seatrain moved into King Leatherbury's barn, he bowed a tendon, and it began to look like a good idea gone lame. We gave him several months off, and when he returned to racing it was at the bottom — a $2,000 claimer at Penn National. He won, and ran a good figure. But after the race Leatherbury told Friedman the horse had aggravated the problem and it was questionable whether he'd be racing much longer.

Seatrain ran two more fair races at the bottom. Now Leatherbury told us that the bow in the tendon had begun to harden and there was a chance of him getting back to his best. We wanted to enter him in a grass race at Delaware Park; the trouble was, his most recent race at Penn National had been a $2,000 claimer, which under the Delaware racing rules was too cheap, making him ineligible to run at that track until he ran for a claiming price of $2,500 or more and finished in the money.

By now it was late August, and Delaware closed for the year shortly after Labor Day, meaning we were going to have to move quickly to find a spot in which Seatrain could regain eligibility. Timonium Racetrack in Maryland had a likely race for $2,500 on August 31, and Seatrain finished second, beaten four lengths, making him eligible for Delaware. But the track had no remaining cheap turf races; the only grass race left for us was a starter handicap on September 11, 1977, the final race of the day and Delaware's racing season.

The other horses in the starter handicap had all been racing for claiming prices of $8,000 to $10,000, and our horse looked overmatched on paper. After all, he'd been competing for $2,500 or less and had run out of the money on turf for a price of $5,000. Leatherbury knew enough about the figures not to dismiss us as screwy for entering Seatrain in this spot, but he saw no point in making the trip up the turnpike to saddle the horse himself, even though it was a Sunday and there was no racing in Maryland that day. He sent a young assistant to the track with the horse.

Friedman, on the other hand, approached the race with high spirits. Sunday was the one day of the week when Delaware had big handles because neighboring tracks were closed, and its patrons were notoriously unsophisticated bettors, making it prime territory for a score. We were secretive about the play to the point of not discussing it with anybody in the office. Friedman was concerned that someone would mention the horse at one of the gaming clubs in Manhattan frequented by several major horseplayers, and one of them would make a trip to Delaware and bet thousands on Seatrain, ruining the price.

Friedman drove down there on race day. In the paddock before the race, the assistant trainer pointed to his *Racing Form* and asked Friedman, "Aren't we in a little deep?"

Friedman was certainly in deep at the betting windows. Having no desire to stir the attention that a Briones-like final betting flash would create, he funneled several hundred dollars at a time into different windows every minute or two, keeping the price on Seatrain relatively steady while accounting for roughly half the entire pool on the horse in win and triple bets. The horse entered the gate at 8–1.

Seatrain showed more early speed than in his previous turf try, sitting about a length off the lead early in the 1⅟16-mile race. Jockey Johnny Adams took him three-wide leaving the backstretch, he reached even terms with the leader turning for home, and drew away through the stretch to win by four lengths. Seatrain paid $19.20 to win, a 34–1 shot finished second to key a $4,680 triple, and Friedman's investment of $6,000 netted him a $50,000 profit.

The win was no fluke. This starter handicap had been split into two divisions, and the time run by Seatrain would have won the other race by ten lengths. The score was a welcome surprise to Friedman, who never felt it was in the bag despite all the meticulous work that went into it — because we knew of so many attempted betting coups that misfired. He was reluctant to try another one, partly because we both believe you run a stable to win races, not to set up bets, and perhaps also because there was a certain satisfaction to retiring undefeated from the betting-coup business.

But eleven years later, opportunity knocked, and Friedman decided to try the door again. A filly named There's A Way, which the Bassfords had claimed on his recommendation, had just run a strong but very buried race at Aqueduct. Friedman persuaded Charles "Nick" Bassford to alter his schedule and give There's A Way an extra rest of almost a month to make sure the filly had time to recover from her effort. He found a spot at Aqueduct, a race for fillies and mares running for a claiming price of $12,000 to $14,000. As he hoped, it was carded as the last race of the day, meaning there would be both exacta and triple betting.

Friedman phoned bets on There's A Way to an associate in Las Vegas, then went to an Off-Track Betting office on Water Street in lower Manhattan to make the remainder of his play. The filly, with Brian Peck riding, was sent off at 41–1. She raced tenth early, and moved up gradually along the rail as the field entered the far turn. She was fifth and rallying strongly in midstretch when another filly bore in sharply, forcing Peck to snatch hold of There's A Way and pull her back to avoid a collision. She then resumed her strong rally, but fell a neck short of catching Ducky Duchesse, the 7–1 winner. The exotics saved the coup: Friedman had reversed his exactas and used There's A Way in every position in the triple; the exacta came back at $508.60, giving him a profit of close to $30,000 in Vegas alone, and the triple paid $5,747, fueling a nice score at OTB.

There is something about owning horses that makes you want to tell people when you think you've got a winner running. You'll tell anyone: relatives, long-ago job colleagues, even total strangers. Horse ownership makes you cock of the walk: you're suddenly an insider, and where's the fun unless you boast to people on the outside about some of what you know?

On Kentucky Derby Day in 1974, I treated myself to an early dinner at Lutèce, New York's austere paradise for gourmets.

Shortly before six, one of the waiters broke the cathedral-like atmosphere by rushing up to the headwaiter, babbling a torrent of French from which I half-recognized two words: "Cahnonahde. Cahnonahde." I didn't need a Berlitz School course to figure he was reporting that Cannonade had won the Derby.

Racing makes all men kin — the air was suddenly chummy. When the waiters approached us, I injected into the conversation the fact that I owned horses. One of them asked, "Does monsieur have maybe something which he thinks maybe might win perhaps soon?" Well, usually we were just routinely running our horses — but right then there actually was one whose line looked quite promising. So I told them a filly named Fortunate Streak would be running in a week or two and should do okay. Sure enough, we found a race in which she got in as the lightweight with Lee Moon riding, and Fortunate Streak won by eight and a half lengths and paid $15.80.

Now look at this event from the point of view of the waiter. A man he has never before seen appears and nonchalantly hands him a miraculous piece of information. The poor guy must have spent the next three years scanning every face that passed the portal, praying for the return of Santa Claus. But I generally dine on Thai takeout.

Three years later, my friend Ellen Willis, whom I met while I was teaching Marxism at the Free University, allowed as how she would enjoy lunch at Lutèce. We were shown to the less desirable tables upstairs. Soon a waiter rushed to our table on a mission that had nothing to do with our food. "Pierre from downstairs — he is so very anxious to speak with you!"

Unfortunately, I had to tell him I was getting rid of my stable. His quest for the Holy Grail had collapsed. At least I left him one for one.

17

Knowing When to Bet

A GOOD GAMBLER approaches his work dispassionately, not allowing himself to be unduly influenced by spectacular scores or crushing defeats. He understands his strengths and weaknesses and makes bets that capitalize on those strengths. He doesn't let his ego dictate his bets. The size of the pot does not influence him.

By such definitions, I am temperamentally unsuited to be a good gambler, although I was successful both at poker and playing horses when I devoted myself to those games.

My FBI file quotes an informant who describes me as "an extremely clever poker player who regularly played winning poker with Pullman porters [actually dining-car men] . . ."

The truth is, I was the best limit poker player in New York thirty or forty years ago — if I needed the money. Without a penny in the bank, I could go into one of the $100-limit games run by Joe Fine and, facing some of the best high-stakes players in the city, almost never lose. But if I was flush going into the game and winning wasn't vital, I'd stay in with dubious hands trying to be cute or brilliant rather than playing it smart and folding.

I'd also run into trouble if I tried to play some of these same guys in the table-stakes games run by Roger Stern, which were the top of the line big-money games in New York during that era. I was moving from a game in which the maximum bet was $100 — $200 if we were really late into the night — into one in which it was common for someone to make a final bet of thousands, and the higher stakes spooked me. I had actually done well in table-stakes games at Harvard, but that changed after I was graduated and the money was suddenly real. At college, your rent and meals are already paid for.

It took me two years to become a consistent winner once I set out to play horses for a living in 1954. But, just as I did in the $100-limit poker games, once I was comfortably ahead of the game, I started being super-clever. I would try to prove my brilliance by making bets I wouldn't normally make because I decided I'd found some inspired reason to break my own rules this once.

There is a term for this: "neurotic gambling." Though I did it only when I was ahead and could afford it, this meant I could never pile up a big profit. My plunges into such activity filled me with self-disgust.

During the late 1950s I went into partnership with a friend named Joe Santini. I typed up a long set of rules and he was entrusted with the task of vetoing any bad bets I proposed. In cases of misunderstanding: no bet. There was always another day. For six or seven weeks, it was a match made in horseplayers' heaven, and we ran a few hundred dollars up to nearly $15,000.

Then things started to get ugly. Feeling rich, I started pushing to come up with "brilliant" bets that were outside my guidelines. I became worn out, spending my emotional energy trying repeatedly to convince Santini that the rules really should have been worded differently and I would die if he vetoed this or that bet. Our profits slowed to a trickle — not enough to sustain his faith in our future. And we both hated the daily battles, which were so obviously neurosis-based. Eventually he became frustrated with trying to protect me from myself and dissolved the partnership, richer at least by a new car.

I continued without him, alternating between being a good

gambler when hungry and a neurotic one when flush. I never tapped out. The half-dozen times when I scraped rock bottom I would wait, sometimes for many days — saving my last few hundred for the perfect overlay that would keep me going. These "final" bets always won, believe it or not.

The overall results of these roller-coaster rides were winnings of perhaps $10,000 a year in the early 1960s — just enough to keep me going. At that point, I was sitting things out politically because the hidebound Communist Party was nothing to be proud about. But as Vietnam developed I became active and I gave sizable sums of money to the antiwar movement. These big donations meant that even when I continued winning I didn't have any money in the bank and couldn't afford a slide into my old neurotic loss pattern.

Suddenly, I became a completely disciplined horseplayer getting a 20-percent return on every dollar I bet, and pulling in about $100,000 a year. It seemed as long as I could find a nonneurotic way to keep myself broke, I could be a well-adjusted gambler. Unfortunately for the therapeutic method, U.S. involvement in Vietnam ended. Fortunately for me, Friedman became the point man.

Long before all this, back in the 1950s, there was a period when I was at the track every day, usually following the horses between New York and Florida. I have fond memories of the track from those early days, especially when my parents were out there and we were watching horses like Tom Fool and Noor and Battlefield and Alerted and Native Dancer.

But as I further refined and expanded *The Sheets,* it involved too much work to allow me time to go to the track. I was breaking down data for a half-dozen or more tracks and betting selectively at all those tracks with bookmakers. Betting and keeping up the figures took almost all my time. I worked until I was tired, slept a while — regardless of the hour — and got up and worked some more. I assume I also ate.

Recently I have done very little betting, aside from my October–November 1996 public challenge to demonstrate *The Sheets,* which showed a 14 percent profit on win bets. My satisfaction comes from the figure work and seeing my judgment validated by other people's results. I never liked the gambling itself. I wouldn't say it's torture, but the extreme ups and downs wear on me. You know you're going to lose most of your bets if the horses you're playing are going off at an average of over 5–1, but I couldn't shrug off those losses. And the big wins are a big high, but I find it an unhealthy high — and it's tinged with a fear that I'll follow with some neurotic bets that will make me hate myself.

Friedman, who bets about $2 million yearly, has much better discipline and seems neither overwhelmed by big scores nor flustered by losing days — though deep down, who knows? I decided to leave the betting to him. I haven't been to a racetrack since 1989, and I can't say I miss it. My rare visits in the '70s and '80s were to watch a horse I owned or managed.

Busy as I was, in the later stages of my betting career I had switched to betting only in the fall season. I aimed to make my year's money betting only on a restricted group of horses with dramatic patterns I considered crème de la crème. These turn up most often between mid-September and early December. So I would sit out most of the year and bet for two and a half months only. Most of those patterns still work — if you have that kind of patience. But do you have it?

It might seem that *The Sheets* would be most effective when handicapping races involving older horses, since clearer patterns would have emerged. But my best bets were actually mostly on two-year-olds — probably because the average bettor can't classify horses with very few races. In fact, my biggest profit pattern came from horses who had made just two starts.

This involves a horse who does not run all that well in his first start, then improves by 1½ points or less in his second start, and turns up in a race where he would have to improve by as much as 7 to 10 points to win. This type of horse, with that small improvement second time out, often delivered the big jump forward, and the odds obviously were very good. This line is still good today, but it seems to me that a lot more of these horses are delivering the good race but being beaten by other, more random jump-ups. Possibly this means that trainers have more control than they used to — draw your own conclusions.

In Friedman's practice, some two-year-old races become good bets as "go-against" situations. One example is when a two-year-old comes into a race off sizzling workouts and is bet down to 3–5 as a result, inflating the value on every other horse in the race. Occasionally that 3–5 shot will run to his workouts, but there are enough things that can go wrong with first-time starters — including the possibility that the workouts took too much out of them — to make tossing out the fast workers a profitable approach in the long run.

Probably the best groups of races to bet involve colts and fillies in the first five months of their three-year-old seasons. Look to bet the ones that equal or exceed their two-year-old peaks fairly quickly. You can eliminate those that are failing to equal their best races as two-year-olds. Once a colt or filly has passed that test, further improvement is likely in four to six weeks, sometimes even sooner. If the horse runs again ten days after the new top, it may deliver or it may react badly, but 2½ to 3 weeks after the new top is enough time to make the horse a solid bet if the odds are right.

When a horse begins its four-year-old season, you expect it to show improvement with the physical maturity and racing experience it's gained. I always thought the closest I could get to a sure thing was a horse who reached a top of, say, 10 as a three-year-old, had a bit of rest, then began its four-year-old campaign running maybe 16 or 17 in its first couple of races and then ran a 14. The forward move was a good sign, but at the same time it was far enough off the horse's peak that you didn't have to worry about it taking too much of a toll. Next race I would expect that horse to be ready for a solid move forward. If it ran a 12, that might be good enough to win; if it matched or surpassed the 10, you should definitely be cashing, and those slower races earlier in the year would have built your price.

The Sheets are particularly effective for handicapping grass races. Most grass races are routes, which offer a truer chance for horses to run their races than sprints, in which momentary trouble can prevent a horse from putting in its true effort on that day. Running on a grass surface also is more natural for horses, so their performances are steadier.

The Sheets also offer a big edge in turf races simply because we have made tremendous efforts to stay on top of the hidden features of the turf courses, from mismeasurements to unreported changes in rail settings to the effects of different run-ups, to plain old mistiming — especially at tracks where they doctor the time to "allow for the rail." Believe me, if you are relying only on published data, you can forget about arriving at good speed figures on the turf. Since turf racing produces more consistent performances than dirt racing, having accurate numbers is a big edge.

In evaluating turf numbers, it is even more important than usual to factor in the likelihood that a horse will lose ground, because the difference in ability among the competitors is often small. As was illustrated by the Grand Flotilla/Bien Bien confrontation in the Hollywood Turf Handicap, you can't always be sure which horses are likely to lose the most ground in a race even if you know their running style. But if a horse has an unfavorable post position and the wrong running style to overcome it, chances are he will lose several lengths because he is forced to go wide on one or more turns.

Horses lose 9 or 10 feet — roughly a length — for each path further outside they run on a turn. In middle-distance route races, two lengths are for us about 1 point. This means if you have a reasonable belief that a horse you're projecting to run a 12 will be two paths wider throughout the final turn than another you expect to run a 13, the latter horse may be a better bet, particularly if he's a longer price.

On the other hand, if the rest of the bettors discount the horse you project to run the 12 because he's in a spot where he figures to lose ground, he may become an irresistible overlay. The flip side of that is that you should remain reluctant to bet a turf horse — or any horse — who figures to save ground but whose form appears to be deteriorating. Declining condition is likely to be more of a negative factor than an advantageous trip can overcome.

Filly-and-mare races tend to be easier to handicap than those involving males, simply because there are more mismatches. We also feel more secure that occasional inexplicably bad single numbers that females throw in can be disregarded if their overall form is good. This allows you to more easily distinguish the contenders from those fillies who have given true indications of going off-form over a series of races and can be readily thrown out.

The fact that stakes races, particularly big ones, attract so many horses shipping in from other tracks makes them fertile territory for handicapping off *The Sheets.* My numbers are going to offer a better and quicker read on the quality of the shippers in relation to the local talent than you will get from their running times and speed figures in *The Racing Form,* as well as illustrating patterns, which give you an indication as to whether a horse is likely to improve that day.

Shippers who aren't running in stakes — particularly at the claiming and preliminary allowance levels — can be hard to assess without good figures. Purse levels vary greatly among tracks, so that a horse who runs at Monmouth in $17,000 allowance races might be entered against a field at Belmont running for a purse of $30,000. Tracks also set different minimum claiming levels: Belmont's rock-bottom price is $12,000, Hollywood Park's is $8,000, Pimlico's is $4,000. Turf claimers at Monmouth run for a minimum price of $16,000, while the minimum price for turf claimers at the major New York tracks is $30,000. For these and other reasons, you can't assume that a horse's claiming-price level at one track means he fits the same race elsewhere.

When confronted with these types of discrepancies, make your decisions based on *The Sheet* numbers the horses are actually running rather than on the purse or the claiming price. This will allow you to find the cases in which that $17,000 allowance horse at Monmouth can beat a $30,000 allowance field at Belmont, and when a horse who had been running in $3,200 claimers at Turf Paradise in Arizona can hold his own against a $10,000 claiming field at Hollywood. Horses shipping in to the "big-money" tracks often go off at inflated odds because most bettors can't evaluate their form and take the easy way out by deciding they can't perform in the big leagues. It's *The Sheets'* job to spot the cases where this isn't true.

There are, of course, many cases where this kind of shipper is not as good as the horses he'll be running against at the bigger track. Further, trainers often take their shot for the fatter purses at the top tracks immediately after their horses have run peak efforts, meaning their horses are likely to bounce even if they measure up to the big-track competition. But my use of on-track observers, development of par times, and painstaking efforts to fix daily variants has meant that a horse getting a 12 on *The Sheets* is putting in the same effort whether he did it at Santa Anita, Keeneland, Hialeah, or Podunk. Rather than puzzle over the disparities in purses or claiming levels, you only have to study the numbers to know how the shippers stack up against the horses you're accustomed to seeing run on your circuit.

It's fine to know the best races to bet using *The Sheets,* but your intelligent decisions may not mean much when really bad weather conditions scare a lot of horses into running gingerly, not going all-out. I always tried to avoid betting races — even those in which I thought I was getting a substantial overlay — when heavy rain or snow was falling or it was extremely windy. The figures show these elements make it a guessing game as to who will run well.

But in situations where the rain has ended but the track is sloppy, you get real overlays by betting a horse in sparkling condition rather than looking for the one with the best numbers. Even if he has no history of running well on a sloppy track, a horse in top condition who hasn't been tired by a recent peak is still likely to run better than horses who are even a little bit suspect on grounds of declining condition. Tailing-off horses will use the slop as an excuse to loaf. Rest is also a big plus in the slop.

One of the more overrated precepts in handicapping is that there are certain horses who love mud and others who hate it. A careful study of *The Sheets* shows that at least 80 percent of the horses are capable of running their top numbers in the mud, and that 90 percent at some point have run badly in the mud. A classic example was Holy Bull, who defeated Dehere during their two-year-old season in the Belmont Futurity over a sloppy track, then ran dismally on a damp surface in the Kentucky Derby eight months later.

If a horse ran a single race in the mud that was consistent with his surrounding races on dry tracks, that would be enough to convince me he could handle an off-track. It wouldn't even have to be one of his faster races: a horse who ran fast-track numbers of 16 and 19, then a 21 in the slop, followed by two 21s on dry tracks, is showing a consistent line, and if his form suddenly turns good, catching another sloppy track should not hurt him.

In the days when I was selectively betting only the very finest condition lines, I didn't care if the horse had never run well in the slop. When they're cranked up, they want to run.

There are only a few horses who are clearly better over a sloppy track. I can think of one filly on whom we made a great deal of money because her trainer rarely ran her in races in which the track was off. Her peak effort in the mud would have disappeared from her past-performance lines in *The Racing Form* by the time she ran on an off-track again — and ran another top. One day she failed to run well in the mud. We were joking that this must be the death knell. Sure enough, two races later, she was actually retired.

Another type of race it's best to avoid is a grass event in which most of the horses are trying that surface for the first time. Breeding is too important an aspect of whether a horse will run well on grass. In a case in which a 2–1 favorite who has shown some ability on grass is facing several first-time turfers, I'd say the choice between betting that horse and sitting out the race depends on the track where it's being run. At a second-tier track like Calder or the Meadowlands, you might conclude that 2–1 on a horse with a proven liking for turf is a good price in that spot. But top tracks like Belmont and Santa Anita have too many potential champions in their maiden or preliminary allowance races. Often these horses win first time on turf, making that type of race a risky bet.

I would never bet a horse with a readable pattern of solid, improving dirt races being switched to the turf. Those horses will get heavy action off their dirt form and they rarely match it when they're switched to grass. Major improvement is far more likely to come from horses switched to the grass because they weren't comfortable on dirt. Their rotten, unreadable dirt form gives you value on the odds board — especially if their breeding is unfashionable but still suggests a turf move-up.

18

A Good Bookie Is Hard to Find

DURING THE MID-1960s, when the Vietnam War spawned the Free University on East 14th Street in Manhattan, I taught a course — using unconventional materials ranging from novels to physics texts — in basic Marxism. I guess students regarded me as a romantic figure — I was raising funds for the causes I believed in by beating a capitalist game. Maybe they figured this was what Robin Hood would have done if there had been pari-mutuel machines in Sherwood Forest.

In reality, it was pretty grubby and far from romantic trying to garner that money. I was always searching for a new bookie after one I beat for a few thousand dollars would quit me — and often shortchange me on the way out.

Off-Track Betting did not arrive in New York until 1971, and even then it didn't suit my needs. I was using *The Sheets* to bet as many as a half-dozen non–New York tracks daily, and the only way to do that was through illegal bookies.

I had always thought you could win tens of thousands before a New York bookie would duck you or stop accepting your bets, but I'd win a few thousand in a week, do it again a few weeks later, and they'd tell me to get lost. I'd constantly be offering friends a finder's fee for digging me up a new bookie.

A Greenwich Village veteran named Teddy Romano handled my earliest action. I learned he was about to leave New York for good at a time when he owed me for a score, and I tracked him down. "I'll have to write you a check," he told me. I naively took this piece of paper, not thinking to ask him why he didn't cash it for me at the liquor store his brothers owned in the neighborhood. Oh, well.

Another of Teddy's clients, a no-visible-means-of-support character named Chuck Connors, was stiffed for a few hundred when Teddy left town, but he was more enterprising than I was. For years he would walk into Romano Bros. liquor store, grab a bottle, and tell them, "This is on your brother's account."

For a while I used a small runner who was getting a commission for the winnings he brought in to a big bookmaker. He soon found that handling my action was leaving him with negative commission. I suppose he thought quitting me would be bad for his image, so he told me one day he would not handle a bet bigger than $20. I asked, "What's going on?" and he smiled and replied, "You know what's going on."

So a friend hooked me up with another runner, and one day I bet $100 across the board on a horse that paid $39 to win, $17 or so to place, and $9 to show — a nice score of about $3,000. The runner came by to pay up, and the money he handed me was way short. I told him, "You must have confused me with some other account." He said, "You'll have to talk to Big Ed." Big Ed told me, "You know my odds limits: I pay twenty, eight, and four." I pointed out that the horse's odds had been less than 20–1 to win, 8–1 to place, and 4–1 to show. Big Ed responded, "No, no, you don't unnastan'. I mean twenty-to-one on the first ten dollars, eight-to-one on the next ten, and four-to-one on everything after that." Big Ed's new math cut the profit to around $1,000, and was clearly his way of telling me to get lost. I suppose I'm lucky I got anything.

Later I dug up another bookie, a guy who was working out of a Village storefront that said "limousine service" — but you never saw any limos. He was offering me the standard 20–1 odds limit that bookies in New York paid on winners, but when I started our association by picking a series of losers, I persuaded him to raise my maximum to 30–1. So one day I hit an $80 horse — who under this setup would be treated as if he paid $62 to win — and went to the limo service to collect the $3,000 I figured I had coming. The bookie wasn't there, and his assistant started to count out the money — calculated on a top payoff of 20–1. I stopped him and said, "My limit is thirty-to-one. I better come back when your boss is here."

When I returned the next day, the employees in the limo office looked scared, and it wasn't out of concern for their boss. They advised me to take the smaller amount — and it was sincere advice. The boss suddenly came barreling out of the back, grabbed me with both hands, and screamed, "Are you trying to tell me how to run my business?" He told the others, "Throw this guy outta here!" Which they did, but not too roughly. Lucky again!

I ran through many more bookies. Years later, my searching led me to a high-stakes poker game on the Upper East Side that was run by some big bookmaker. I got to the apartment, and the scene had a Las Vegas feel to it, with sexy-looking women bringing drinks to the men sitting around the card table. For about half an hour I stood there watching the game and waited for this heavyset, jowly, middle-aged bookie to acknowledge me. Finally he removed the cigar from his mouth and said, "Don't you remember me?" And I suddenly realized: this was the trim, young, small-time "you know what's going on" runner from my youth, now grown into a full-sized bookie. And no, he was not interested in cutting into his prosperity by accepting me as a client.

Getting cut off by a bookie was known in the gambling world as "getting your diploma." Those poker players were pretty impressed — from what they could see, I was getting my diploma without even making a bet!

Then, just as I was despairing of finding a reliable bookie, I was approached by a man calling himself Ralph Atlas. In his struggling past, his mob friends had called him Buster from Brooklyn. He proposed to handle all my action. He dealt with large operations all over the United States, where he could lay off our bets while profiting by adding on big money of his own. In his own self-interest, he treated me right. Once I knew I could bet with the expectation of getting paid, I went a step further. With a talented associate named Jeff Langbert making the picks, I set up a mutual fund for horseplayers. Our investors bought shares. For each $1,000 they were given a $10 across-the-board bet on any horse we liked. Their deposits were put into individual savings accounts, which soon totalled $250,000, mostly from friends and acquaintances. Half the profit went to me and Jeff.

Jeff wasn't a superselective bettor like I was. He found a lot of small-edge bets. This greatly increased the action we were giving Ralph, and he began treating me like a very important client. One night he took me out, along with Jeff and his wife, for an evening at Regine's, then a fancy dinner-dance spot, picking me up in his Rolls-Royce. We arrived at Regine's, where Jeff and his wife were outside waiting. During the drive I had been joking that Jeff — basically an ill-kempt games-club hustler — would look so disreputable he wouldn't be seated. Now Ralph and I burst out laughing, because Jeff was wearing a suit that cost $14 and was shiny and frayed from too much pressing. But — serves me right — when we tried to enter the club, it was I whom the maître d' stopped. My classy English houndstooth sport jacket didn't match my slacks, and the place had a suits-only rule.

With his mob background, Ralph wasn't accustomed to being detained at club entrances. We tried to reason with the maître d' for a couple of minutes. Then we beseeched a higher-up he summoned. But now Ralph was out of patience. He glared at the man and said slowly, rasping, biting off his words, "Look . . . I think . . . it's . . . gonna . . . be . . . ALL . . . RIGHT."

And in we went.

Now in theory, law-enforcement officials regard bookmaking as a serious offense, but in those days, before the Knapp Commission hearings of the 1970s showed that much of the NYPD was being paid off by bookmakers to allow them to operate, pinches were relatively infrequent.

There was at least one big bust however. A major bookie operation based in Nassau but servicing New York City was raided — because the FBI's phone tap on me for my left-wing political activities led the Feds to the scene!

Shortly after I began phoning in bets to this outfit, I got a call from the clerk who handled my action. Sounding frazzled, he asked me to go over what I had bet that day, explaining that the Nassau headquarters was invaded by the FBI and the slips on which they recorded bets were grabbed.

"They can't understand what happened," the clerk said of his bosses. "They've been paying off the Nassau County cops for twenty-five years and never had a problem. But this was the feds!"

Evidently the politically motivated wiretap the FBI used on my phone had recorded my calls to the bookie operation, and they must have decided, Why not make ourselves look like real crime fighters?

I didn't mention any of this to my man. From then on I called him from pay phones.

19

Big Hits, Near Misses, and Moving Violations

ONE RACE shortly after we met that made Friedman a believer in *The Sheets* involved a pick I gave him named Desfile, a $3,000 claimer running at Atlantic City in mid-September of 1967. We lost: the horse finished seventh by ten lengths while going off 119–1. It wasn't an inspiring effort, but the sheet for the horse suggested he was moving toward a good race, and this single bad effort should be disregarded. Next out the horse would be a prime pattern play.

A week later, the horse turned up in a similar race at Atlantic City. It again figured to go off 100–1 or better, and since no bookie was going to offer me better than 30–1, my only choice was to board a bus from the Port Authority and head down to the track. My typical bet at the time was $40 across the board, but for this excursion I was carrying $1,000 and ready to bet most of it.

Desfile was running in the fourth race that day, facing most of the same horses he'd lost to last time, plus a shipper from Timonium named Blue Brother. In his last race, Blue Brother had run fourth by nine lengths against $3,250 claimers in Maryland, and I wasn't particularly worried about him though I had no sheet.

Edgy with anticipation, I wandered down to the concrete apron of the track, where I engaged in a conversation with a group of hard hats who had taken the day off. I told them I was there primarily to bet the fourth race. Naturally they asked whom I liked. I couldn't resist telling them I was betting Desfile — I figured when they saw the odds they would think I was nuts. And they did.

When the betting opened, Desfile was 90–1. I bet $50 to win on him and the pool was so small that he dropped to 30–1 on the next flash of the tote board. Then a few minutes later, with no one else betting him, he drifted back to 60–1. This time I bet $100, and his price dropped once more. I continued betting each time his price hit 60–1, and when the betting pools closed, that's where he was.

With $400 to win, $200 to place, and $100 to show, I had accounted for roughly half the action on the horse. Without my money, he'd have been 120–1. (There were no exotics.)

They broke from the gate in the 1⅛-mile race, and Blue Brother, the shipper whom I and most of the bettors had dismissed at 40–1, went right to the lead, with Desfile not too far behind. By the time they'd gone six furlongs, Desfile had moved into second and opened some ground on the rest of the field, and all that separated me from a titanic score was this ridiculous shipper from Timonium, still coasting on the lead.

They turned for home and Desfile narrowed the gap, getting to within a length of Blue Brother by midstretch. Meantime, Blue Brother was drifting further and further to the outside of the track, and if I'd had the foresight to bring a baseball bat with me, I'd have been able to whack him as he passed me running close to the outer rail. However, he straightened out and managed to win.

But the fact that he was almost 40–1 meant the place and show prices on both horses were huge, with Desfile paying $54.60 to place and $29.80 to show. My $700 bet returned $6,910 even without the horse winning.

During the bus ride back, I mentioned to an old man sitting alongside me that I'd made the trip down just to bet Desfile. I showed him the big check I was carrying. He told me, "You keep betting horses like that, son, you're gonna go broke."

The truth was, the figures were so good and offered such an edge over the other printed material — principally *The Racing Form* — that was available to bettors in the 1960s and 1970s that you were going to have your share of cases where the obvious favorite on *The Sheets* was going off at 15–1 or better. Alas, no more — we have forced too many people to see the light, and the edge is less.

A few years later, there was a racetrack strike in Maryland, leading horsemen and bettors down there to move up to Garden State Park for close to five months. Friedman recalls it as the greatest protracted betting opportunity he's seen: Jersey bettors with no good read on the Maryland shippers, Maryland bettors unfamiliar with Garden State's idiosyncrasies and the hometown horses, and us with figures that gave us all the necessary comparisons. Charge!

An even more frequent patron at Garden State during that strike was Richie "The Big Man" Schwartz, who had become our first betting customer after observing the success Friedman was having. By this time he was paying me almost $100 a day for copies of *The Sheets* for whatever track he was playing. He could afford it; the size of his bets was one of the reasons we called him The Big Man.

The other was his physical bulk. He was quite large, in a funny, nonathletic way that makes me think of the basketball player Bryant "Big Country" Reeves. Schwartz was partial to Hawaiian shirts and old Cadillacs.

A few other guys who enjoyed hanging around my office talking horses and sometimes doing work for me transformed what had been a solo practitioner's operation into a social club. The demands of maintaining and upgrading the figures limited my ability and willingness to leave the office to go to the track. But Friedman (who was betting for both of us) and Schwartz became the ringleaders in a merry road company that, because bettors in New York tended to be the most sophisticated, was frequently traveling out of town to find the best overlays.

The Big Man was not the best of traveling companions, for a variety of reasons. He had an immense appetite, but he would always suggest splitting the check with the rest of the table, even though the other diners had eaten half as much and were not betting or winning as much as he. He was also so indifferent to the economic needs of waiters that Friedman used to volunteer to leave the tip simply to spare the party the wrath of the servers if there was ever a return trip.

Richie isn't a schemer. He just doesn't realize the impressions he leaves. One day Lou Rose, who today is our clocker/observer in New Jersey, was driving him to the track. They were running late, and there was a horse they liked in the first, so Schwartz had Lou drop him off at the track entrance. He took off before Lou could remind him to add on a small piece to his bet. Lou parked and got inside the track just in time to hear the bell signaling the close of betting. Their horse won, giving Schwartz a huge score, and as they headed for the track dining room, Richie commiserated with Lou, then declared, "Lunch is on me . . . but you'll have to pay the tip."

In those years, the good bets were as likely to be in the early races as in the last race triple, and since none of us was an early riser, this created problems anytime the track was further away from Manhattan than Belmont Park. Running late brought out two of Schwartz's other vices: an aversion to getting gas in advance if there was no one with him to pay their share, and the daring to speed through toll booths on the Garden State Parkway if stopping for a minute to pay might mean blowing a double at Monmouth or Atlantic City.

The toll-dodging occasionally would send an attendant running after Schwartz's car shaking his fist and screaming, but he was never apprehended. He also managed, one day when traffic backed up for blocks on the residential streets leading to Hialeah, to get there in time by driving his car over the lawns of outraged homeowners for several blocks.

Of course, these tactics made it simple for Friedman when Schwartz during the 1970s asked him to give a name to his racing stable. Thereafter, Richie's steeds raced under the banner of the Run-a-toll Stable.

Friedman also has been known to ignore the rules of the road when making the daily double is at stake. He was speeding through the streets of Atlantic City shortly before post time one afternoon when a motorcycle cop pulled him over and, sizing up the vehicle's occupants quickly, asked, "What's the rush? You got something in the double?"

"The two and the four in the first with the six in the second," Friedman replied. "Well, drive carefully," the cop cautioned, and then sped off in the direction of the track. Friedman arrived on time, and the double paid $280.

By the early 1970s, both my father and I were operating stables, and I was selling *The Sheets* to a small coterie of owners, trainers, and bettors. The harder I worked to refine the figures, the better we all did. Friedman was doing better making bets for both of us than I had on my own.

At this point, the only time I was testing my betting judgment against my office's inner circle was during the Triple Crown races. Generally Friedman did best — it was his living, after all. But the 1975 Preakness put me temporarily in the lead — even though it wasn't because my handicapping was better than his.

Going into the Preakness that year, Foolish Pleasure was both an obvious and deserving favorite. He had overcome an impossible post to win the Wood Memorial, then improved slightly to win the Kentucky Derby two weeks later, and still figured to have something left heading to Pimlico.

Master Derby, on the other hand, looked like a horse who, on past numbers, had an outside shot to complete the exacta. Sent off at 5–1 in the Derby, he'd raced in close quarters early, rallied from ninth to be third at the quarter pole, but then flattened out, finishing six and three quarter lengths behind Foolish Pleasure in fourth, with Avatar and Diablo separating them.

But Master Derby was one of two horses whose owners thought enough of their chances to pay a heavy supplemental fee that was required if horses were not earlier nominated to run in the Preakness. More important, on *The Sheets* his line gave him a small chance to pop a winning effort, so all our circle was using him as a saver.

Personally, I didn't care about the best way to beat the race — I wanted to beat the other guys. Cashing along with them wouldn't satisfy me. I decided that the best chance for a score that I alone would have lay with Master Derby.

So instead of using him lightly in my exacta combinations with Foolish Pleasure, I made Master Derby my key horse. In contrast to his ride in the Derby, jockey Darrell McHargue kept Master Derby out of trouble by getting good position early, and he moved to the front turning for home and was able to prevail by a length over Foolish Pleasure's late charge. When they crossed the finish line, I became disoriented. I turned from my TV set and said shakily, "I think . . . I've just made a fortune." By my standards, I had: the exacta paid $111.60 and I made more than $10,000 on my bet, mainly motivated by a desire to show off.

A couple of months later, destiny brought me a horse who it seemed had been named in anticipation that someday I would own horses. Marxism — O holy name! — shipped in to New York from Philadelphia Park to run in a 1¼-mile race for $7,500 claimers. I put up the money and claimed him. He ran fifth by seventeen lengths that day, but I was convinced that improvement was coming shortly. Also, he was a three-year-old, and the figures showed this to be one of those rare years where the three-and-up claimers were weaker than those limited to three-year-olds — so I had another potential edge.

Sixteen days later, I had Preston King skip the obvious three-year-old spots, enter him in a mile race against older $12,000 claimers, and put an apprentice named Roger Velez on him — and Marxism won by seven lengths and paid $24.40. I ran him again eight days later, this time for a price of $16,000 going 1$\frac{1}{16}$ miles, and he opened a five-length lead in early stretch before tiring and finishing second. Two weeks later, we entered Marxism for the same price but this time going six furlongs, and he won by three and a half lengths, paid $10.40, and was claimed, giving me an $8,500 profit on the claim along with about $20,000 in purses plus what we'd won betting.

The tale seemed like it would make a cute article for the Communist Party's *Daily Worker*, so I called the paper, explained that I was the nephew of Rachel Ragozin (a charter member of the party), and I'd had this nice success when I took over a horse named Marxism. When I finished my story, the communist on the other end of the phone screamed, "You own him? We've been making money like crazy betting on him!"

I couldn't say whether Marxism's being with fellow travelers was what accounted for his breakthrough as a racehorse. But in his first three starts after he was claimed from me, the horse finished last each time.

I had entered 1977 on a high note, with Frampton Delight closing out the previous year winning the two stakes races at Aqueduct, netting me close to $100,000 in purse money. But there was trouble on the western horizon — Friedman had lit out for California that winter. He was taking a royal bath at Santa Anita because he was unfamiliar with the trainers and unaware that horses coming off six-week layoffs there — in contrast with New York — were likely to run well.

At the end of January, he called to tell me just how bad things were going. The numbers were not pretty, but I recall being more interested in telling him about a race that had just been run for $5,000 claimers over the inner dirt track at Aqueduct. The lines of two horses in this bottom-of-the-barrel race had impressed me, and since they finished seventh and eighth, I knew their quality would be invisible to the betting public. The horse who ran seventh, Jersey Giant, had been 38–1, and Livid Purple had been six and a half lengths further back at 17–1. Individually, I told Friedman, either horse would offer terrific value the next time he ran, and if they wound up in the same race, a major score might be made in the exacta or triple.

A week later, February 7, Friedman had some personal business to attend to in New York, and he flew into Kennedy Airport. When he arrived, he called the office, learned both horses were entered in the ninth race that afternoon, and jumped in a cab for the quick trip from JFK to Aqueduct. Someone was dispatched to the track with a set of *The Sheets* (in those days we didn't sell them on-track).

Both horses were 20–1 on the morning line. The crowd was even less impressed, sending Jersey Giant off at 61–1 and Livid Purple at 65–1. Speedy Flier, who had been fifth against those two as the 7–5 favorite in his last start, again was the chalk, this time at 5–2. Friedman decided to key Livid Purple in his triple combinations, using him in each position with several of the other eleven entrants.

Pat Day (not yet a star) took Livid Purple right to the lead from his outside post and was engaged to his inside by Grand Gamble, the 7–2 third choice in the betting. They dueled around the turn, and as they straightened away, Livid Purple — with Day showing the knack for saving a horse for the stretch run that would become his trademark — began to edge away. Grand Gamble suddenly snapped a leg, falling in the path of three longshots racing on the inside part of the track. Speedy Flier, who was unaffected by the spill, began to close in, with Jersey Giant, Friedman's other big longshot, moving into third.

Friedman was shouting encouragement throughout the stretch run to Livid Purple as his lead slowly diminished, but as the horses neared the wire, he ceased his exhortations and realized that no one else was screaming. There was dead silence as Livid Purple crossed the wire a nose in front of the favorite.

Livid Purple paid $132 to win; the triple came back for $52,459. The silence at the track was telling: while six people at OTB had managed to hit the triple, Friedman held the only winning ticket sold at Aqueduct.

It turned out that two other people who worked for me should have had this triple and didn't. Bernie Wishengrad worked out a four-horse box the night before, using the two 60–1 shots as well as Speedy Flier, then crossed it out while muttering, "Ahh, I never hit these damn triple bets."

The other guy was Jerry Brown, who would later break with

me to sell horse-rating sheets that look strangely like mine. The night before the race, Jerry had been in the office and put together a series of bets on the entire card at Aqueduct. He phoned his bets to an acquaintance named Mario who had access to a bookie in Brooklyn. For exotic bets that were likely to pay higher odds than the bookie covered, however, Mario made trips to OTB, using money Jerry had in a running account.

Jerry was a night owl who slept late. Mario called him just before noon the following day and told him he didn't have enough cash to cover all the exotic bets, so he was going to put in the early races and would reinvest any winnings Jerry had on the ninth race triple. Jerry said something like, "Yeah, yeah," and went back to sleep. Well, all his early bets went down, and there went $50,000.

Friedman used the race as a springboard out of his California slump, won handsomely that summer at Atlantic City, and then engineered the Seatrain coup at Delaware on September 11. Twelve days later, he would strike again.

A Uruguayan horse named Lebon had made his American debut at Belmont Park on September 9, running 1⅟16 miles for a claiming price of $10,500 off a five-month layoff. He opened up at 50–1 in the betting, but the odds dropped steadily, and a surge of late money, including a single $10,000 bet, drove the price down to 7–1 at post time. Lebon settled in eleventh in the twelve-horse field early and stayed there, losing the race by eleven and a half lengths.

It turned out that on *The Sheets* this was another "buried" race. The first six finishers had all run faster than usual, obscuring the fact that, considering the layoff, Lebon's race was a promising debut. The heavy betting action in the last two minutes also struck us as very significant. Although the horse was five years old and had run fairly often in Uruguay, the situation was akin to those my father always regarded as prime next-out bets: a first-time starter heavily played for no discernible reason — meaning the money was probably bet by insiders.

On September 23, Lebon turned up in the ninth race, a 1¼-

mile turf race, running for a price of $16,000 (the cheapest price Belmont then permitted for turf horses). There is no grass racing in Uruguay, but horses from South American countries have often flourished when put on turf after arriving in North America, so we thought Lebon had a decent chance to run well on turf. The favorites in the field had been running hard all season and seemed on the downgrade, and if he could improve just 3 points over his post-layoff tune-up race two weeks earlier, he had a good shot to win. This certainly wasn't asking for miracles.

Lebon stayed at 50–1 virtually throughout the betting. Friedman was hesitant to make a win bet on him, remembering the deluge of late money in his previous race, so he confined his betting to triples, keying Lebon with the rest of the field and then playing a separate set of triples keying Georgetown, who was also fresher than most of the field and was going off at 22–1.

When they left the gate, Lebon was closer than in his debut, racing seventh early in a tightly bunched field. The pace was slow, and by the time they had gone half a mile, he had carried rider Larry Adams into third, just a length off the lead. A quarter-mile later he was two lengths in front, and he just kept on going, winning the race by four lengths. Li'l Tommie, the 4–1 second choice in the betting, closed for second, and Georgetown — our other key — outfinished two other horses to get third and give Friedman a second winning ticket on the triple.

The only person to make more money on the race than we did was the horse's secret owner, Mark Gerard. Gerard, a society-owner veterinarian who treated Secretariat, had bet $1,300 to win and $300 to show on Lebon, bringing him a return of about $76,000. But if you deduct his intercontinental expenses and the earlier $10,000 bet, we made more.

Less than a month later, Gerard's coup began to unravel. A woman who made the $10,000 bet in the horse's first race decided she had been double-crossed, and a Uruguayan newspaperman had his suspicions aroused when he saw a photo of "Lebon" in the winner's circle. Their complaints led the New York Racing Association to launch an investigation. They learned that the

NINTH RACE
Bel
Sept'ber 23, 1977

1¼ MILES (inner turf). (1:58⅘). CLAIMING. Purse $10,000. 3-year-olds and upward. 3-year-olds, 118 lbs.; older, 122 lbs. Non-winners of two races at a mile and a furlong or over since Aug. 15 allowed 3 lbs.; of such a race since then, 5 lbs. Claiming price, $18,000; 2 lbs. allowed for each $1,000 to $16,000. (Races when entered to be claimed for $14,000 or less not considered.)

Value to winner $6,000; second, $2,200; third, $1,200; fourth, $600. Mutuel Pool, $127,322. Off-track betting, $195,964. Triple Pool, $129,826. Off-track betting Triple Pool, $347,856.

Last Raced	Horse	Eqt	A	Wt	PP	¼	½	¾	1	Str	Fin	Jockeys	Owners	Odds to $1
9 Sep77 ^{5}Bel^{11}	Lebon		5	113	2	7½	3½	1^{2}	1^{2}	1^{2}	1^{4}	LAdams	J B Morgan	57.00
15 Sep77 ^{6}Bel^{4}	Li'l Tommie	b	8	117	7	10^{h}	11^{3}	10½	$9^{1\frac{1}{2}}$	5½	$2^{1\frac{1}{2}}$	LPincayJr	H Jacobson	4.00
29 Aug77 ^{4}Bel^{6}	Georgetown	b	3	113	11	5	7^{h}	8^{h}	7^{h}	4^{h}	3½	JVelasquez†	Rokeby Stable	22.20
8 Sep77 ^{5}Bel^{7}	Rigamarole		6	115	10	$11^{1\frac{1}{2}}$	9½	$9^{1\frac{1}{2}}$	8^{1}	$6^{1\frac{1}{2}}$	4no	JCruguet	Mary-Jean Stable	6.50
10 Sep77 ^{2}Bel^{1}	No Distress		5	117	3	$2^{1\frac{1}{2}}$	4^{h}	3½	2½	2½	5^{h}	MVenezia	P Wise	2.40
8 Sep77 ^{5}Bel^{8}	Yvetot	b	9	113	6	6^{h}	8^{5}	6½	4^{3}	3½	6¾	RIVelez	W K Gumpert	11.80
16 Sep77 ^{8}Med^{2}	Framarco		3	114	9	12	12	12	11½	9^{2}	$7^{1\frac{1}{2}}$	LSaumell†	R Coto	18.70
19 Sep77 ^{5}Bel^{7}	Gallant Stevie	b	3	113	4	$4^{1\frac{1}{2}}$	$5^{1\frac{1}{2}}$	5^{h}	5½	8^{h}	8^{1}	ASantiago	W R Kampfer Jr	9.20
2 Sep77 ^{4}Atl^{1}	Pier		7	115	8	3^{h}	2½	2½	3^{1}	7^{1}	$9^{1\frac{1}{2}}$	EMaple	Valerie Widmer	5.00
1 Aug77 ^{9}Sar^{7}	Panegirico		7	112	12	8^{8}	6½	7^{3}	6^{1}	$10^{1\frac{1}{2}}$	$10^{1\frac{1}{4}}$	JLSamyn^{5}	T P Whitney	17.90
16 Sep77 ^{6}Bel^{8}	Rock Dancer	b	4	113	5	9^{2}	10½	11^{3}	12	11^{3}	$11^{3\frac{3}{4}}$	DMontoya	M Garren	37.60
9 Sep77 ^{9}Bel^{2}	Ligur	b	6	105	1	1^{h}	1½	4^{2}	$10^{1\frac{1}{2}}$	12	12	ENavedo^{7}	Saddle River Stable	17.90

†Five pounds apprentice allowance waived.

OFF AT 5:33½ EDT. Start good. Won handily. Time, :25, :50⅕, 1:14⅘, 1:35⅖, 2:05. Track good.

$2 Mutuel Prices:			
2-LEBON	116.00	60.00	16.80
7-LI'L TOMMIE		6.20	5.60
11-GEORGETOWN			13.40

$2 TRIPLE (2-7-11) PAID $29,855.00.

horse racing as Lebon was actually Cinzano, who had been the Uruguayan champion as a three-year-old in 1976 while winning seven of eight stakes races. Before the probe was over, Cinzano was barred from racing, the NYRA's track veterinarian said that at least two other South American horses who had run successfully in New York were ringers, and Gerard was brought to court (he served no time). The FBI queried us too (see page 17) but gave us a clean bill.

With all this, our score was just the usual sheet handicapping. In fact, if the South American had been scratched, Friedman would have collected on a sizable triple via Georgetown.

My own next — and luckiest — big horse-race venture involved a $40,000 bet I *didn't* make. The Jockey Club Gold Cup, run October 6, 1979, at Belmont, would match the four-year-old Affirmed against Spectacular Bid, that year's Derby and Preakness winner. By my numbers the three-year-old was running slightly faster than Affirmed in most of his starts. He had run a 1 in his previous race, a point faster than any of Affirmed's best races. His condition line, though not exciting, looked fine. He was the legitimate favorite — but Affirmed was going to be the public choice at odds-on.

The week of the race, Lou Wolfson, who owned Affirmed, was making noises around Belmont that he wanted to make a big bet on his horse but not through the mutuel machines, because Affirmed figured to be 3–5 without a penny of his money. Word got back to Friedman and me. We liked the idea of the poor boys with golden figures going mano a mano with the millionaire owner of Harbor View Farm. Everybody in the office put up some money, and I threw in most of the $50,000 we were going to risk.

Connie Merjos, one of the most highly respected men in the New York racetrack community, offered to serve as middleman and to arrange the bets. The fairest way would be a system called double-booking: Wolfson would bet on Affirmed and we would have to pay him the track odds if he won; the same would apply to our bet on Spectacular Bid.

Wolfson initially refused; he wanted an even-up bet, $50,000 against $50,000. But we considered that small-time chiseling, since Spectacular Bid was sure to go off a much better price than Affirmed. The morning of the race, I authorized Merjos to make a counteroffer: we would give him 4–5 odds, better than he would get from the mutuels or any bookmaker. If he really wanted to bet, this was generous. If he was just spouting off, or was getting cold feet because he had learned something about who we were, there would be no action.

I wasn't letting all this stop me from a day's work — so I stayed in the office in Manhattan. And since there were no public phones inside the track in those days, there was no way for me to learn from Connie whether Wolfson had accepted our proposition.

So, in the dark about whether we had $50,000 — $40,000 of it my own — riding on the race, I headed over to the Lion's Head, a storied Greenwich Village saloon, to watch it. At this point late in the afternoon, there were three other customers in the bar, all falling asleep, and a baseball game was on the TV. I knew the bartender had an attitude and wouldn't like me pushing in, but I had to ask whether he planned to switch over to the horse race. He said, "Yeah, don't worry, there's plenty of time."

Ten minutes before post time he switched over. Five minutes later he had to show me who was boss by hopping back for a look at the ballgame. That — plus nervousness about the bet — did it. I picked my drink up high, and smashed it to the floor behind the bar at his feet. Glass and ice cubes flying, I stalked out, walking quickly over to The Corner Bistro a few blocks away, which had a TV tuned to the race.

It was only a four-horse field, but one of the other two entrants was Coastal, who had swooped by Spectacular Bid in the Belmont to deny him the Triple Crown. Still, it seemed like strictly a two-horse race. As I expected, Affirmed went off 3–5; Spectacular Bid was a shade higher than I figured at 7–5.

The race began, and it looked suspiciously like the Belmont — the Affirmed-Alydar Belmont. Pincay put Affirmed on the lead in nice, leisurely fractions, and eventually Shoemaker moved Spectacular Bid to the outside (groan) to mount a challenge. In early stretch, he moved to within a half-length of Affirmed, but he never looked like he would go by. Affirmed edged away late to win by three quarters of a length.

I stood there, devastated. Believe it or not, what really bothered me was that my judgment had been shown to be faulty. The money was secondary, and so when I got word later that Wolfson had declined the bet, I honestly didn't feel that much better.

A year later, I made and won my biggest bet, on a sport which I hardly follow, and by betting against someone I greatly admired. The wager — the only one I ever made on a prizefight — was governed by one of my basic ideas derived from experience handicapping horses: look for value when the crowd is betting someone who should be a throw-out.

The contender was Larry Holmes; the throw-out was Muhammad Ali. Ali was fighting against the advice of his doctor. Holmes to me was a legitimate fighter. That's all I knew; I didn't really follow boxing.

What I could see was that Ali at that point was a shot athlete whose support in the betting was coming mainly from wealthy Hollywood well-wishers. I had lived long enough to see other great aging athletes try to go on a bit too long — Don Budge, Joe Louis, Stymie. I couldn't conceive of losing this bet. I put up $51,000 in Vegas to win $30,000, and the money was never at risk.

Most of our biggest scores have come on races no one would confuse with Triple Crown events. When you do this professionally, you know there are lots of other races besides the championship ones, and you're not particular about which ones bring in the biggest profits. That said, there's still something special about being right on the money — at a huge return — on a race that draws wide public attention. In Friedman's case, he had the satisfaction of doing it not in a seminar before a couple hundred people familiar with *The Sheets,* but in the pages of *The Racing Form* the day of the 1996 Belmont Stakes.

Friedman was writing an occasional column for *The Racing Form* analyzing some of the bigger stakes races, including the Triple Crown events. He had liked Editor's Note and Louis Quatorze best in the Derby, won by Grindstone — another horse he liked who was part of an entry with Editor's Note. He went with Editor's Note again in the Preakness but backed off Louis Quatorze, much to his regret afterward.

But in the Belmont, he still liked Editor's Note, even as others were writing off the horse as a plodder who never quite ran big enough to win. His faith was unshakable. I agreed. He was not swayed when Gary Stevens — whose agent, Ron Anderson, uses *The Sheets* and was persuaded by our feelings about the horse's line to have Stevens choose Editor's Note from among the Lukas three-year-olds — was injured and had to be replaced by Rene Douglas.

For second, he picked Skip Away. Others, noting Skip Away did not qualify on Dosage and had failed to gain on Louis Quatorze in the stretch run of the Preakness, wondered whether he could go 1½ miles. Friedman, however, figured the doubts about Skip Away going a distance would merely produce better odds.

His pick for third was My Flag, a filly from Shug McGaughey

who seemed a bit slow but whose line suggested she was ready to run a lifetime best, particularly racing with a good five weeks' rest.

He did not make Louis Quatorze, the Preakness winner, one of his top picks, figuring he would bounce. Friedman was even more negative on Cavonnier, who had run by far his lifetime top when he lost by a nose in the Derby and then backed up with a tepid Preakness effort. Many public handicappers thought Cavonnier was ready to rebound. But Friedman thought even the relatively dull race in the Preakness was so superior to the horse's pre-Derby numbers that it might have hurt Cavonnier. And his Derby figure — more than 5 points better than he'd ever run before it — was such a jump that Friedman believed as the likely favorite the horse was a great bet-against. Jamies First Punch also figured to bounce.

That's how he wrote it in *The Racing Form* before heading off to a small track in New England to bet and watch the Belmont. There he discovered that Editor's Note was 5–1, half the price he'd been expecting, but the horse's line looked so good that he had no second thoughts and placed a heavy win bet.

Midway on the backstretch, Cavonnier took a bad step and had to be pulled up, perhaps confirming Friedman's judgment that the first two legs of the Triple Crown had taken too much out of him. Louis Quatorze bounced out of the money.

In midstretch it was clear that Editor's Note and Skip Away would duel to the end; the TV monitor did not yet show that My Flag was going to be a clear third. Friedman had an anxious moment when Skip Away surged back into the lead in the final sixteenth, but then Douglas urged Editor's Note to the front for good.

Friedman had publicly picked the triple cold — the $2 payoff was $914. It was the equivalent of hitting three homers in the last game of the World Series or scoring 60 points in the NBA championship game — something neither you nor anyone else is likely to do again anytime soon.

Because he bet much more heavily to win than on the triple, Friedman made a nice score but not one of his biggest; certainly

Len Ragozin "The Sheets"™

EDITOR'S NOTE 93

10 RACES 95

12 RACES 96

95		96	
12"	AWCDDWL		
.8+	s AWBEDWL		v AWWODWL
14-	vs AWSADWL		s AWBEDWL
14-	wt AWTPDWL		w AWLDDWL
8	vw AWBEDWL		vs AWSrDWL
24+	AWSrDWL		Vs AWSrDWL
18"	vs AWSrDWL		
16	Vw MSMTDWL		
^21"	[t MSCDDWL	5-	Vws------DWL
.25-	VsT MSCDDWL	6"	Y AWP·DWL
		5	Vsb AWCDDWL
		F′6"	s AWKEDWL
		5	AWGFDWL
		8	t AWGPDWL
		6	v AWGFDWL

Len Ragozin — "The Sheets"™

SKIP AWAY 93

6 RACES 95 — 12 RACES 96

6 RACES 95		12 RACES 96	
11+	vAWAQHHe		
13	vAWBEHHe		
13-	VQAWMEHHe		wAWBEHHe
			wAWMDHHe
			vt AWSrHHe
15-	wMSMTHHe		
			vw AWMTHHe
=20+	vs AWMTHHe		
			w AWTD23
27+	YS MSMTHHe	6	v ←——— HHe
		4+	AWP1HHe
		9	V AWCDHHe
		'2	w AWKEHHe
		6-	AWGPHHe
		F9	wt[AWGPHHe
		32"	Z AWGFHHe

DEC NOV OCT SEP AUG JLY JUN MAY APR MAR FEB JAN

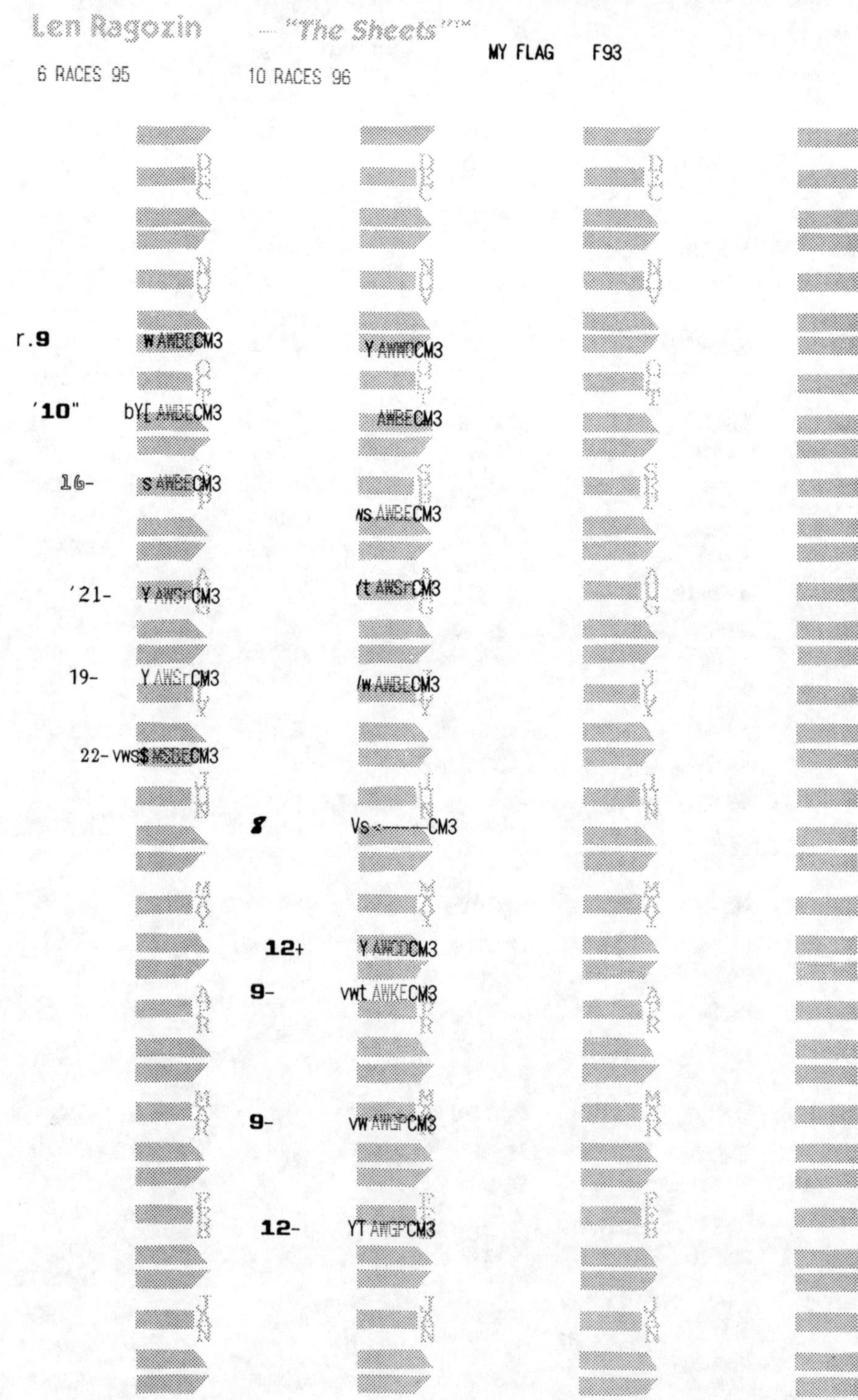

Len Ragozin
"The Sheets"™
MY FLAG F93
6 RACES 95
10 RACES 96

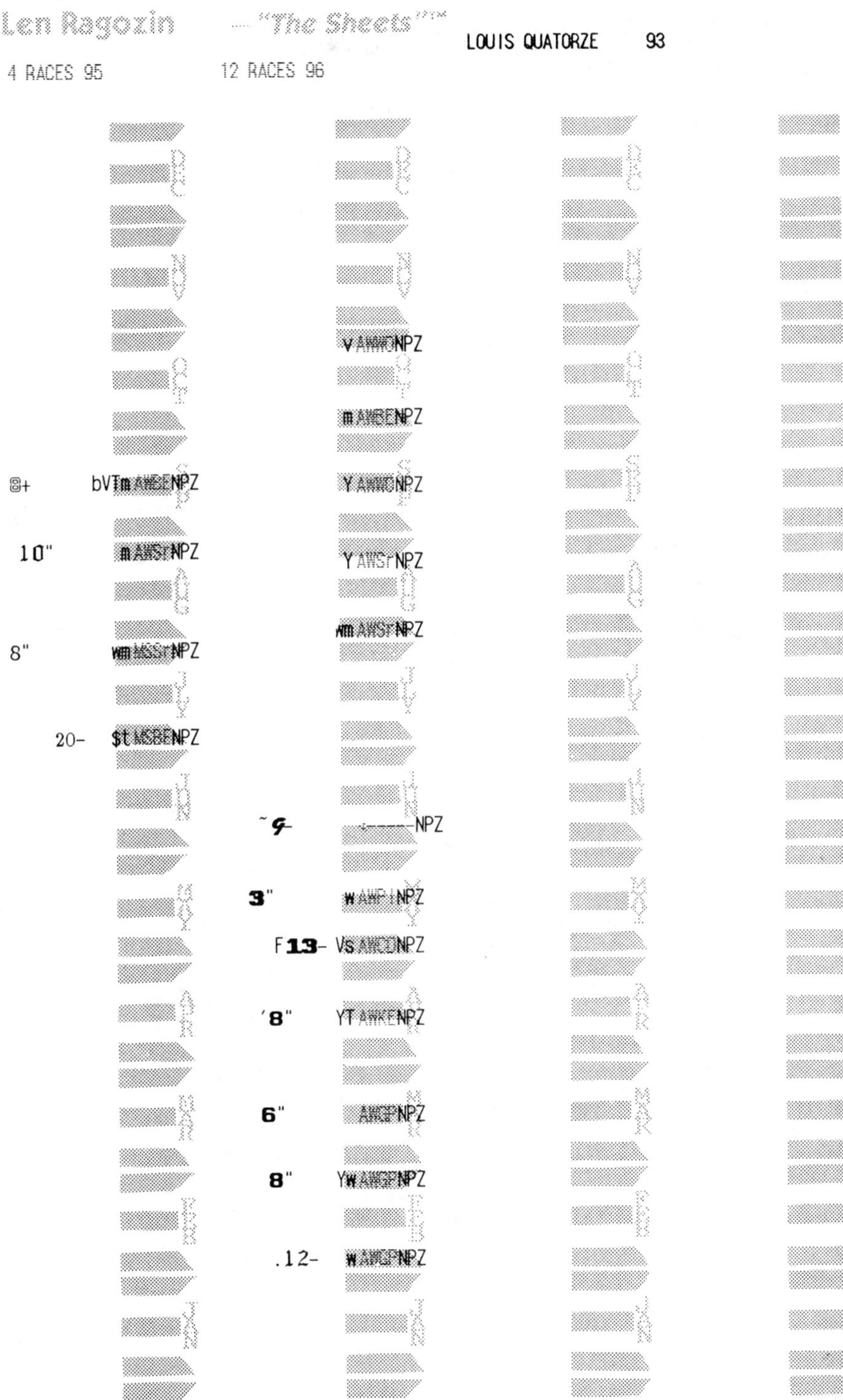
Len Ragozin — "The Sheets"™
LOUIS QUATORZE 93
4 RACES 95
12 RACES 96

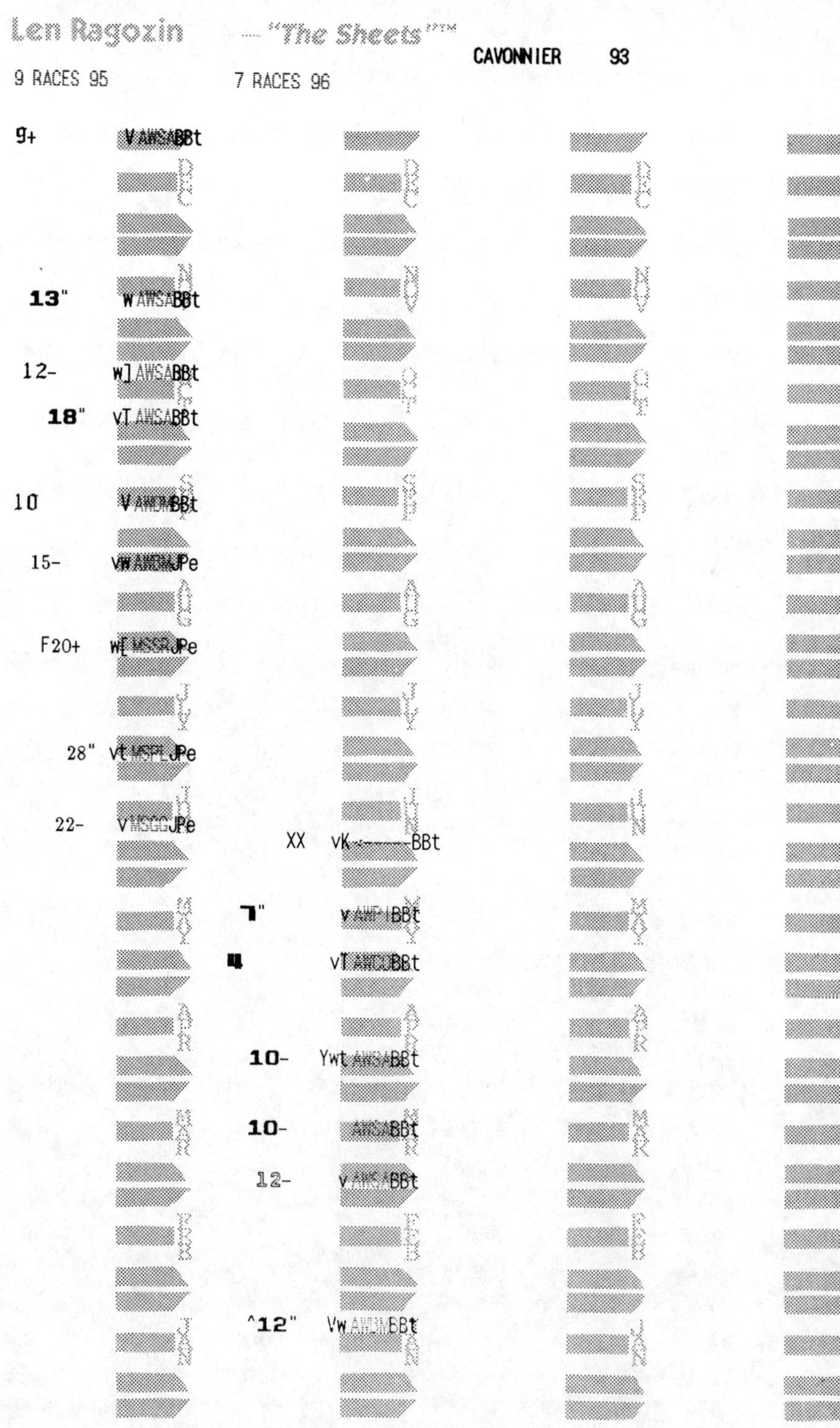
Len Ragozin
"The Sheets"™
CAVONNIER 93
9 RACES 95
7 RACES 96
9+ V AWSA BBt
13" W AWSA BBt
12- w] AWSA BBt
18" vT AWSA BBt
10 V AWDM BBt
15- vw AWDM JPe
F20+ w[MSSR JPe
28" vt MSPL JPe
22- V MSGG JPe
XX vK BBt
7" v AWP BBt
4 vT AWCD BBt
10- Ywt AWSA BBt
10- AWSA BBt
12- v AWSA BBt
^12" Vw AWDM BBt
DEC
NOV
OCT
SEP
AUG
JLY
JUN
MAY
APR
MAR
FEB
JAN

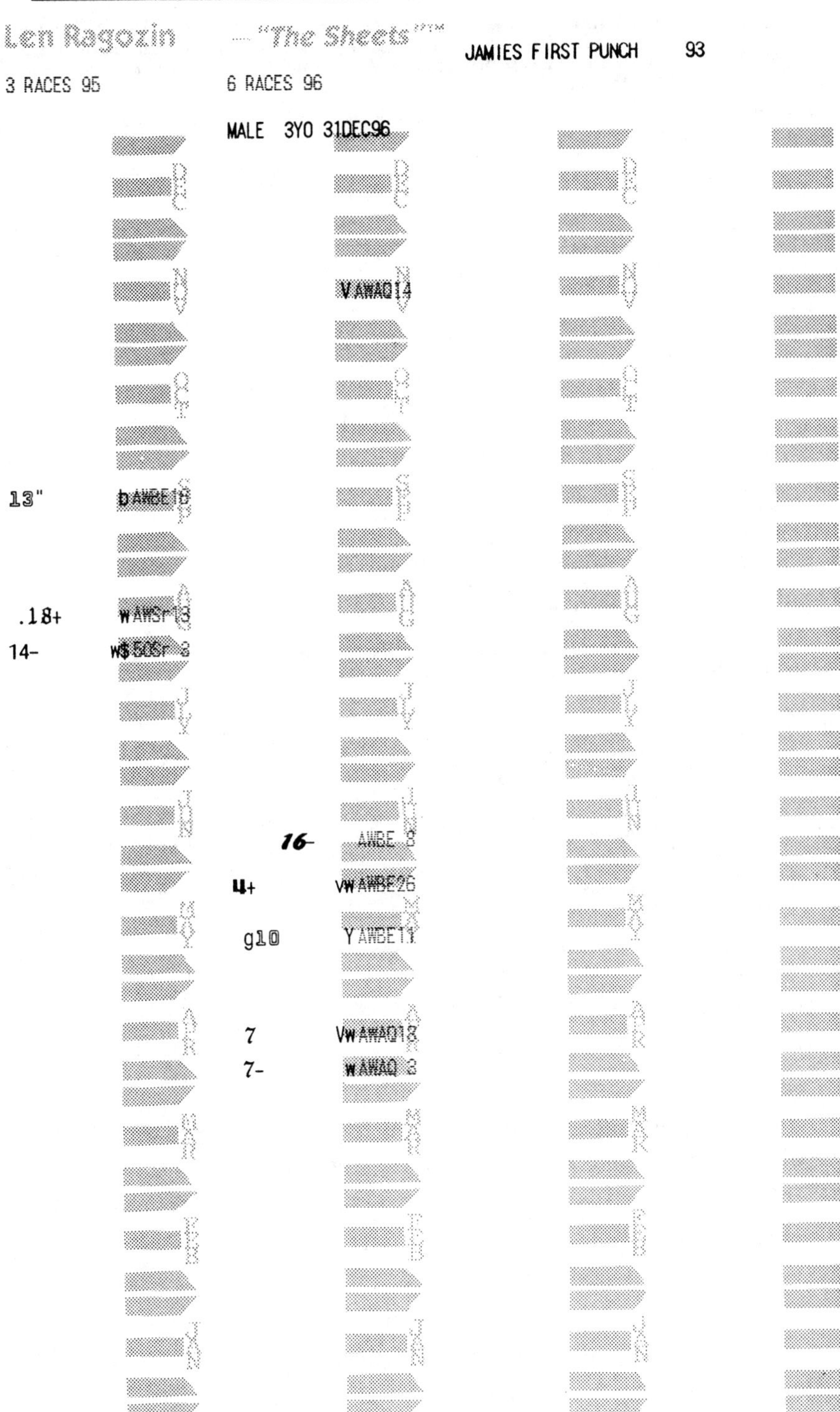
Len Ragozin — "The Sheets"™
JAMIES FIRST PUNCH 93
3 RACES 95
6 RACES 96
MALE 3YO 31DEC96
VAWAQ14
13" bAWBE10
.18+ wAWSr13
14- w$50Sr 3
16- AWBE 8
u+ vwAWBE26
g10 YAWBE11
7 VwAWAQ18
7- wAWAQ 3

NINTH RACE
Belmont
JUNE 8, 1996

1½ MILES. (2.24) 128th Running of THE BELMONT. Purse $500,000 added (plus up to $36,000 NYSBFOA). Grade I. 3-year-olds. By subscription of $600 each to accompany the nomination if made on or before January 20, or $6,000 if made on or before March 30, $5,000 to pass the entry box, $5,000 to start with $500,000 added.

Value of Race: $729,800 Winner $437,880; second $145,960; third $80,278; fourth $43,788; fifth $21,894. Mutuel Pool $5,706,641.00 Exacta Pool $3,864,546.00 Trifecta Pool $3,533,837.00

Last Raced	Horse	M/Eqt.	A.	Wt	PP	¼	½	1	1¼	Str	Fin	Jockey	Odds $1
18May96 ^{10}Pim^{3}	Editor's Note	Lb	3	126	7	$1^{1\frac12}$	12^{2}	5^{hd}	$2^{\frac12}$	2^{5}	1^{1}	Douglas R R	5.80
18May96 ^{10}Pim^{2}	Skip Away	Lb	3	126	13	$5^{\frac12}$	6^{3}	2^{hd}	$1^{1\frac12}$	$1^{\frac12}$	2^{4}	Santos J A	8.00
3May96 ^{9}CD^{5}	My Flag		3	121	9	12^{hd}	13^{2}	9^{2}	7^{2}	$3^{\frac12}$	3^{6}	Smith M E	7.70
18May96 ^{10}Pim^{1}	Louis Quatorze	L	3	126	12	$4^{1\frac12}$	3^{2}	$3^{2\frac12}$	3^{2}	4^{4}	4^{2}	Day P	a-6.10
18May96 ^{10}Pim^{7}	Prince of Thieves	Lb	3	126	6	9^{1}	$8^{1\frac12}$	6^{1}	$5^{\frac12}$	5^{3}	5^{8}	Bailey J D	6.60
15May96 ^{6}Bel^{1}	Rocket Flash		3	126	4	$8^{\frac12}$	10^{hd}	$10^{\frac12}$	$9^{2\frac12}$	8^{5}	6^{1}	Maple E	f-41.50
11May96 ^{7}Spt^{1}	Natural Selection	b	3	126	2	2^{hd}	$2^{\frac12}$	1^{hd}	$4^{\frac12}$	$7^{\frac12}$	7^{2}	Romero R P	22.50
26May96 ^{9}Bel^{1}	Jamies First Punch		3	126	5	7^{hd}	7^{hd}	8^{2}	8^{3}	6^{2}	8^{2}	Velazquez J R	5.90
18May96 ^{10}Pim^{6}	In Contention	L	3	126	11	$10^{1\frac12}$	9^{1}	$11^{2\frac12}$	10^{3}	9^{10}	9^{16}	Bravo J	36.00
12May96 ^{6}Bel^{1}	Traffic Circle	Lb	3	126	10	$13^{1\frac12}$	11^{1}	12^{1}	$12^{1\frac12}$	11^{4}	$10^{6\frac12}$	Chavez J F	f-41.50
18May96 ^{7}Pim^{1}	Saratoga Dandy	L	3	126	1	14	14	13^{3}	$11^{2\frac12}$	$10^{\frac12}$	11^{nk}	Davis R G	a-6.10
11May96 ^{10}Bel^{1}	Appealing Skier	L	3	126	8	$3^{\frac12}$	1^{hd}	$7^{\frac12}$	13^{16}	12	12	Migliore R	37.50
25May96 Dnr^{2}	South Salem	Lf	3	126	3	1^{hd}	4^{1}	14	14	—	—	Krone J A	37.00
18May96 ^{10}Pim^{4}	Cavonnier	L	3	126	14	6^{2}	5^{1}	$4^{2\frac12}$	6^{hd}	—	—	McCarron C J	3.00

South Salem:Eased; Cavonnier:Lame
a-Coupled: Louis Quatorze and Saratoga Dandy.
f-Mutuel Field: Rocket Flash and Traffic Circle.

OFF AT 5:33 Start Good. Won driving. Time, :23^{2}, :46^{4}, 1:10^{4}, 1:35^{4}, 2:02, 2:28^{4} Track fast.

$2 Mutuel Prices:

6-EDITOR'S NOTE	13.60	6.50	4.30
10-SKIP AWAY		8.20	6.20
8-MY FLAG			5.50

$2 EXACTA 6-10 PAID $107.50 $2 TRIFECTA 6-10-8 PAID $914.00

Ch. c, (Apr), by Forty Niner–Beware of the Cat, by Caveat. Trainer Lukas D Wayne. Bred by Fawn Leap Farm Inc (Ky).

EDITOR'S NOTE unhurried while outrun early, moved up outside approaching the end of the backstretch, continued his rally while four wide approaching the stretch, drifted out after catching SKIP AWAY nearing the final furlong, then outfinished that rival. SKIP AWAY reserved after coming away in good order, eased inside SOUTH SALEM just after entering the backstretch, came out five wide to split horses approaching the far turn, opened a clear lead nearing the stretch and fought it out gamely. MY FLAG slow early, rallied in the four path approaching the stretch, but wasn't able to gain on the leaders through the final furlong. LOUIS QUATORZE racing with mud calks, raced forwardly into the first turn while well out in the track, remained prominent for more than nine furlongs and tired badly. PRINCE OF THIEVES away slowly, moved up between horses to reach a striking position midway on the far turn but lacked a further response. ROCKET FLASH dropped back along the inside around the first turn and failed to be a serious factor. NATURAL SELECTION saved ground while showing good early foot, held on well until near the stretch and had nothing left. JAMIES FIRST PUNCH never far back while saving ground, was finished when he angled out wide entering the stretch. IN CONTENTION had no apparent excuse. TRAFFIC CIRCLE broke slowest of all and failed to reach contention. SARATOGA DANDY racing with mud calks, was never close. APPEALING SKIER raced in the four path while showing early foot but was finished before reaching the far turn. SOUTH SALEM hustled along after the start, stopped badly after entering the backstretch and was eased when unable to keep up. CAVONNIER well placed while five wide around the first turn and into the backstretch, rallied while continuing wide racing into the far turn, then pulled up lame after entering the stretch.

not on a par with Seatrain in that cheap turf race at Delaware Park or There's A Way in that race for New York's bottom-level filly-and-mare claimers.

But as you might suppose, everybody who does this has his pride, and a public pick like this is a once-in-a-lifetime thing. In addition to all the congratulations from people who knew him, there was that peculiar joy that comes when all the hard work results in everything falling into place just as you'd figured it.

There were two more potentially great scores that got away from our crowd, involving the 1990 and 1991 Derbies. The 1990 Derby had the elements of a prime score: a co-favorite who looked very beatable, and a longshot who off the sheets was one of the two prime contenders.

The overrated co-favorite was Mister Frisky, a colt from Puerto Rico who was undefeated in thirteen starts down there. He then was shipped to California to win three stakes races, the most recent being the Santa Anita Derby by four and a half lengths. The only problem was, Mister Frisky wasn't the fastest horse in the field, and his line suggested he would back up rather than improve. His numbers in California suggested he was no match for Summer Squall, the eastern horse who was co-favorite, and would have trouble beating several others in the field.

Most public handicappers gave Unbridled a chance to be third at best. He had won a slow Florida Derby on the same day that Summer Squall had run a strong second going seven furlongs against Housebuster, who would be the odds-on favorite in the Breeders' Cup Sprint a year later. Then, when they met in the Blue Grass Stakes in both horses' final Derby prep, Summer Squall had beaten Unbridled by three and three quarter lengths. Comparison handicapping seemed to show Unbridled as extremely unlikely to turn the tables.

Looks were deceiving — but not the wind and ground corrections I used to rate the field's past performances. In the Florida Derby, Unbridled had to contend with a stiff wind in his face for over half the race, while Summer Squall, running in a sprint from the chute, had the wind at his back most of the way. As a result, despite the much superior raw time Summer Squall posted, I had given him a number just 2 points better than I gave Unbridled for his slow 1⅛ miles. In the Blue Grass, Summer Squall had been in front virtually the entire way while Unbridled had to circle wide on the final turn. Despite Summer Squall's comfortable margin of victory, I rated his performance just a ½ point better than the third-place finisher.

Unbridled had also shown encouraging development during the early part of his three-year-old campaign, and it seemed possible more would come on Derby Day. Summer Squall was also going to have to overcome Post 13 in a fifteen-horse field.

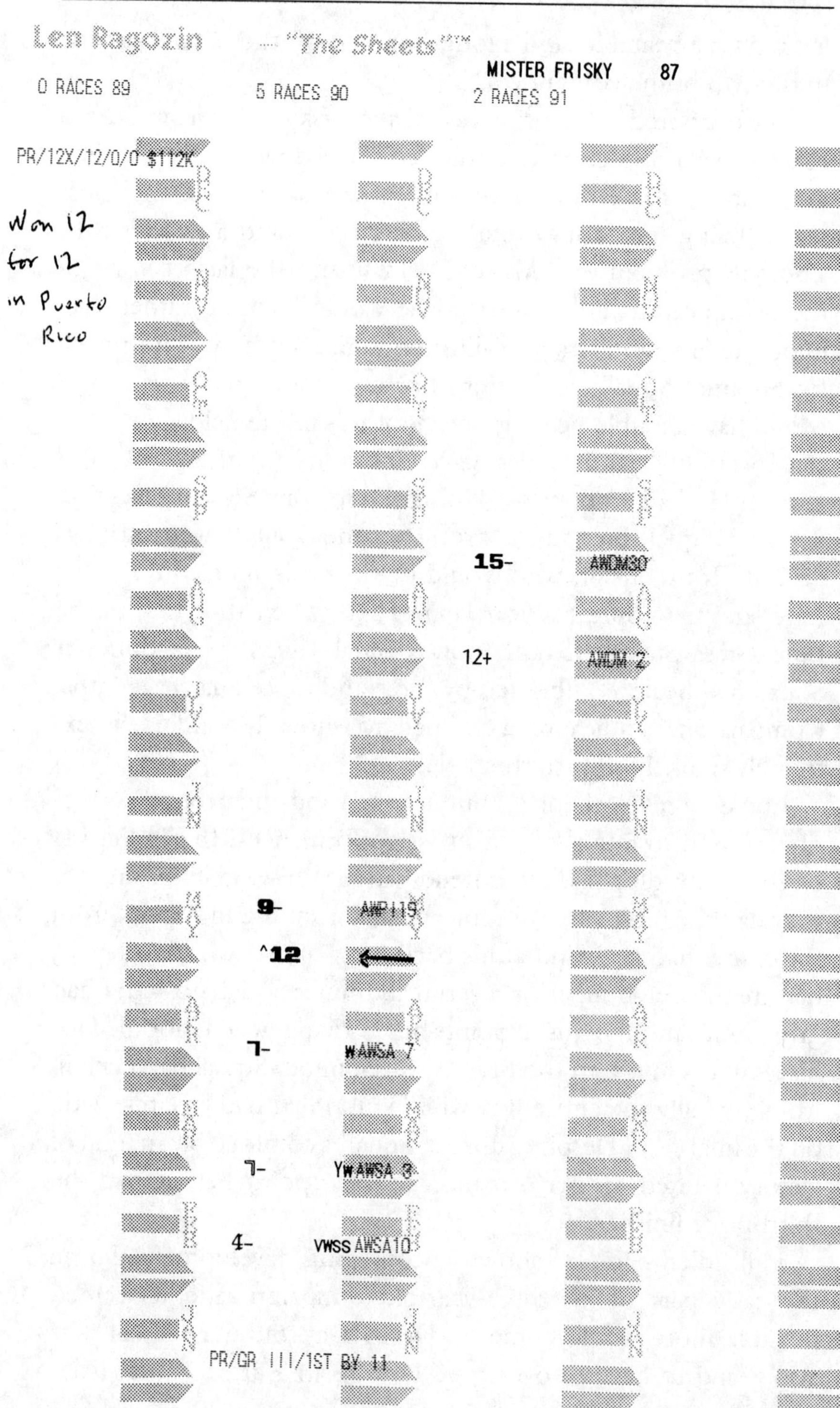
Len Ragozin
"The Sheets"™
MISTER FRISKY 87
0 RACES 89
5 RACES 90
2 RACES 91
PR/12X/12/0/0 $112K
Won 12 for 12 in Puerto Rico
15- AWDM30
12+ AWDM 2
9- AWP119
^12
7- wAWSA 7
7- YwAWSA 3
4- VWSS AWSA10
PR/GR III/1ST BY 11

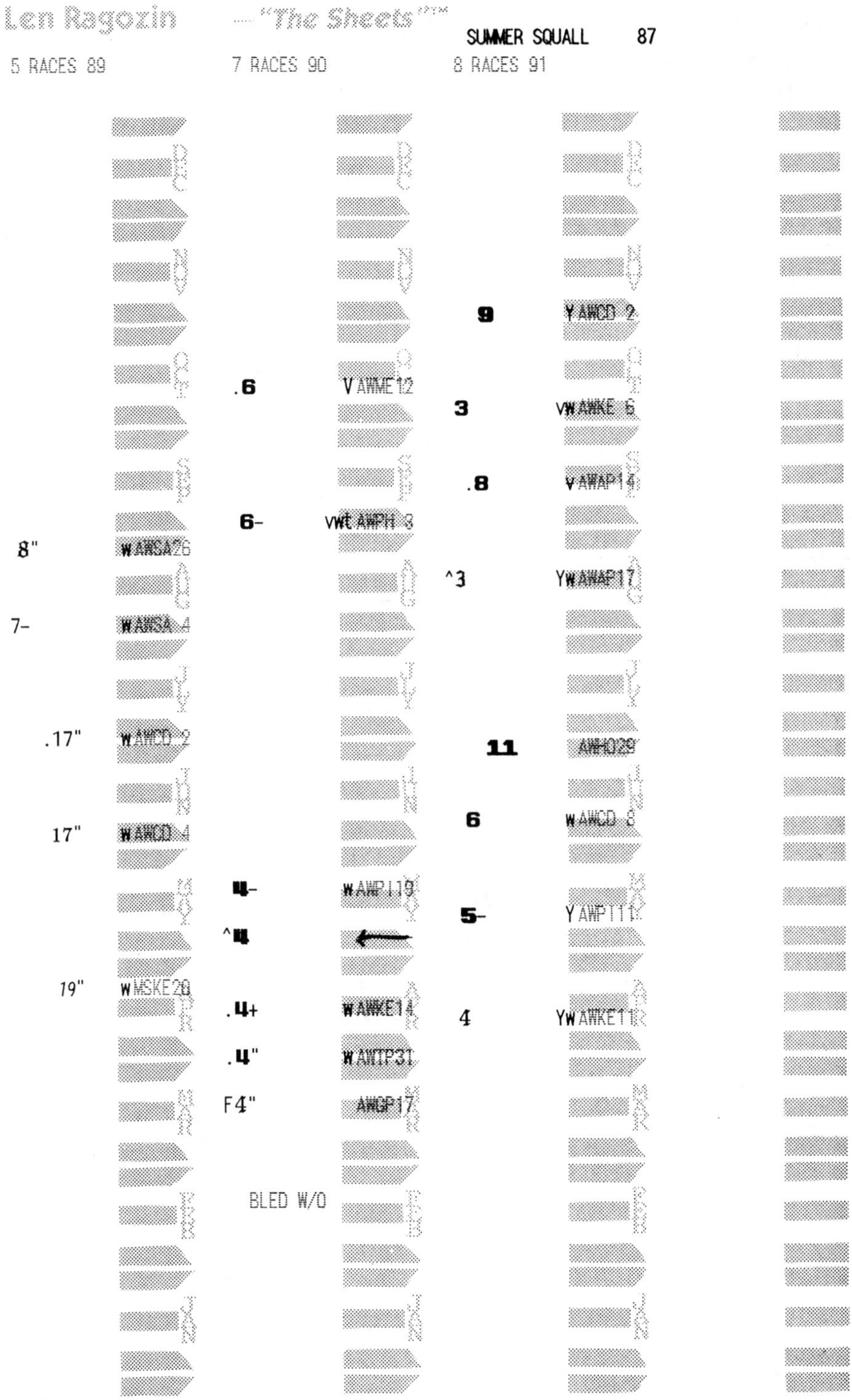

Len Ragozin — "The Sheets"™

SUMMER SQUALL 87

Month	5 RACES 89		7 RACES 90		8 RACES 91		
DEC							
NOV					9	Y AWCD 2	
OCT			.6	V AWME12	3	VW AWKE 6	
SEP			6-	vwt AWPH 3	.8	v AWAP14	
AUG	8"	w AWSA26			^3	Yw AWAP17	
	7-	w AWSA 4					
JLY	.17"	w AWCD 2			11	AWHO29	
JUN	17"	w AWCD 4			6	w AWCD 8	
MAY			4-	w AWPI19	5-	Y AWPI11	
			^4	←			
APR	19"	w MSKE28	.4+	w AWKE14	4	Yw AWKE11	
			.4"	w AWTP31			
MAR			F4"	AWGP17			
FEB			BLED W/O				
JAN							

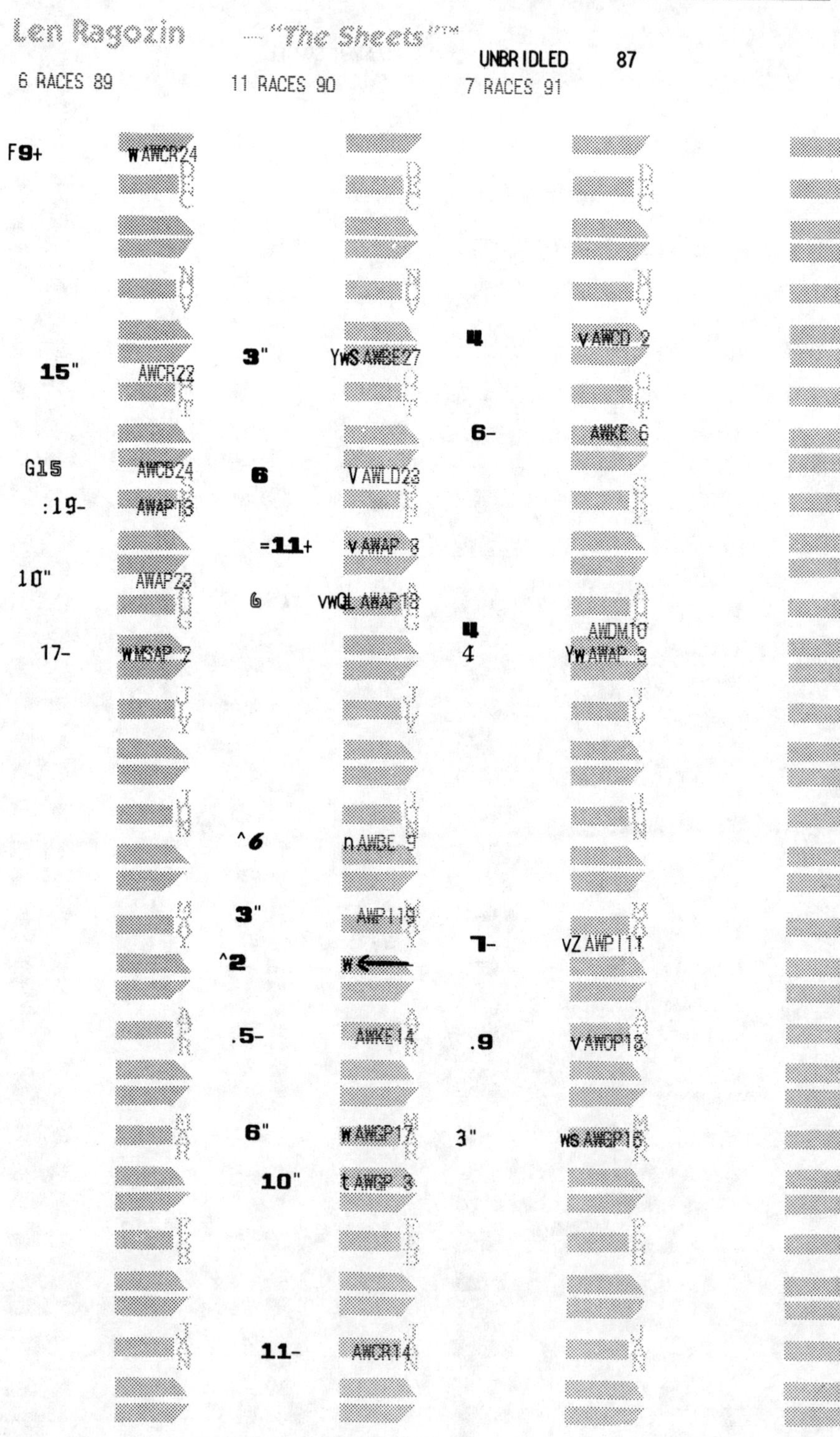
Len Ragozin "The Sheets"™
UNBRIDLED 87
6 RACES 89
11 RACES 90
7 RACES 91
F9+ wAWCR24
15" AWCR22
G15 AWCB24
:19- AWAP13
10" AWAP23
17- WMSAP 2
3" YwS AWBE27
6 V AWLD23
=11+ vAWAP 8
6 vwQL AWAP13
^6 n AWBE 9
3" AWP I 19
^2 w
.5- AWKE14
6" w AWGP17
10" t AWGP 3
11- AWCR14
4 vAWCD 2
6- AWKE 6
4 AWDM10
4 YwAWAP 3
7- vZ AWP I 11
.9 v AWOP13
3" WS AWGP16

Though we considered Summer Squall the legitimate favorite, our Derby seminar encouraged most of our followers to take the odds on Unbridled for at least some of their money.

When Unbridled at 10–1 swept by the field on the final turn to draw away from Summer Squall as Mr. Frisky faded to eighth, we did fine on both the win payoff and the exotics. But a day or two after the Derby, we got a piece of news that made Unbridled's $23.60 win payoff at Churchill Downs seem like chump change. At El Comandante racetrack in Puerto Rico, the fans had unloaded with a vengeance on the hometown hero, making Mr. Frisky 2–5. They let Summer Squall go at a shocking 12–1, but the head-slapper was learning that Unbridled paid $93.50. It was something either Friedman or I should have anticipated and capitalized on by booking a flight to San Juan. I was more guilty because I had seen something similar before, when U.S. favorite Floyd Patterson had ended up a 12–1 underdog in Sweden for his heavyweight championship rematch with Swedish Ingemar Johannsen. Once again, home-country odds had offered the ultimate overlay, and we had missed it.

A tragic, last-chance miss on a big score came a year later. My father, a month shy of his ninetieth birthday, loved Strike the Gold in the Derby. Slowed by age, Harry by then was doing almost no handicapping, but we had the sheets for the likely Derby starters ready a week before the race, which gave him the time he needed to work out his play. I myself wasn't crazy about Strike the Gold because he'd improved so substantially in his previous three starts. I didn't think he could sustain his form, and he figured to be an underlay. Be that as it may, he was the horse my father keyed.

We were in agreement on the other horses, and he set about preparing a large, complicated triple play. A day before the Derby, *New York Newsday* published a preview section that included a listing of the field by the letters by which you could bet them at OTB. My father filled out a slew of betting slips using those letters. The trouble was, OTB had just changed its system of assigning letters to the Derby's coupled entries, and *Newsday* had

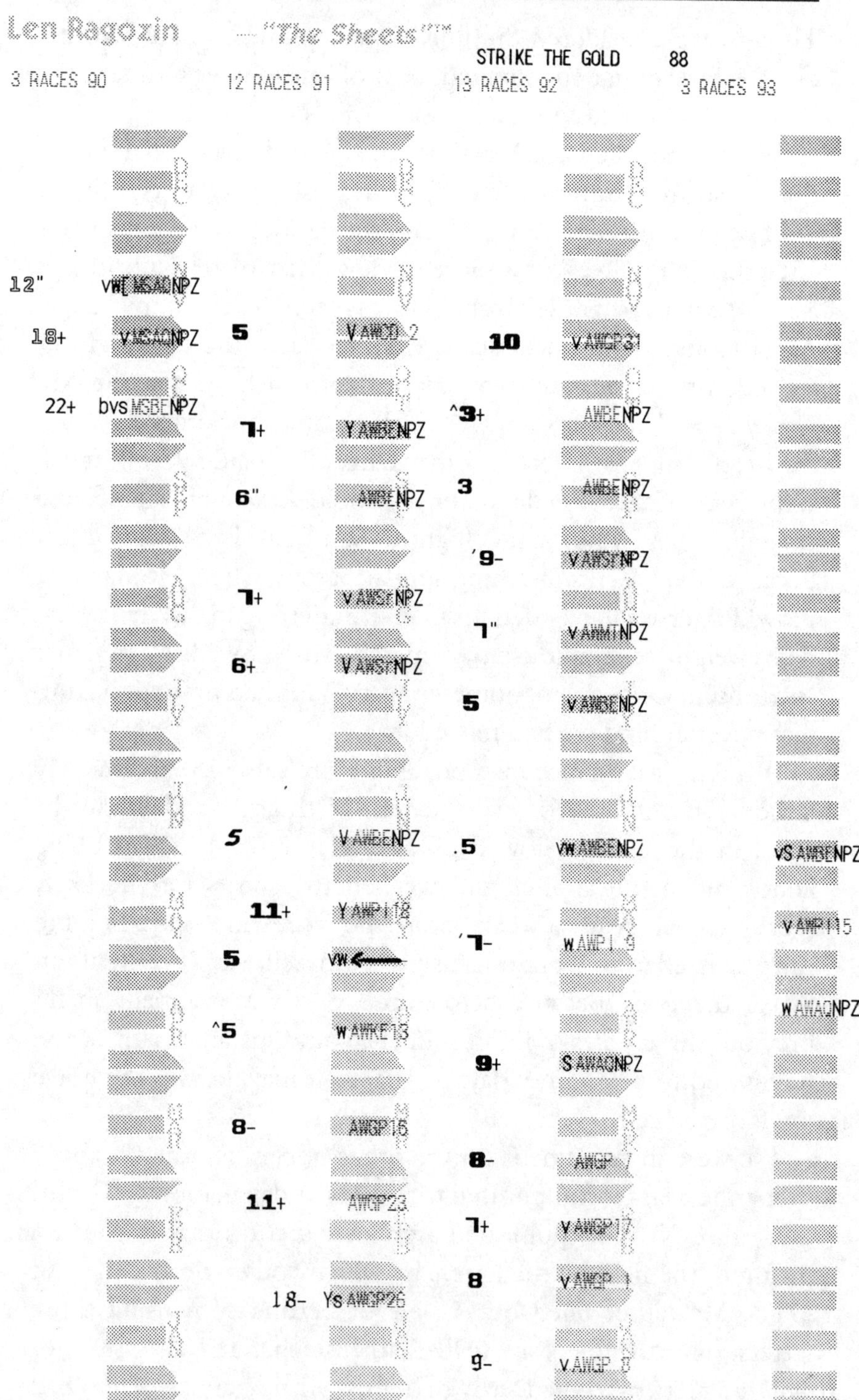

Len Ragozin — "The Sheets"™

BEST PAL 88

8 RACES 90

- 9 VwAWHO 9
- 11" vAWBE1Jy
- 12 wAWSA 7
- 10 vwAWDM12
- 11- vwAWDM22
- 10+ vwLAWDM27
- 14 AWGG23
- 18 wMSHO18

10 RACES 91

- =3" vAWHO30
- 6 vAWSA 9
- 7" vAWLD22
- 3" vwAWDM10
- 6 wAWHO 7
- 8 AWHO13
- 9" AWPL12
- 6 ←
- 6 vAWSA 6
- ^7 YAWSA 8

5 RACES 92

- ´6 AWPL 9
- 1- VwAWOP11
- 3- vwAWSA 7
- 3- vwAWSA 9
- 3" VwAWSA18

8 RACES 93

- AWSA 6
- vwAWSA16
- AWDM21
- wAWHO 3
- AWHO31
- AWOP10
- /tAWSA 6
- vAWSA24

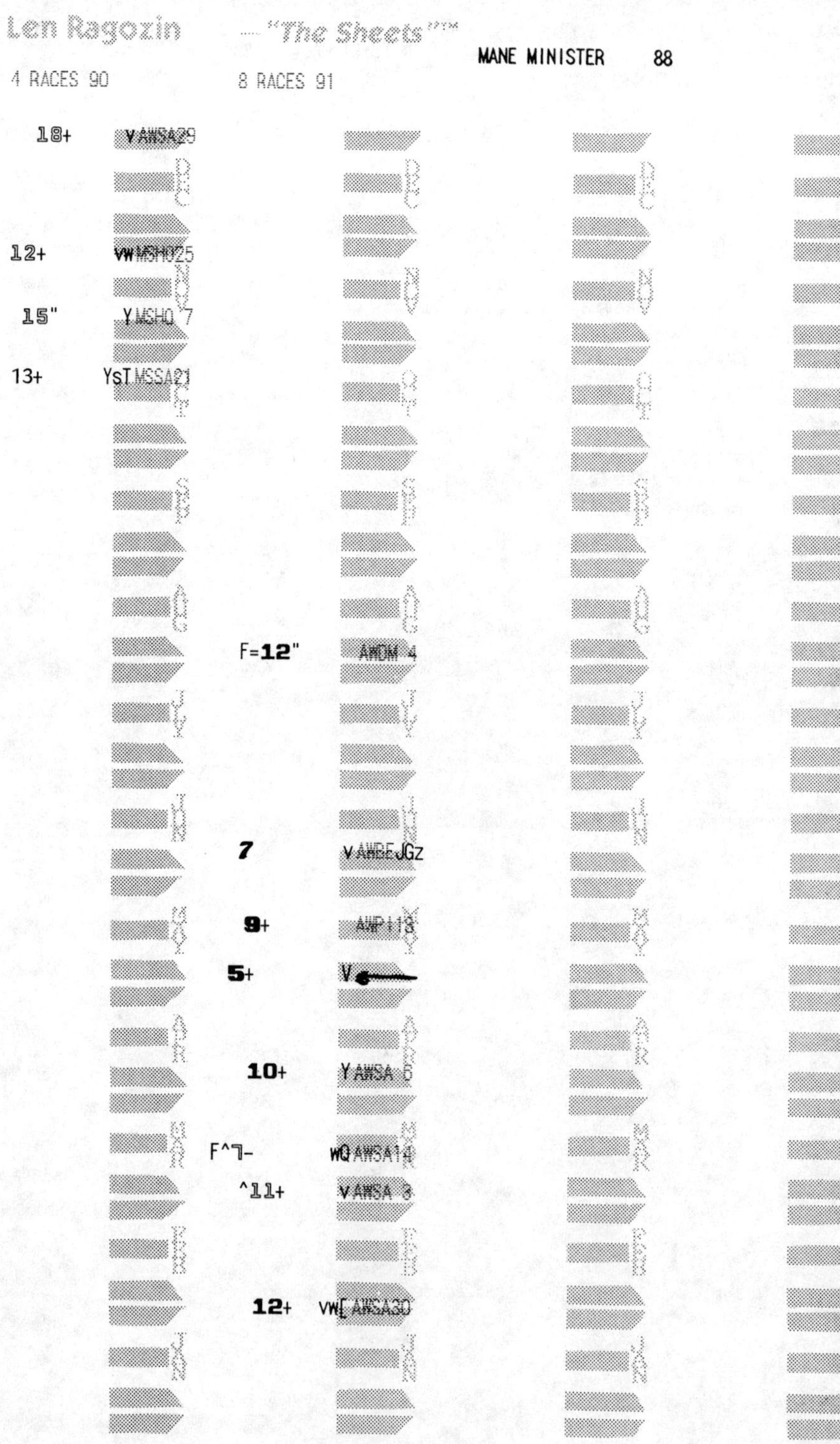

Len Ragozin
"The Sheets"™
MANE MINISTER 88
4 RACES 90
8 RACES 91
18+ VAWSA29
12+ VWMSHO25
15" YMSHO 7
13+ YsT MSSA21
F=12" AWDM 4
7 VAWBEJGZ
9+ AWP113
5+ V
10+ YAWSA 6
F^7- wQ AWSA14
^11+ VAWSA 3
12+ VW[AWSA30

Kentucky Derby

EIGHTH RACE
Churchill
MAY 4, 1991

1 ¼ MILES. (1.59^{2}) 117th Running THE KENTUCKY DERBY. (Grade I). $500,000 Added. Scale weight. 3-year-olds; with an entry fee or $10,000 each and a starting fee of $10,000 each. Supplemental nominations may be made in accordance with the rules, upon payment of $150,000. All fees will be paid to the winner. $500,000 added shall be paid by Churchill Downs Incorporated as the Added Purse. The winner shall receive $250,000, second place shall receive $145,000, third place shall receive $70,000 and fourth place shall receive $35,000

Last Raced	Horse	M/Eqt.	A.	Wt	PP	¼	½	¾	1	Str	Fin	Jockey	Odds $1
13Apr91 ^{8}Kee^{1}	Strike the Gold	B	3	126	5	$12^{1\frac{1}{2}}$	12½	10^{2}	6½	2½	$1^{1\frac{3}{4}}$	Antley C W	4.80
6Apr91 ^{5}SA^{2}	Best Pal	LB	3	126	15	10½	8^{hd}	8^{1}	7^{2}	5^{2}	$2^{1\frac{3}{4}}$	Stevens G L	5.20
6Apr91 ^{5}SA^{4}	Mane Minister	LBb	3	126	10	$8^{1\frac{1}{2}}$	10^{3}	5^{hd}	4½	$3^{1\frac{1}{2}}$	3^{hd}	Solis A	86.90
13Apr91 ^{7}GG^{1}	Green Alligator	Bb	3	126	8	16	16	15^{1}	13^{1}	9^{2}	4¾	Nakatani C S	f-16.30
13Apr91 ^{8}Kee^{2}	Fly So Free	B	3	126	1	4½	4½	3^{hd}	3^{1}	4½	$5^{1\frac{3}{4}}$	Santos J A	3.30
20Apr91 ^{9}OP^{4}	Quintana	LB	3	126	16	9^{hd}	13^{5}	$12^{1\frac{1}{2}}$	8^{hd}	$8^{1\frac{1}{2}}$	6½	Cordero A Jr	28.50
21Apr91 ^{3}Due^{2}	Paulrus	LB	3	126	11	14^{2}	14^{3}	14^{hd}	14^{1}	$11^{2\frac{1}{2}}$	7^{hd}	Sellers S J	f-16.30
6Apr91 ^{5}SA^{3}	Sea Cadet	LB	3	126	4	1^{hd}	1½	1^{hd}	1½	1^{hd}	8^{2}	McCarron C J	15.90
20Apr91 ^{9}OP^{2}	Corporate Report	B	3	126	12	3^{hd}	3^{hd}	4^{1}	2^{hd}	6^{hd}	9^{2}	Day P	8.70
21Apr91 ^{8}Kee^{1}	Hansel	LB	3	126	6	5½	6^{3}	$7^{1\frac{1}{2}}$	5^{hd}	7^{hd}	10^{hd}	Bailey J D	2.50
20Apr91 ^{8}Aqu^{3}	Happy Jazz Band	B	3	126	14	13^{1}	11^{hd}	13½	12½	12^{1}	11½	Asmussen C B	107.80
20Apr91 ^{8}Aqu^{2}	Lost Mountain	Bb	3	126	9	11^{5}	7½	$9^{1\frac{1}{2}}$	$9^{1\frac{1}{2}}$	10^{3}	$12^{8\frac{1}{2}}$	McCauley W H	72.60
20Apr91 ^{8}Aqu^{7}	Another Review		3	126	13	7^{hd}	9½	$11^{1\frac{1}{2}}$	10^{hd}	13^{hd}	13^{nk}	Madrid A Jr	f-16.30
27Apr91 ^{9}CD^{1}	Alydavid	LB	3	126	2	6½	5^{1}	6½	11^{1}	14^{2}	$14^{1\frac{1}{2}}$	Black C A	17.80
13Apr91 ^{8}Kee^{6}	Wilder Than Ever	B	3	126	3	15^{hd}	15^{hd}	16	15^{1}	15^{8}	15^{16}	Deegan J C	f-16.30
26Apr91 ^{5}Kee^{1}	Forty Something	LBb	3	126	7	2^{1}	$2^{1\frac{1}{2}}$	2^{2}	16	16	16	Seefeldt A J	f-16.30

f—Mutuel field.

OFF AT 5:36. Start good. Won driving. Time, :23^{1}, :46^{2}, 1:11^{1}, 1:37^{2}, 2:03 Track fast.

$2 Mutuel Prices:

4–STRIKE THE GOLD	11.60	6.20	5.40
10–BEST PAL		6.40	5.40
7–MANE MINISTER			25.60

$2 EXACTA (4–10) Paid $73.40. $2 PICK THREE (2–7–4) PAID $54.20.

Ch. c, (Mar), by Alydar—Majestic Gold, by Hatchet Man. Trainer Zito Nicholas P. Bred by Calumet Farm (Ky).

STRIKE THE GOLD, unhurried while outrun into the backstretch, was caught in close quarters between horses nearing the end of the backstretch, angled out to make his run, circled the leaders leaving the far turn and proved clearly best while drifting out under left handed pressure. BEST PAL, reserved early while racing along the inside, was looking for room behind the stretch to loom boldly inside the final furlong and bested the others while coming out slightly near the finish. MANE MINISTER moved up outside horses approaching the end of the backstretch, continued his rally while racing five wide into the stretch but wasn't good enough in a long drive. GREEN ALLIGATOR, outrun until near the stretch, moved through inside horses after straightening away for the drive and continued on with good energy while swinging out from behind a wall of horses late. FLY SO FREE came out slightly after the start brushing ALYDAVID and bothering WILDER THAN EVER, remained along the inside while close up into the backstretch, leaned in forcing LOST MOUNTAIN into the rail at the far turn, came out between horses to make a bid nearing the stretch and weakened. QUINTANA, outrun early, was checked sharply between horses nearing the far turn, swung out after recovering, raced wide into the stretch, then lacked the needed response. PAULRUS, without speed much of the way, passed tired horses while saving ground. SEA CADET, away alertly, saved ground while showing speed, made the pace into the stretch and gave way. CORPORATE REPORT, prominent early while racing outside the leaders, loomed boldly between horses approaching the stretch, then was tiring when brushed by HANSEL approaching the final furlong. HANSEL, well placed while five wide into the backstretch, remained within easy striking distance for a mile and ducked in while tiring brushing CORPORATE REPORT. HAPPY JAZZ BAND failed to be a serious factor. LOST MOUNTAIN, in close after the start, was moving well along the inside when forced into the rail at the far turn losing all chance. ANOTHER REVIEW tired while racing wide and tightened it up on QUINTANA nearing the far turn. ALYDAVID, brushed by FLY SO FREE following the break, raced forwardly to the far turn and tired. WILDER THAN EVER, steadied following the start, was never close. FORTY SOMETHING prompted the pace to the far turn and stopped badly.

Owners— 1, Brophy-Condren-Cornacchia; 2, Golden Eagle Farm; 3, McCaffery & Toffan; 4, Fowler A; 5, Valando Thomas; 6, Garber Gary M; 7, Hermitage Farm; 8, V H W Stables (Lessee); 9, Overbrook Farm; 10, Lazy Lane Farms; 11, Straus Medina Ranch; 12, Loblolly Stable; 13, Buckland Farm; 14, David's Farm; 15, Cottrell R H; 16, Morrell Sam F.

Trainers— 1, Zito Nicholas P; 2, Jory Ian P D; 3, Gonzalez Juan; 4, Johnson Murray; 5, Schulhofer Flint S. 6, Cross David C Jr; 7, Penrod Steven; 8, McAnally Ronald; 9, Lukas D Wayne; 10, Brothers Frank L; 11, Gleaves Philip; 12, Bohannan Thomas; 13, Campo John P; 14, Hauswald Philip M; 15, Churchman John E Jr; 16, Vardon Reginald S.

been unaware of the change. Their letters were wrong. So when my father arrived at OTB the afternoon of the Derby, the clerk started to punch out his tickets, then stopped and said, "There's no letter O," which was the letter *Newsday* listed for Best Pal, Harry's second choice.

That was when my father became aware that *Newsday*'s letters were all out of sync. With a half-hour left until post time, the clerk tried to recast all the bets, but Harry was using so many combinations that the process became difficult and upsetting. Finally Harry told him, "Forget the triples. Just give me $500 to win on Strike the Gold." Then he threw in a few exacta combinations.

Well, Strike the Gold won at 9–2, with Best Pal — my own choice in the race — second at 5–1, giving my father a $72 exacta in addition to his win bet. But the very plausible Mane Minister had run third at an incredible 86–1, triggering a $4,176 triple at OTB on which my father would have had eighteen tickets except for the fouled-up slips. If the bet had gone in as he planned it, he would have collected about $75,000 on the race, even allowing for the fact that his bet would have shortened the triple price. A newspaper error had torpedoed what would have been the greatest score of his life — his last Derby, and the perfect finish for his career as an analyst.

I have to say my father handled it very gracefully, with hardly a complaint about his misfortune. Very few could have taken it as well. Of course, he bet much more on the Preakness than he otherwise would have, and he didn't hit it.

But, that's racing.

Epilogue: Final Speculations . . .

SO, WHERE DO WE GO from here? What's ahead for thoroughbred racing itself, for handicappers and bettors, and for the Ragozin *Sheets*?

Just a few years ago, racing appeared to be dying — and with good reason. When I was growing up, and well into my young manhood, the racetracks had an effective monopoly on legal gambling. If you wanted to bet, you went to the track. Oh, yes, there were bookies who would take a bet on a prizefight or a college basketball game — but to Mr. and Ms. Average Citizen this was still outside the line of conventional respectability.

Along came television. Sports, especially football and baseball, gave you a full afternoon of entertainment at home. On this new medium, racing couldn't compete in fan interest. And as the home appeal of televised sports settled in, the idea of having a bet going while you watched the game became socially acceptable, even though technically still illegal. Your bet on the Giants got you so much more entertainment than a bet on a horse race — it was just no contest. On top of this, legal lotteries ate up more gambling dollars. The long-run outcome of this seemed so obvious that, a few years ago, I put a price tag on my business for an interested buyer. Lucky for me, his backers didn't quite come up with the money.

Now, however, I think the outlook is decidedly different. Perhaps I should have seen this before, but at any rate there's no doubt that — once you are gambling in a casino or simulcast atmosphere — racing rebounds with a big advantage not available in other sports: a series of quick results. It's sort of like a sports slot machine. The old boring half-hour between races is gone because of multitrack simulcasting. It's constant action. And this positive feature, operating now at casinos and simulcast outlets, will carry over into the upcoming era of interactive TV home-betting. It's still true that the average fan at the racetrack is well over fifty years old. But, away from the live action, there's a younger wave of figure guys who should supply enough betting handle to keep the sport going.

Actually, *The Sheets* may prove to be racing's lifeline. If you look at the big players in Las Vegas, almost all of them buy my data. The *Racing Form* recently did a front-page piece on the two biggest. Both use *The Sheets.* I presume that professionals like this would not be pushing millions through the windows without a good record of profits behind them. *The Sheets* provide them with a reasonable approach, and their example gives heart to a generation of players who will — I hope — be following their lead.

Anyhow, for the forseeable future racing is not about to shut up shop. Even though it gets a much smaller percentage of the national gambling dollar than it used to, the absolute figure continues to rise, and I assume that home-betting plus casino vacationers will supply enough "sucker money" that the pros can still find their profits. If not, of course, the pros will be cannibalizing each other — and the betting input could shrink.

Meanwhile, Las Vegas casinos have created a more level playing field for the horse-race bettor. Sports betting is attractive to pros because it creams off a very small percentage for the "house" — about 4 percent of the total bet. Meanwhile racing takes 15 to 25 percent or more. But now Vegas is giving rebates to large horse-race bettors, thus making racing a more reasonable proposition to serious gamblers. The casinos keep saying they aren't doing this anymore and/or they are planning to outlaw it soon, but as of this writing people say that they are getting it. But even if it is officially outlawed, don't tell me a man who bets over a million dollars a month isn't going to find a casino owner somewhere in the United States who will give him a kickback to get all that action!

So if racing is here to stay, are *The Sheets* just resting on their laurels? If you could hang around our office, expecially in the late afternoon, when I come in but the others haven't left yet, you'd find many an animated conversation that centers on various problems whose solution would improve the quality of the figures. Yes, they're awfully good already, but we keep treating racing as a very "live" base of data, and we recognize that what we are inputting is not perfect, especially at certain tracks that don't seem to care much about the statistics they put out. (Unfortunately we can't afford a full-time expert observer at every medium-to-small track.)

In our push toward perfection, the big advance I made in 1995 was to begin working with time-coded videotapes. I imprint a time-code number on each frame of the race video. This means I can use slow motion and freeze-frame on my VCR to get exact timing of every horse in every race *and* exact timing of an off-poorly, when a horse is tardy coming out of the gate. I have been doing this work personally at a few tracks, and when I have learned all I think I can learn about this approach, we will spread it to more tracks and have it in reserve to check questionable data at *all* tracks.

Meanwhile, when the phone rings at night in my office — by which time I am usually the only one there, since I prefer to work in silence — I answer, and often the customer on the other end sounds surprised that it's me. Why? Because some of my main competitors busily spread the rumor that I long since gave up working on the figures and that it's all mechanical now (!) — with a little help from a few flunkeys. Well, let me assure you I am not yet in the grave or the armchair.

In 1995 my personal analysis of videotapes solved some problems regarding the Saratoga turf run-ups that my on-track observers had been unable to pinpoint for me, presumably because their view was obstructed by trees. The track's timing of some turf at Saratoga uses an employee with a stopwatch, not a teletimer, so private clocking from the gate plus knowledge of the exact distance (run-ups) is essential for accuracy. Using time-coded tapes, and working out TV perspective corrections to allow for the fact that the sixteenth-poles (distance markers) are a few feet removed from the hedge or railing along which the horses are actually racing, I was able to improve upon our older estimates. None of this required great genius, but it did require dedication and hard work — drawing straight lines on my TV screen radiating from the camera site to the sixteenth-poles on both sides of the course (the dirt-course sixteenth-poles are *outside* the turf course, which helps you solve the perspective problem). I learned enough from doing all this that we should now be able to do perfect clocking via TV at tracks where we don't have an on-site observer to measure the run-ups.

Speaking of improvements, 1995 was the time to question *all* our fundamental formulas — because we were switching over to a better computer and investing a lot of time and money in new programming. The most interesting result of this questioning: a decision to treat slow races as if they were actually *longer* races. Remember, the *Sheet* figure says that 1 point equals a lot more time at (say) 1½ miles than at six furlongs, and by the same token 1 point equals slightly more time even at six and a half furlongs than at six furlongs. In other words, every jump or bound that an inferior horse takes eventually puts him slightly further behind a superior horse, so the same racing ability reflects more time differential the longer the race goes on. Well, from that point of view, why should a six and a half-furlong race run on a fast track and timed in 1 minute and 18 seconds be any different from a *six*-furlong race run on a deep winterized track and timed in the same 1:18? The horse is out there just as long and works just as hard.

We made a patchwork correction in our old computer to test

the idea of treating these cases as being equivalent, and are satisfied that this is the right approach. In most cases, these new formulas give results "only" ¼ point or ½ point different than what we formerly got — and only on the slow races. You could live without it — but there will be days when it helps you make a more accurate variant. So this is a good example of how we keep striving toward complete accuracy long after our figures have demonstrated the ability to help players toward a successful attack on the game.

With the advent of the new computer we will finally get around to making a "pace" figure available to customers who are interested in the question of who ran faster in the earlier portion of the race. We think this affects the outcome of races in only a very small portion of the races, and should not become a mainstay of anyone's handicapping. But if people want to do research along these lines, the pace figures currently available by other methods are useless — because they don't include wind corrections. *Final* times of races are protected from outrageously large wind corrections because much of the course traveled by the horse cancels out in terms of wind. They run right-to-left on the backstretch and left-to-right through the stretch. But a fractional time, on which pace is based, can be almost all in one direction. Just look at how the first ¼ mile or even ½ mile of an average sprint is run. A reasonable tailwind could slice five-fifths off the time, while the next day a headwind could *add* that same full second to the fractional time. The pace analyst would be forced to treat these two races very differently, although the horses were actually doing the same thing. Our pace figures — if you live long enough to see them! — will be the *beginning* of the possibility of accurate pace analysis.

To tell the truth, it's hard for me to expect any dramatic improvement in betting results from all this work on pace, because it's hard to believe that our gang has been beating such a tough game all these years while ignoring any fundamental reality. My hunch is that pace is not fundamental to proper analysis. But I will be happy to provide accurate pace figures: first, to let people really attack the problem properly so we can find out how much validity there is in pace theories; second, because accurate pace figures will help you to "pre-chart" a race and know when you have a situation where a certain horse will gain a clear lead easily and have a favorable, ground-saving journey rather than battling two other front-runners to his inside and racing wide. This would surely be good to know.

My biggest achievement of the past two years, however, is a detailed set of rules, computerized to generate bets from the sheets. Don't start salivating — I'm not selling it! But I used it to demonstrate *The Sheets'* power when I announced that I would make a two-month casino foray in the fall of 1996.

When the SPORT-STAT outfit (see page 33) found that profits could be made on *The Sheets* by computer-searching only the horse's most recent three races, the long-standing opinion shared by me and my associates — that a computer system to beat the horses was a practical impossibility — was a bit shaken. However, we all get so much enjoyment from our personal approaches to betting that none of us wanted to buckle down and try to improve upon SPORT-STAT's admittedly oversimple system.

But my best friend and ex-wife, Marion Buhagiar, whose opinion I greatly respect, urged me to make the effort and offered to do the eventual dry-run testing herself. I was still reluctant. But one day I remembered an old computer program that I had devised to help us use nonclaiming races in estimating the daily track variant. This program arrived at a par time for a nonclaiming race by looking at the past figures for each horse. Well, in a way it was trying to predict what these horses would run next out. And it had different rules for different ages, distances, and sexes. So, I already had the beginnings of a pick-the-winner program, and could go to work to improve upon it. Which I did.

I began writing rules, hand-testing results, rewriting, retesting — you get the idea. The rules were a detailed version of the principles described in this book. A year later I had almost a hundred pages of rules and couldn't work up the energy to test them any more because it was too laborious to run all the rules by each horse. It was time to take up Marion on her offer to run tests on her computer.

Meanwhile, during the very period when all this was going on, the Las Vegas casinos began offering rebates to large horse-bettors. This now meant that if the system did nothing more than break even, a good profit was available based on the rebates.

Yes, the newspapers were recently full of the great achievement of the IBM programmers who developed Deep Blue — the chess program that won a game against world-champion Kasparov. But isn't beating racing via computer a noteworthy achievement? I don't quite know how to claim my trophy, however. I would be happy to challenge Beyer or any leading public handicapper to fight things out with my system — but I doubt very much that anyone with a reputation would accept the dare. I would have everything to gain and little to lose, while they would be in the opposite position.

So, I am still turning over ideas for showing my baby off to the world. Step one was a publicized visit to the casinos in October–November 1996. I announced that I would bet sheet data from computerized rules for two months. I faxed my bet list to the *Racing Form* around noon daily, so I didn't have the final odds. I made $17,110 on my 414 win bets, which totaled $124,200. That is, by inputting to the computer nothing but *The Sheets* and the track program, I made a 14 percent profit on win bets in a publicly monitored trial. *The Racing Form* ran an article on the results, but that's all the public recognition I got. I guess I'll have to cast a small statue and give myself the first "Lenny" award for computer handicapping.

After my mechanical-system betting foray, Len Friedman called my attention to Andy Beyer's recent book, *Beyer on Speed*, in which he states that (1) you can't win without paying attention to pace (fractional time) and track bias (track surface helping certain types of horses); and (2) you positively can't win by applying a set of mechanical rules to a set of speed figures.

Since I had just performed these impossible feats, I decided to read the book and find out where I had gone wrong. For my own malicious enjoyment, I give you some quotes from Beyer's book:

> No factor . . . can conceal and distort the true ability of horses so much as track bias. No factor can render speed figures so meaningless. . . . All serious bettors therefore pay keen attention to this aspect of the game.

So, it seems I was not a serious bettor. Not only that, in a considerable number of races my figures were "meaningless." The Ragozin figures must certainly be amazingly better than anyone else's to have overcome these disadvantages and produced a 14 percent win-bet profit in a lengthy public trial.

> If a strong bias does exist, though, there is one all-important rule that every horseplayer should heed: Don't fight it.

Well, at least I didn't "fight it." I couldn't, because *The Sheets* don't include that information.

> Is it reasonable to anticipate improvement or decline in a horse's figures based on what the pace of today's race is likely to be?
>
> The answer, indisputably, is yes.

I don't trust guys who say "indisputably" instead of proving their argument. Examples can be found to back up any theory, so the test of pace theory has to be in one's results. In the SPORT-STAT study previously discussed, pace figures were subjected to the same investigation as the figures of Beyer, Thoro-graph, and Ragozin. The pace-figure results were at the bottom of the list. This fact may not be completely conclusive, since pace practitioners could object to the simplicity of the selection system employed. But, when put alongside the fact that I have shown substantial profit to be available without using pace, it certainly puts a question mark after that word "indisputably."

As for me and my associates:

> Their single-minded focus on numbers alone is what led me to dismiss them as a bunch of kooks. . . . Ragozin's insights into the nature of horse racing are indeed brilliant, but, like his hero

> Karl Marx, he turned his view of the world into a rigid, almost suffocating dogma.

Beyer goes on to explain that pattern analysis can be valid only because the numbers show how the horse's real-life physical condition is changing (true). But, says Beyer, Ragozin et al. are "mesmerized" by the numbers themselves and ignore the real world.

Now, this is a really low blow. Just look through this book. We have also made many instructional tapes. Almost all our discussion of handicapping revolves around analyzing changes in the physical condition of horses. *Of course that's what the figures show* — and he says *we* are "mesmerized" out of this reality.

Horses' growth, injuries, illnesses, recoveries — this is precisely what we study through accurate numbers. In fact, I would argue that it is Beyer who treats horses as machines by assuming in his handicapping that a horse will generally repeat its best effort unless there is a change in the track bias or pace or "trip." It is relatively unimportant to him that the horse might have changed physically (for the better or worse) as a result of the effort put out in a recent race.

However, recognition of the fact of physical change creeps in through the side door and makes a muddle of Beyer's thesis that races run under "bad" circumstances will be followed by a rebound. For instance, he picked Badger Land to win the 1986 Preakness because of his bad trip in the Derby. Fair enough — nobody picks winners all the time. But when the horse ran badly in the Preakness, he says that it must have been physically drained by that Derby in which the unfavorable circumstances developed. Well, if an unfavorable-circumstance race can either knock a horse out *or* set him up for a great bet next out, where are you?

After detailing the horrible trip Badger Land had in the Derby and how impressive it was that he came in fifth after all this trouble, Beyer called him a "mortal lock" to win the Preakness. But when he ran badly, Beyer jumped the fence to say,

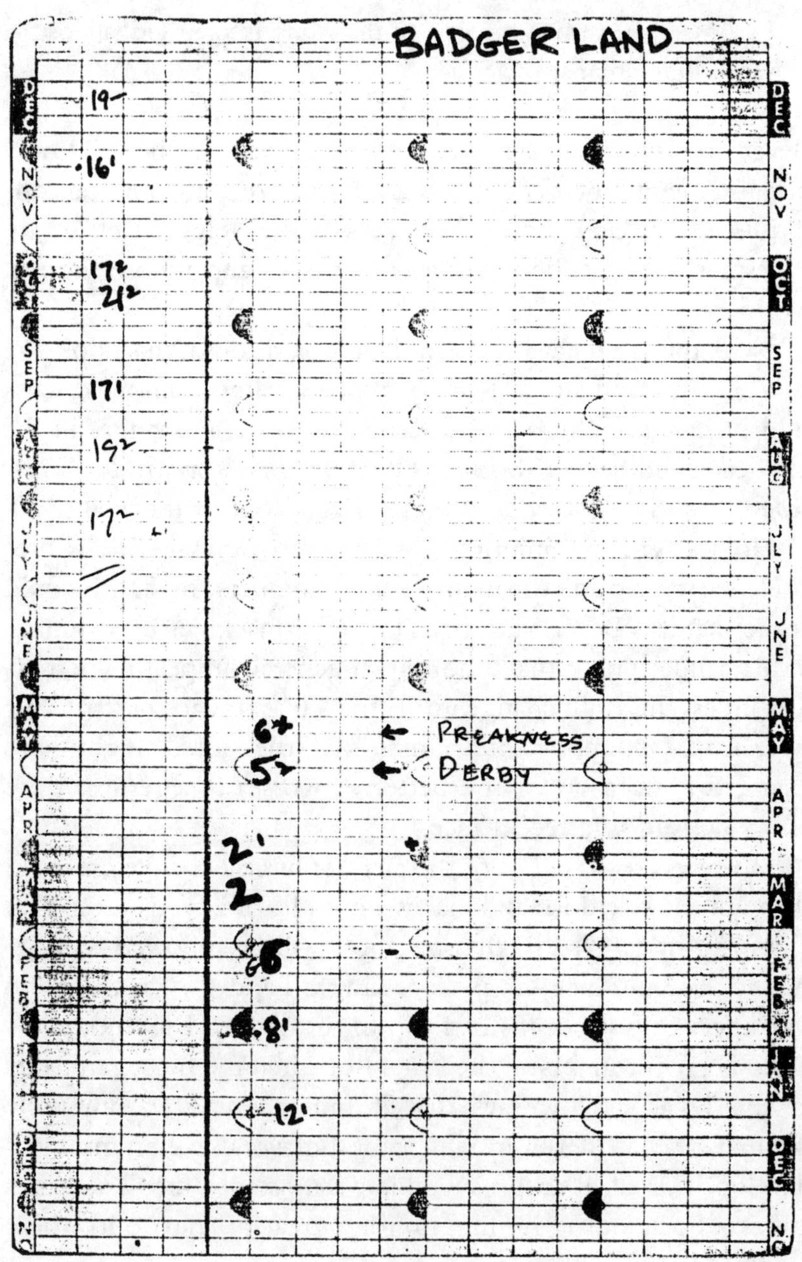
BADGER LAND
DEC
NOV
OCT
SEP
AUG
JLY
JNE
MAY
APR
MAR
FEB
JAN
DEC
NO
19
16'
17²
2²
17'
19²
17²
6²
5²
PREAKNESS
DERBY
2'
2
6B
8'
12'

> But a bedraggled Badger Land, suffering from the effects of that stressful race in Louisville, barely picked his feet up in Baltimore.

Having trashed his own trip-theory, Beyer then wants to prove that we, also, couldn't have expected Badger Land to run badly in the Preakness:

> Badger Land . . . had not run exceptional speed figures, which, according to Ragozin's theories, would have foretold a decline.

That last sentence is another low blow. Maybe by *Beyer's* figures Badger Land had not previously run exceptionally. By *our* figures (which Beyer evidently didn't bother to check out), he surely had peaked out and was declining (see sheet on the facing page). In our 1986 Triple Crown forecasts, we picked against him with no difficulty. The type of unfair comment made on Badger Land is repeated throughout the book. That is, Beyer shows a winner he picked, then says that our methods of analysis would have rated the horse negatively. The trouble is, he applies our methods to *his* speed figures, which lack corrections for weight, wind, ground loss, and gate timing and are fuzzy for other reasons discussed earlier in this book.

Len Friedman pulled out our sheets for all the winners used by Beyer to knock our methods, and found that by our figures most of them actually looked good. In fact, he started to write an analysis of each case, which we were going to include in this book. Unfortunately, we both fell asleep reading it — so we left it out. But if you want copies of the sheets involved, we will gladly send them to you. Call us at (212) 674-3358.

Even while he is tossing mud upon my head, Beyer, in effect, admits that the advice he gave on handicapping for thirty years was wrong because he didn't believe in analyzing patterns and derided us for doing so.

He begins by saying that bettors need a way to find bets based on speed, but not so obvious that their odds get hammered. He asks how this can be done; then he says that my approach — pattern-analysis of condition — is an answer that has influenced a generation of handicappers (even though I didn't write columns or books!). He continues:

> Can past patterns of speed figures really predict the future?
>
> I used to snicker at the idea, telling readers of the Sheets that they might as well study tea leaves. When the *Racing Form* undertook its [computer] study of the Beyer Speed Figures, I had the chance to examine some patterns and determine if they had any bearing on a horse's future performance . . .
>
> . . . [The study] verifies Ragozin's premise — which I had always doubted and often derided — that patterns of past figures may indeed be meaningful. It suggests that many such patterns may exist. And it confirms Ragozin's central tenet that a peak performance is apt to be followed by a decline.
>
> . . . Students of the Sheets are decades ahead of me in the search for such form cycles.

OK, Andy, you were man enough to admit it.

* * * * *

As you can see, I still get a big kick out of analyzing thoroughbred racing. How long I can keep going, I can't say. My father was still innovating in his mid-eighties, but I don't know if I want to try to match that record.

Even if by now I've gone about as far as I personally care to go, I certainly have opened up the game for fun and profit to a whole generation of analyst-gamblers. And my team, my organization, has an internal vibrancy that I am confident will lead to more frontiers being breached in the future whether or not I personally lead the attack.

So that's my life. I was lucky — I enjoyed it. Good luck to you.